Praise for Multiple Streams of Income

"*Multiple Streams of Income* is a smart, instructional read for anyone just beginning, or well on their way to financial freedom. You can't go wrong with this book. It's right on target."

Michael Gerber
Founder and Chairman,
The E-Myth Academy

"Reading this book is in itself a transforming experience. The financial principles are as sound as the Rock of Gibraltar and are explained with such clarity you will never forget them. You get inside the mind of one of the great entrepreneurial thinkers of our time and see just how he turns ideas into profits. Few successful multimillionaires are also successful at writing books that clearly explain how others can succeed. As a teacher with an abundance of brilliantly organized, fascinatingly relevant lessons on how to create wealth, Robert Allen is unsurpassed."

Scott DeGarmo
Former Editor in Chief and Publisher,
Success Magazine

"I have tremendous respect for Robert Allen's ability to teach people how to make a lot of money. His latest book, *Multiple Streams of Income,* contains a wealth of information."

Robert T. Kiyosaki
Author, *Rich Dad, Poor Dad*
Chairman, Cash Flow Technologies

"Twenty years ago, Robert Allen showed us how to get rich in real estate with no money down. Now, he shows us exactly how to become financially independent in the twenty-first century economy by developing multiple streams of income. This is a great book. Every working person in America could benefit from reading it."

Michael B. O'Higgins
Financial Advisor
Author, *Beating the Dow*

"Robert Allen's book, *Multiple Streams of Income,* is provocative and should be read cover to cover by everybody from the entrepreneurial or investing novice to the most experienced and seasoned of us. It will be difficult to come away without new, profitable information, but for many, just the kick in the butt to be more aggressive in diversifying could prove very valuable."

Dan S. Kennedy
Author, *How to Succeed in Business by Breaking ALL the Rules*

"The information contained in the first paragraph of page 297 alone is worth 100 times the price of this book."

Gary Halbert
Author, *The International Gary Halbert Letter*

"This book promises multiple streams of income but actually delivers mulitple streams of *mountains* of income. I am astounded by the abundance of wisdom in every chapter—enjoyable quotations, easy-to-understand graphs, simple rules to follow, websites to check for free, and references to others who have used these proven systems successfully. This book will truly guide ordinary people to create and keep multiple streams of lifetime income. Bravo, Bob. You have done it again. You are the financial mentor to the world's aspiring millions."

Raymond Aaron
Author, *Vast Profits for the 1990's*

"Bob Allen has done it again with his new book, *Multiple Streams of Income*. It's the best treasure trove of multiple ways to make money, save money and protect money that I have ever seen. If you can't make money with this book, check your pulse. You're dead."

Larry Williams
Author, *How to Outfox the Foxes*

"Bob Allen has the unique ability to teach proven moneymaking systems while motivating the student to take action. I have personally seen Bob's information transform thousands of lives for the better—including my own. In the past 10 years I've purchased over 800 properties using the information you'll find in this book. I highly recommend his books to my own students. I'm sure he has another best-seller in *Multiple Streams of Income.*"

John R. Burley
Author, *Automatic Wealth*
audio program

"Robert Allen is an information alchemist. He has the ability to distill complex information into simple formulas that get results. In the 13 years that I've known him and worked with him, I've witnessed how his teachings have directly compelled countless people to create substantial wealth and happiness in their lives. He is one of the great money mentors of our time."

Donald Wolfe, M.A.
The Vision Coach
C.E.O. Consultant and Corporate Trainer

"*Multiple Streams of Income* is a must-read book. If you're looking for the financial freedom you deserve, do so by first reading this book and educating yourself on how to play the game and play it successfully."

Marshall Sylver
Author, *Passion, Profit & Power*

"Very few people have influenced my life more than Robert Allen and one of the most profitable things I learned from him was the importance of multiple streams of income. This book will change your life. Read it and then give it to your children."

Ron LeGrand
Author, *Fast Cash with Quick Turn Real Estate and Cash Flow Generator*

"Bob Allen understands how to get other people's efforts, assets, and money working hard for you. In his new book, *Multiple Streams of Income,* he shows you 10 powerful ways to create income streams that anyone can use successfully to create financial freedom and security."

Jay Abraham
Author, *Getting Everything You Can Out of All You've Got*

Multiple Streams
of Income

ROBERT G. ALLEN

John Wiley & Sons, Inc.

Published by John Wiley & Sons, Inc., New York.
Published simultaneously in Canada.

Library of Congress Cataloging-in-Publication Data:

Allen, Robert G.
    Multiple streams of income/Robert G. Allen.
      p.   cm.
    Includes index.
    ISBN 0–471–38180–2 (cloth : alk. paper)
    ISBN 0–471–21887–1
    1. Money. 2. Income. 3. Finance, Personal. I. Title.
HG221.A415 2000
332.024'01—dc21   99-058145

Printed in the United States of America.

10 9 8 7 6

CONTENTS

Dear Reader of *Multiple Streams of Income:*

For the past 20 years, through my best-selling books and international seminars, I've taught thousands of people how to achieve financial freedom. Now it's your turn.

In these pages, I'm going to teach you how to earn multiple streams of *lifetime* income. More specifically, you'll learn 10 different ways to earn these extra income streams. These are not just ordinary streams of income. You'll learn how to create the kind of residual income streams that flow into your life 24 hours a day—even while you sleep. You'll learn how to create these special streams of income . . .

- ✔ on a part-time basis.
- ✔ working right from your own home.
- ✔ using little or none of your own money.
- ✔ with few or no employees.
- ✔ using simple, proven systems that really work.

In addition, I will show you how to . . .

- ✔ gain control of your finances.
- ✔ earn high rates of return—18 percent, 36 percent, and as high as 50 percent—using little-known financial strategies, some even guaranteed by the government!

✔ earn as much as $1,000 a day right from your own home.

✔ make an extra $50,000 to $100,000 a year for life.

✔ perhaps even become a lifetime multimillionare.

What will all of this get for you? A lifestyle that gives you the freedom to do what you want, when you want, with whomever you want. There is a Spanish saying that captures the essence of this lifestyle:

"Salud, Dinero y Amor y Tiempo para disfrutarlo"
(health, money, and love, and the time to enjoy them).

If this is what you want, let's work together to make it happen in your life.

Prosperously, your money mentor,

Robert Allen

ACKNOWLEDGMENTS

There are so many people to thank, so many friends to acknowledge. First and foremost, I acknowledge the sacrifice that my family made during my long hours of research and writing. Daryl, Aimee, Aaron, and Hunter, I love you forever.

Next, I want to acknowledge those who helped me in the research for this book: Tom Painter, Dr. Stephan Cooper, William Donoghue, J.J. Childers, John Childers, Ted Thomas, Daren Falter, Bob and Joyce Gatchel, Maryam Chaney, Ken Kerr, Collette Van Reusen, Saul Klein, Stan Miller, Mark Hulbert, Steve Shellans, Michael O'Higgins, Chris Parks, and all my many friends at USANA.

I owe a debt of gratitude to all the fabulous people at John Wiley & Sons, North Market Street Graphics, and Nightingale/Conant who helped me turn the raw ore of my ideas into precious metal.

I want to make a very special mention of the graduates of my advanced mentoring program who became the sounding board for these strategies. They helped me hone the rough edges of the material and make it more presentable to the world. Many incredible success stories have already come from this group, and I have no doubt that most of them are on track to financial freedom using these ideas and techniques. I call this special group my protégés. Thanks to all of you.

Charlie Abbott	Ed Allen	Robert Anthes
Robert Abel	Robert Ambs	Jan and Allison Aul
Linda Adams	Kerry and Russ	David Baross
Fedrico Aguirre	Anderson	Steve Bartholomew

James Bauch
Donald Bauer
Laura Bauske
Ronald Beach
Jacob Beck
John Bedosky
Renod Bejjani
Bonita Bell
Victoria Benoist
Shelly Bergbower
Mark Bergeron
Jim Berry
Norma Betancourt
Robert Beverage
Brett Beyers
Barbara Black
Benjamin Blackmon
Terri Blake
Lee Bordenave
Vance Borton
Brent Boyd
Catherine Brooks
Jerry Buchs
Byron Camp
Cooper Campbell
Mark Campbell
Pat Cannon
Joseph Castellano
Barbara Castle
Genaro Castro
Robert Catterton
Rosanne Cellini
David Cerminaro
Michael Chapman
Arasu Chellaiah
Steve Childs
Ross Church
Frank Ciarcia
Bob Clarke
Earl Cochran
Aflinda Coke
Georgia Coman
Diane Conklin
Tracy Cooke
Greg Corkins
Robert Cormier

Arnold and Katy Cox
James and Barby Crear
Terry Crim
Patrick Cunningham
Aden Curtis
Carl Cutrone
Eric Dale
William Dambach
Jim Davis
Marcia Davis
Tracy Davis
George Day
Jack Doran
Larry Wayne Dorough
Bill Dugger
Walter Edge
W. P. Edwards
Paula Elmer
Kazim Emini
Rebecca Engel
Tom Esper
Mike Estes
Madeline Faulkner
Gregg Fleming
Ray Freeman
Mark Freund
Keith Gallaher
M. Arthur Garmon
Bertha A. Garza
Roseanne Gillespie
Scott Goddard
Jason Gounaris
Scott Gray
Edward Green
Lupe Green
Leslie Greenfield
Kimberly Greer
Philip and Gary Griner
Fred Grube
Garry Haase
David Hacke
Idaline Hall
Michael Hall
Reta Harbaugh
Robert Hardy
Chris Hartle

Valeria Hazziez
Bruce and Karin
    Henderson
John Herb Jr.
Kathy Hermanson
Rubin Hernandez
Herbert Holcombe
Linda Hollander
Steven Hollingsworth
David Hoover
Margaret Hoover
Lynn Horner
Charles Howe
Hugh Hughes
Louise Hughes
James Hurrle
E. M. Hurtado
Curt Hutchings
Susan Hutchinson
David Ingvoldstad
Vernon Jackson
Terry Jacobson
Cindy Jameson
Jim Jasper
Mike Jay
Diane Jean
Joseph Jerryton
Erik Johnson
Kathleen and Kelly
    Johnson
Sharon Johnson-Burrell
Hattie Jolin
Kevin Jones
Win Jones
Kian Kasra
Donna Kasuska
David Kavaljian
Mark Kehrig
Iain Kelly
Brian Key
Kay and Maxie Key
Blanche Khan
Darja Kiara
Bruce Kirkberg
Robert Knaus
Glen Korell

Joseph Kraut
Bruce Lasner
Jeanne Laudenberg
Charles Lax
Michael Lemmons
Elayne Lieberman
Tad Lignell
Colleen Lilly
John Lloyd
Chuck Loderbauer
Craig Loree
Bryan Lovejoy
Brent Loyd
Ron and Joyce Loyd
James Luce
Richard Lundquist
Lynn Lyons
Bob and Bonnie
    Macioroski
Ed Maksimowicz
Ofelia Mancera
Leah Markstein
Jean Martin
Collin Mayers
Patricia McCallum
Lori McCool
Mike McDermott
John and Peggy
    McGee
Chris McGowan
Sebastian Mellone
Cheryl Merritt
Jim Milnes
John Molinari
Walter Moller
Douglas Monie
Christine Moreno
Harvey Morgan
Ron Mueller
Ed Narmore
Bradley Nelson
Randall Nelson
Bernard Newns
Ann Noble
John Norbert

Hannah Norcross
Don Norgren
Carol O'Conner
Spencer Ohleyer
Akintunde Oni
Juan Ortiz-Moyet
Darryl Owens
Albert Padley
Christine Pearson
Rick Penrod
Kathy Perciful
Bruce Peshek
Larry Peterson
Dale Petry
Ramon Picazo
Ronald Pippin
Rhea Pivetti
Bob Pogorelc
Greg Pohl
Eddie Powell
Joseph Rabbia
Gerald Steve
    Rebagliati
Rosemary Recker
James Reese
Gary Rehak
James Reid
Maureen Reville
Jim Reyes
Bob Ribelin
Michael Rizzolo
Phillip Robbins
Diane Roberts
Bill Rohrs
Silva Roque
Carole Royal
Reynaldo Ruiz
Charles Runels
George Saffas
Jeff Saito
Katherine Schaffer
Steve Schenck
Jach Schiller
Bob Schumacher
David Schweppe

Susan Secord
Steve Seifert
Muyi Shogbuyi
Paul Simsic
Robert Sloan
Bill Smith
Chester Smith
James Smith
Tony Sparks
Kim Stanley
Joel Stein
Joseph Steinhouser
Jan Stephan
Rick Stoddard
Dave Strayer
Charles Strickland
Brian Strong
Janice Tabbut
Helen Tang
Richard Tiedemann
Jim Tollison
Trudy Trexler
Bob Trimble
Marvin Tye
Charles Wagner
Rubin Wald
Robert Walker
Keith Walter
Mike Warren
Martha Washburn
Ann and Scott Webb
Karen Wedding
Steve Wellman
Bob and Barbara
    Wexler
Steve White
Russell Whitehead
John Whitley
Thayne Wilkins
Shelly Williams
Daryl Windland
Bernard Worby
Art Zavala
James Zifchock

I've got some good news and some bad news.

First, the good news. If you're like the average North American, earning at least $25,000 a year, then in your lifetime *over $1 million* will flow through your fingers. That's a lot of money. In other words, you're already on track to be a lifetime millionaire.

Now for the bad news. If you're like most people, you'll spend it all and, after a lifetime of earning, end up with almost nothing. How can that be?

Frankly, nobody teaches us about money. We receive no formal education in the most critical of all life skills—how to become financially successful. Did you ever, in all your years of public education, attend a class entitled "Money 101"? Why isn't such a class mandatory in every elementary school?

How have you learned what you know about money? You picked it up, a piece here . . . a tip there. You absorbed attitudes from your parents, from the media. You observed the examples of friends. You proceeded through trial and error . . . the school of hard knocks. What you learned was haphazard, mostly wrong, and certainly out of context. Most of the books you read about the subject probably overwhelmed you with details or bored you with useless facts. If you're like most, you're confused and frustrated.

Yet money is one of the most important subjects of your entire life. Some of life's greatest enjoyments and most of life's greatest disappointments stem from your decisions about money. Whether you experience great peace of mind or constant anxiety will depend on getting your finances under control. Your relationships will be greatly affected. In fact, most divorces in our society result from disagreements about money. Understanding money—how to make it and keep it—is absolutely essential to your life, to your relationships, to your happiness, to your future.

Still, there are some people who seem to be naturally good at managing money. The same $1 million flows through their fingers, and they seem to know how to keep some of it and even make it grow—in some cases, a hundredfold more than the average person.

Do these people work 100 times harder? Are they 100 times smarter? Of course not. They just know how to play the game. You see, *money is a game* . . . a very important game. If you know the rules, you win. If you don't know the rules, you lose. As physician George David said,

> Wealth *is when small efforts produce big results.*
> Poverty *is when big efforts produce small results.*

In this book, you will finally learn how to play the money game . . . and win. If you follow these simple strategies, you can enjoy a banquet of prosperity throughout your life . . . followed by a financially secure retirement. You will learn a simple system for controlling your finances. You will learn how to invest your surplus funds without losing sleep at night. You will learn how to create multiple streams of lifetime income. You will learn how to oversee your growing financial empire in as little as 10 minutes a day. You will learn how to leave a financially secure future to your family and loved ones.

You may wonder how I qualify to be your instructor. I started in the 1970s, perhaps just like you, with a dream of becoming financially independent. After graduating with an MBA from Brigham Young University in 1974, I began investing in small real estate ventures and parlayed a tiny nest egg into a multi-million-dollar net worth in a few short years. Along the way, I also suffered my share of setbacks. I've not only made millions but lost millions . . . and made them back again. I know from the school of hard knocks what works and what doesn't.

I shared my powerful systems in the number one *New York Times* best-seller, *Nothing Down: A Proven Program That Shows You How to Buy Real Estate with Little or No Money Down.* This book became the all-time real estate investment classic used by beginning investors. I also wrote two other major best-sellers, the number one *New York Times* best-seller, *Creating Wealth,* and *The Challenge.* In promoting this last book, I made the bold statement:

> Send me to any unemployment line. Let me select someone who is out of work and discouraged. In two days' time, I'll teach them the secrets of success, and in 90 days they'll be back on their feet with $5,000 cash in the bank, never to set foot in an unemployment line again!

*The Challenge** is the true story of how I selected three people from the unemployment lines of St. Louis, Missouri, and taught them the secrets of financial success. . . . And, yes, they were able to achieve incredible success in 90 days. One of the couples went on to earn over $100,000 in the 12 months that followed. To celebrate, I took them on *Good Morning America* with me.

What I am about to share with you is the result of having worked with thousands of successful people over two full decades. I have seen people go from living on the streets to living in mansions . . . from driving a taxi to being driven in limousines.

Although my most famous book is about real estate investing, the book you now have in your hands will show you how to create wealth in many different ways . . . from multiple sources. Actually, there are three great wealth-creation mountains. I call them *money mountains.* Each mountain is distinct from the others, and yet each share similar characteristics. The mountains are the *investment mountain,* the *real estate mountain,* and the *marketing mountain.*

From this mountain range of money mountains, there are at least 10 separate and distinct streams of income flowing into your growing reservoir of wealth. Each stream was carefully chosen using a formula I call the *money tree formula.* In this book, I will teach you the 9 characteristics of the ideal stream of income. Then I will teach you exactly how to profit from each of these streams. The goal is for you to add at least one new stream of income to your life each year. Eventually, these streams will overflow your life with prosperity and freedom.

The first question people usually ask at this point is, "Why multiple streams?"

The Wisdom of Multiple Streams of Income

How many streams of income did it take in the 1950s for a family to survive? *One.* Today, very few families can survive on less than two streams of income. And even that won't be enough in the future. It's a volatile future. You'd be wise to have multiple streams of income flowing into your life.

Prosperous people have always known this. If one stream dries up, they have many more to support them. Ordinary people are much more vulnerable. If they lose one of their streams, it wipes them out. And it takes them years to recover.

In the future, you will need a *portfolio of income streams*—not one or two—but many streams from completely different and diversified sources,

---

* Although my first two books were number one *New York Times* best-sellers, *The Challenge* is my favorite and, I think, my best book. I'll send you a free copy if you'll pay the shipping and handling. Call my office at 801-852-8700.

so that if one streams goes, you'll barely feel the bump. You're stable. You have time to adjust. You're safe.

Do you have multiple streams of income flowing into your life at this time? Maybe it's time to add another one.

In this book, I'll teach you the nitty-gritty strategies and techniques for developing 10 separate streams of income. But first, let's make sure that your streams flow from a wellspring of true and sound financial principles.

CHAPTER 1

*The greatest mathematical discovery
of all time is compound interest.*
ALBERT EINSTEIN

Easy Money: Financial Freedom on a Dollar a Day

It all starts with a single unit of money.

In the United States, Canada, Australia, Hong Kong, and New Zealand, it's the dollar. In Great Britain, it's the pound. In France and Switzerland, it's the franc. In Germany, it's the mark. In Japan, the yen.

Wherever you are, reach into your wallet or purse and dig out some of your own paper currency and examine it. Rub it between your fingers. Feel the texture. Bring it to your nose. Does money smell? Examine the images. Notice the serial numbers. Turn it over. Notice the strange symbols. What do they mean? Imagine that you're looking at it through a microscope. Read every single word. This simple piece of paper doesn't appear to be worth much. Inflation erodes its value daily. So what if you waste it or lose it or throw it away.

But wait a minute. Can this ordinary piece of paper money be worth more than meets the eye? Could it be a magic ticket to a more abundant life of anywhere/anytime/anything you want? One thing's sure: How people feel about these silly pieces of paper makes a huge difference in how they enjoy life's great banquet of prosperity.

When you've finished reading this chapter, I promise that you'll never think of money in the same way again. Ever. You see, prosperous people don't think of money as just colored pieces of paper adorned with pictures of famous dead people. They imagine it as seeds—money seeds—with the power to grow into money trees, bearing fruit to fulfill every one of their dreams. And they are absolutely right.

Every dollar bill is a money seed. Just as a tiny acorn contains the power to grow into a mighty oak tree, each dollar bill has the power to grow into a mighty money tree. You can grow one of these money trees . . . on as little as a dollar a day. Could you afford that?

If you follow the advice in this book, you will soon have your own majestic money tree, growing right in the center of your future dream home. Imagine that! Branches of your money tree are growing along the ceiling and spreading into every room of the house. Every few feet along each branch are ripening money fruits that pop open once or twice a day releasing crisp $100 bills. As the $100 bills fall from the tree, they float into money baskets throughout the house. All night long you hear the pop, pop, pop of the ripening money fruits. You might think the sound would keep you awake, but it's a very soothing sound. Your money tree produces fruit 24 hours a day. While you sleep. While you work. While you play. While you eat. It never stops. An endless stream of cash flow. Whenever you need money, you just take whatever you want from one of the baskets. Get the picture?

If you destroy an acorn, the potential oak tree inside also dies. Every time you waste one of those silly pieces of paper money, it's just like destroying a potential money tree. That's why it is so important to preserve and protect each of these money seeds. (See Figure 1.1.)

So how much is one of those seeds really worth? That depends on how long you let it grow and at what rate of growth. Let's suppose you take a single dollar and put it into a special bank account that will let the dollar grow, untouched by taxes and fees. How long will it take for this *single dollar bill* to grow into *$1 million?*

That depends on the interest rate that the bank account pays. If it's like ordinary bank accounts, then it's going to take a long, long time. Table 1.1 shows you how long it takes for a single dollar bill to grow into $1 million at various interest rates.

**TABLE 1.1 A Single Dollar
Grows into $1 Million**

Interest Rate	Time in Years
0%	Never
3%	468
5%	284
10%	145
15%	99
20%	75

FIGURE 1.1　Your money tree.

As you can see, at bank rates of 3 percent it will take 468 years for a single dollar bill to grow into $1 million. What? Not planning on living 468 years? Relax. We're not done with that dollar bill yet. We've got to supercharge it. How can we do this? Rather than just planting one money seed, could you plant them more often? Could you afford to put away a dollar a day? Thirty bucks a month! You can do that.

Table 1.2 shows the number of years it takes for a dollar a day to grow into $1 million at various interest rates. Wow! A dollar a day becomes $1 million in the span of a normal lifetime.

Suppose you'd invested a dollar a day starting on the day you were born. Table 1.3 shows what you'd have at age 66. A dollar a day grows

TABLE 1.2　A Dollar a Day Grows into $1 Million

Interest Rate	Time in Years
3%	147
5%	100
10%	56
15%	40
20%	32

TABLE 1.3 A Dollar a Day Compounded at Various Rates for 66 Years

Interest Rate	Cumulative Savings
0%	$24,000
3%	$77,000
5%	$193,000
10%	$2.7 million
15%	$50 million
20%	$1 billion

into *$1 billion* by the normal retirement age! That's a whole forest of money trees. You're Ross Perot in embryo! And what makes this happen? The power of *compound interest* makes a few dollars a day grow into enormous sums of money. Einstein himself said, "The most powerful invention of man is compound interest."

But suppose you don't want to wait for 66 years. Okay, there's another way to speed up the process. Could you plant two or three seeds a day? Or five? Or ten? What does that do? Well, let's cut right to the chase. If you put away 10 lousy bucks a day and put it in the right mutual funds or stocks or real estate and let the clock tick at 20 percent, you're a millionaire in just 20 years! (Pop, pop, pop, pop.) Excited yet?

Now, I can hear the skeptics saying, "No one can sustain a 20 percent rate of growth for 20 consecutive years. It's not possible!" Well, Warren Buffett, the stock market genius, was able to do it for over 40 consecutive years. When you've finished reading this book, you'll know that it's not only possible for you, but entirely within the reach of anyone with discipline and a few financial skills. You don't have to be a financial genius. You don't have to own a big company. You can do it from your kitchen table using the money that you're now foolishly throwing away. If you just divert a few of your ill-spent dollars and funnel them into some well-timed investments, you can achieve financial success.

TABLE 1.4 How Various Amounts per Day Can Grow into $1 Million

Savings per Day	3%	5%	10%	15%	20%
$1	147 yrs.	99 yrs.	56 yrs.	40 yrs.	32 yrs.
$2	124	85	49	36	28
$3	112	77	45	33	26
$4	102	71	42	31	25
$5	95	67	40	30	24
$6	90	63	38	28	22
$7	85	61	37	27	22
$8	81	58	36	26	21
$9	77	56	35	26	21
$10	74	54	34	25	20

I'll bet you'll think twice before you throw away one of those silly green pieces of paper. It's like throwing away the seed to a $1 million money tree.

Every time you save one of those money seeds, you start sowing your way to wealth. The most important lesson of this chapter is to change your attitude about money, especially those $1 bills. I have no doubt you can save $30 per month . . . even on the most meager budget. Over time, you will want to increase this to $100, $200, or $300 a month or more. The more the better. The more the faster. How many seeds do you think you could save and invest every day? Table 1.4 and Figure 1.2 show you how a few dollars a day can grow into $1 million.

How to Earn an Extra Million in Your Lifetime

The real key is to keep socking away the money. Let the numbers whisper their silent but relentless message. Consistency. Day in, day out. Save. Invest. Save. Invest. It might be boring. It might be dull. It might be hard to do. No matter. Just do it.

I met a young man in Chicago who had made the decision to make his future bright by dimming his desires today. He worked full time, as did his spouse. If they had been like normal (broke) young married couples, they would have pooled their two pay-

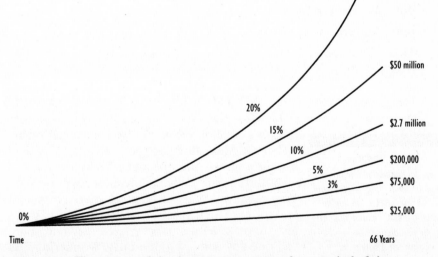

FIGURE 1.2 The power of tiny investments over a long period of time.

checks and bought a new car (with a fat monthly payment), stretched themselves into "too much house," and stressed out for the next 30 years. Instead, this young couple made a very smart choice. They lived on her paycheck and saved his entire monthly $2,000 paycheck. They put the money into well-selected mutual funds and watched the cash begin to pile up. This is true prosperity.

Our parents were right. We cringed when they told us, "Live on less than you earn. Invest the surplus. Avoid debt. Build long-term security." This may not be the exciting get-rich-quick rabbit, but the tortoise laughs slowly all the way to the bank. So, with that tortoise mentality firmly in place, let's start building some specific plans for the future.

Setting Some Specific and Realistic Financial Goals

First of all, you have five decisions to make about your money seeds:

Target: How much total money would you like to accumulate?

Amount: How many dollars a day can you squeeze out of your life?

Rate: What interest rate can you earn on your invested dollars?

Time: When would you like to reach your goal?

Purpose: What is your financial purpose?

For example, suppose you decide you want a $1 million nest egg in 20 years. Your ultimate purpose is to quit your job and spend your life working with the youth in your church. According to Table 1.5, one scenario would be to invest $10 per day at 20 percent per year to reach your goal:

Target: $1 million

Amount: $10 per day

Rate: 20 percent

Time: 20 years

Purpose: Church youth

Using the charts in Table 1.5, I'd like you to come up with a reasonable scenario for your wealth-building plan. To do so, use the worksheet that follows and fill in the blanks for your target financial goals. Make sure you spend some quality time asking yourself the question, "Why do I really want this money? What is my ultimate purpose?" Your moneymaking will be much more successful and meaningful if you have a clear purpose. If it's just "to make a lot of money," you may find yourself one day with a lot of money, wondering, "Is this all there is?"

Financial Target Worksheet

What is my target investment goal? $ _____

How much can I invest per day? $_____ per day

How long am I willing to invest?   _____ years

What is my target interest rate?   _____ %

Why is it important to me to achieve this goal?

_____

_____

_____

_____

The sooner you start, the richer you are immediately! Hey, wait a minute! This sounds too good to be true! A few dollars a day and you can become a millionaire? If this is so easy, why aren't all of us millionaires? Well, the truth is, we all *could* be millionaires, but most of us lack the simple discipline to make small daily deposits over long periods of time. And then, of course, we procrastinate getting started.

Let me show you the terrible cost of procrastination. Suppose you had the discipline to sock away $200 a month (about $7 a day) over a 20-year period of time with a target interest rate of 20 percent. How much could you accumulate? According to my calculator, $200 per month at 20 percent for 20 years grows into $632,000. Not bad!

Now, suppose instead of starting this year, you wait a year to get started. This leaves you only 19 years of growth instead of 20. According to my calculator, you would have only $516,000 in your bank account in 20 years. That's $116,000 less than you could have had if you had started on schedule. In other words, your procrastination cost you $116,000 in future dollars!

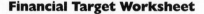

$$$

WIT & WISDOM
How did a fool and his money get together in the first place?

Procrastination is expensive! For each of the 365 days that you waited, your future portfolio was shrinking by over $300 (116,000 ÷ 365 = $317.81). In other words, every day you procrastinate costs you $300 (or $13 an hour, 24 hours a day).

What if you were to invest the same $200 per month over 30 years? The cost of waiting that extra year is now a whopping $842,803. Waiting an extra year costs you almost $1 million in future dollars. That's over $2,000 a day, or almost $100 per hour, 24 hours a day. *Every day you wait . . . every hour you delay . . . is like burning up future money!*

Do it now. Do it regularly.

One final word: *consistency.* How much you invest is not as important as consistently investing that amount over a long period of time. If you miss a payment or two, no big deal. But let me show you what happens when you mess with the formulas. Suppose you could invest $200 month for 20

TABLE 1.5 Wealth-Building Plan*

Assuming 5% interest

Savings per day	5 years	10 years	15 years	20 years	30 years	41 years	45 years	54 years
$1	2	5	8	13	25	50	60	100
$2	4	10	16	26	50	100	120	200
$3	6	15	24	39	75	150	180	300
$4	8	20	32	52	100	200	240	400
$5	10	25	40	65	125	250	300	500
$6	12	30	48	78	150	300	360	600
$7	14	35	56	91	175	350	420	700
$8	16	40	64	104	200	400	480	800
$9	18	45	72	117	225	450	540	900
$10	20	50	80	130	250	500	600	1.0
$11	22	55	88	143	275	550	660	1.1
$12	24	60	96	156	300	600	720	1.2
$13	26	65	104	169	325	650	780	1.3
$14	28	70	112	182	350	700	840	1.4
$15	30	75	120	195	375	750	900	1.5
$16	32	80	128	208	400	800	960	1.6
$17	34	85	136	221	425	850	1.0	1.7
$18	36	90	144	234	450	900	1.1	1.8
$19	38	95	152	247	475	950	1.2	1.9
$20	40	100	160	260	500	1.0	1.2	2.0

Assuming 10% interest

Savings per day	5 years	10 years	15 years	20 years	30 years	41 years	45 years	54 years
	3	6	13	25	75	200	300	1
$2	5	12	25	50	150	400	600	2
$3	8	18	38	75	225	600	900	3
$4	10	24	50	100	300	800	1.2	4
$5	13	30	63	125	375	1.0	1.5	5
$6	15	36	75	150	450	1.2	1.8	6
$7	18	42	88	175	525	1.4	2.1	7
$8	20	48	100	200	600	1.6	2.4	8
$9	23	54	113	225	675	1.8	2.7	9
$10	25	60	125	250	750	2.0	3.0	10
$11	28	66	138	275	825	2.2	3.3	11
$12	30	72	150	300	900	2.4	3.6	12
$13	33	78	163	325	975	2.6	3.9	13
$14	35	84	175	350	1.0	2.8	4.2	14
$15	38	90	188	375	1.1	3.0	4.5	15
$16	40	96	200	400	1.2	3.2	4.8	16
$17	43	102	213	425	1.3	3.4	5.1	17
$18	45	108	225	450	1.4	3.6	5.4	18
$19	48	114	238	475	1.4	3.8	5.7	19
$20	50	120	250	500	1.5	4.0	6.0	20

| Assuming 15% interest | | | | | | | | |
Savings per day	5 years	10 years	15 years	20 years	30 years	41 years	45 years	54 years
$1	3	10	20	50	100	250	1	5
$2	5	20	40	100	200	500	2	10
$3	8	30	60	150	300	750	3	15
$4	10	40	80	200	400	1.0	4	20
$5	13	50	100	250	500	1.3	5	25
$6	15	60	120	300	600	1.5	6	30
$7	18	70	140	350	700	1.8	7	35
$8	20	80	160	400	800	2.0	8	40
$9	23	90	180	450	900	2.3	9	45
$10	25	100	200	500	1.0	2.5	10	50
$11	28	110	220	550	1.1	2.8	11	55
$12	30	120	240	600	1.2	3.0	12	60
$13	33	130	260	650	1.3	3.3	13	65
$14	35	140	280	700	1.4	3.5	14	70
$15	38	150	300	750	1.5	3.8	15	75
$16	40	160	320	800	1.6	4.0	16	80
$17	43	170	340	850	1.7	4.3	17	85
$18	45	180	360	900	1.8	4.5	18	90
$19	48	190	380	950	1.9	4.8	19	95
$20	50	200	400	1.0	2.0	5.0	20	100

| Assuming 20% interest | | | | | | | | |
Savings per day	5 years	10 years	15 years	20 years	30 years	41 years	45 years	54 years
$1	3	12	35	100	250	750	5	50
$2	6	24	70	200	500	1.5	10	100
$3	9	36	105	300	750	2.3	15	150
$4	12	48	140	400	1.0	3.0	20	200
$5	15	60	175	500	1.3	3.8	25	250
$6	18	72	205	600	1.5	4.5	30	300
$7	21	84	240	700	1.8	5.3	35	350
$8	24	96	275	800	2.0	6.0	40	400
$9	27	108	315	900	2.3	6.8	45	450
$10	30	120	350	1.0	2.5	7.5	50	500
$11	33	132	385	1.1	2.8	8.3	55	550
$12	36	144	420	1.2	3.0	9.0	60	600
$13	39	156	455	1.3	3.3	9.8	65	650
$14	42	168	490	1.4	3.5	10.5	70	700
$15	45	180	525	1.5	3.8	11.3	75	750
$16	48	192	560	1.6	4.0	12.0	80	800
$17	51	204	595	1.7	4.3	12.8	85	850
$18	54	216	630	1.8	4.5	13.5	90	900
$19	57	228	665	1.9	4.8	14.3	95	950
$20	60	240	700	2.0	5.0	15.0	100	1,000

*Numbers in unshaded boxes are in thousands of dollars. Numbers in shaded boxes are in millions of dollars.

years with a target rate of return of 20 percent. You are pretty good at socking the money away for a few months, and then you read an ad in the paper for a great deal on a new car. In order to be able to afford the new car, you decide to lower your savings rate from $200 a month to $100 a month. In 20 years, instead of having $632,000 sitting in the bank, you'll have only $316,000 and a very old car. That's $316,000 less. Is your new car worth that much? If you invest wisely today, you'll be able to pay cash for any car you want 20 years from now. Deferring gratification for a while will allow your money tree to grow. When you prematurely pick the fruit from your money tree, you stunt its growth and dramatically reduce the time it takes for you to enjoy a fully matured, fruit-bearing money tree.

You can do the most good for the greatest number of people, yourself included.

Let's examine the money trees of some of the last century's most famous billionaires. You'll have to admit, they knew how to grow money trees. What did they do with their wealth? Almost every one of them set up a foundation that would outlive them. These foundations are like money tree forests that continue to thrive long after the money tree farmers are gone.

In the *World Book Encyclopedia,* under "Foundations," you'll discover that there are over 24,000 charitable foundations set up in the United States alone, dispensing yearly charitable grants to needy groups and organizations of almost *$5 billion.* The top 10 foundations are as follows:

	Assets	Annual Giving
Ford Foundation	$4.8 billion	$170 million
Getty Trust	3.7 billion	160 million
Kellogg Foundation	3.1 billion	75 million
MacArthur Foundation	2.3 billion	105 million
Lilly Foundation	1.9 billion	57 million
Johnson Foundation	1.8 billion	95 million
Rockefeller Foundation	1.6 billion	45 million
Pew Charitable Trusts	1.6 billion	90 million
Mellon Foundation	1.5 billion	67 million
Kresge Foundation	1.1 billion	42 million

The Ford Foundation was established in 1936, yet decades later is still giving away more than a $100 million a year to needy causes. No matter what your attitude toward the wealth of the Fords, Rockefellers, or Gettys, you've got to admit that hundreds of thousands of people (even you) are benefiting each day from the legacy of these great money masters. The fruits from their money trees continue to bless the world.

You can have a major, positive impact on future generations.

If you learn the secrets of these successful money masters, eventually you, too, will be able to leave a legacy that will outlive you. Although leaving a $100 million fortune may be the furthest thing from your mind today (you'd probably rather make an extra $10,000 this year), I encourage you to imagine what your future foundation might look like. Answer the following question: *Once you have achieved your financial goals and lived a long, prosperous, happy, and healthy life, how do you want your money invested so that it can have the greatest positive impact on future generations?*

$$ $$$ $$

WIT & WISDOM
Money is like manure. You have to spread it around or it smells.

J. PAUL GETTY

_____

_____

_____

_____

_____

In the purest sense, money is a spiritual concept. It contains the power to do so much good. Imagine the benefit that you could provide to future groups of worthy people. Imagine your own posterity—your own great-great-grandchildren—a century from now. How could they benefit from your wise financial, spiritual, and intellectual legacy? If you won't do it for yourself, at least do it for them.

Now let's look at that dollar bill one more time. This simple money seed contains the power to bless you and countless future generations. But only if you'll start now. The future is counting on you. A wealthy future is awaiting you. It's worth the sacrifice. Remember, it all starts with a single unit of money.

I wish I had the power to reach more people with the message that you've just read. Why don't they teach these things in school? I feel so strongly that more people should learn these concepts that I've made this entire chapter available free on my web site. If you'd like to share it with someone else—your family, for example—just go to www .multiplestreamsofincome.com and click on the *Free chapter* link.

Now that you have the right respect for each of those priceless money seeds, let me show you specifically how to turn each of them into $1 million money trees. Join me in the next chapter and let's get started.

CHAPTER 2

The way to wealth, if you desire it, is as plain as the way to market.
It depends chiefly on two words, industry and frugality;
that is waste neither time nor money, but make the best use of both.
BENJAMIN FRANKLIN

The 10-Minute Millionaire

In the previous chapter you learned how easy it could be for you to be financially free. A few dollars a day compounded over a long period of time . . . anyone can do that. You *could*—but *will* you? Do you have the will for it? It's easy to dream. But do you have the discipline to do it . . . a dollar at a time? To weaken your will, the "world of stuff" beckons: "Buy this. You need this now. Spend, spend, spend." What do prosperous people do when faced with the relentless siren song of instant gratification?

Prosperous people practice seven financial secrets. I call them *secrets* not because very few of us are aware of them, but because very few of us use them. The secrets are, in reality, skills . . . essential money skills that all wealthy people practice. I believe that if you learn these skills, wealth can flow into your life . . . multiple streams of increasing prosperity. Wouldn't that be nice? Money to buy whatever you want . . . houses, cars, travel, freedom. Surplus to share with the people you care most about. Security. Peace of mind. That's what these skills will bring you.

Throughout this book, you'll learn how to cut through the blinding blizzard of financial information swirling around you every day and focus on the seven essential money skills that will take you to financial security. I call these skills *money skills*. (See Figure 2.1.)

The first three money skills form the foundation of all financial success. Without them, none of the other skills have power. If you don't value money, you won't make the effort to control it. If you can't control it, you

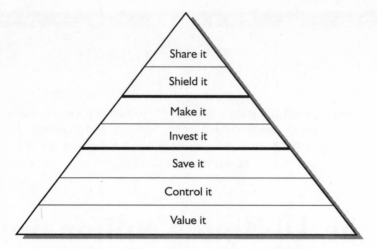

FIGURE 2.1 **The seven essential money skills.**

won't be able to save it. And if you can't save it, there won't be any surplus to invest. If you don't understand investing, you'll be a less effective entrepreneur. Therefore, you won't have any money to shield. And if you don't have any to shield, you won't have any to share.

You may be tempted to skip over this chapter and get to the real "moneymaking" chapters, but please be patient. This is the foundation-building stage of financial freedom. For many years I have taught real estate investing seminars in which people learn how to buy millions of dollars worth of property for little or no down payment. I find that a certain percentage of people who buy property are then unable to manage the cash flow of that property.

I remember one student who was especially impatient. He didn't want to waste time learning basic money management skills. He wanted to make some "real money" and then hire someone to take care of his money. By asking him a few pointed questions, I discovered that his personal finances were in shambles. Here was a person living in financial chaos, lacking the discipline even to balance his own checkbook, who could hardly wait to acquire a 50-unit apartment building so he could get rich quick. If he thinks his money problems are bad now, wait till he adds the problems of managing a 50-unit apartment building. That would multiply his financial chaos by 50!

So, whether you're starting from scratch or doing well financially, we're going to begin at the foundation and build sound financial management skills. Then we'll move to the next stage of wealth. I want you to build on a strong foundation of proven financial strength. If you can manage the pennies in your life, then you'll be ready to manage the millions that will soon be flowing into your life. If you can't manage the pennies, even though millions may come, you won't be able to hang onto them. As proof, I simply point to the dismal experience of lottery winners. If they had simply followed the ideas in this chapter, many of those lottery millionaires, instead of being broke, would be multimillionaires today.

In Chapter 1, you learned the first and most basic money skill . . . how to *value* it. Warren Buffett, one of the world's wealthiest investors, has two important rules: (1) Never lose money. (2) Never forget rule 1. He hates to lose money because he is keenly aware of the *future value* of each squandered dollar. For him, a $1,000 loss today represents the loss of millions of future dollars.

Money Skill 1: Value It

The following quote explains how billionaire John D. Rockefeller taught his children to value money:

> John D. Rockefeller, Jr., was certainly not trying to save money when he decided to pay an allowance to his five sons. According to son Nelson, "We got 25 cents a week, and had to earn the rest of the money we got." To earn part of that extra money he raised vegetables and rabbits. . . . "We always worked," according to Nelson. All the boys were required to keep personal daily account books. They were required to give 10 percent of their income to charity, to save 10 percent, and to account for all the rest. They had to balance their account books every month and to be able to tell what happened to every penny they earned. Nelson went on to serve as Governor of the state of New York for many years, and, ultimately, became Vice President of the United States. One of his brothers, David Rockefeller, Chairman of the Chase Manhattan Bank, says, "We all profited by the experience—especially when it came to understanding the value of money."*

Interesting. You'd expect that these kids, raised in the lap of luxury, wouldn't need to learn these things. Yet Rockefeller wanted his kids to understand money. He taught them a specific pattern for dealing with their money. There is a lot of wisdom in what he did.

The necessity for *work*:	When you earn it, you value it.
The importance of *charity*:	Give away the first 10 percent.
The need for *saving*:	Pay yourself the next 10 percent.
The power of *accountability*:	Account for every penny.

In addition to valuing money, Rockefeller was teaching his kids how to control their money. And that's the second of the seven money skills.

* Ken Davis and Tom Taylor, *Kids and Cash,* Oak Tree Publications, 1979.

Money Skill 2: Control It

The first step in gaining control of your finances is to set up a simple system for organizing your financial life. You may already have a system for controlling your finances. Maybe you use one of the popular computer programs such as Quicken or Microsoft Money. Even so, I think you could learn a lot from a simple system I call Streams and Leaks.

Most people have one simple stream (or main source) of income: their job. This income flows into the reservoir of their life, but the reservoir has leaks and the money flows out through them. Most everyone spends every penny they earn and then some. Obviously, the only way to have overflowing prosperity in your life is to plug up those leaks and to add more streams . . . to have *multiple streams of income.* It is critical to plug leaks *and* keep streams flowing. How many financial streams do you have flowing into your life? How many leaks are there in *your* reservoir? (See Figure 2.2.)

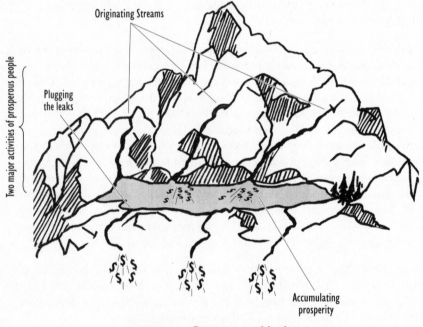

FIGURE 2.2 Streams and leaks.

Let's look at plugging up the leaks first. Then we'll focus our attention on how to keep the streams flowing. I have condensed the many ways you can spend money into 10 categories, or leaks. I've kept the categories simple and broad; if they get too complicated, you'll ignore them. Even when using a computer finance program like Quicken, you can organize your expenditures into these 10 categories. It's easy to remember the categories. They are listed in order of priority.

The first leak, or category (using the Rockefeller model), is called *giving.*

This represents your contributions to church, charity, and others. This category is number 1. I find it interesting that Rockefeller taught his kids to give the *first* 10 percent of their earnings to others. To learn why I believe he chose to do this, visit my web site at www.multiplestreamsofincome.com and enter the keyword God and money.

After you pay the first 10 percent to your "silent partner," you pay yourself. The next 10 percent of your money belongs in category 2: *self.* In the classic, *The Richest Man in Babylon,* George S. Clayson tells the story of the wise investor whose primary rule was, "A part of all you earn is yours to keep." How true. Most of us save out of what's "left over." Prosperous people save *first* and then live on what's left over. This makes a huge difference.

After you pay 10 percent to others and 10 percent to yourself, the third category, number 3, is *taxes.* (See Figure 2.3.)

1. Giving   2. Self   3. Taxes

FIGURE 2.3   The first three leaks.

After the first three categories, what is the next most important expense of your life? Category 4 is your *shelter* . . . in the form of house payments or rent.

The fifth category is *household* expenses such as food, clothing, television, and the normal expenses of living in your residence. This will amount to your largest category.

Then comes category 6: *auto.* You need transportation. Every time you pay for gas, transportation, and repairs to your vehicles, or make car payments, you should organize these expenditures in category 6.

Next is category 7: *fun and entertainment.* Whenever you spend money away from home on movies, fast food, travel, or toys, you should think of these expenditures as part of category 7, the number for fun.

Then comes category 8, all forms of *insurance:* health, life, disability, liability, personal possessions, homeowners, and so forth.

Miscellaneous expenditures (including payments toward debt) come under category 9, *debt/miscellaneous.*

And finally, there is category 10: *business* expenditures.

As you can see, all of your expenditures can be summarized into just 10 broad categories. (See Figure 2.4.)

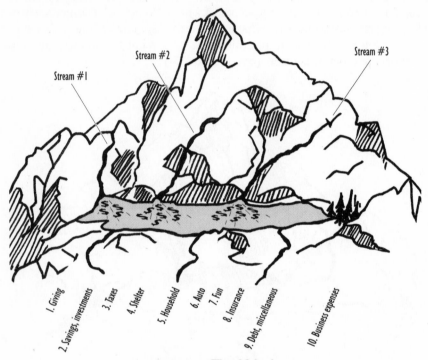

FIGURE 2.4   The 10 leaks.

You spend money only a few times a day. And yet those few decisions can make all the difference between poverty and wealth. Let's examine the actual act of spending. Let's dissect a typical money transaction, or *money event.* If you could dissect a normal money event, what would it look like? Let's examine Figure 2.5.

Prosperous people have a unique attitude toward each money event. During a typical transaction, they complete a few extra key activities. In doing so, they spend a few extra minutes per money event. I believe that it is these few extra key minutes that make all the difference. That's why I call this the *millionaire minute.*

Would you invest a few extra minutes per money event if you knew it would eventually help you become financially free? Here is how people who are good with money approach a money event:

$$$ You Can't Delegate This to Anyone $$$

The subject of budgeting and saving and penny-pinching seems tedious to most of us, yet these skills or habits must become part of your life if you ever hope to achieve any measure of financial success. Don't give me your old excuses. Don't you dare tell me you're not good at math, or that you hate to balance your checkbook, or that you don't have a head for numbers, or that you never went to college, or that you don't know how to use a calculator, or that your spouse takes care of that stuff, or that you don't have the time, or that life is short and you'd better enjoy it while you can. Odds are, you're going to live well past retirement age, and you must plan for it by taking charge of your finances *now*.

Have you ever walked past a penny on the sidewalk and not picked it up because it was just a penny? The truth is, hidden beneath that penny is a stack of a million pennies. Pick up that penny and invest it immediately. Make the decision that, starting today, you will no longer go into debt to support your lifestyle. You're going to live below your means . . . no matter what. It may take you months to turn your spending patterns around. For an oil tanker to change course 180 degrees takes many, many hours and hundreds of miles to accomplish. You're like that tanker—it will take time to turn your financial bad habits into good ones, so be patient with yourself.

1. They plan the purchase. As with airline tickets, the longer the planning horizon, the cheaper the purchase.

2. They expect, ask for, and often get a discount.

3. They expect, ask for, and always get a receipt.

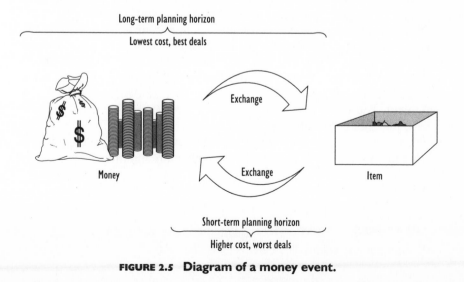

FIGURE 2.5 Diagram of a money event.

$$$ Financially Challenged versus Financially Prosperous $$$

Financially Challenged	Financially Prosperous
A day late and a dollar short	Abundance and time freedom
Short planning horizon—impulse buying	Long planning horizon
Planning wants and procrastinating needs	Planning needs and procrastinating wants
Paying retail	Paying wholesale
Not getting a receipt	Getting a receipt
Not categorizing a receipt	Categorizing a receipt
Not filing a receipt	Filing a receipt

4. They always examine the receipt for errors.

5. They immediately write on their receipt a category number.

6. They balance their accounts to the penny.

7. They file the receipt as soon as they get home.

All told, on average, the millionaire spends about a minute or two more per transaction than the poor person. This takes no more than 10 minutes per day. But what a savings in time and money! The millionaire saves from 10 to 20 percent by comparison shopping. What if you could lower your annual spending by 20 percent without a lot of sacrifice? By investing an extra minute to record the transaction and to file it properly, you have at your fingertips a vast source of information. You know your current account balances. You can compare your spending to previous months, and you'll notice trends. You are more aware of your actual spending. This gives you much greater control of your finances.

You can calculate your tax consequences in minutes, not days. You can back up your tax decisions with instant documentation. In case of dispute, you know where, when, and how you spent your money, and you have a receipt to prove it. You are in control. And the resulting peace of mind creates a feeling of power. This increases your confidence, creativity, and judgment. You make fast, correct, decisive decisions. This gives you that secret millionaire's advantage.

From now on, every time you spend money, take a few extra minutes during that money event to practice the millionaire minute:

Plan your purchase.

Get a discount.

Get a receipt.

Examine your receipt.

Categorize your receipt.

Balance your account.

File your receipt.

Setting up your filing system is simple. Get 10 manila folders and number them from 1 to 10. At the end of the day, quickly file your categorized receipts into one of the 10 manila folders. If a receipt is a household expense, file it in folder number 5. If it is for entertainment, file it in folder number 7. Where would you file a receipt for an automobile expense? How about a business expense? Do this and you'll be in control of your expenses in a few short weeks.

Why go to all this trouble? In Chapter 1, I explained the power of compound interest—how just $1 a day can grow into millions given enough time. By practicing the millionaire minute, you will be able to *find* that extra $1 to $10 a day to fund your investment program. You can grow wealthy on the money that is *already* flowing through your fingers.

Most people don't practice the millionaire minute; therefore, they don't plan their purchases. This alone increases their living expenses by at least 10 percent. In addition, they don't collect receipts. And if they do, they throw their loose receipts into a shoe box. At the end of the year, doing their taxes is a real chore, taking time and extra money for their accountant to sort out—more lost money.

Just how much are those lost receipts worth? Suppose you buy a pen and instead of throwing away the receipt you actually keep it, categorize it, and file it for tax time. Now you have proof of a tax-deductible expense for your home-based business. You can deduct this expense from your income *before* you calculate your taxes. What is this worth to you? *An immediate 30 percent return on your money!*

If you're in the 30 percent tax bracket, every dollar you categorize as a tax deduction gives you a 30 percent return on your money. Did you get that? Hello? Where can you today get an instant 30 percent guaranteed return on your money? When you get and keep the receipt for a tax-deductible expense and then deduct that expenditure on your taxes, you're making 30 percent on your money. This 30 percent return on your money is the kind of thing that turns ordinary people into millionaires. Start today to gain greater control over your money by doing the millionaire minute. . . . You'll be amazed.

I've created a special form that you can use to give yourself a financial tune-up. It's called a MoneyTracker. (See Figure 2.6.) I promise that if you'll use the MoneyTracker for 30 days, you'll be amazed at the confidence it will build in your ability to control your finances. After 30 days, you can continue to use the MoneyTracker or go back to

$$$

WIT & WISDOM
All progress is based upon a universal innate desire of every organism to live beyond its income.
EDMUND BURKE

WIT & WISDOM
Things turn out best for the people who make the best of the way things turn out.
TY BOYD

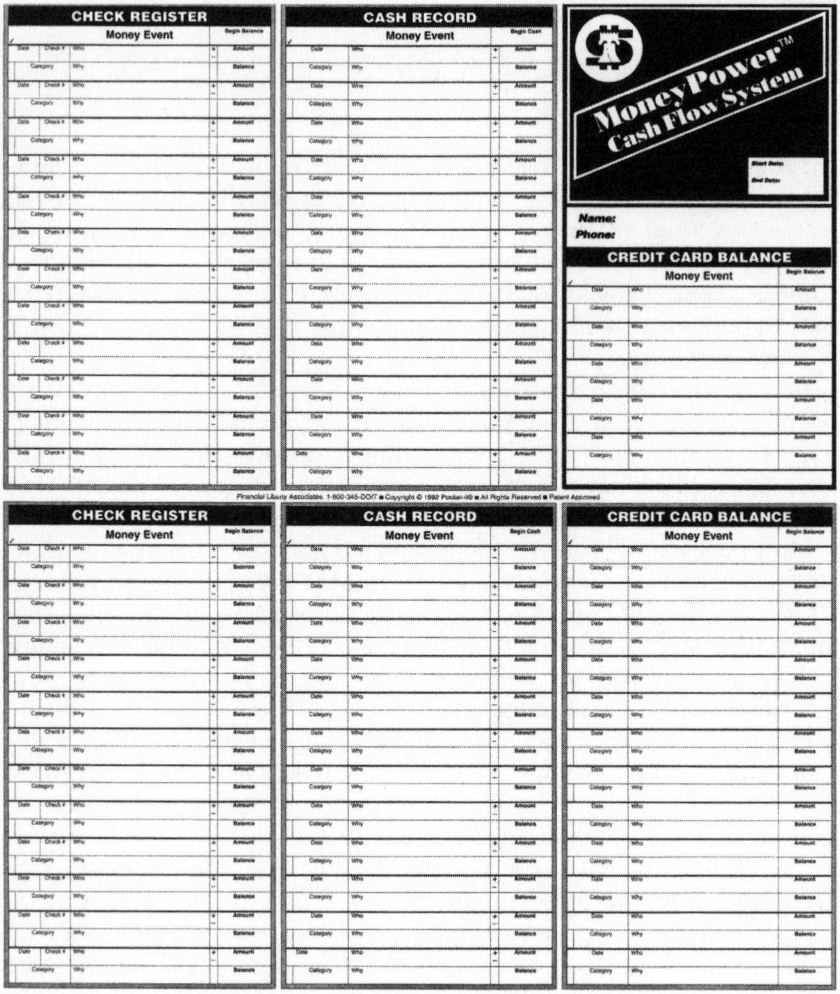

FIGURE 2.6 The MoneyTracker form.

your old ways of doing things, but every six months you should use the MoneyTracker for another 30 days to sharpen your skills. If you'd like to download a fully printable copy of the MoneyTracker, visit my web site at www.multiplestreamsofincome.com and enter the keyword MoneyTracker.

Money Skill 3: Save It

The key to financial planning is cash-flow management. You've not only got to get the cash to flow into your reservoir, but you also have to manage the leaks so that there is money left over at the end of the month. This monthly surplus is the secret to financial growth. The surplus can be invested. The object of the money game is to accumulate enough investments so that the income from these investments will eventually support you. The third money skill is to save your surplus. (See Figure 2.7.)

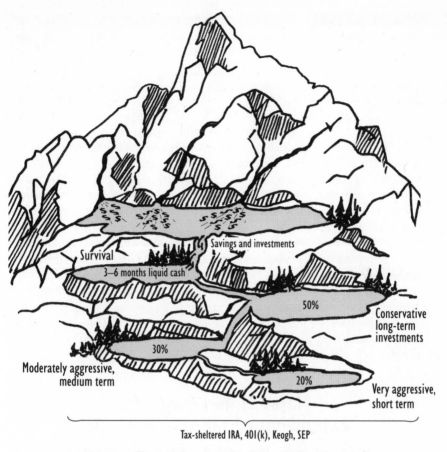

Savings and investments

Survival

3–6 months liquid cash

50% — Conservative long-term investments

30% Moderately aggressive, medium term

20% Very aggressive, short term

Tax-sheltered IRA, 401(k), Keogh, SEP

FIGURE 2.7 Financial reservoir with overflow basins.

There are two meanings for the word *save:* (1) to pay less for your purchases, as in "Safeway *saves* you more!"; (2) to create a surplus, as in "I need to *save* some money for retirement." Some people are good at the first save.[1] They like to shop for bargains. But they are terrible at the second save.[2] Wealthy people are great at both. They *love* to save[1] money—to buy things wholesale, to get a good deal, to get a bargain. They *hate* to pay retail for anything. And now you know why. Each wasted dollar destroys a forest of future money trees.

But they don't stop there. You see, anyone can save money by buying at a discount, but do they save[2] the money that they save[1]? That's the hard part. A friend of mine quit smoking and was bragging about the $50 a month she was saving[1] by not smoking. I asked, "Where is the $50?" She didn't know. She had saved[1] the money, but she hadn't saved[2] it . . . put it away. When you save[1] money by changing your buying habits, take that money out of your purse or wallet to get it out of your spending grasp.

[1] The first definition of *save.*
[2] The second definition of *save.*

You won't even miss it. Put it into a savings[2] jar, and frequently deposit this money into your savings[2] account. That's when you've truly saved[1]/saved[2] it.

Suppose you normally buy your gasoline from a certain gas station. Then one day you notice a new gas station that sells gas 10 cents a gallon cheaper. With a 10-gallon purchase, you should have saved[1] about a dollar. But, you only notice the benefit of that savings when you take the second step and save[2] it. Therefore, when you go to the cash register to pay for the gasoline, physically take that saved[1] dollar out of your wallet or purse and put it into a savings[2] envelope. You can put the envelope into the side pocket of your car door and let your savings[2] accumulate until you have $25 to $50. Don't be tempted to spend it. You need to transfer those savings into your long-term savings[1] account . . . and from there into your investment account . . . and from there into your various investments (mutual funds, stocks, bonds, real estate, etc.).

You can literally become a millionaire on the money you're wasting. There are thousands of ways to save[1] money. A popular mutual fund company has prepared a list of 50 simple ways to save $50. It's an excellent list, and you'll find it at the end of this chapter. But two *major* ways to save money are not found on the list.

Major Money Saver 1:
Extend Your Planning Horizon

When asked for his secret, billionaire businessman J. Paul Getty said, "I buy my straw hats in the fall." He didn't buy his straw hats in the spring when the sun was hot and these hats were popular and expensive. He bought them in the fall when they were unpopular and cheap. He used this same philosophy with every purchase . . . his oil wells, his businesses, his buildings, his corporate jets, and his art collections. He had a "wholesale" mentality. He saw into the future and scheduled his buying for the cheapest time. He bought when nobody wanted and sold when demand was high.

To obtain such bargains, you need to lengthen your planning horizon. Poor people have disorganized, short-term planning horizons. Rich people have organized, long-term planning horizons. The more scheduled you are into the future, the cheaper your life is going to become. You've

got to begin to organize your life like a major corporation. The average American corporation operates on 5-year planning horizons. The average Japanese corporation operates on a 150-year planning horizon. You might wonder how the Japanese know what is going to happen in 150 years. They don't have to. Remember, the future is not something that happens. The future is something that you *make* happen.

You need to start immediately to extend your planning horizon. If you normally plan a week in advance, extend it to 30 days. If you normally plan a month in advance, extend it to three months. If you normally plan a year in advance, extend it to five years. The further into the future you plan, the cheaper your life will become.

Of course, your well-laid plans almost never come to fruition as you envision them. The purpose is not to come up with a plan laid in cement but to go through the process of planning. I recommend a minimum planning horizon of 90 days. Here's how.

Many people spend a few minutes planning their day. This is an excellent idea, but there is a better way. Instead of just planning your daily activities, look at your calendar 90 days out from today and ask yourself, "What do I need to do today to make sure that the things I need 90 days from now can be purchased smarter?" Scan over the 90-day period to see if you'll need any airline tickets. Does anyone have a birthday? What about other gifts? What about food? What about office supplies? This one simple habit could lower your cost of living dramatically.

Successful money managers know instinctively how much easier it is to save a dollar than to make an extra one. To earn a dollar in net profit, you have to deal with employees, paperwork, hassles, advertising, customer relations, inventory, taxes, red tape, risk, and so on. This is hard. But saving a dollar can be done in the blink of an eye, just by cutting out an unnecessary expense. Both a dollar earned and a dollar saved drop to the bottom line. They look the same. But it is much easier to control your expenses than to increase your income.

$$$

WIT & WISDOM
A bank in New York City is now making it possible to buy and sell stock using their ATM machines. This is great—it gives muggers a chance to diversify their portfolios.

DAVID LETTERMAN

Poor people today always seem to run "a day late and a dollar short." If you're a day late you'll always be a dollar short. Why? Because procrastination is expensive. It forces you to pay retail prices. Organized people are automatically better off financially because they have time to schedule their expenditures, to "buy their straw hats in the fall."

In other words, if you want to learn to control your money, you have to learn how to control your time. That's the meaning of the phrase, "Time is money." So the first key to controlling your money is to learn to control your time. And the key to controlling time is to extend your planning horizon.

Major Money Saver 2: Schedule Some Plastic Surgery

Would you like to learn how to cut your living expenses by 20 to 30 percent in 30 seconds? You would? Well, take out all of your plastic credit cards, put one away for emergencies, and cut up the rest. Statistics have shown that this simple exercise will automatically and almost effortlessly cut your living expenses by an average of 30 percent over the next 12 months. Why? Because credit cards provide easy access to purchasing power. If you remove the easy access, you remove the temptation to spend. Thus, your overall spending will automatically decline.

> **$$$**
> **MONEY TALK**
> Sow a thought, reap an act.
> Sow an act, reap a habit.
> Sow a habit, reap a character.
> Sow a character,
> reap an eternal destiny.
> DAVID O. McKAY

With the money you're save/saving plus the 10 percent you pay yourself off the top, you should be able to fund your lifetime $1 million investment program.

Imagine a series of basins into which money is siphoned from your reservoir. The first basin should be your emergency basin. Let your 10 percent flow there first, until you have at least three months' worth of living expenses saved. You'd be surprised how many people in this country are only one paycheck away from homelessness. Don't let that be you. This money should be in the safest place possible—probably in an insured bank account—at the highest interest rate you can find while still having access to your money within 30 days. After this first basin is filled up, the stream of 10 percent will overflow into one of three additional basins—labeled *conservative investments, moderately risky investments,* and *very risky investments.* The older you are, the more money you

> **$$$**
> **MONEY TALK**
> The secret of financial success
> is to spend what you have
> left over after saving,
> instead of saving what is
> left after spending.

should have in the conservative basin. The younger you are, the more risk you can take. Study Figure 2.8, and I'll see you in the next chapter.

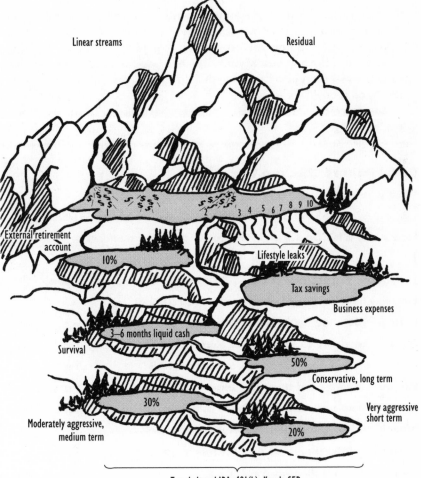

FIGURE 2.8 Your complete financial picture.

$$$ Fiscal Fitness Checkup $$$

Suppose, for a moment, that you're a medical doctor. A patient comes to you for an annual physical checkup. You ask the usual questions. You poke here, probe there, and, within a short time, you have a pretty good idea of the patient's health.

It's time for a visit to the money doctor. Instead of *physical* examinations, let's give you a *fiscal* examination.

What is fiscal health? It is being a wise steward over your money. What is your track record with money? Honestly. Are you good at causing money to flow into your life? Are you good at controlling money from flowing out of your life? Are you good at accumulating assets? Are you good at avoiding debt? In short, are you able to make and keep money?

Complete the Fiscal Fitness Checkup that follows, to see how well you're doing.

Fiscal Fitness Checkup Worksheet

What is your approximate monthly income? (Circle one)

  $1,000 $2,000 $3,000 $4,000 $5,000 $6,000 $7,000 $8,000 $9,000 $10,000+

How stable is it? (On a scale from 1 to 10, circle one number)

1   2   3   4   5   6   7   8   9   10

(1 = income is extremely shaky   10 = income is extremely reliable)

How much money do you save monthly? (Circle one)

0–100$ 200   300   400   500   600   700   800   900   1,000+

Did you contribute to a retirement plan last year?	Yes	No
Do you reconcile your checkbook at least monthly?	Yes	No
Do you categorize and track your expenses monthly?	Yes	No
Have you paid any late charges in the past 90 days?	Yes	No
What is the estimated value of everything you own?	$ _____	
What is the total amount of all of the money you owe?	$ _____	
Do you own more than you owe?	Yes	No

What % of your debt is for investment assets?   % _____
  (Investment assets generally go up in value: real estate, stocks, education, etc.)

What % of your debt is for consumer assets?   _____%
  (Consumer assets generally go down in value: cars, furniture, stereos, TVs, etc.)

Does credit card debt exceed 10% of your total debt?	Yes	No
Do you have liquid cash equal to 3 months' expenses?	Yes	No
Do you pay your credit card balance off every month?	Yes	No

50 Ways to Save $50 a Month*

1. Shop with a list—and stick to it.

2. Just say NO to ATMs with fees—plan ahead for your cash needs.

3. Does your bank charge high fees? MOVE YOUR ACCOUNT.

4. Pay off that credit card balance!

5. If you must carry a credit card balance, shop around for a card with a lower rate.

6. Look for lower premiums on your insurance policies.

7. Consider higher deductibles for your home and auto insurance.

8. Do you have private mortgage insurance? If you've built up 20% equity in your home, you can cancel it.

9. Use a mail-order pharmacy for long-term prescriptions.

10. "Doc, can I get that as a generic drug?"

11. Check all medical and hospital bills for errors—many insurance companies offer rewards.

12. Rent—never buy—something you'll only use a few times.

13. Turn your yard into a department store—have a rummage sale.

14. Switch long-distance carriers—then switch again.

15. Call waiting? Not usually? Cancel those add-on phone services you don't need.

16. E-mail your friends instead of calling.

17. Skip the movies—rent a video instead.

18. Dine out? Eat in.

19. Lunch is "in the bag"—or it should be.

20. Don't buy that book! Exercise your library card.

21. Free up space in your mailbox—cancel that magazine subscription you never read.

22. Watch a parade or have a picnic—free entertainment is often the best.

23. Turn your car into a "chat room." Carpool to work.

24. Join the "bus crowd" and avoid cab fare.

25. Buy airline tickets in advance—and always stay through Saturday. You'll have more fun and it's a lot cheaper, too!

26. Quit that health club—join the local gym instead.

27. "COUPONS" & "DOUBLE COUPON DAYS." Enough said.

* Copyright Strong Funds. Used by permission. For free information, check 1-800-368-1030 and www.eStrong.com.

28. What's in a name? Buy generic instead.

29. Skip the paper towels—wash your cloth ones instead.

30. Watch out for "convenience" foods—they're expensive and not as healthy for you anyway.

31. Join a warehouse club.

32. "Scan" those scanners and receipts—mistakes do happen.

33. Avoid "pricey" specialty stores.

34. Comparison shop "on-line."

35. Gotta trunk? Buy in BULK.

36. Premium gas for your car? Most run fine without it. Check your manual to be sure.

37. Forget the words "automatic car wash"—do it yourself and get some fresh air.

38. Use that quick-change oil and lube service on the corner instead of a full-service garage.

39. Never pay extra for service contracts or extended warranties—the manufacturer's warranty is usually sufficient.

40. Cancel that premium channel you never watch—or cancel cable TV altogether.

41. Don't touch that thermostat—put on a sweater instead.

42. Take a shower instead of a bath.

43. Only run a full dishwasher.

44. Have an energy audit done on your home—some companies offer them for FREE.

45. Never pay extra for car rental insurance—you're probably already covered by your credit card or regular car insurance.

46. DON'T PLAY THE LOTTERY—the odds of getting hit by lightning are better than your chances of winning.

47. Time to refinance your home? Keep an eye on interest rates.

48. Pay yourself first—set aside a dollar a day.

49. Buy a "piggy bank" for all the spare change you keep finding in your couch.

50. Don't spend your next pay raise—INVEST THAT MONEY INSTEAD.

CHAPTER 3

*I think it is a man's duty to make all the money he can,
to keep all that he can, and give away all that he can.*
JOHN D. ROCKEFELLER, SR.

The Money Tree Formula: How to Create *Lifelong* Streams of Cash Flow

Building upon a solid foundation of the first three money skills, let's assume that you've decided to add another stream of income flowing into the reservoir of your life. You could always get another part-time job, but that's not the kind of income I'm talking about. You certainly don't want to get stuck on somebody else's treadmill. You want the kind of streams that you can own.

I'm talking about *residual income*. That's a fancy term for a "recurring" stream of income that continues to flow whether you're there or not. I've heard too many small business owners say, "I haven't taken a vacation in five years." There's something wrong with that picture. I don't have anything against hard work. But after a few short years of hard work, you should be free to have your streams of income forwarded to your mailbox in Tahiti. Get the picture?

Two Types of Streams: Linear and Residual

Not all streams of income are created equal. Some streams are linear, and some are residual. Your answer to the following question tells you whether your income streams are linear or residual: *"How many times do you get paid for every hour you work?"*

If you answered, "Only once," then your income is *linear*. Income streams from a salary are linear. You get paid only once for your effort.

And when you don't show up for work, neither does your paycheck.

With *residual* income, you work hard once and it unleashes a steady flow of income for months or even years. You get paid over and over again for the same effort. Wouldn't it be nice to be compensated hundreds of times for every hour you work?

For example, I wrote a book in 1980 called *Nothing Down: How to Buy Real Estate with Little or No Money Down.* I put in over 1,000 hours of hard work writing *Nothing Down* before I earned a single penny. Teenagers working at McDonald's earned more than I did. But I wasn't looking for a salary. I wanted a royalty. So I was willing to sacrifice. It took over two years before the money started to flow. But it was worth the wait. I've now earned millions of dollars in royalties. And the checks are still flowing decades later! That's the power of residual income: It keeps flowing and flowing and flowing.

Here's another example. Have you seen that tiny battery tester on the Duracell battery? I'm told that the inventor presented his idea to the big battery companies. Most turned him down, but Duracell saw the genius of it and agreed to pay just a few pennies per battery pack for his idea. Now he has earned millions, because those residual pennies add up. In essence, he invested many hours of his time to create the concept, to package it, and then to sell it. Now it generates a raging river of residual riches to him and his family. And the best part about it—*he doesn't have to be there!* It flows without him.

Linear versus Residual: Do You See the Difference?

The secret of the wealthy is not that they have more money but that they have more *time* freedom. Because many of their streams are residual, they have time to spend on anything they want.

When you view people's lives through the filter of *residual* income, many groups of people aren't as wealthy as they appear. Doctors and dentists don't earn residual income from their labors. Their income potential is capped. They can see only a fixed number of patients in a day. And they have to be there for every single one of them. That's linear.

The same holds true for top salespeople, chiropractors, and attorneys. Most of them don't enjoy the power of residual income, either. They may appear to be rich, but they're on a treadmill just like the rest of us.

What percentage of your income is residual? If you're smart, you'll start shifting your income streams from linear to residual. This will give you the time freedom to do what you want when you want. And that starts with turning on at least one new residual stream every year.

There are many, exciting new ways of creating residual income.

Do you know who Warren Buffett is? He's the smartest stock picker in history and the wealthiest investor in the world, with a net worth in the tens of billions. What if Warren Buffett himself were to call you on the phone and give you a hot stock tip. He tells you to sink every penny into a certain stock. He says that he's invested a couple of hundred million of his own money and he feels the stock is a sure bet to double or triple in value. What would you say to him? "Sorry Warren, but I like to pick my own stocks by throwing darts at the *Wall Street Journal!*" Would you listen to the master or continue to do things your own way?

> **$$$**
> **WIT & WISDOM**
> I'd gladly participate in any experiment to test the effects on me of sudden great wealth.
> ASHLEIGH BRILLIANT

Well, I'm no Warren Buffett, but through my books and seminars I've probably helped to create as many millionaires as he has. If I were to guess, it's probably in the thousands. And this book contains all of my "hot streams" for the new millennium. It's where I've sunk a huge amount of my own time and effort. I am about to share with you the best opportunities I've seen in 20 years. They are certain to create many residual millionaires in the next 10 years. You could be one of them.

The Money Tree Formula

The first step to picking the right income streams is to pass them through the filter of the money tree formula—the nine essential characteristics of the ideal income stream.

Having a money tree assumes that you have an inexhaustible, effortlessly generating stream of cash flow that requires little or none of your presence. In order for this to occur, you must be in a position to create, control, and own that stream of income. Another way of saying the same thing is, you must become an entrepreneur . . . a businessperson. You may still retain your employee position, but on the side, as a way of protecting your long-term financial future, you need to create additional streams of income—ASAP.

I remember watching TV recently as a couple was being interviewed about being laid off from their long-term jobs. The wife looked out of the screen and said, with tears in her eyes, "For 17 years we worked hard for our security, and now we're out in the cold. It's not fair." I wanted to reach through the television set and tell her that for 17 years she had only the illusion of security. She wasn't secure—she just thought she was.

Working for someone else, unless you own a piece of the profits, is not security. It's just the *illusion* of security.

If you're going to become a home-based entrepreneur, you'd better learn which businesses have the potential for creating lifetime streams of income and which ones are just a dead-end way to make a few extra bucks before they fizzle out and die. I'd like to teach you a formula for the perfect business in the new millennium. I call it the *money tree formula* and it will be very easy for you to remember because it spells the word **MONEYTREE.**

M in the Money Tree Formula Stands for *Multiple Streams of Income*

The first goal in starting your own home-based business is to add another stream of income to your life as a safety net in case other of your streams of income dry up. The home-based business you select should be a source of more than just one stream of income. It should eventually become a source of multiple streams of income all by itself.

For example, suppose you're considering buying an existing restaurant. What is its potential for growth? Can you add more shops? Is your idea franchisable? Can one of your food entrées be sold nationwide as a frozen item? Can you license your special cooking secrets to other restaurants? Is there a cookbook possibility in there somewhere? What about bottling and selling your special sauces? Get the drift? Don't even consider a business that doesn't have expansion potential for additional streams of income. That's why the first *M* in the formula is intended to remind you of *multiple streams of income.*

O in the Money Tree Formula Stands for *Outstanding*

If your product, service, or information isn't distinguishably excellent or unique it will eventually become a casualty of competition. The goal of creating a money tree is to do the work once and to have the money flow for the rest of your life. What good does it do to create a business and eventually have it succumb to competition? In order for your source of income to survive through the next 10 recessions (as there will be many more recessions in your lifetime), you must select a product, service, or source of information that has the possibility to be permanently and per-petually profitable. When times get tough, people gravitate to either price or quality. Don't get stuck in the middle. That's a sure formula for disas-ter. And don't compete with the rest of the world on price. Make sure the quality of your produce is outstanding . . . the best you can offer at a fair price. This will give you a good chance of succeeding in the long term.

N in the Money Tree Formula Stands for *Nothing Down*

Why nothing down? Well, your down payment doesn't have to be com-pletely zero . . . but as little of your own money as possible. If you're like most people, you probably don't have a couple hundred thousand dollars lying around to invest in your business. But what if you do have a nice chunk of cash? Should you run out and find a business to match your money and launch it? I think that one of the greatest curses is to have a lot of money to put into a new business.

Suppose you want to buy a hot franchise. It might cost you $100,000, and that's just for the franchise rights. Then, you need to purchase inventory, leasehold improvements, special equipment. And what do you get? For most franchises, you get the right to be tied to a business 12 hours a day, to manage a lot of undereducated, under-motivated employees, and make a steady paycheck for yourself. In a sense, you are just buying yourself a job. Why spend tens of thousands of dollars of your own money just to buy yourself a job . . . with a lot of risk?

I'm going to show you businesses that you can launch with little risk, little or no money down, and the possibility of creating what I call "walk-away" cash flow—money that flows to you whether or not you show up.

> **━━━ $$$ ━━━**
> **WIT & WISDOM**
> You miss 100% of the shots you never take.
> WAYNE GRETZKY
>
> **WIT & WISDOM**
> Live within your income even if you have to borrow to do it.
> JOSH BILLINGS

E in the Money Tree Formula Stands for *Employee-Resistant*

That's right. . . . You don't want employees. Employees are dangerous! They begin to feel they are entitled to their jobs. ("You can't fire me. I own this job.") The rapid increase in employee/employer litigation should be enough to convince you that you want to find a home-based business that you can do by yourself, with a very low employee-to-income ratio.

I used to be the president of a seminar company with over 200 employees. I made the decision to downsize when one of the employees sued me for age discrimination. He was in his late 60s when he came to work for us, and when we laid him off during an economic downturn, he slapped us with a $500,000 lawsuit. We settled out of court for $2,000, but that was the last straw. I decided to never again put myself in a position where one disgruntled employee with a smart attorney could take it all away.

Today, I have zero employees. I make as much today as I used to make—with 200 times less hassle. I like it that way. All my streams of income can be monitored from a telephone anywhere in the world in only a few minutes a day.

A friend of mine, Dan Kennedy, puts it this way, "When it comes to employees, hire slow and fire fast." Most businesspeople do just the opposite. They hire fast and fire slow. I say, try to find money tree businesses that don't require any employees. Then you don't have to worry about either hiring or firing. If you need help, outsource.

Y in the Money Tree Formula Stands for *Yield*

The streams you choose should be high-yielding, high-profit cash cows. Six years ago, a friend of mine, Collette, started such a home-based business. In less than a year she was making about $10,000 per month.

What's more, this business is a money tree business. It would generate cash flow even if she stopped working! But why stop when she is having so much fun? Today, after six years, she has grown her business till she now *nets* over $1 million a year.

What's the yield on that kind of income? It's the equivalent of having *$20 million* in the bank earning 5 percent interest! That's my idea of yield. In this book I'll be sharing exactly how Collette did this, and we'll look at other businesses that offer the same kinds of money tree characteristics.

T in the Money Tree Formula Stands for *Trend* and *Timing*

Starting a business against the trend is like swimming upstream. Running a business is hard enough without trying to swim against the current. When you choose a business that is *with the trend,* it's like floating downstream with the current. How do you select a business that's on trend?

The first time I started a business was just after college. I started buying real estate, and as luck would have it, the timing was perfect. The baby boomers wanted to own real estate, and the demand drove prices upward. Anyone who owned property made a killing. You could almost do no wrong.

Then, I started teaching people how to buy real estate with little or no money down. My little classified ads brought hordes of calls. It was a feeding frenzy. I was on trend. My seminar businesses took in more than $100 million in the next decade.

The secret is to get in front of a trend and ride the wave. The biggest wave of our century is the baby boom—76 million people born between 1946 and 1964. This generation is four times the size of the previous generation. As this mass of humanity rolls forward through time, it creates a huge demand wave. Picking businesses at the leading edge of this age wave has created thousands of fortunes. You need to make sure that your new business is leading this trend and not following it. It can make a huge difference in your lifestyle.

R in the Money Tree Formula Stands for *Residual*

We've already talked about the importance of this part of the money tree formula. But to emphasize this concept even further, let's compare it to an escalator. Have you ever walked *up* a down escalator . . . the wrong way? When you walk up the down escalator, you have to walk fast just to stay in the same place. And to get to the top, you have to walk at double speed. People on the up escalator don't have to work hard at all. They just stand there holding the handrail and the escalator takes them to the top. (See Figure 3.1.)

The up and down escalators represent the two kinds of income that you can earn: linear income and residual income. Our economy is a down escalator. You work hard for your money, but with

Which Escalator Are You On?

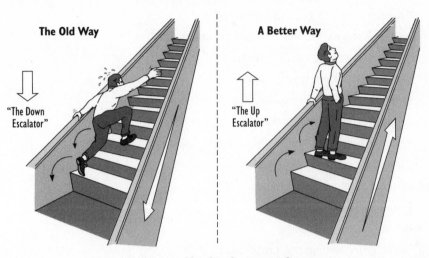

The Old Way

"The Down Escalator"

A Better Way

"The Up Escalator"

FIGURE 3.1   Up the down escalator.

inflation you have earn 3 to 5 percent more next year just to stay in the same place. But this puts you in higher tax brackets. The more you make, the more they take. You seem to work harder and harder without making any progress. Your bank account balance earns 2 percent and your credit card balance costs you 20 percent. You're going in the hole 24 hours a day. You wonder why you can never catch up. And if you stop, the escalator just takes you right back down to the bottom.

That's what it's like to earn linear income. When I think of this kind of income, I'm reminded of the stratagem for catching monkeys in Africa: Natives take a coconut and cut off one end to make a small hole just large enough to allow a monkey's fist to enter. The other end of the coconut is attached to a long cord. They place a few peanuts inside the coconut, place the coconut in the middle of a clearing, and hide behind a tree to wait for the monkeys to come. The monkeys come and smell the peanuts inside the coconut shell. One monkey reaches inside the shell and grabs the peanuts, but now the fistful of peanuts is too large to escape the hole in the coconut. Then the native yanks on the cord and hauls that silly monkey to captivity because the monkey will not let go of those peanuts to save his skin.

Are you working for peanuts? If you're walking up the down escalator, you are caught in a monkey trap. What you want is up-escalator income. Which escalator are you on? Here's a list of the many types of residual income that you want to be exploring:

Savers earn interest.

Songwriters earn royalties on their songs.

Authors like myself earn royalties from their books and tapes.

Insurance agents get residual business.

Securities agents get residual sales.

Network marketers get residual commissions.

Actors get a piece of the action.

Entrepreneurs get business profits.

Franchisors get franchising fees.

Investors get dividends, interest, and appreciation.

Visual artists get royalties from their creations.

Software creators get royalties.

Game designers get royalties.

Inventors get royalties.

Partners can get profits.

Mailing-list owners get rental fees.

Real estate owners can get cash-flow profits.

Retired persons can get pensions.

Celebrity endorsers get a percentage of gross profits.

Marketing consultants get a percentage of profit or gross revenue.

When you go to bed tonight, ask yourself this question, "What percentage of my day did I spend creating residual income?" If the answer is zero, you're in trouble. You'd better wake up tomorrow and get busy. We'll learn more on residual income later. For now, I hope you see why it's such a vital part of our money tree formula.

E in the Money Tree Formula Stands for *Essential to Everybody Every Day*

Whichever home-based business you select, try to pick a product or service that's essential, or is perceived as essential, by a large and very motivated segment of society. Let me give you the real reason that real estate has always been a great wealth-creation vehicle and a prime source of residual income for hundreds of thousands. It fits the money tree formula. Check it out for yourself and you'll see why.

Whatever product you choose to market, just make sure it's essential. The more people who need it and the more often they need it, the more successful your business can become.

The Final E in the Money Tree Formula Stands for *Enthusiasm*

You've got to love what you do. If you hate what you sell, you'll never be any good at it. The prime admonition from Gary Halbert, one of the all-time great marketing gurus is this: *Sell what you love.* Truth is, you'll never be truly great unless you do.

Well, there you have the nine major characteristics of the money tree formula. These nine characteristics are essential to the kind of hands-off, hassle-free businesses that create lifelong streams of cash flow. In this book, we'll be exploring in depth the 10 practical businesses that fit this formula perfectly.

Now, what about earning a salary? Being an employee may be an honorable and even enjoyable way to earn income, but it doesn't fit the money tree formula. . . . It doesn't flow 24 hours a day. To earn the special kinds of income streams that you'll learn about in this book, you need to think less like an employee and more like an investor and an entrepreneur.

Even as an employee, you must learn to think of yourself as a *free agent.* Just as in sports, where athletes lease their skills to a specific team on a temporary basis, you will eventually be leasing your skills—your mind, your experience, your body—to needy employers. You must become a one-person consulting business, leasing your services out to the highest-bidding team on a short-term contract basis. Your financial stability will come from investing 10 percent of your earnings on the side. For that, you need to think like an entrepreneurial businessperson. For many of us, this is a foreign experience.

A hundred years ago, about 90 percent of our ancestors were entrepreneurs. Now the number is between 10 and 20 percent. By moving from the farms to the factories, we delegated our freedom to large, centralized organizations. We got soft. We lost our entrepreneurial skills. And now that the new paradigm of the world is changing, we've been forced "back to the farm" so to speak—back to individual responsibility. The whole world is moving away from centralized authority of every kind. With downsizing, companies are splitting into profit teams: smaller PT boats instead of lumbering battleships. Many of those who have been downsized are realizing that being an employee is even riskier than being in business for themselves. That's what fueled the incredible home-based business revolution of the 1990s, when home-based businesses were being created at unprecedented rates.

The definition of an *entrepreneur*—a person who sells a product or a service for profit—is much too broad for our discussion here. Most entrepreneurs own businesses that are nothing more than glorified monkey traps . . . sweatshops that simply provide jobs for the owners. They don't have the freedom to come and go as they wish. They are tied to their one-person businesses. That is not my idea of fun.

— $$$ —
WIT & WISDOM
80% of success is showing up.
WOODY ALLEN

— $$$ —
WIT & WISDOM
Behold the turtle.
He makes progress only when he sticks his neck out.
JAMES BRYANT CONANT

— $$$ —
WIT & WISDOM
When a friend asked W. C. Fields for a loan, he replied: "I'll see what my lawyer says, and if he says yes, then I'll get another lawyer."

What you and I are trying to create is much more powerful. We want residual income—lifetime streams of income that we do not have to manage. We want the same thing that Garry Trudeau, the famous cartoonist, stated as his ultimate goal: "To create a lifestyle that does not require my presence." We want to create income streams that don't require our presence. You're not trying to create income, to be a mom-and-pop business or a corner grocery store with regular hours. You want up-escalator income that flows to you . . . whether or not you get up this morning.

Can you see the distinction? I hope so, because it's critical. If you start out with this goal in mind, then you will be able to see through the thousands of business opportunities that get thrown at you every day and zero in on only those specific businesses that will achieve your goal of money tree income.

For instance, open any income-opportunity magazine that you find on most major newsstands. You'll see lots of ads for businesses such as carpet cleaning, upholstery repair, auto detailing. Hard work. Requires you to be there. Sure, you might earn a good income, but is it linear or residual? Is it monkey trap income or money tree income? Will your efforts eventually create a lifetime stream of income when you stop working? If not, it's a monkey trap business that will require long hours trying to go up the down escalator. Unless you can figure out a way to turn it into a money tree, keep looking.

Which Kind of Entrepreneur Are You?

There are special breeds of entrepreneurs—specialized, residual, money tree entrepreneurial enterprises. Here are my names for them:

Intrapreneurs

Extrapreneurs

Infopreneurs

Autopreneurs

You're probably going to fit naturally into one or more of these categories. The following questions will help you determine your own special niche.

Are you good at influencing the decisions of others? Do people take your advice easily? Do you like to give recommendations to others? Would you be a good spokesperson for a specific product or service that you really believed in? Do you feel your ideas have enough value that someone should pay you for them? Do you enjoy selling? If so, you'll probably be most suited as an *intrapreneur.*

Do you see yourself as an artist? Do you enjoy creating? Do you like to entertain? Are you good at creating solutions to problems? If so, you would probably be great as an *extrapreneur.*

Do you enjoy organizing and simplifying information? Do you enjoy teaching? Can you explain complicated subjects easily? Is it important to you to help others improve the quality of their lives? Would you consider yourself to be an idea person, good at brainstorming solutions to problems? Do you like to write? Are you a good communicator? Do you like to read? If so, you are most likely an *infopreneur*.

Are you a good saver? Do you like to squeeze the last ounce of benefit from a situation? Do you enjoy seeing your money grow while you sleep? Do you like to analyze numbers? Do you like to make deals? Do you enjoy finding bargains? Are you good at comparing differing projects to make a decision? Are you good at putting people or properties together? Do you like to turn a sow's ear into a silk purse? Do you like to improve a deteriorated situation? Do you like to own things? If so, you would be a good *autopreneur*.

Intrapreneur Skills: To Influence, to Persuade, to Lead

An intrapreneur remains inside a corporation, not as an employee but as a consultant, commissioned salesperson, or part owner. For those who like the feeling of playing on a team, this is an ideal choice.

Insurance agents get residual business.

Securities agents get residual sales.

Network marketers get residual commissions.

Corporate managers get stock options.

Extrapreneur Skills: To Be Creative, to Entertain

Songwriters earn royalties.

Actors get a piece of the action.

Visual artists get royalties from paintings.

Game designers get royalties.

Celebrity endorsers get a gross percentage of profits.

Inventors get royalties.

Infopreneur Skills: To Organize, to Simplify, to Teach

An infopreneur is a person who makes money selling information. The primary product is data, knowledge, skill, or specialized information. This is where you turn your ideas, knowledge, and experience into cash.

Authors like myself earn royalties from their books and tapes.

Marketing consultants get a percentage of profit or gross revenue.

Franchisors get franchising fees.

Software creators get royalties.

Internet content providers get advertising revenues and royalties.

Autopreneur skills: To Analyze, to See Hidden Value, to Invest

Unlike traditional entrepreneurs who create businesses that sell (as one of my associates calls them) "hard, lumpy objects," the autopreneur is looking for ownership of automatic streams of income without hassle. We'll get back to this later.

Entrepreneurs generate business profits.

Savings account owners earn interest.

Investors get dividends, interest, and appreciation.

Discount mortgagors earn interest.

Tax lien certificate holders earn interest penalties.

Mailing-list owners get rental fees.

Company pension plans offer income flow.

Venture partners get a percentage of profits.

Real estate owners can get cash-flow profits.

To review, then, you need to start thinking more like a money tree entrepreneur and less like an employee.* Now that you've come to this realization, meet me in the next chapter to learn about money mountains.

---

* For more on how to make the move to free-agent thinking, see www.multiplestreamsofincome .com, keyword Free Agent.

CHAPTER 4

*We are the opening verse of the opening page
of the chapter of endless possibilities.*

RUDYARD KIPLING

The Mountain Range of Financial Freedom: The Three Great Money Mountains

There are three great financial-freedom mountains. Each mountain is uniquely different from the others. Yet each mountain is extremely important to your long-term financial success. Investing in the entire mountain range will give you both the safety of diversification and constant exposure to the hottest opportunities.

From each of these money mountains flow separate streams of income. As Figure 4.1 shows, there are 10 separate income streams. The goal is to have several streams from each money mountain flowing into the reservoir of your accumulating prosperity.

In coming chapters, I'm going to take you to the source of each of these fountains of financial freedom. Remember, these streams are not just ordinary streams of income. Each stream is carefully screened using the money tree formula from Chapter 3. You want streams that flow into your life 24 hours a day—even while you sleep. In later chapters I'll show you how to create these special streams of income on a part-time basis, working right from your own home, using little or none of your own money, with few or no employees, using simple, proven systems that really work.

Just a word of caution before we begin. Each of these three broad money mountains contains thousands of legitimate opportunities, with hundreds of separate moneymaking techniques and dozens of moneymaking formulas. Any one of the mountains could take years to learn and master.

The purpose of this book is not to give you an encyclopedic grasp of the entire mountain range of money. If you're like most people, you're already

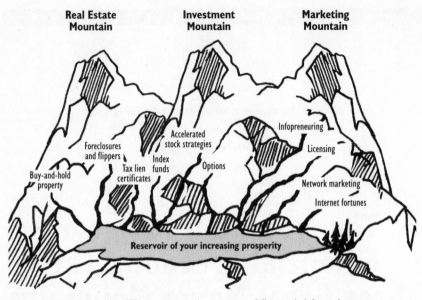

FIGURE 4.1   The mountain range of financial freedom.

inundated with too much information. Too many *Wall Street Journals* left unread, too many *Money* magazines piled high in a corner, too many financial offers stuffed into your mailbox, too many web sites overbrimming with data, too many books stacked on your nightstand, too many financial advisors clamoring to advise you. It can be overwhelming. People who are overwhelmed generally do nothing. As the saying goes, "A confused mind always says no."

Whenever you get overwhelmed, just remember the 80/20 principle: *Only 20 percent of the things you do give you 80 percent of your results.*

You don't need to know 100 percent of the facts about money. You need to know only the 20 percent of the facts that will give you 80 percent of your results. Focusing on a few critical activities will give you enormous leverage. Your goal is to be confident enough to launch at least one new income stream a year. By doing this, you'll generate amazing results while most everyone around you is drowning in details or paralyzed with fear.

The Real Estate Mountain

For example, let's take the real estate mountain. This is a tremendously important piece of your lifelong financial-freedom plan. There are hundreds of books on how to make money in real estate. I should know—I've written three of them. Each of these books is filled with dozens of strategies, techniques, and tips. Quite frankly, there is too much to know. . . . I've been studying the real estate field for 20 years and I'll never know it all.

However, *anyone can know enough to take action,* because any branch of real estate investing boils down to the 20 percent of information that gives you 80 percent of your results. What are the critical few factors in real estate investing? There are three:

Finding

Funding

Farming

If you want to be successful in real estate investing, you need to know how to find bargain properties, how to fund those properties, and then
how to farm them . . . or to harvest the profits
from each deal. In your own city there are thousands of properties for sale, yet you can eliminate
99 percent of them from consideration by first
determining which of them are the best bargains.
Then you focus on how to raise the funds to
acquire them. Finally, you decide whether to keep
them for long-term profit or flip them for short-term gain. It may sound
oversimplified, but frankly, that's the world of real estate investing in a
nutshell. Find it. Fund it. Farm it.

The Investment Mountain

The same is true for the investment mountain. There are over 10,000
individual stocks in the stock market and almost as many mutual funds (a
special selection of a variety of individual stocks). There is a bewildering
assortment of moneymaking methods to apply to these stocks. Do you
use fundamental analysis or technical analysis? And what about the bond
market? Or certificates of deposit with varying terms and interest rates?
All of this information gets updated and changed *every minute* of every
business day. You *can't* know it all!

But you *can* determine the 20 percent of the facts that will give you 80
percent of your results. Just as in real estate, there is a basic formula. No,
it's not buy low and sell high. Most likely, you'll be buying high and selling
even higher. Here is what you need to know:

Screening and filtering

Timing in

Timing out

Using simple, understandable filters, you can sift through the gravel of the
market and uncover a nugget or two. Using the power of inexpensive (how
about free?) tools, you can know *exactly* when to buy and *precisely* when
to sell. The results will astound you. When you're finished with this book,
you may know *less* overall data about the market than the average investor,
but you'll possess the key knowledge for making consistent profits.

The Marketing Mountain

How can you select the right business opportunities for this time in your life? There are tens of thousands of "deals" floating around out there. First, pass them through the screen of the money tree formula and you'll dramatically lower the chances for failure. But even after the screen, there are hundreds from which to choose. I've done some of the screening for you and narrowed your choices to just four emerging fields of business. Each field has the potential to create untold numbers of success stories. I expect you to be one of them.

The Internet

The field of network marketing

The concept of infopreneuring

The idea of licensing

The fundamental activity behind all of them is marketing. That's why I call it the *marketing mountain* and not the entrepreneurial mountain or the home-based business mountain. Whether you're selling a set of ideas, a service, or a product, nothing happens without marketing. Without marketing, even the best of books languish in a dusty garage. Without marketing, your web site is nothing more that a multimedia billboard in a corner of your basement. Without the oxygen of marketing, you're business is DOA (dead on arrival).

In the marketing mountain, you'll learn the three key marketing activities:

Targeting

Baiting

Lifetiming

$$$ Knowing Where to Tap $$$

A machine in a factory broke down and an expert was called in to fix it. He took a few minutes to assess the problem, took out his hammer, and tapped twice. The machine started up again immediately. He turned to the supervisor and said, "That'll be $500 please." The supervisor, furious with such a high bill for so little work, demanded an itemized statement. The bill arrived the next day. It read as follows:

Tapping with a hammer:	$ 1.00
Knowing where to tap:	$499.00
Total:	$500.00

TABLE 4.1 Fundamentals of the Money Mountains

Real Estate Mountain It's all about the *deal!* What?	Investment Mountain It's all about the *timing.* When?	Marketing Mountain It's all about the *customer.* Who?
Finding deals	Filtering and screening	Targeting (finding hungry fish)
Funding deals	Timing in (when to buy)	Baiting (creating irresistible bait)
Farming deals	Timing out (when to sell)	Lifetiming (creating lifetime customers)

You'll learn what these words mean and how to implement them in any business that you're involved in . . . from large to small.

As you look at Figure 4.1, which of the money mountains do you want to climb? The answer is, of course, all of them. But each mountain is different and thus requires a unique set of skills. (See Table 4.1.) Some of these skills you already possess. Some you will be required to develop. Where should we begin?

The first and most basic of the money mountains is what I call the *investment mountain.* It is where you should start. Come. Let me show you where to tap.

CHAPTER 5

*Don't gamble; take all your savings and buy some
good stock and hold it till it goes up, then sell.
If it don't go up, don't buy it.*
WILL ROGERS

YOUR FIRST STREAM
Success in the Stock Market:
Investing for Total Idiots

In Chapter 2, I shared with you the seven skills/secrets of prosperous people. The first three were (1) value it, (2) control it, (3) save it. In this chapter you will be learning the fourth skill: Invest it.

Investing is distinctly different from the fifth skill: making it. Investing is primarily a passive process. It doesn't involve the active buying and selling of products or services. It simply involves the buying and selling of passive financial instruments such as stocks, bonds, options, certificates of deposit, and so forth. To be a great investor you don't have to transact business in the normal sense—and you don't have to deal with people. You can be anonymous. You can do everything from behind a computer screen with a modem and a telephone. Although investing can be done in minutes a day, the results are accumulated and compounded over long periods of time.

It is such an important skill that I've included it in the mountain range of wealth as the *investment mountain*. If the investment mountain is characterized as passive, then the other two money mountains (*real estate* and *marketing*) are definitely more active. They are the "making-it mountains." They involve active participation for months, even years, to get their streams up and running. You have to deal with people: negotiating and persuading and marketing. More about these mountains later. First, let's master the investment mountain.

I'll make the assumption that you are following the "reservoir model" and that your survival account is now fully vested with three months of emergency cash. A consistent 10 percent of your income is available to flow into the remaining investment basins. Now you're ready for the markets!

Let's explore the myths and realities of the world's financial markets. As I said in Chapter 4, there are thousands of stocks and mutual funds to choose from—and the data about these investment vehicles is changing every minute of every business day. You can't know it all, so don't even try. Don't let the overwhelming amount of data cause you any concern whatsoever. Focus only on your three simple tasks:

Filtering

Timing in

Timing out

These three tasks represent the three critical questions that you need to answer if you're going to be extremely successful in the stock market:

How can I know which stocks to buy? (Filtering out the good ones)

How can I know when I should buy them? (Timing your purchases)

How can I know when I should sell them? (Timing your sales)

This chapter will answer each of these critical questions. When you've finished reading this chapter, you're going to feel confident and well on your way to stock market success.

But let's pop your bubble before we begin. I don't want you to entertain the notion that you are going to learn how to "beat the market." By *beating the market,* I mean being able to pick a set of stocks or mutual funds that will outperform the traditional indexes such as the Dow Jones Industrial Average, the S&P 500 or the Wilshire 5000, which are the traditional thermometers of the investment world. When you listen to the news, you will constantly be hearing phrases like this: "The Dow is up 100 points." "The S&P 500 was off 5 today." "The broad averages were mixed." "The Wilshire 5000 has been trending sideways for several weeks." Just what are these benchmark averages, and why should you care? The Dow Jones Industrial Average (DJIA) is a complicated formula that represents the average of the stock prices of 30 of the largest companies on the New York Stock Exchange (e.g., General Motors, Wal-Mart,

Disney). It's often confused with representing the entire market of over 10,000 stocks. The S&P 500 is the average of the top 500 companies from all of the three stock exchanges. The S&P 500 is just a broader snapshot of the entire market. It represents companies that are worth about 75 percent of the value of the entire stock market. And the broadest view of all is the Wilshire 5000, a composite of all stocks of the top 7,000 companies. All told, there are over 10,000 stocks to choose from, including many over-the-counter stocks not yet listed on one of the three major U.S. stock exchanges (New York Stock Exchange, American Stock Exchange, and Nasdaq). Of these three averages, the one to beat is the S&P 500. A money manager looks like a genius if he or she can make his or her portfolio of stocks produce a higher percentage return (or a lesser loss) than the percentage return generated by the S&P 500 average.

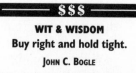

━━━ $$$ ━━━
WIT & WISDOM
The best way to predict the future is to invent it.
ALAN KAY

You may be surprised to learn that 75 percent of all of the smartest money managers in the world, working 20 hour days, with huge research staffs, powered by the most advanced computers, have not been able to consistently beat the market. Of the remaining 25 percent, most were just able to keep pace with the market (but when you factor in commissions and fees you're still a net loser).

A handful of the rest, and I do mean a handful, were able to beat the market by a substantial margin. But to pull off this feat year in and year out is next to impossible. You'd have to be an outright genius like Warren Buffett, or someone possessed with uncommon common sense like Peter Lynch

━━━ $$$ ━━━
WIT & WISDOM
Buy right and hold tight.
JOHN C. BOGLE

(now retired), or believe that God is on your side like Sir John Templeton (now retired). In the history of the markets, only a tiny number of long-term superstars, out of millions who have tried, have been able to tame this tiger. That's why they so are famous (and so rich). You and I, with our puny brains, are not going to best the best of the best. So give up on that notion. It'll save you a lot of sleepless nights, money spent on investment advisory services, countless hours studying boring stock market tables, or precious minutes perusing exciting stock market newsletter offerings. Some people—a brilliant, lucky few—might be able to beat the house, but the odds against you and I doing it are lottery-like.

Let me say it again: You can't beat the market. Give up now, before you begin. As Ashleigh Brilliant said in one of his cartoons, "I feel so much better now that I've given up hope." Having said this, I know that if you are a naturally competitive person, you don't want to believe what I just said. You want to be the next Peter Lynch or Warren Buffett. Okay. In the next two chapters, I'll show you some ways to take some of your high-risk money, say 20 percent, and perhaps hit a home run or two. But for now, let's be content with walks, bunts, and singles.

━━━ $$$ ━━━
WIT & WISDOM
You wonder why fund managers can't beat the S&P 500? Because they're sheep, and sheep get slaughtered.
GORDON GEKKO (MICHAEL DOUGLAS) IN THE MOVIE WALL STREET

Notice that I didn't say you couldn't make money in the market. In fact, you can make *huge* amounts of money in the market. In the long run, it's probably the surest way for you to amass an extra million or two in your lifetime.

The Road to Winning

I'm going to show you a method for winning in the stock market. It's the idiot's approach. The lazy way. The simplest way. Ironically, the best way. Study Figure 5.1. It shows the history of the stock market for the past 50 years. This chart contains all you need to know to be a consistent winner. You should deduce three powerfully obvious lessons from this chart.

Obvious Lesson 1: The Longer You Invest, the Lower Your Risk

Notice the dips in Figure 5.1. Suppose you happened to sink your entire inheritance into the market at the top of one of the peaks, just before a huge dip, like the one in 1974. With the hindsight of history, it's obvious that the storm was eventually going to blow over. (It didn't seem so at the time, I remember. That's the year I graduated from college and the storm was still raging.) The best strategy would have been to just strap yourself to the mast and hold on through the gale. This would have brought you through safely to a continuing cadence of escalating profits. You can always win if you just hang on long enough—*every single time!*

Will this trend continue into the future? Who knows? At worst, the market could collapse into a steep decline from which the world will never recover. (Sounds ridiculous, doesn't it, considering all this bloody century has seen and survived?) Maybe the market will take a breather and lan-guish for a decade. That's sounds more plausible. But even so, if you give yourself a long enough time frame, the overwhelming odds are that things will eventually improve . . . and keep on improving.

The chart in Figure 5.1 also reveals that the shorter your investment

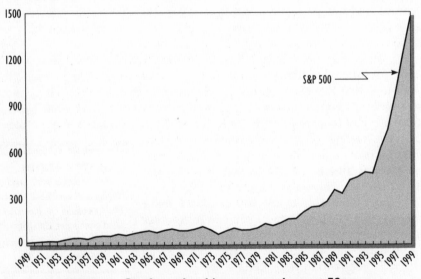

FIGURE 5.1   Stock market history over the past 50 years.

horizon, the greater your risk. Suppose you got into the market and things started to look bad. Instead of holding for the long run, you got spooked and jumped out after only a year. What would be the odds of your success? Look at Table 5.1.

From 1950 through 1999, there have been only 11 years in which the overall market (as measured by the S&P 500) lost ground. That's about one losing year for every four winning years. Over three quarters of the years have been winners. What does that tell you? The odds of winning are in your favor. Nonetheless, on a short-term basis, you have about a 22 percent chance of losing all or part of your money. One chance in four. Russian roulette with a four-chambered handgun. That's too high a risk to take in the short run.

If you could hold on for five years, you would lower the risk of loss to about 15 percent. There were very few five-year periods in the past half century in which you would have ended up with a net loss. If you hold for 10 years, the risk of loss is less than 1 in 20. The same logic holds true for 15-, 20-, and 25-year holding periods. The longer you invest, the lower your risk. In fact, a 25-year holding period has been shown to give you a zero risk situation.

Would you like to invest your money without risk? Then the most important decision you could make today is to get into the market and *stay there* for at least 25 years. Lock that decision in your mind and throw away the key. Take a lesson from the smartest stock picker in history, Warren Buffett: "My favorite holding period is . . . forever." That's why Buffett is a billionaire and your stockbroker is just a broker.

We just answered one of the three critical questions for the beginning investor who is planning to put some money into the stock market.

Question: When should I sell?

Drum roll. . . . The envelope, please.

Answer: Sell somewhere between 10 and 25 years from now.

TABLE 5.1 50 Years of Winning and Losing with the S&P 500 Not Including Dividends

1950	21.8%	1960	–(3.0)%	1970	0%	1980	25.9%	1990	–(6.6)%
1951	16.5%	1961	23.1%	1971	10.8%	1981	–(9.7)%	1991	26.3%
1952	11.8%	1962	–(11.8)%	1972	15.7%	1982	14.7%	1992	4.5%
1953	–(6.6)%	1963	18.9%	1973	–(17.4)%	1983	17.3%	1993	7.1%
1954	45.0%	1964	13.0%	1974	–(29.7)%	1984	1.4%	1994	–(1.5)%
1955	26.4%	1965	9.1%	1975	31.6%	1985	26.4%	1995	34.1%
1956	2.6%	1966	–(13.1)%	1976	19.2%	1986	14.6%	1996	20.1%
1957	–(14.3)%	1967	17.6%	1977	11.5%	1987	2.0%	1997	31.0%
1958	38.1%	1968	10.0%	1978	1.1%	1988	12.4%	1998	26.7%
1959	8.5%	1969	–(11.4)%	1979	12.3%	1989	27.3%	1999	19.5%

If you're not going to do this for the long term, don't start. Get used to the idea of arriving in the future and having no money there to greet you.

Now, take another look at Figure 5.1. What else does it tell you?

Obvious Lesson 2: If You Can't Beat 'Em, Join 'Em

In the past 10 years, out of 6,000-plus professionally managed mutual funds, only about 20 were able to beat the 10-year performance of the S&P 500 after expenses and fees. (See Table 6.2. on page 67.) They deserve honorable mention. (Just because they made the list this year doesn't guarantee that they will continue to be on the list.)

Whenever I mention this short list of winners, people always perk up. For the wrong reasons. The lesson is not to bet your money on the top 20 rabbits in the race. The lesson is that 5,980 other rabbits, racing with all their might, couldn't outpace the lowly tortoise. The risk of picking the right rabbit in 6,000 is ridiculous compared to the no-brainer of simply placing your bet on the tortoise. In stock market terms, what is the tortoise? It's the S&P 500.

By now, you've heard of index funds. One of the most popular index funds is a special mutual fund made up of all 500 stocks in the S&P 500. What a great concept. If you can't beat the market, then buy the whole market. Bet that the entire market will continue to go up . . . *in the long run,* of course. There are so many advantages to investing in index funds compared to the average professionally managed equity mutual fund.

Index Fund	Professionally Managed Mutual Fund
Lower costs, 0.2 percent	Higher costs, 2.0 percent or more
Low portfolio turnover	Higher portfolio turnover
Low transaction fees	Higher transaction fees
Low tax consequences	Higher tax consequence

For the average unsophisticated investor, the no-brainer approach is to buy a few carefully selected index funds and forget about them. Here's the answer to another of the three critical questions.

Question: Which stocks should I buy?

Drum roll. . . . The envelope, please.

Answer: All of them.

Buy an index fund made up of all the stocks in the market. Table 5.2 shows a few examples.

Odds are, with this approach you'll do just as well as the vast majority of professional fund managers and perhaps much better. You don't have to agonize for months over which stocks to buy and when. Just choose one from the following list and forget about it for 10 to 25 years.

And that brings us to the final question: When should I buy? Another look at Figure 5.1 gives you the answer. The obvious answer is, *immediately!*

Obvious Lesson 3: The Sooner You Buy, the Richer You Can Become

The sooner you buy, the longer you have your money at work and the more money you have to compound. Take 50 percent of your monthly savings and sock it away into your chosen index fund(s). Do this every month without fail for the rest of your life.

If you'll do this—even if you do *nothing else* I describe in this book—then in due time the floodgates of prosperity will pour into your life. The goal of the following chapters is to open those floodgates much sooner. But if all of your short-term "hare-brained" schemes come to naught, this "tortoise" strategy will have you slowly giggling yourself toward a prosperous future.

If you're like most folks, you don't have a lump sum lying around. You're forced to invest in periodic payments over time. When you invest a fixed amount every single month for a long period of time, you're actually practicing a rather sophisticated strategy called *dollar cost averaging*. Look at Figures 5.2 and 5.3 and tell me which of the two mutual funds looks like the best moneymaking opportunity.

TABLE 5.2   Top Categories of Index Funds

Name of the Fund	Stock Symbol	Telephone Number	Web Address
Funds that track the S&P 500 Index			
Vanguard Index 500	VFINX	800-662-7447	www.vanguard.com
Fidelity Spartan Market	FSMKX	800-544-6666	www.fidelity.com
Dreyfus Basix S&P 500	DSPIX	800-782-6620	www.dreyfus.com
Transamerica Premier Index	TPIIX	800-892-7587	www.transamericafunds.com
Funds that track the Wilshire 5000 Index			
Vanguard Total Stock Market Index	VSTMX	800-662-7447	www.vanguard.com
T. Rowe Price Total Equity Market Index	POMIX	800-225-5132	www.troweprice.com
Fidelity Spartan Total Market	FSTMX	800-544-6666	www.fidelity.com
Funds that track the Morgan Stanley EAFE Index (Europe, Australasia, Far East)			
Vanguard Intl Equity Index Emerging Mrkts	VEIEX	800-662-7447	www.vanguard.com
Dreyfus International Stock Index Fund	DIISX	800-782-6620	www.dreyfus.com
Funds that track the Lehman Brothers Aggregate Bond Index			
Vanguard Total Bond Market Index	VBMFX	800-662-7447	www.vanguard.com
Dreyfus Bond Market Index Fund	DBIRX	800-782-6620	www.dreyfus.com

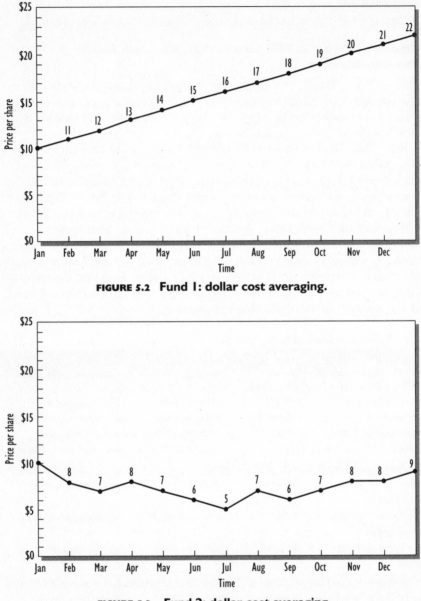

FIGURE 5.2 Fund 1: dollar cost averaging.

FIGURE 5.3 Fund 2: dollar cost averaging.

Fund 2 outperforms fund 1 by a substantial margin. How can that be? It surely doesn't look that way. The answer is simple: As the price was dropping, the fixed $100 investment purchased a larger number of shares. Even though the share price never reached its starting point at the beginning of the year, the total value of the portfolio increased substantially because of the shares purchased at lower prices.

TABLE 5.3   Year-end summary*

	Fund 1	Fund 2
Total dollars invested	$1,200	$1,200
Total number of shares purchased	71.3	160.09
Value of each share at year-end	$22	$9
Total value of investment	$1,426	$1,521.81
Total return on investment	18.83%	26.81%

*Assuming a periodic payment of $100 each month for 12 months.

Of course, these are contrived examples (lies, damned lies, and statistics!), but you can clearly see the value of a decline in the stock price, assuming that the price eventually recovers. With dollar cost averaging, you're actually hoping for a price decline every once in a while. It gives you a chance to buy more shares at a cheaper price. That is why you can look at temporary stock market slumps as positive events in your long-term investment horizon.

Dollar cost averaging works only if you continue buying—especially during the bad times—and hold on until good times return. If you stop buying during the bad times, you lose your advantage when things rebound.

Here's the number one reason that dollar cost averaging* is so powerful: It completely eliminates the need to guess when you should buy. It takes away the need for *market timing.*

What is market timing? If you're really smart (or have a lot of time on your hands), you can try to forecast the highs and lows in the market. At the peak, when the market is just beginning to dip from its highs into a trough, market timers say you should cash in your chips and park your money in some risk-free checking account. Then, when the market hits bottom and starts to bounce back, that is the precise time for you to buy with both hands. Sounds easy, but only a handful of investors have been smart enough to do it.

For example, during the entire decade of the 1980s the S&P 500 Index gained 17.6 percent annually, with frequent dips and spurts. During this period there were 2,528 trading days. A full 28 percent of the entire profit for the decade was generated in just *10 days.* If you had been trying to time the market and happened to miss those 10 critical days, you would have lost 28 percent of your gain for the entire decade![†]

---

* If you're a beginning investor and would like a free report on the basics of investing in the stock market, including basic definitions and seven basic investment strategies for beginners, go to www.multiplestreamsofincome.com and enter the keyword 7 Strategies, or call my office at 801-852-8700.

[†] Burton G. Malkiel, *A Random Walk Down Wall Street* (New York: W.W. Norton & Co., 1999), p. 163.

With dollar cost averaging, you don't have to be smart. You can be a total idiot and still win. You just buy every month, month after month. You buy during the good times. You buy during the bad times. You don't care what the headlines are saying. You ignore the experts on TV. You don't get jealous when you hear that one stock (out of 10,000!) tripled in price that day. A lot of other investors also bought the one that dropped by two-thirds on the very same day. You just blindly and ignorantly do what you have always done—buy, buy, buy. The average price of your continued buying will give you a wonderful average long-term return. This, of course, assumes that the past 50-year history of 11 percent compounded annual stock market gains continue for the next 50 years into the future. This is not necessarily a sure bet! You'll have to decide whether this is a safe bet for you.

Let's review what we've learned:

- You must start your investing program immediately.
- Index funds are the safest, simplest way to invest in the market.
- Dollar cost averaging is convenient and smart for most of us.
- Long-term investing is far less risky than short-term investing.

The question is, how much of your disposable savings should you invest in index funds. I recommend that you put at least 50 percent of your savings there. What about the other 50 percent? You're going to spread it into two other reservoirs or basins. (See Figure 5.4.)

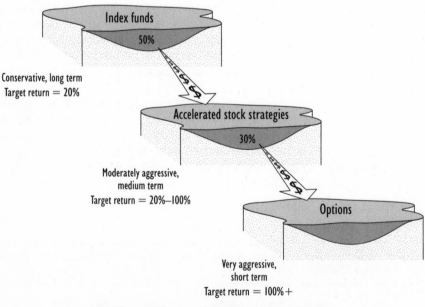

FIGURE 5.4 Your various investment basins.

The information in this chapter is just enough to get you started, but certainly not enough to form a firm foundation for investing. As you begin your study of this fascinating field, you will find that the books you read will be polarized along a continuum of investment theories. One theory—the *efficient market theory*—holds that stock prices are extremely efficient and that it is difficult if not impossible to buy stocks at bargain prices and therefore almost impossible to beat the market. At the other end of the spectrum are those who hold that the market is inefficient and that it is possible to beat the market with superior knowledge, techniques, and strategies.

The Efficient-Market Group	The Beat-the-Market Group
A Random Walk Down Wall Street Burton G. Malkiel (New York: W.W. Norton & Co., 1999)	*One Up on Wall Street* Peter Lynch and John Rothchild (New York: Simon & Schuster, 1994)
Common Sense on Mutual Funds John C. Bogle (New York: John Wiley & Sons, 1999)	*Buffettology* Mary Buffett (New York: Fireside, 1997)

The two books in the efficient-market group clearly explain how it is almost impossible to beat the market over any length of time. The two books in the beat-the-market group clearly explain how two superstar investors were able to beat the market year in and year out. I encourage you to read all of them. They will give you the view from both ends of the spectrum.

Both theories have compelling arguments. Which side of the fence you come down on depends on your own personality. If you aren't interested in the markets and want the fastest, safest, easiest way to invest for the long term, then invest all your money in index funds and I'll see you in 30 years. You can skip over the next two chapters in the book and proceed directly to the real estate mountain.

If you're a natural autopreneur—if you love to tinker with numbers and analyze data, if you'd like to learn to think like Warren Buffett, and if you love the challenge of trying to magnify your investment returns—then I recommend that you join me in Chapter 6, where I'll show you how to invest the other, more aggressive portion of your investment portfolio.

Index funds, dollar cost averaging, long-term investing. . . . You've probably heard all of this before. But have you done anything about it?

Stop reading right now. Pick up the phone and call one of the index funds listed on page 55. If you prefer to do your own research, go to one of the mutual fund tracking services (e.g., www.morningstar.com) and look up all of the index funds that are available through various fund families.

This shouldn't take you more than 30 minutes. Throw a dart and pick one.

Call the toll-free number of the fund you selected and have X dollars automatically deducted from your bank account every single month for the rest of your life. (Relax, you can always change your mind.)

Most likely, the company has account representatives available 24 hours a day . . . which means that you have no more excuses. You can do it right now. Operators are standing by. Don't even wait to finish reading this sentence. Stop and do it now.

(*Pause . . .*)

You didn't stop reading, did you? Why not? You say that you already own an index fund? Okay, then *you* can continue to read.

As for the rest of you, what's your excuse? You say you haven't set up a savings program yet?

All right, could you afford $50 a month? Would that break your budget? Gotcha! Here's an index fund that will start you out for only $50, with a minimum investment of $50 a month thereafter. No more excuses.

Transamerica Premier Index
(TPIIX) 800-892-7587
www.transamericafunds.com

Now go pick up the phone and get this over with. You'll feel much better when this is behind you. I'll be right here when you get back. Go.

(*Pause of about 30 minutes . . .*)

Now, doesn't that feel good? Reach your left hand over your right shoulder and give yourself a big pat on the back. Just keep it up and I'll see you 25 years from now. Let's have dinner in Paris. You're buying, right? Say yes. You can afford it.

CHAPTER 6

Those who understand compound interest are destined to collect it.
Those who don't are doomed to pay it.
TOM AND DAVID GARDNER, THE MOTLEY FOOLS

YOUR SECOND STREAM
Accelerated Stock Strategies: Six Ways to Magnify Your Returns

So, you want to be more aggressive with your investments? Well, hold onto your hat. We'll start slow, but by the end of this chapter we'll be flying at Mach 3. This chapter will teach you how to invest the portion of your stock portfolio designated for your moderately aggressive basin—earning 20 to 100 percent on your money annually.

I encourage you to put a fire wall between each of your investment basins. Never dip into your long-term basin to fund a shortfall in your short-term basin and vice versa. Each basin is sacred, designed for a specific use.

Using baseball language, your long-term, low-risk basin is designed for walks, bunts, and singles—10 to 20 percent return per year. Your medium-term, moderately aggressive basin is for doubles and triples—20 to 100 percent per year. Your short-term, highly aggressive basin is for home runs—100 percent per year and more.

In this chapter, let's learn how to beat the market. Wait a minute! In Chapter 5, I told you it was *almost* impossible to beat the market. Yes, it's almost impossible . . . over a long period of time. But a large number of people have done it on a short-term basis, and some people are doing it this very second. Don't believe me?

Just for fun, stop reading, fire up your computer, and log on to www.morningstar.com. Morningstar is one of the top performance-tracking services for mutual funds and stocks. Best of all, it's free. On the main page, scroll down to Tool Box and click on Fund Selector. When prompted, you want to scan All Funds for one-year returns. For example, on the day I did this search, there were 9,082 mutual funds of all types, from which the computer produced a list of the hottest funds for the previous 12 months. Table 6.1 shows the top 20 funds on the list. The top fund boasts a one-year total return of 471.68 percent. That's not a typo: over 400 percent! The last fund on the list boasts 201.21 percent. If you had picked any of these 20 funds, you would have more than doubled your money in that year. Wow! But 20 funds out of a universe of over 9,000

TABLE 6.1 Morningstar Top 20 Funds*

Ticker	Name	1-Year Total Return
NGTIX	Nicholas-Applegate Global Techno I	471.68
MSCGX	MAS Small Cap Growth Instl	317.44
VWEGX	Van Wagoner Emerging Growth	300.56
NEVIX	Nevis Fund	296.61
ATCHX	Amerindo Technology D	268.69
VWPVX	Van Wagoner Post-Venture	260.28
MFITX	Monument Internet A	260.24
WJSAX	Warburg Pincus Advisor Japan Sm Co	256.85
WPJPX	Warburg Pincus Japan Sm Co Comm	255.82
VWTKX	Van Wagoner Technology	249.31
FJSCX	Fidelity Japan Small Companies	249.28
BMCIX	BlackRock Micro-Cap Equity Instl	241.19
BMEAX	BlackRock Micro-Cap Equity Inv A	239.77
BRMBX	BlackRock Micro-Cap Equity Inv B	237.15
BMECX	BlackRock Micro-Cap Equity Inv C	237.04
WWWFX	Internet	226.51
VWMCX	Van Wagoner Micro-Cap	212.36
TIFQX	Firsthand Technology Innovators	212.31
UOPIX	ProFunds UltraOTC Inv	205.41
UOPSX	ProFunds UltraOTC Svc	201.21

Courtesy of Morningstar. Used with permission.

*Chicago-based Morningstar, Inc. is a leading provider of investment information, research, and analysis. Its extensive line of Internet, software, and print products provides unbiased data and commentary on mutual funds, U.S. and international equities, closed-end funds, and variable annuities. Established in 1984, Morningstar continues to be the industry's most trusted source on key investment issues of the day. For more information about Morningstar, visit www.morningstar.com or call 800-735-0700.

funds is only one-fifth of 1 percent. That's like betting on a horse with odds of 500 to 1. Would you risk the rent money for that? Sure seems tempting, doesn't it?

Some people view the entire universe of mutual funds as a horse race. Some funds race off ahead while the rest of the pack trails. Then the lead horse surrenders the lead to another pony who sprints to the front. This lead pony then falls back as yet another contender surges ahead. All the way around the track the horses keep exchanging the lead. In this race, however, there are more than 9,000 horses, and the race ends on December 31 every year.

One of the horses is called the S&P 500, which represents the top 500 companies in North America, if not the world. All other horses are trying to beat this horse. In most years, the vast majority of horses finish far behind the S&P 500 horse, especially when you factor in taxes and operating costs. Those horses that beat the S&P 500 do so only temporarily. But, as the Morningstar list in Table 6.1 shows, a handful of horses finish spectacularly in the short run. The question of this chapter is, how can we locate these horses?

In the next few pages, I'll share with you six ways (systems, really) for finding funds and stocks that have the highest probabilities for not only beating the market but trouncing it. We'll start with the easiest suggestion.

System 1: Let the Master Himself Manage Your Money

Who is the master of the investment world? Warren Buffett. He is, without question, the greatest stock investor of all time. I first learned of Buffett about 10 years ago, when the stock of his holding company, Berkshire Hathaway (stock symbol BRKA), was selling for an astronomical $10,000 a share. It was then, and still is, the single most expensive stock in the world. Buffett doesn't believe in splitting his stock price, so if you want to own a piece of it, you must write a very large check for even a single share. Figure 6.1 is a stock chart showing the growth of Berkshire Hathaway. In essence, Berkshire is Buffett's own mutual fund.

At this writing, Buffett is 69 years old (b. August 30, 1930). How much longer will he be a market force? Will the magic be lost forever when he's gone? Who knows? If you're willing to take the chance that Buffett will be around for another 20 years then you, too, can own a piece of him. A $10,000 investment with Buffett when he began in the mid-1950s would now be worth over $200 million! When he passes on to the "Big Board in the Sky," his stock price will probably take a temporary dip (this is just my guess), but then the results should continue pretty much as they have for years. Why? The cochairman of Berkshire is

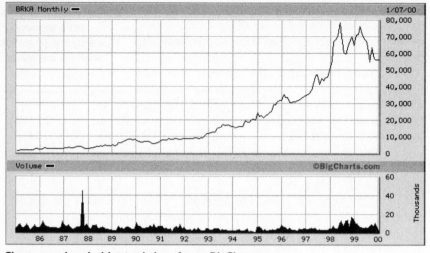

Chart reproduced with permission of www.BigCharts.com.

FIGURE 6.1 **Growth of Berkshire Hathaway stock.**

Charlie Munger, who is less public but certainly as important to the success of Berkshire. The companies that he and Buffett have selected are exceptional long-term winners. The Berkshire Hathaway management team consists of only 12 people, all thoroughly trained in the Buffett methodology. As Buffett himself has written:

> On my death, Berkshire's ownership picture will change but not in a disruptive way: First, only about 1% of my stock will have to be sold to take care of bequests and taxes; second, the balance of my stock will go to my wife, Susan, if she survives me, or to a family foundation if she doesn't. In either event, Berkshire will possess a controlling shareholder guided by the same philosophy and objectives that now set our course. . . . You can be equally sure that the principles we have employed to date in running Berkshire will continue to guide the managers who succeed me. Lest we end on a morbid note, I also want to assure you that I have never felt better. I love running Berkshire, and if enjoying life promotes longevity, Methuselah's record is in jeopardy.*

The preceding quote comes from an *Owner's Manual* found at www.berkshirehathaway.com. It includes a description of the 13 guiding principles behind the success of the Buffett style of investing. Buffett further states in the *Owner's Manual:*

> Charlie and I cannot promise you results. But we can guarantee that your financial fortunes will move in lockstep with ours for whatever period of time

---

* Berkshire Hathaway, Inc. *Owner's Manual.* A message from Warren E. Buffett, Chairman and CEO, January 1999.

you elect to be our partner. We have no interest in large salaries or options or other means of gaining an "edge" over you. We want to make money only when our partners do and in exactly the same proportion. Moreover, when I do something dumb, I want you to be able to derive some solace from the fact that my financial suffering is proportional to yours.

By the way, if the high-octane Berkshire Hathaway (BRKA) is too rich for your blood, you can always buy the Berkshire Hathaway B shares . . . called Baby Berkshires (BRKB). They were created in 1996 to fill the void of those who couldn't afford the Mama stock. Each Baby Berkshire is ⅒₀ of the price of the A shares, with a few less benefits. Figure 6.2 shows what the stock looks like.

A quote from the Berkshire home page is appropriate here: "If you don't know jewelry, know the jeweler." I'd add, "If you don't know horses, know the jockey." Warren Buffett is the winningest stock jockey of all time.

If you want to learn how to do what Buffett has done and perhaps even duplicate it yourself, then you must read *Buffettology,* the book I recommended in Chapter 5.

System 2: Select Mutual Funds with the Longest-Term Track Record

If you don't want to bet on Buffett's selection of stocks in Berkshire Hathaway, then perhaps you'd like to choose another mutual fund to beat the market. Let's assume you could select only one of two funds. One fund has consistently beaten the market with a 20 percent per year compounded annual return for the past 10 years in a row, compared to 17.2

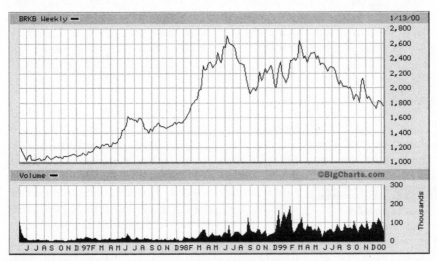

Chart reproduced with permission of www.BigCharts.com.

FIGURE 6.2 Growth of Baby Berkshire stock.

percent for the S&P 500. The second fund earned a whopping 176 percent in the past 12 months alone . . . outpacing the entire 10-year track record of the market in a single year! You're at the betting window, trying to choose between these two horses. Do you go with the hot hand or the consistent winner? Make your choice. The horses are at the gate, restless in their stalls. You rapidly juggle the numbers in your mind. If the hot fund could repeat its performance for only a few more years, you would be rich. Images of yachts and jewels and exotic places bounce around your brain. You could get used to that.

Get rich slow, or get rich fast? This choice is thrust in your face every day. You read a *Money* magazine ad boasting that this new fund burst out of the gate and grew at 52 percent in its first year (in the fine print, you read the familiar caveat, "Past performance does not guarantee future results"). On the next page, a similar ad boasts a much lower one-year return: 16.5 percent. You flip back and forth between the ads. . . . They both seem so real, so seductive. All things being equal, wouldn't you choose the fund with the bigger number?

Now take another look at the list of 20 funds in Table 6.1. Here's a list of winning thoroughbreds. Why don't you just throw a dart at the funds on this list? Remember, by the time that you read about these spectacular results in the press, the race has already been run. Can these horses do it again?

For the answer to this, we dig a little deeper into Morningstar and find out how many of these winning funds were on the list in previous years. This narrows the choices down dramatically. Only 2 of the 20 were on the list three years in a row. If you had been smart enough three years ago to sink all of your money into either of these funds, the odds are about one in seven thousand that you would have selected the hot fund. If you go back 5 years, none of the funds did well 5 years in a row.

Now, we're starting to see the problem. More than likely, the hot fund this year will not repeat its success the next year. In fact, if we look at the list of the highest-producing funds in each of the previous 1, 3, 5, and 10 year periods, not one fund made the top 20 in all of the time periods. Not one! In other words, the hot horse was not able to remain at the front of the pack. Of course, this is hindsight, but it sheds some light on the problem.

Choosing a fund based on a short-term track record simply doesn't work. In fact, it might even be an indicator that this is the *last* fund you should be putting your money into. Excellent short-term results may be the clue that you should run for cover. It would be nice to be on the horse when it surges to the front of the pack and then ride it for all it's worth. But how can you find this fund *before* it makes its move? That's the trick. There is a way to do it. . . . But it's fairly risky, so I'll save it for later in the chapter. For now, let's go for the more conservative alternative over the past 10 years.

There have been funds that have beaten the market, year in and year out, over a long period of time. And it's relatively easy to find them. Once again, we turn to Morningstar and a screen of all the funds in the Morningstar database for the highest total return over the past 10 years. On the day I searched, there were 1,630 funds that had been in existence for the previous 10 years. Table 6.2 shows the top 20 funds.

This list is for illustration purposes only. By the time you read this book, the list will be obsolete and you'll have to go to the Internet for the current screens. In fact, when you perform your new search, it will be instructive to see how different the funds are compared to those in Table 6.2.

Here's the question: How have these funds been able to pull off such long-term spectacular results? Was it the manager? Was it the fund strategy? Was it because of the bull market? Will they do as well in a bear market? Will any of these funds do as well in the next 10 years as they have in the past 10?

TABLE 6.2 Morningstar Top 20 Funds, with 10-Year Track Record*

Ticker	Name	10-Year Total Return
FSELX	Fidelity Select Electronics	34.64
FDCPX	Fidelity Select Computers	31.34
FSPTX	Fidelity Select Technology	30.34
FTCHX	Invesco Technology II	27.75
FSCSX	Fidelity Select Software & Comp	26.88
PRSCX	T. Rowe Price Science & Technology	26.79
SLMCX	Seligman Communications&Information A	26.38
ALTFX	Alliance Technology A	26.35
SPECX	Spectra	25.92
RSEGX	RS Emerging Growth	24.71
JAVLX	Janus Twenty	24.33
ACEGX	Van Kampen Emerging Growth A	23.48
EQPGX	Fidelity Advisor Equity Growth Instl	22.74
MSIGX	Oppenheimer Main St Growth & Income A	22.24
KTCAX	Kemper Technology A	22.22
TISHX	Flag Investors Communications A	22.21
FSPHX	Fidelity Select Health Care	22.17
TWCUX	American Century Ultra Inv	22.11
VGHCX	Vanguard Health Care	22.11
UNSCX	United Science & Technology A	22.08

Courtesy of Morningstar. Used with permission.

*See footnote, Table 6.1.

Obviously, they've done something right. Let me give you two ways to narrow the list of 20 down to the one, two, or three that you might be willing to put some of your money into.

1. *Expense ratios.* All things being equal, the fund on the list with the lowest expense ratio will probably have an edge in the long run. For exhaustive proof of this point, read *Common Sense on Mutual Funds* by John Bogle.

2. *Industry group performance.* All things being equal, the fund that has consistently performed in the top quartile compared to all other funds in the same market segment will probably have an edge over the next 10 years.

Take a look at Figure 6.3. When it comes to quartile analysis, John Bogle, elder statesman of the index fund industry, has this to say in his excellent book, *Common Sense on Mutual Funds:*

> When I evaluate mutual funds (and I have looked carefully at many hundreds of them during my long career), I like to look at a fund's ranking among other funds with similar policies and objectives. . . . Morningstar Mutual Funds makes these comparisons easy. It shows, in a simple chart, whether a fund was in the first, second, third, or fourth quartile of its group during each of the preceding 12 years. . . . For a fund to earn top performance evaluation, it should have, in my opinion, at least six to nine years in the top two quartiles and no more than one or two years in the bottom quartile. I would

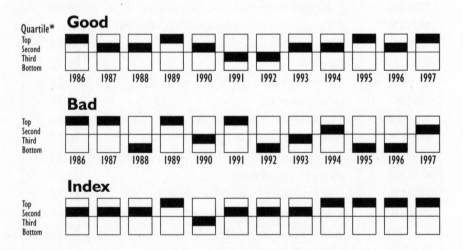

*Quartile within *Morningstar* style category.

Courtesy of Morningstar. Used with permission. (See footnote, Table 6.1.)

FIGURE 6.3 Morningstar performance profiles: consistency.

normally reject funds with four or five years in the bottom quartile, even if offset by the same number in the top quartile.

All of the preceding criteria can be determined with a little more digging in the Morningstar data. To replicate the analysis, you'll need to either become a subscriber to Morningstar (which offers a 12-week trial for $55) or become a Premium Morningstar member at www.morningstar.com or call 800-735-0700. But relax. At this writing, a premium membership was only $9.95 per month with the two first weeks free. So you could feasibly sign up for the service, check it out, get your data, and be gone for $10 or less. I think, once you've seen how it works, you'll enjoy it enough to continue to be a member. Also available are powerful one-page summaries of each fund that Morningstar follows. Each report costs only $3.

If you want to take a little more risk and venture beyond the plain-vanilla index funds described in Chapter 5, then this would be a sound strategy. There is no guarantee that a fund you select this way will continue to be a winner in the future. But it stacks the odds in your favor . . . and probably gives you a better chance than a monkey throwing darts at a newspaper (if that makes you feel any better).

System 3: Select Only Financial Advisors with the Longest Track Records

I've been to a racing track only a handful of times in my life. A friend of ours owned a racehorse and invited us to Del Mar to watch it run (it finished fifth). As we walked onto the grounds, there were several booths of people hawking handicapper newspapers that offered advice on which horses to bet on. Supposedly, these experts had taken all factors into consideration (the horse, the jockey, the track, the weather, etc.) and were willing to share their top picks—for a price. Although the stock market is not a betting track, there are hundreds of experts who will sell you their analyses.

You'd have to have lived in a cave for the past year not to have received a boxcar full of junk mail touting this or that expert's system for making huge returns from the stock market. These offers sound almost too good to be true. I've gone through my junk-mail file of past newsletter offerings and culled a handful of headlines and claims for you:

*"305% . . . 503% . . . 95% . . . 147% . . . 377% . . . 526% . . . 818% . . . .
These figures are not misprints. They are some of my recent profits. . . .
Profits that yielded an incredible annual return of over 100% for
four years in a row!"*   [Cost for the subscription, $199]

*"In an account entered in a trading contest with actual money,
I turned $1,072 into $151,000 in 8 months. That even beats Hillary. . . ."*
[Cost for 12 weeks of e-mail, $699]

*" 'Paul,' he said. 'I did it. I invested just like you said.
And I want to thank you because . . . I just made $300,000 in one day!' "*
[Cost of the subscription for 1 year, $995]

"How to Make a Million Dollars in the Stock Market."
[Cost for the system, $195]

*"If you do not want to double or triple your money
within 12 months, please throw this letter away
right now."* [Cost for the subscription, $2,500]

*"One select group of traders, using one secret trading system,
piled up a huge 426 Million Dollar profit in 1998. . . . In fact, these
winning traders have made at least 100 Million Dollars per year
for the last decade!!"* [Cost for the seminar, $2,500]

Hey, who needs Warren Buffett? All you need to do is plunk down a few
hundred bucks and you, too, can be a millionaire. Are any of these offers
legitimate? I don't know. Here's what I do know: Before I spend a dime
on any advisory service, I'm going to buy some low-cost information
insurance by getting an inexpensive subscription to the *Hulbert Financial
Digest* (www.hulbertdigest.com).

$$$

WIT & WISDOM
Wall Street is the only place
that people ride to in a Rolls-
Royce to get advice from
those who take the subway.

WARREN BUFFETT

Just as Morningstar tracks individual stocks and
funds, the *Hulbert Financial Digest* provides a
benchmark with which to compare an advisor's
long-term track record. Mark Hulbert has been
tracking the success of newsletter services for 20
years. He's seen a lot of flakes come and go. He
currently tracks the success and/or failure of over
450 newsletter portfolios each month. Now you
can compare the hype in their mailing pieces with
the cold, hard facts of reality. And it's well worth
the price—normally $135 for a 12-month subscription, but currently
offered at a special price of only $59. Cheap insurance.

Mark Hulbert is our watchdog and, in my opinion, has done the most
to clean up the industry. Here is one of the most important lessons he has
learned over the past 20 years of comparing the rhetoric with reality:
Avoid the hot-handed advisor.

As with mutual funds, the hottest hands this year will almost always
cool off next year. For example, in 1998 the best-performing newsletter
portfolio gained 192.8 percent. Wow! Let me get my checkbook! But,
writes Hulbert, "In my experience, huge one-year returns are almost
impossible to sustain." And he proves it with some impressive research.
He says:

To illustrate how unprofitable it would be to invest this year on the basis of
last year, I constructed a hypothetical portfolio that exploited one-year
returns. Each January 1, this portfolio would invest in the best-performing
portfolio from the previous year. It would follow this portfolio for 12

months, and on the subsequent January 1 start following whatever portfolio had done the best over that year.[1]

How well did the "hot-hand" portfolio do? Between 1991 and 1998, the years of the test, this portfolio had an annual *loss* of 40.3 percent compared to a gain of 20.2 percent for the broad market Wilshire 5000 Index. For example, the big winner in 1991 was the *Granville Market Letter,* with 244.8 percent. The very next year it proceeded to lose 84.3 percent. Did you get that? Chasing the hottest advisors' previous portfolios, as many neophytes are tempted to do, produced huge losses.

Hulbert then tried a different approach. Rather than focusing on one-year results, he decided to find out what would happen if he used only portfolios from newsletters with the best track records over the previous five years. This time the results were much better—17.7 percent over the same eight-year period of the test—but still below the market's annual average of 20.2 percent.

> **$$$**
> **WIT & WISDOM**
> I pretend to work.
> They pretend to pay me.

Using the same logic, he began to test newsletter portfolios from letters that had an excellent 10-year record. They did even better: 20.4 percent annualized returns compared to the broad market index of 20.2 percent. Still, you could have saved your newsletter subscription fee, bought a no-hassle index fund, slept better at night, and still done extremely well compared to the smartest of the experts.

Hulbert summarizes:

> These results are exactly what we should expect, if we believe that longer track records tell us more about an adviser's abilities than shorter ones. And they clearly do. When focusing on one-year returns, it's virtually impossible to tell the difference between an adviser whose return was the result of genuine ability and one who merely was lucky. When focusing on returns over ten years (or longer), in contrast, luck plays a much less dominant role . . . Chase last year's top performers at your peril.[2]

> **$$$**
> **WIT & WISDOM**
> First Law of Personal Finance:
> Bills travel through the mail
> at twice the speed of checks.

So, what should you do? Well, if you really want to learn how to hit some doubles or triples on your own, it wouldn't hurt to take some batting lessons from some of the best in the industry. The *Hulbert Financial Digest* lists the top five newsletter performers over four different periods of time: 15 years, 10 years, 8 years, and 5 years. Taking into consideration the long term ("That old dog sure can hunt!") and the short term ("Whatcha done for me lately?"), three newsletters make most of the lists, with the following total annual returns:

---

[1] *HFD Introductory Booklet,* "Why You Should Ignore Short-Term Gains," p. 3.
[2] Ibid.

	15-year	10-year	8-year	5-year
The Prudent Speculator (tracked since 1980)	19.9%	—	27.4%	29.3%
OTC Insight (tracked since 1987)	—	28.5%	26.5%	37.1%
Timer Digest (tracked since 1988)	—	19.7%	22.2%	26.0%
Compared to the Wilshire 5000	18.0%	16.4%	18.5%	24.2%

Caveat! The preceding returns are not adjusted for risk. Notice how these returns compare to the Wilshire 5000, which is the return that you would have received if you had bought an index fund of the entire stock market and just held on. The portfolios of stocks recommended by the newsletters carried a much higher risk while generating only a few more percentage points in return. Is this risk worth it? The *Hulbert Digest* illuminates issues like these so that an investor can make more-informed choices.

As for mutual funds, is there a way to hop from one hot fund to another in the short term like jumping from one winning horse to the horse that is overtaking it? How do you find such funds? One of the most useful aspects of the *Hulbert Digest* is Hulbert's Performance Scorecard for Mutual Fund Letters, in which he lists the top five mutual fund newsletters over a 10-year period of time and an 8-year period of time. The following three newsletters make both lists:

	10-year	8-year
Timer Digest (tracked since 1988)	21.2%	22.6%
The Chartist Mutual Fund Letter (tracked since 1989)	16.9%	17.9%
No-Load Fund-X (tracked since 1980)	15.2%	18.0%
Compared to the Wilshire 5000	16.4%	18.5%

Still, I'm curious about how some of these newsletters have been able to do so well for so long. It's obviously not just luck. I want to know how they did it. Don't you? Many of these newsletters offer a free trial letter. It's worth a peek. To find out which letters are tracked by the *Hulbert Digest,* go to www.hulbertdigest.com and click on Newsletter Profiles. This will give you a complete listing, with available links to their actual web sites.

The *Hulbert Newsletter* is excellent for people who want the do-it-yourself approach. If, however, you have a fairly large sum of money and you're looking for someone to manage it for you, then here is a tip. I've recently learned of a newsletter that tracks the performance of money managers who use the principles of market timing to manage actual customer accounts with real money in real time. In other words, this newsletter doesn't track the *advice* of a newsletter guru, it tracks the money manager's actual, *real-dollar performance* with his or her clients' money. It's called the *MoniResearch Newsletter.* The editor for almost two decades has been Steve Shellans. If you have a large amount of money you want to put under management, this newsletter is an excellent resource to help you select the right person or firm for the job. Check out the web site at www.moniresearch.com. I think a trial subscription for two issues is $55.

When I showed Steve Shellans this chapter for his comments, he sent me the following e-mail, which I believe is instructive:

> In one particular context, I disagree with your premise: "Only select financial advisors with the longest track record." This is good advice for the newsletter advisors tracked by the *Hulbert Digest,* but not necessarily for money managers. Here is why. Mutual Funds hate market timers. Some reject them completely, others tolerate them while they are still small. Therefore, all money managers using market timing and who manage actual client accounts have a finite capacity for accepting new money. The bigger they get, the more difficult it becomes to find mutual funds which will accept them. The good market timers attract the most capital. The better they are, the more people send them money. Here are three actual examples of top-notch money managers we began tracking in the *MoniResearch Newsletter.* In the month after they were written up, they brought in $50 million, $30 million, and $15 million, respectively. In the *Newsletter* there is a Closed Performance Table showing the managers who had to close their programs to new money when they could find no more mutual funds who would accept them. You will see that their performance numbers are better than the population as a whole. What is even more startling is the fact that the very best managers are not to be seen at all! When they become "saturated" they ask me to drop them out of our newsletter completely because they don't want the bother of people calling them to open accounts. [Tough problem!]
>
> There is another mechanism operating that leads me to disagree with the "long track records" premise—at least as it applies to actual money managers. When a manager first starts out, perhaps with $1 to $2 million under management, he is lean, hungry and aggressive in his trading. But after he amasses a couple of million under management, his attitude changes—his primary goal is not to rock the boat. That is, not to make mistakes. So his style becomes more conservative. His performance numbers go down, but he doesn't alienate many clients.
>
> Therefore, for clients who wish to use a money manager who is a market timer, I feel the best strategy is this. Put your money with the hot hands and shooting stars. Spread your money over several such managers to reduce risk. Monitor their performance on an ongoing basis. If performance deteriorates (for whatever reason), leave and move the money to another manager. As you might expect, the managers themselves dislike this concept, but in my experience this is in the client's best interests.

There you have sage advice from two newsletter publishers (Hulbert and Shellans) who spend their lives tracking the success of some of the world's smartest investment advisors and money managers.

Now let me introduce you to a gentleman who is both an advisor and a money manager.

System 4: Let Your Portfolio Go to the Dogs

In 1990, an investment book appeared that caused quite a stir. It's called *Beating the Dow: A High-Return, Low-Risk Method for Investing in the Dow Jones Industrial Stocks with as Little as $5,000* by Michael O'Higgins with John Downes. This is what his publisher said about the book:

> By following a simple formula . . . investors could beat the pros 95 percent of the time by putting 100 percent of their money into the "dog" stocks of the Dow. Not only did this formula work for nearly a decade, but the publication of *Beating the Dow* spawned a veritable industry, including websites, mutual funds, and $20 billion worth of investments, elevating the theory to legendary status.

It has become so legendary that people have given this strategy the name "Dogs of the Dow." Table 6.3 shows you how well this approach has worked over the past 27 years, updated to January 1, 2000.

O'Higgins's approach is deceptively simple. Rather than rooting around in 10,000 individual stocks to find the ones with the greatest chance of success, he urges us to narrow the universe to only the 30 stocks that make up the Dow Jones Industrial Average—the most widely followed stock index in the world.

From this universe, he shows you how to find the few stocks on the list that have the highest probability of increasing in value in the next 12 months. All of this research takes 10 minutes per year. You make your choice, invest your money, and don't do a single thing until the next year, when you perform the same simple 10-minute calculation and reshuffle your portfolio. Sound too hard for you? Now you know why his book became so popular. People are still talking about it over a decade later. In his most recent book, *Beating the Dow with Bonds*, Mr. O'Higgins states:

> My stock-picking system for beating the Dow is predicated upon the idea that the out-of-favor, or "worst"-performing, companies on the Dow (my pet Dow Dogs) do a lot better over time than the top, or "best"-performing, ones. My Five-Stock formula is the simplest way of outperforming the Dow with that strategy. It uses a combination of the highest-yielding and least-expensive stocks to structure a five-stock portfolio; this has the incidental advantage of requiring less capital because of fewer stocks and lower prices.

The list on page 75 identifies the 30 companies that make up the Dow Jones Average, along with how well their stock performed in 1999.

TABLE 6.3 Beating the Dow

Year	BTD 5 Stock	BTD 10 Stock	DJIA
1973	19.60%	3.90%	−13.10%
1974	−3.80%	−1.30%	−23.10%
1975	70.10%	55.90%	44.40%
1976	40.80%	34.80%	22.70%
1977	4.50%	0.90%	−12.70%
1978	1.70%	−0.10%	2.70%
1979	9.90%	12.40%	10.50%
1980	40.50%	27.20%	21.50%
1981	0.00%	5.00%	−3.40%
1982	37.40%	23.60%	25.80%
1983	36.10%	38.70%	25.70%
1984	12.60%	7.60%	1.10%
1985	37.80%	29.50%	32.80%
1986	27.90%	32.10%	26.90%
1987	11.10%	6.10%	6.00%
1988	18.40%	22.90%	16.00%
1989	10.50%	26.50%	31.70%
1990	−15.20%	−7.60%	−0.40%
1991	61.90%	39.30%	23.90%
1992	23.10%	7.90%	7.40%
1993	34.30%	27.30%	16.80%
1994	8.60%	4.10%	4.90%
1995	30.50%	36.70%	36.40%
1996	26.00%	27.90%	28.90%
1997	20.50%	21.90%	24.90%
1998	12.30%	10.60%	17.90%
1999	−4.70%	3.60%	26.96%
Cumulative	**12649.79%**	**7529.34%**	**3106.26%**
Annualized	**20.50%**	**18.14%**	**14.27%**

The 30 Stocks That Make Up the Dow Average and How They Performed in 1999

Alcoa	122.6	Exxon Mobil	10.2	McDonald's	5.0
American Express	62.2	General Electric	51.7	Merck	−8.9
AT&T	0.6	General Motors	21.6	Microsoft	68.4
Boeing	27.0	Hewlett-Packard	66.5	3M	37.6
Caterpillar	2.3	Honeywell	30.2	J.P. Morgan	20.5
Citigroup	68.1	Home Depot	12.4	Philip Morris	−57.0
Coca-Cola	−13.1	Intel	38.9	Procter & Gamble	20.0
Disney	−2.5	IBM	17.0	SBC Communications	−9.1
DuPont	24.1	International Paper	25.9	United Technologies	19.5
Eastman Kodak	−8.0	Johnson & Johnson	11.2	Wal-Mart Stores	69.8

Why these 30 stocks? You can see that they are extremely successful companies that will be around for decades to come. The only trick is to determine which of them is going to do the best over the *near term*. Look at the list again. Without a crystal ball at the beginning of the year, how could you know which of these stocks to invest in and which to avoid? With hindsight, it's easy to see the winners and losers. The best one increased in value by 122.6 percent and the worst one lost 57.0 percent in value. O'Higgins's approach is to create a small portfolio of five stocks that, as a group, have the greatest probability of outperforming the 30 stocks as a whole. Here is how O'Higgins tells you to do this:

1. Buy a copy of the *Wall Street Journal* showing the closing prices on the last business day of the year. (Actually, it shouldn't matter which 12-month period you choose as long as you do it consistently.)

2. Use the Dogs of the Dow worksheet (Figure 6.4), and gather information about the closing stock price and the dividend yield for that day.

3. Rank the yields by circling the 10 highest yields.

4. Rank the circled stocks from 1 (highest yield) to 10 (lowest). You have now identified the 10 highest yielders in the Dow.

5. Identify the lowest-priced high yielders. Put a checkmark next to the five circled stocks with the lowest closing prices. You have now identified the five stocks combining the highest yield with the lowest prices.

If even these steps seem like too much work, simply go to the web site www.dogsofthedow.com and look up the current Dogs of the Dow list. All of the selections and day-to-day performance records are right there for you . . . free. (What did we do before the Internet?)

Some people have written that the Dogs of the Dow approach has gotten so popular that it has lost its edge, as the most recent performance results seem to indicate. O'Higgins himself has refined his approach in his recent book entitled *Beating the Dow with Bonds.* In this book, he still touts the power of his five-stock portfolio, but feels that the entire market is currently overpriced. Therefore, he counsels that there are many years when an investor should not be in stocks at all . . . but would do substantially better with either a fully vested position in U.S. Treasury bills or U.S. government zero-coupon bonds. He states:

> . . . my Beating the Dow Five-Stock Strategy is still the stock-picking system to beat when the investment class of choice is determined to be stocks. But . . . it no longer responds sufficiently to the overall needs of investors in today's market because it is only one-third of a strategy. My new strategy of allocating assets among and between the three major investment sectors closes the loop by being more well-rounded. It is the complete strategy for winning, not just in today's market conditions but all market conditions.*

* Michael B. O'Higgins with John McCarty, *Beating the Dow with Bonds: A High-Return, Low-Risk Strategy for Outperforming the Pros Even When Stocks Go South,* 1999, p. 150.

FIGURE 6.4 Dogs of the Dow Worksheet

	Symbol	Dow Stock	Closing Price	Yield	Rank	Lowest Rank	Execution Price	Closing Price End	Dividends	Total Return
1	AA	Aluminum Co. of America								
2	AXP	American Express								
3	T	American Tel. & Tel.								
4	BA	Boeing								
5	CAT	Caterpillar								
6	C	Citigroup								
7	KO	Coca-Cola								
8	DIS	Walt Disney								
9	DD	Dupont								
10	EK	Eastman Kodak								
11	XON	Exxon Mobil								
12	GE	General Electric								
13	GM	General Motors								
14	HWP	Hewlett-Packard								
15	HON	Honeywell								
16	HD	Home Depot								
17	INTC	Intel								
18	IBM	Int'l Business Machines								
19	IP	International Paper								
20	JNJ	Johnson & Johnson								
21	MCD	McDonald's								
22	MRK	Merck								
23	MSFT	Microsoft								
24	MMM	Minnesota Mining & Mfg.								
25	JPM	JP Morgan								
26	MO	Philip Morris								
27	PG	Procter & Gamble								
28	SBC	SBC Communications								
29	UTX	United Technologies								
30	WMT	Wal-Mart Stores								

In other words, O'Higgins recommends switching your entire investment portfolio into one of three investment vehicles: the five Dogs of the Dow Stocks, U.S. Treasury bills, or U.S. government zero-coupon bonds. Knowing when to switch from one investment vehicle to another is a fairly simple process.

Step 1. On or about January 1, buy the latest issue of *Barron's* weekly financial newspaper.

Step 2. Locate the section of the paper that lists the Standard & Poor's Industrial Index. You're looking for last week's Earnings Yield %, as illustrated in Figure 6.5.

Step 3. Locate the latest U.S. Treasury bond price quotations. You're looking for the most recently issued U.S. Treasury bond scheduled to mature in 10 years, as illustrated in Figure 6.6.

Step 4. Do some simple math. Add 0.30% to the number from step 3. Then compare this number to the figure circled in step 2. If the stock yield (2) is higher than the bond yield (3), this is your signal to invest your money in stocks that year. Just follow the five Dogs of the Dow strategy mentioned earlier.

If, however, the bond yield is greater than the yield on stocks, this tells you that stocks are overpriced and ripe for a correction. Your money should be invested elsewhere. Exactly where you invest your money depends on the price of gold. (Don't ask me why, but O'Higgins has done the research to back up his selection.)

Step 5. Go to the section of *Barron's* which lists the Gold and Silver prices and note last week's price of gold per troy ounce. Also, circle the price of gold as of one year ago, as illustrated in Figure 6.7.

INDEXES' P/ES & YIELDS

DJ latest 52-week earnings and dividends adjusted by the Dow Divisors at Friday's close. S&P Sept. 4-quarters earnings and indicated dividends based on Friday close. DJ and S&P latest available book values for FY 1998 and 1997.

	Last Week	Prev. Week	Year ago Week
S&P Ind Index	1760.34	1774.82	1403.98
P/E Ratio	39.03	39.35	35.86
Earns Yield, %	2.56	2.54	2.79
Earns $	45.10	45.10	39.15
Divs Yield %	.97	.98	1.22
Divs $	17.08	17.39	17.13
Mkt to Book	9.11	9.18	8.17
Book Value $	193.30	193.30	171.86

FIGURE 6.5 *Barron's* showing the earnings yield for the S&P Industrial Index.

U.S. Notes and Bonds

Rate	Mo/Yr		Bid	Asked	Fri. Chg.	Ask Yld.
$6^3/_8$	May	00n	100:09	100:11		5.52
$8^7/_8$	May	00n	101:16	101:18	−1	5.07
$5^1/_2$	May	00n	99:28	99:30		5.63
$6^1/_4$	May	00n	100:07	100:09		5.62
$5^3/_8$	Jun	00n	99:25	99:27	−1	5.66
$5^7/_8$	Jun	00n	100:02	100:04		5.63
$3^7/_8$	Jan	09i	97:21	97:22	−2	4.18
$5^1/_2$	May	09n	95:27	95:28	+ 15	6.08
$9^1/_8$	May	04-09	110:25	110:29	+ 8	6.26
6	Aug	09n	99:15	99:16	+ 14	6.07
$10^3/_8$	Nov	04-09	116:31	117:03	+ 10	6.28
$11^3/_4$	Feb	05-10	123:21	123:27	+ 9	6.28
10	May	05-10	116:22	116:26	+ 9	6.29
$12^3/_4$	Nov	05-10	131:13	131:19	+ 11	6.28

FIGURE 6.6 *Barron's* showing U.S. Treasury bond quotes.

Step 6. Compare the price of gold last week to the price of gold one year ago:

If the price of gold is higher last week than last year, then invest 100 percent of your available money in U.S. Treasury bills due to mature a year from now.

If the price of gold is lower last week than a year ago, then invest 100 percent of your available money in U.S. government zero-coupon bonds that are due to mature in 20 years or more.

Then, according to O'Higgins,

Sit back, relax, and do nothing but watch your returns come in for the next twelve months. Then, on or about January first of next year, go out and buy *Barron's* again, and revisit your investment strategy. . . . Follow the same procedure every year thereafter. And that's all there is, folks, to my new Beating the Dow with Bonds strategy. Told you I kept it simple.

GOLD & SILVER PRICES

Handy & Harman	12/10	12/03	Year Ago
Gold, troy ounce	280.60	282.75	290.80
Silver, troy ounce	5.16	5.13	4.74

Base for pricing gold or silver contents of shipments and for making refining settlements.

FIGURE 6.7 *Barron's* showing gold and silver prices.

To show you how powerful this strategy would have been over the past 30 years, O'Higgins includes a chart with the impressive results shown in Table 6.4.

TABLE 6.4 Comparison of Beating the Dow with Beating the Dow with Bonds

Year Ended	Indicated Strategy	DJIA Return*	BTD 5 Stock[†]	O'Higgins's New Strategy[‡]
31-Dec-69	1 Year T-Bills	−11.60%	−10.09%	7.57%
31-Dec-70	30 Year Zeros	8.76%	−4.72%	24.33%
31-Dec-71	1 Year T-Bills	9.79%	5.03%	3.99%
29-Dec-72	1 Year T-Bills	18.21%	22.16%	5.37%
31-Dec-73	1 Year T-Bills	−13.12%	19.64%	6.76%
31-Dec-74	BTD 5 Stock	−23.14%	−3.80%	−3.80%
31-Dec-75	BTD 5 Stock	44.40%	70.10%	70.10%
31-Dec-76	BTD 5 Stock	22.72%	40.80%	40.80%
31-Dec-77	BTD 5 Stock	−12.70%	4.50%	4.50%
29-Dec-78	BTD 5 Stock	2.69%	1.70%	1.70%
31-Dec-79	BTD 5 Stock	10.52%	9.90%	9.90%
31-Dec-80	BTD 5 Stock	21.41%	40.50%	40.50%
31-Dec-81	1 Year T-Bills	−3.40%	0.00%	13.25%
31-Dec-82	30 Year Zeros	25.79%	37.40%	156.12%
30-Dec-83	1 Year T-Bills	25.68%	36.10%	10.03%
31-Dec-84	30 Year Zeros	1.05%	12.60%	20.44%
31-Dec-85	30 Year Zeros	32.78%	37.80%	106.90%
31-Dec-86	1 Year T-Bills	26.92%	27.90%	5.92%
31-Dec-87	1 Year T-Bills	6.02%	11.10%	5.21%
30-Dec-88	1 Year T-Bills	15.95%	18.40%	8.99%
29-Dec-89	30 Year Zeros	31.71%	10.50%	45.25%
30-Dec-90	30 Year Zeros	−0.58%	−15.20%	0.33%
31-Dec-91	30 Year Zeros	23.93%	61.90%	35.79%
31-Dec-92	30 Year Zeros	7.35%	23.20%	7.82%
31-Dec-93	30 Year Zeros	16.74%	34.30%	37.80%
30-Dec-94	1 Year T-Bills	4.98%	8.60%	7.15%
29-Dec-95	30 Year Zeros	36.49%	30.50%	63.80%
31-Dec-96	1 Year T-Bills	28.61%	26.00%	5.49%
31-Dec-97	30 Year Zeros	24.74%	20.02%	29.22%
31-Dec-98	30 Year Zeros	17.93%	12.33%	23.83%
31-Dec-99	30 Year Zeros	26.96%	−4.66%	−22.04%
Annual		13.05%	17.69%	21.97%

*Dow Jones Industrial Average 31-year average total return.
[†]Beating the Dow 5 "Dogs" strategy total return (including dividends).
[‡]Beating the Dow with Bonds strategy.

As soon as the Dogs of the Dow became popular, other people came out of the woodwork with their own selection processes for picking the right stocks from the Dow 30. The Motley Fool duo of David and Tom Gardner came up with a variation called the Foolish Four that they track on their web site.

As you learned in the list on page 75, there is a huge difference between the top stock of the Dow 30 and the bottom one (122.6 percent and −57.0 percent is a massive swing of 179.6 percent). Therefore, it's worth the effort to come up with any kind of system that works.

According to Morningstar, several mutual funds use some of these strategies: Strong Dow 30 Value (SDOWX), and, of course, O'Higgins's own mutual fund called the O'Higgins Fund (800-548-1942).

I've shared these first four strategies with you to show you that there are specific systems for beating the market. If you uncover new and potentially more powerful systems, I'd love to hear about them. My e-mail address is webmaster@robertallen.com.

$$$

WIT & WISDOM
There is no security
on this earth. There is
only opportunity.

DOUGLAS MACARTHUR

Opportunities are usually
disguised as hard work,
so most people don't
recognize them.

ANN LANDERS

System 5: Consider Enhanced Index Funds

So far, we have looked at four strategies:

Strategy 1: Riding the coattails of a *single* time-tested brilliant investor, the legendary Warren Buffet

Strategy 2: Relying on the management of mutual funds with the best *long-term* track records

Strategy 3: Relying on the financial advisors with the best *long-term* track records

Strategy 4: Buying the lowest-price, high-yielding Dogs of the Dow

I asked my friend and mutual fund guru Bill Donoghue what he thought of these strategies. Bill is one of the world's premier financial advisors over the past 20 years and author of 10 national best-sellers with, 1.2 million copies of his books in print, including the *No-Load Mutual Fund Guide* and *Donoghue's Mutual Fund SuperStars*. Here is what he wrote:

Well, Robert, as an investor you have to make your money in the future, not in the past. Your choices are all time-tested favorites and well respected among the wisest investment advisors. However, each of those strategies assumes the past is indicative of the future. Already the past decade has shown that older, once-exciting mutual funds and strategies have become too large to maintain their competitive advantage. Today, they hold too many

of the same securities. Age often brings wisdom and respect, but not necessarily the ability to re-create success.

Then he added, "The day of the stock picker is over; the day of the index
picker has arrived." Donoghue reached this conclusion because of several
major trends that have been overlooked by many financial advisors:

Trend 1. Over the past 5 to 10 years, only 18 of 3,772 managed no-
load domestic stock funds have been able to beat the average performance of the Standard & Poor's 500 Composite. With all their
so-called sophisticated investment analysis and investment savvy,
99.5 percent were unable to beat a simple S&P 500 index fund like
Vanguard 500 Index Investors.

Trend 2. The baby boom generation is investing more and more of its
retirement savings in the stocks of fewer and fewer companies. The
500 largest corporations in America (the S&P 500) of today are
probably the "S&P 2000" of a decade ago. This demand, focused on
fewer and fewer stocks, is driving the prices of large-capitalization
stocks higher and higher.

Trend 3. There is a greater and greater concentration of investor dollars in index funds like Vanguard 500 Index Investors, which is now
the largest fund in the world with $90 billion in assets. Most of the
growth in value in the past decade has been confined exclusively in
the large-cap stock market defined by the S&P 500 Composite and
the Nasdaq 100—the 100 largest over-the-counter (OTC) stocks.

Trend 4. Over the past few years, we have seen that the emergence of a
new breed of mutual fund allows the individual investor to take
advantage of these trends, which are likely to continue well into the
new millennium: *enhanced index funds.*

What Is an Enhanced Index Fund?

To answer this question, we need to do a little review from the previous
chapter. This is so important that I want to make sure you truly understand these concepts.

A stock market *index* usually describes the weighted total market value
of a specific group of stocks. Here are some examples:

- The *Dow Jones Industrial Average* is a large-cap* index of 30 large-
company industrial stocks.

- The *S&P 500 Composite* is a broader large-cap index (the 500
largest stocks, which make up about 70 percent of market valuation).

---

* *Cap,* or *capitalization,* is the total current market value of a company's outstanding stock.
Large-cap means large companies, *mid-cap* refers to middle-sized companies, and *small-cap*
refers to relatively smaller companies. All of these indices are based on stocks listed on major
stock exchanges such as the New York Stock Exchange, the American Stock Exchange, or
the Nasdaq.

- The *Nasdaq 100 Composite,* also referred to as "OTC" (over the counter), is a mid-cap index.

- The *Russell 2000* is made up of the 3,000 largest stocks less the largest 1,000; therefore, it is a small-cap index.

The term *index fund* refers to a mutual fund that invests its portfolio with the investment objective of tracking or duplicating the movements of a specific stock index. Vanguard 500 (VFINX) is such a fund; its objective is to approximate the total return of the S&P 500 Composite Index.

The term *enhanced index fund* refers to a mutual fund that invests its portfolio in an attempt to earn a multiple of the index it tracks. For example, the Rydex Nova fund (RYNVX) has an investment objective of earning *1.5 times the return of the S&P 500.* Investing in the *actual* stocks included in the stock market index would achieve a total return only equal to or close to the index. To earn 1.5 times the index, it is necessary to invest about 10 percent of the fund's portfolios in overnight options and futures and 90 percent in overnight repurchase agreements (repos) as defined by their investment strategy. Repos are one of the very safest investments available (both the purchase of and the agreement to repurchase the underlying securities a day or so later are executed simultaneously). The futures and options give the fund its investment power and, at the same time, its volatility.

Did you catch that? In other words, an enhanced index fund has a way of *supercharging* the returns of an index fund. This also means that, from time to time, it may supercharge your losses. However, *if* you invest in an index fund because it is broadly diversified and beating nearly all of the managed mutual funds, and *if* you think the stock market will continue to rise, and *if* you are willing to be patient for the long term, why not attempt to earn 1.5 times as much as an ordinary index fund (as in the case of Rydex Nova)? The ride may have a few more and larger bumps along the way, but you will arrive in a brand-new Cadillac instead of on a bicycle.

Here's what *Business Week* said about enhanced, or leveraged, index funds in an article by Andrew Osterland entitled, "Here's Where the Dough Really Rises" (January 18, 1999). (If you want to read the entire article, go to www.businessweek.com and click on Search Past Issues.)

> Call them index funds on steroids. Offered by such companies as Rydex Series Trust, ProFunds Advisors, and Potomac Funds, they promise outsize returns by buying and selling index options and futures rather than just stocks. Last year, these leveraged index products accounted for 2 of the 10 best-performing mutual funds. . . . Leveraged funds, most of which are quite small, guarantee serious extra bang for your buck—125%, 150%, even 200% of index returns. The bang comes from derivatives—index options and futures that can be bought with only a small down payment on a contract's value. A targeted return is achieved by combining options and futures with cash and underlying stocks. . . . (ProFunds) UltraOTC fund, which seeks to double the return of the NASDAQ 100 index, jumped 185.3% last year,

while Potomac OTC Plus rose 104.2%. Leverage, of course, cuts both ways. (UltraOTC) plunged when the market sold off in the third quarter last year. . . . "As exciting as it can be on the upside, it can be equally as bad on the downside," says Kevin McDevitt, an analyst with Morningstar Inc. . . . While these funds weren't designed for mom and pop, they are attracting a wider audience. A growing number of individuals, rightly or wrongly, feel sufficiently savvy to handle the huge risks.

The first family of mutual funds to offer enhanced or leveraged index funds was Rydex. (www.rydexfunds.com). Today, Rydex offers several enhanced index funds that attempt to earn a multiple of various major indexes. As I mentioned earlier, the Rydex Nova fund seeks to deliver 1.5 times the performance of the S&P 500. Figure 6.7 is a chart for Rydex Nova.

Enhanced index funds can also be designed for the investor to bet *against* the index. The Rydex fund family also offers Rydex Ursa ("the Bear" in Latin—get it?), which seeks to deliver minus 1.0 times the performance of the S&P 500. That is, if the S&P 500 rises 1 percent, Ursa seeks to lose 1 percent. If the S&P 500 falls 1 percent, it seeks to earn 1 percent.

In other words, Rydex Nova is designed for investors who wish to speculate that the S&P 500 will *rise,* and Rydex Ursa is designed for those who speculate it will *decline.* Every day, both funds make the same bets: Ursa bets the market will fall and Nova bets the market will rise. Each investor will have a leveraged position to earn 1.5 times the move in the index if they are right or lose 1.5 times the move in the index if they are wrong. It is up to the investor (or his or her advisor) to choose the fund in

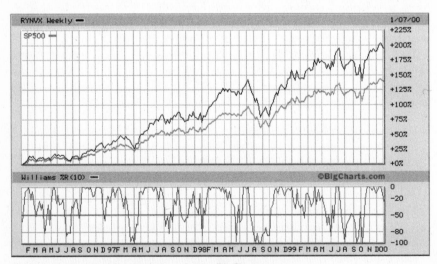

Chart reproduced with permission of www.BigCharts.com.

FIGURE 6.7   **Chart of Rydex Nova.**

which he or she wishes to invest. The fund's managers simply provide the investment vehicles, not the advice.

Other fund families, like ProFunds (www.profunds.com), offer even more highly leveraged index funds:

S&P 500–Based Funds	Beta	Benchmark
UltraBull (ULPIX)	2.00	Twice S&P 500 Index
UltraBear (URPIX)	−2.00	Twice Inverse S&P 500 Index

Nasdaq-Based Funds	Beta	Benchmark
UltraOTC (UOPIX)	2.00	Twice the NASDAQ 100 Index
UltraShort OTC (USPIX)	−2.00	Twice the inverse of the NASDAQ 100 Index

What Does This Mean For Investors?

The strategic implications are obvious. According to Donoghue, if the trend toward the domination of the stock market by the S&P 500 largest stocks continues, and if that stock market sector continues to rise, why not bet on the S&P 500 continuing to rise and earn 1.0 to 2.0 times the return of the S&P 500?

If, over the long term, over 99.5 percent of all of the *managed* funds have not been able to beat an *unmanaged* index fund like Vanguard 500 Index Fund, then put your money there and forget the managed funds.

If investing in the Vanguard 500 Index is good, then investing in Rydex Nova, which seeks to earn 1.5 times the S&P 500's return, may be better. If Nova is better, then investing in ProFunds UltraBull, which is geared to earn 2.0 times the S&P 500 return, might be better still.

At least that's the way it's supposed to work in theory. Most of the leveraged funds have difficulty reaching their targeted goals. Goals may be inspirational, but only performance is spendable.

What's the Downside?

What if the stock market goes into a dive—a steep correction? That's where reading the market's momentum is everything. If you can recognize the correction early in the game and get out of the market or into a negative beta fund, you can make some extra money. If you can recognize the recovery as well, you can make excellent money from the volatility. Both are very difficult and emotional trends to detect and act upon, even by professionals.

And this is where Donoghue shines. Donoghue's advisory firm, W. E. Donoghue & Co., Inc. (WEDCO), has been managing money since 1986 and currently has over $100 million under management (their minimum relationship is $100,000). Using unique and proprietary (i.e., secret) formulas, Donoghue has created a portfolio of enhanced index funds, which he calls his Bull and Bear Portfolio. By moving in and out of certain funds at very specific times, his Bull and Bear Portfolio earned 222.5 percent in 1999. These returns were net of all investment costs and management fees. For the same time period, the S&P 500 was up only 22.1 percent.

His longtime friends have been begging him for years to share these secrets with people outside his inner circle. As of this writing, he is considering writing a newsletter called *Donoghue's Power Portfolios* with a weekly e-mail/fax ActionGram. I hope he does, because I'll certainly be a subscriber. If he ever does decide to share his wisdom, I'll try to twist his arm and send you a free copy. (Check www.multiplestreamsofincome.com under the keyword Donoghue, or call my office at 801-852-8700.)

In the meantime, Donoghue recommends that a good middle ground to beat the S&P 500 is to put 60 percent of your money in ProFunds UltraOTC or UltraBull and the rest of your money in your favorite income investment. The total of the two should exceed the Nasdaq 100 or the S&P 500 return, respectively. If either reaches its goal of earning twice the index, a 60 percent position should earn at least as much as the index. If you take the other 40 percent and invest it in your favorite income fund, you are almost certain to have a total return in excess of the index, and, if the current index fund leadership trend continues, you'll equal or beat the return of nearly every managed stock fund in America.

More important, you have the potential of beating the S&P 500 without the event risk (the risk of a single event, like negative news or rumors of news about a single company, impacting a stock) of a single, speculative stockholding. Effectively, you may enjoy greater returns than in a single stock with the broader diversification among the stocks in the index.

Are enhanced or leveraged index funds for you? They may be an interesting alternative for aggressive investors. Do your homework and read the mutual fund prospectuses before investing, of course. Caution: All of the preceding benefits are derived from profits earned from securities. Past performance does not guarantee future profits. Investment should be made only with the advice of a qualified financial professional.

System 6: Consider High-Powered Stock Sector Funds

When a professional investor looks at the entire market, he or she can view it either vertically or horizontally:

Vertically. By size or market capitalization. You choose among various index funds (large-cap, mid-cap, and small-cap domestic stock indexes; European or Asia stock indexes; or returns tied to the value of the 30-year Treasury bond).

Horizontally. By industry or market sector. You choose among various sector funds (Utilities, Energy, Energy Services, Electronics, Financial Services, Technology, etc.).

What Is a Sector Fund?

Investor's Business Daily lists stocks in 196 industry groups or sectors. Depending on the economy, industry groups can be either "in demand" or "out of favor" with the market. If an individual stock happens to be in an industry grouping that is out of favor, it may have a dampening effect on those stocks' price performance. And vice versa.

Managers of sector funds try to build a portfolio of the strongest stocks in a single sector. Investment advisors who serve as managers of portfolios of sector funds, like Donoghue, try to invest in a few of the strongest sectors for their clients. The funds won't change their stripes, regardless of market trends, but the investment advisor can change the funds he or she holds.

If you look at a list of the hottest mutual funds in the past decade, you'll always find several sector funds. For example, Table 6.5 is a listing from

TABLE 6.5 Morningstar Top-Performing Funds in a Recent 10-Year Period*

Ticker	Name	10-Year Total Return
FSELX	Fidelity Select Electronics	34.64
FDCPX	Fidelity Select Computers	31.34
FSPTX	Fidelity Select Technology	30.34
FTCHX	Invesco Technology II	27.75
FSCSX	Fidelity Select Software & Comp	26.88
PRSCX	T. Rowe Price Science & Technology	26.79
SLMCX	Seligman Communications&Information A	26.38
ALTFX	Alliance Technology A	26.35
SPECX	Spectra	25.92
RSEGX	RS Emerging Growth	24.71
JAVLX	Janus Twenty	24.33
ACEGX	Van Kampen Emerging Growth A	23.48
EQPGX	Fidelity Advisor Equity Growth Instl	22.74
MSIGX	Oppenheimer Main St Growth & Income A	22.24
KTCAX	Kemper Technology A	22.22
TISHX	Flag Investors Communications A	22.21
FSPHX	Fidelity Select Health Care	22.17
TWCUX	American Century Ultra Inv	22.11
VGHCX	Vanguard Health Care	22.11
UNSCX	United Science & Technology A	22.08

Courtesy of Morningstar. Used with permission.

*See footnote, Table 6.1.

Morningstar of the top-performing funds over the past 10 years, showing their average return per year. It's pretty impressive. Notice how many of them are sector funds . . . and which fund family dominates the list.

Fidelity Select Portfolios currently has the largest selection of sector funds, offering a choice of 39 individual sector portfolios, which range from the multi-billion-dollar conservative sector funds like their Utilities portfolio to smaller, more speculative sector funds like Medical Delivery.

Fidelity Select Portfolios is unique in that it charges a one-time sales charge of 3.0 percent to invest in the program. Once your money is invested, there are no new sales charges unless you invest more money in the program. The one-time sales charge, however, gives you the "run of the house." Fidelity's house is a mansion. It has hundreds of funds to choose from. I asked Bill Donoghue how he decides which ones to watch. He replied,

> We follow about 60 sector funds, defining the word "sector" a bit liberally. We follow the Fidelity Select Portfolios, single-country international stock funds, regional international stock and bond funds, and some specialty funds, which Fidelity offers. Fidelity Export is a fine example. Once we have paid the 3.0% entrance fee, we might as well use all of the funds available to us.
>
> Some investors don't want to pay loads of any kind so they choose to use the much more limited lists of no-load sector funds at Rydex and INVESCO. We are watching those families, but currently we like the broad range of choices we see at Fidelity, where we have more clout for our clients because we have millions of their money at Fidelity.

Consider the sector chart in Table 6.6 and make your own choices.

Looking back at the Morningstar chart in Table 6.5, it looks like technology has been hot for the past 10 years. But will it *still* be hot in the next 10?

Remember, I told you earlier in this chapter that choosing a fund based on a short-term track record simply doesn't work. It would be nice to be riding the horse when it surges to the front of the pack. But how can you find this fund as it begins to make its move? That's the trick. How can you know which of these sector funds is going to be hot in the near future? Once again, we turn to our mutual fund guru, Bill Donoghue, for the answer. He writes,

> In what investment fund(s) shall I invest? Ah, that is THE great investment question. The answer is actually surprisingly simple. Follow the stock market's price trends. The market itself will tell you where it is paying the best returns. Regardless of stock market "experts'" predictions, the stock market's movement is the reality with which we work. The market is always right. Sometimes, finding the stock market's direction and future trend is simply looking at where it has been recently.

The *long-term* trend in the stock market is obviously upward. Inflation alone will most likely drive the market up over time. In the very *short term*

TABLE 6.6 Sector (Industry) Funds from Fidelity, Invesco, and Rydex

Sector	Fidelity Select	Invesco Portfolios	Rydex
1. Electronics	Electronics	—	Electronics
2. Technology	Technology	Technology	Technology
3. Biotechnology	Biotechnology	—	Biotechnology
4. Developing Comm.	Developing Comm.	—	—
5. Computers	Computers	—	—
6. Telecommunications	Telecomm.	Telecomm.	Telecomm.
7. Energy Services	Energy Services	—	—
8. Software & Computers	Software & Comp.	—	—
9. Energy	Energy	Energy	Energy
10. Natural Gas	Natural Gas	—	—
11. Utilities	Utilities Growth	Utilities	—
12. Multimedia	Multimedia	—	—
13. Precious Metals & Min.	Precious Metals	—	Precious Metals
14. Gold	Gold	Gold	—
15. Medical Equip & Sys.	Medical Equip & Sys.	—	—
16. Paper & Forest	Paper & Forest	—	—
17. Brokerage & Investments	Brokerage & Inv.	—	—
18. Health Care	Health Care	Health Sciences	Health Care
19. Industrial Materials	Ind. Materials	—	—
20. Financial Services	Financial Svcs.	Financial Svcs.	Financial Svcs.
21. Insurance	Insurance	—	—
22. Banking	Banking	—	Banking
23. Home Finance	Home Finance	—	—
24. Medical Delivery	Medical Delivery	—	—
25. Bus. Svcs. & Outsrcg.	Bus/Svcs. & Outsourcing	—	—
26. Cyclical Industries	Cyclical Industries	—	—
27. Food & Agriculture	Food & Agriculture	—	—
28. Leisure	Leisure	—	—
29. Air Transport	Air Transport	—	—
30. Automotive	Automotive	—	—
31. Industrial Equipment	Industrial Equipment	—	—
32. Chemicals	Chemicals	—	—
33. Consumer Industries	Consumer Industries	—	—
34. Defense & Aerospace	Defense & Aerospace	—	—
35. Construction & Housing	Construction & Housing	—	—
36. Environmental	Environmental	—	—
37. Retailing	Retailing	—	—
38. Natural Resources	Natural Resources	—	—
39. Transportation	Transportation	—	—

Fidelity Select Portfolios (1-800-544-8888) $2,500 minimum initial purchase per fund, 3.00% one-time sales charge on new money, fee tracking applies, minimum hold 30 days or 1.5% redemption charge.

INVESCO (1-800-525-8085) $1,000 minimum initial purchase per fund, no-load.

Rydex (1-800-820-0888) $25,000 minimum initial purchase per fund, no-load.

(day to day), the stock market can be very unpredictable. Some days it is up, some days it is down. But, contrary to what most believe, even in a bull market, the stock market is down about 40 percent of the days.

That Sweet Spot!

But, ah, somewhere there is a middle ground where you can identify the "sweet spot" among *intermediate-term* trends—where the advice is "just right" to make profits most of the time. That's all you need: to pick up the intermediate-term trends, the trends that, most of the time, last for weeks on end. Even then, you can expect to identify only about 60 to 70 percent of the trend. You will, of course, miss the beginning of the trend because it will just have started. You will, of course, miss the reversal of the trend because the trend takes time to establish itself. However, if you can find that sweet spot, the intermediate-term time period over which you can identify the greatest portion of the trend most of the time, then you have added some significant value to your investment strategy. If you can then combine that analysis with leveraged investments such as enhanced index funds and carefully selected sector funds, you can magnify that advantage into a major investment opportunity.

How major of an opportunity? Donoghue manages two portfolios of sector funds: his Diversified Sector Fund Power Portfolio and his Targeted Sector Fund Power Portfolio.

The *Diversified Sector Fund Power Portfolio* chooses four funds from a universe of 60 sector funds and stays with those as long as they remain in the top 10. The universe he chooses from includes 38 Fidelity Select Portfolios plus selected specialty funds, international single-country funds, and regional stock and bond funds.

The *Targeted Sector Fund Power Portfolio* selects a *single* fund from a limited universe of five carefully screened sector funds—a tighter focus, but at the same time it has the potential of earning greater returns.

Over the past 12 months, using what he calls *reality-based momentum investing,* his portfolios have been up 86.7 percent and 96.1 percent, respectively. I couldn't get him to reveal all his secrets, but Bill has graciously agreed to share with you a few tips to help you choose a portfolio of selected sector funds to enhance your investment returns:

> Using our special brand of *reality-based momentum investing,* we focus on only the most recent price trends to identify the funds whose value is accelerating at the greatest rate and then we remain invested in those investments until another investment's current price uptrend is stronger. This often means that rather than "overstaying our welcome" in a specific fund whose momentum is slowing, we most often reinvest our money in a different sector, which is taking new leadership. Most trades are initiated for a positive reason (new leadership) rather than a negative reason (reversal of trends). There are, of course, no guarantees; our track record speaks for itself.
>
> If you're trying to accomplish this task by yourself, here is some specific advice, which I hope will be of use to you. . . .

Allow me to give you an oversimplified version of how my analysts and myself go about selecting investments for our three Power Portfolios.

First, we select our fund universes:
For the Diversified Sector Portfolio we select among a universe of 60 sector funds.
For our Targeted Sector Portfolio we select among a universe of 5 carefully selected noncorrelated (they don't move in concert) sectors.
For our Matrix Bull and Bear Portfolio we select from among 38 Rydex Index Trust Funds.

Then we rank the funds' performance by comparing how fast their returns are accelerating. To do this we take, for example, each fund's annualized performance over the past, say, seven days and compare it to their performance over, say, the past twenty-eight days. If it is earning profits faster in the past week than in the past month, then its performance is accelerating, growing faster and faster. We rank the funds in each universe and then select

- The top four funds in the Diversified Sector Fund Portfolio's universe
- The single top fund in the Targeted Sector Fund Portfolio's universe
- The single top fund in the Bull & Bear Power Portfolio universe

Finally, as long as the four funds we picked in Diversified remain in the top 10 and we hold for at least our minimum period, we stick with them. If one drops out of the top 10, we replace it with the best fund that we don't own. In the other universes, we require the fund stay in the top two or we drop it. These strategies all have minimum holding periods, which avoids a lot of volatility.

We make these decisions each week. Evaluating each day or each month would, according to our research, cause us a lot of unnecessary losses. A week seems to be a comfortable review period.

We then keep an eye on each strategy to see if we are satisfied with its performance. After all, it is only a mechanical strategy, and we manage people's hard-earned money. However, it would take something extraordinary to override our successful strategies.

Well, I hope you have enjoyed this very valuable peek into the mind of a top money manager. As you can see, Donoghue has done his homework. If you want to view how his funds have performed recently, visit www.donoghue.com at your leisure. Remember to read his prospectus and talk with his personal asset managers before determining which combination of Power Portfolios is for you or whether you should try to do this yourself.

To summarize, Donoghue's approach is to tap into the rhythm of the market and let the market tell him where it is going. So far, his returns are impressive. However, this active trading can generate a lot of "tax consequences," or short-term profits on which taxes must be paid in the current year. Donoghue's strategies may have the potential to earn more after taxes than most strategies do before taxes, so that may not be a major issue. In addition, when we get to Chapter 15 and discuss saving money on your taxes, I am going to ask Bill Donoghue to tell you how your portfolio profits can be 100 percent income tax deferred and possibly even 100 percent income tax free! You won't want to miss this.

Investing strategies in the new millennium are going to be very exciting, and well they should be. We are all facing the reality that we will "live longer and prosper." Hmmm, that has a familiar ring to it.

CHAPTER 7

> *The safest way to double your money is to fold it over once and put it in your pocket.*
> **ELBERT HUBBARD (1856–1915)**

YOUR THIRD STREAM
Double Your Money in the Market: How to Multiply Your Investment Dollars

In the last few chapters we have talked about how to invest 80 percent of your investment mountain dollars into long- and intermediate-term investments such as index funds, aggressive mutual funds, and stocks. In this chapter, I'll show you where I believe some of the remaining 20 percent of your dollars should go. This is your most aggressive portfolio. To do this, we'll shorten our time frame, narrow our focus, and (hopefully) double our money. Yes, there are ways to double your money in the market—if you're willing to take some extra risks and employ the power of leverage.

Leverage. Interesting word. What does it mean? The root word is *lever.* Archimedes, the Greek genius who lived about 200 B.C., discovered that with levers and pulleys he could move huge objects with a small amount of force. He is said to have boasted, "Give me the place to stand, and a lever long enough, and I will move the *earth.*"

Leverage in the financial world means controlling a large amount of wealth with a small amount of money. How does leverage work? First, we'll look at a real estate example, then the stock market.

Let's assume that two families buy their first $100,000 home. Mr. and Mrs. Cash use a $100,000 inheritance and pay cash for their home. Mr. and Mrs. Leverage put down $10,000 and arrange for a $90,000 mortgage. Let's assume that both homes appreciate $5,000 in value almost immediately.

The Cash family earns a return on their investment of 5 percent ($5,000 ÷ $100,000 = 5% profit). The Leverage family has the power of leverage on its side. Since they invested only $10,000, the return on their investment is 50 percent ($5,000 ÷ $10,000 = 50% profit). Of course, prices could decline and then leverage would work in reverse. But because real estate prices tend to increase over the long term, most homeowners end up with long-term gains.

The power of leverage gives the beginning investor the ability to control a lot of real estate with only a small amount of money. (See Figure 7.1.) The power of leverage employed with the stable nature of real estate is a long-term surefire winner. It is, without question, the reason that a large percentage of the personal wealth in the world is accumulated in the average family's single-family home.

Can you apply leverage to the stock market? Absolutely. Any stock investor, using his or her stock as collateral, can borrow up to 50 percent of the value of the stock to buy more stock. This is called buying on *margin*. The problem with buying individual stocks on margin is that, unlike real estate, stocks are volatile. That is, stocks often show wide swings in price over a short time span. Real estate is generally exempted from this degree of volatility. In the short term, this volatility in stocks can be very dangerous to your wealth. It's like betting your rent money on the spin of the roulette wheel. However, the use of leverage in the stock market can be very powerful.

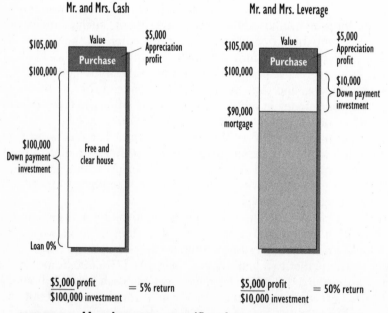

FIGURE 7.1   How leverage magnifies the return on investment.

In Chapter 6 we talked about several ways to multiply your rate of return by using "enhanced" index funds. In this chapter, I'll share with you another way to use leverage in the stock market that, if used with prudence, can produce spectacular returns.

Let me return to real estate to provide an example. In the beginning of my real estate investing experience, I stumbled onto a technique that made a nice profit for me. I was learning the ropes of real estate investing by working as a licensed real estate agent. My boss was a real estate appraiser named Paul Brown. One day a client came in to

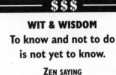

$$$

WIT & WISDOM
To know and not to do
is not yet to know.
ZEN SAYING

request an appraisal on a four-acre piece of vacant ground. As he was leaving, he stopped to chat and mentioned the following details: The land had been donated to a local church many years earlier when the property was nothing but a cow pasture. In the ensuing years, development had cropped up around the pasture, and its value had significantly appreciated. The church was in no hurry to sell the property and just wanted to determine its approximate value. The man hinted that the church might be willing to sell an option on the property. "What's an option?" I asked. He explained it to me this way:

> Suppose your boss appraises this property today at $200,000. The church has two choices. It can list the property with a Realtor for $200,000 and wait for an offer. Suppose several months go by and someone offers us $200,000. After commissions of about $12,000 we'll net about $188,000. That's the first choice. The second choice would be to sell an option on the property. Suppose an investor wants to give us $10,000 for the right to lock in the price for a year at $200,000. If this investor is able to sell the property to someone else for more than $210,000, then they get to keep the difference as a profit. How does the church win? It gets a full $200,000 in cash *plus* the option money of $10,000. And it doesn't have to pay a penny in commissions. Obviously, this is a win-win situation.

I was intrigued but skeptical. We parted company, but I continued to stew over the numbers. As an agent, I had been trained to have sellers give *me* a listing. But this seller wanted me to pay *him* $10,000 *up front*. If I couldn't sell it, I'd lose everything. It seemed extremely risky. But I had a powerful hunch to move forward.

I went to visit the gentleman and made one of the most fateful decisions of my life. I told him that I didn't have $10,000 but that I would give him $5,000 if he would lock in the price at $200,000 for one year. After a moment's thought, he agreed. We shook on it and I left.

$$$

WIT & WISDOM
Lottery: A tax on people
who are bad at math.

There was only one problem. I didn't have the $5,000 and I didn't know where I could get it. Again, on a hunch, I took a dentist friend over to look at the property. I told him that if he put up the money, I would handle finding a buyer. He didn't have $5,000 either, but he thought he could borrow it from his banker. So we formed a partnership. He would come up with the money and I would guarantee him a 100 percent profit if there was a profit or I would guarantee to pay his loan to the bank if things didn't pan out.

A few days later, when I signed my name to that option, I knew my neck was really on the line. If I couldn't move the property I would be stuck for the entire $5,000 loss.

To my great relief, 11 months later I found a builder who was looking for just such a property on which to build an apartment building. He offered $275,000 in cash. I readily accepted. At the closing, the church received its $200,000 in cash. My dentist friend received $12,000, which paid back his bank loan and put a nice profit into his pocket. After costs, my broker and I split the remaining $60,000 in cash. (I was still single, so I took my $30,000 profit, bought a VW bus in Germany, and toured Europe with a couple of buddies.)

Everybody won. The church made more money than it would have by listing the property for sale. My partner doubled his money. And instead of a small commission, I made a $30,000 fee for taking the risk and putting the transaction together. This was my first exposure to options.

When it comes to the stock market, the concept of options is exactly the same. Some owners of stock are willing to sell an option on their stock for a fee. The seller of the option gets immediate income from the sale of the option, and the buyer of the option gets the right but not the obligation to buy the stock at a future date at a fixed price. If the stock increases in value enough, the person who bought the option can profit. If the stock doesn't increase in value on or before a future date, the option expires and the money is lost.

Sounds risky—and it is. But just as in my real estate example, if you play your cards right, you can win . . . and win big.

Profit Multiplier 1:
Writing Covered Calls

To show you how this works, let's pretend that you are a long-term employee of XYZ Company. In your company retirement plan you have accumulated 1,000 shares of XYZ stock over the years. Each share is worth $6, so your portfolio is worth $6,000. Every month, you've been accumulating stock tax free (dollar cost averaging like the millionaire next door), with no intention whatsoever of selling your stock. You're happy to let it compound away till retirement day.

But then one day your stockbroker, in reviewing your financial statement, sees that you own 1,000 shares of XYZ at $6 a share. She asks you if you might consider "writing some covered calls." "Covered what?" you ask. She explains that because you own the stock, you can sell an option to someone else and earn some immediate short-term income. She tells you that people are willing to give you 50 cents a share today for the right to buy a 30-, 60-, or 90-day call option at $7 a share. That could generate $500 in income immediately (1,000 shares × $0.50 = $500). Since these short-term gains occur in your tax-sheltered retirement account, you can defer the tax consequences.

"Why should I consider such a plan?" you ask. Well, the obvious benefit, she explains, is that instead just letting your stock sit there earning dividends, you could earn extra money on the same stock by selling an option against it. If someone is willing to give you $500 immediately for the option, you can earn an immediate 8.3 percent on your money ($500 ÷ $6,000 = 8.3%). You don't have to wait an entire year as you do with a CD or a bond. The money is deposited the very next trading day into your brokerage account. You make an instant $500!

Wait a minute! There must be a catch somewhere. Why would anybody do that? Well, suppose the person (let's call him Tom) buying the option has a strong belief that XYZ stock is going to increase in value substantially in the next 30 days. He thinks it might go to $8 per share. Acting on this belief, he could do one of two things:

1. Tom could buy 1,000 shares of the stock today for $6,000 and hold on for 30 days. If it goes up to $8 per share, he could sell out and reap a $2 dollar profit per share, or $2,000 less commissions. That would be a quick 33 percent on his money in 30 days. Not bad. But what's the downside? Suppose the stock declines instead to $5 per share or lower. That would wipe out $1,000 or more of value. By buying the stock, Tom could make $2,000 or more on the upside, and on the downside he might lose $1,000 or more.

Is there another way?

2. Suppose, instead of paying $6,000 to *buy* the stock, the investor buys an *option* on 1,000 shares of stock with a locked-in price of $7. The cost would be only $500. With leverage, Tom controls $6,000 worth of stock for only $500. If it goes up to $8 a share, then he could exercise his option, sell the 1,000 shares for $8,000, pay you $7,000, and pocket $1,000 for himself. Of course, he invested $500 to buy the option, so his net profit is $500. (See Figure 7.2.)

Notice how leverage doubled the return on Tom's investment. A $500 investment returned a $500 profit, or 100 percent on his money, *in only 30 days!*

But wait, what's the downside? Well, if the stock doesn't increase in value in 30 days, the option expires worthless and our investor Tom loses the entire $500—poof, up in smoke. Why would Tom take such a risk?

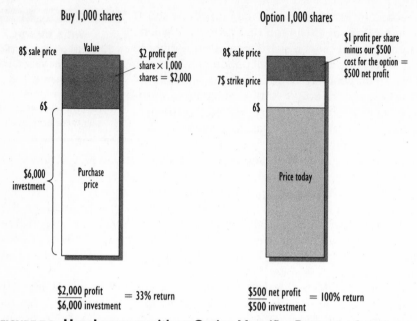

FIGURE 7.2 How Leverage with an Option Magnifies Return on Investment

Three reasons: (1) Maybe he doesn't have the $6,000 to buy 1,000 shares of XYZ but wants to take advantage of a potential upward movement in the stock. (2) Maybe he doesn't want to put $6,000 of his money at risk where there is a chance that the stock could lose more than $1,000 if things didn't turn out. (3) Or maybe he wants to have a chance of earning huge rates of return . . . 50 percent or more on his money. For whatever reason, there are thousands of Toms out there who are willing to assume this risk. I'll show you how to find them shortly.

Now, a little terminology is in order. One option contract controls 100 shares of stock. Ten contracts would, therefore, control 1,000 shares of stock. In the preceding example, Tom would have bought 10 option contracts.

There are two kinds of options: *calls* and *puts.* In our example, Tom bought a call option: the right to buy (or *call*) a specific stock at a specific price. Investors buy calls when they expect the price of the underlying stock to go up. A put option is the exact opposite: the right to sell a specific stock at a specific price. Investors generally buy *puts* when they expect the underlying price of the stock to go down. In this book I will be talking only about call options.

The $7 price that Tom locks in for XYZ stock is called the *strike price.* And the $500 Tom paid for the option is called a *premium.*

All option contracts expire on the third Friday of every month. If you are buying a September call contract, you need to understand that the option expires on the third Friday of September.

If Tom calls his broker in August and wants to buy 10 contracts with a strike price of $7.00 that will expire in about 30 days, he will say something like this: "I'd like to buy 10 contracts of XYZ September $7.00 calls." He is informed that the premium is $.50 per share, or a total of $500. If the stock increases in value beyond $7.50, he could earn a nice profit.

Now, where do *you* fit into this picture? In our example, you own 1,000 shares of XYZ. You are willing to sell (or *write*) call options on your shares to magnify your return. You phone your broker and say something like this: "I want to write 10 contracts on XYZ September $7 calls." The broker enters the order, sells the 10 option contracts, and deposits the money (minus a small commission) into your account the next day.

Here's the picture on the day you sell the option contracts to Tom:

You	Tom
You own 1,000 shares of stock.	He wants the option to buy your 1,000 shares.
You sell (write) 10 call contracts.	He buys 10 call contracts.
You receive $500 in 24 hours.	He invests $500.
You earn an immediate 8.3 percent.	He waits to see what the stock will do.

Let's look at three possible scenarios in 30 days.
Scenario 1: Your $6 stock appreciates in value to $8.

You	Tom
You get "called out."	He exercises his option.
You have to sell your stock to Tom for $7 a share.	He buys your stock for $7 a share.
You receive $7,000 cash from the stock sale.	He resells it immediately for $8.
You make $1,000 profit from the sale of the stock.	He makes $1,000 from the sale of stock.
You keep the $500 from the sale of the option.	He deducts the $500 cost of the option.
Your total profit is $1,500, or 25 percent.	His total profit is $500, or 100 percent.

If you had held your stock instead of selling the options, your portfolio would now be worth $8,000. But since you sold the option and collected the $500 premium, you gave up your right to the fast price appreciation. Why did you do this? You decided that a bird in the hand was worth two in the bush, so you're happy with your decision. Everybody wins.

Scenario 2: The stock price remains at about $6.

You	Tom
The options you sold expire.	His option contracts expire worthless.
You have no more obligation to sell your stock.	He loses his entire $500 premium.
You earned $500, or 8.3 percent, on your $6,000.	His loss is 100 percent.
You are free to repeat this process.	Oh, well. Better luck next time.

With the right stock, you could do this several times a year and add an extra 10 to 50 percent return to your existing portfolio.

Scenario 3: The stock price declines below $6. The result is exactly like scenario 2. Since you're buying this stock to hold for the long term, you don't mind the short-term fluctuations up or down. You're like Warren Buffett. You just continue to buy and hold.

In other words, you and Tom are betting against each other. If Tom wins, he pockets the short-term profit. If you win, you pocket the premium. So why would you be willing to play this game? Here's the secret: According to some experts, the options expire worthless about 80 percent of the time. You pocket the premium 8 out of 10 times. Suppose you were to play roulette with those odds—80 percent of the time you win and 20 percent you lose. How soon would you like to start?

Still, there is risk. If the stock increases substantially above the strike price, you lose the potential profit. You still make some of the profit plus your premium, but the big profit goes to the person who buys your option. But remember, this doesn't happen very often. Most of the time, even if you lose, you don't lose much. And if you win, you win instantly. The only reason you might not want to play is if you were certain that the stock would really increase dramatically in price that month.

This is the perfect scenario for a person who already owns stocks and plans to keep them. You sell an option when you want the opportunity to multiply your returns. I heard a rumor (whether true I don't know) that Warren Buffett made some substantial money by selling covered calls on his Coca-Cola stock. Perhaps this is one of the reasons he was able to make his fortune grow at over 22 percent compounded annual rate of return for 40 years in a row.

— **$$$** —

WIT & WISDOM
Surplus wealth is a sacred trust which its possessor is bound to administer in his lifetime for the good of the community.

ANDREW CARNEGIE

What I just described is the technique of *writing covered calls.* To *write* and to *sell* mean the same thing. *Covered* means that you own the stock.

What if you don't have 1,000 shares of XYZ just sitting around gathering dust so you can write some covered calls? Here's a plan for you. Let's say you have $10,000 in high-risk money that you want to invest. You realize that you could lose this money. But since you've already set up your survival basin and your long-term and intermediate investment basins, you're willing to assume more risk for a higher return.

Your goal is to find the perfect stock to buy with the express intent of writing covered calls. You buy 1,000 shares of ABC stock at $9 per share, for a total of $9,000. Then you sell 10 contracts of ABC $10 calls with an expiration date about 30 days in the future. The premium is 50

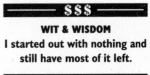

WIT & WISDOM
I started out with nothing and still have most of it left.

cents per share. You still own the stock, but you have sold a 30-day option, earning an extra $500, or an immediate 5.6 percent on your money. It is deposited into your brokerage account the very next day. Not bad for a one-day return.

Now you have to wait for 30 days to find out what's going to happen. Will you be able to keep your nice profit? Or will you lose some of the potential upside profit? Or will the stock decline in value? Let's review what could happen.

Scenario 1: The stock increases in value to $11. Your stock gets called out at $10 per share and you receive a check for $10,000. This gives you a profit of $1,000 plus the $500 premium on your calls. That's a tidy $1,500 in profit on your investment, or 16.6 percent in one month!

What was your risk? You risked the lost profit that you might have earned above the $10 strike price. But, as they say, a bird in the hand is worth two in the bush. Wouldn't you take a guaranteed 16.6 percent profit today over the slight chance that you might earn an even larger profit in 30 days? The answer is yes.

Scenario 2: The stock hovers at around $9 per share for the entire 30 days. The option expires and you keep the $500 premium. You earn 5.6 percent on your money in 30 days. You can write another 10 calls the very next day and do the same thing all over again.

$$$

WIT & WISDOM
When your ship finally does come in, how come the IRS is on the dock unloading it?

Scenario 3: The stock drops to $8 per share. The option expires and you keep the $500 premium for your trouble. Your stock loses $1,000 in value, but the $500 option premium hedges your loss. You lose a total of only $500 in 30 days. But you still own the stock. . . . It might bounce back.

In the best case, you make a sure $1,500 profit but lose out on the chance to make a larger profit. In the next-best case, you make a sure $500 profit. In the worst case, your stock loses $1,000 of its value but your premium cuts your losses in half. So writing the covered call was an excellent way to hedge your possible loss while giving you an excellent chance of earning a nice profit. It's the perfect strategy. And you can do this *over and over and over again.*

Have I gotten your attention? If you were excited about the possibility of earning a long-term 11 percent a year in index funds, then the possibility of earning 5 to 25 percent *a month* or more should keep you awake at night.

Well, now that I've gotten you excited, let's bring you back down to earth. What I have just described has been practiced for decades by a lot of very smart people . . . many of whom have lost a lot of money. If you're just a novice, you'd better go into this with your eyes open. What if you buy a stock that drops dramatically in value in those 30 days while you're waiting for the outcome? Your $5,000 nest egg could fall out of the carton and break. There are real risks associated with this strategy. You have to know what you're doing or you will be another skeleton in the options graveyard. The goal is to win big when you win and lose small when you lose. Enough hypothetical examples. Here's a true story with true profits.

Although I'd heard about options for years, I was actually mentored in these techniques by a retired chiropractor by the name of Dr. Stephen Cooper. I thank him for opening my eyes to the profit potential in options and for teaching me (and now you) a system that works. Ironically, Dr. Cooper retired because he permanently injured his back helping a friend lift a boat. He sadly closed his practice and was forced to find another way to earn a living to support his family. He always had a love of the stock market, so he plunged into study with a fury. He didn't have any time to waste. After a crash course in the ways of the market, he settled on options as his best bet. He reviewed the literature, attended some seminars, and discovered that many of the popular seminar methods were either too risky, too unrealistic, or outright dangerous. But several techniques seemed to make serious sense. One of those techniques was covered calls.

Dr. Cooper had been watching the stock of a company named Organogenesis. The stock was selling at $17.50 a share, with strong earnings growth. He bought 1,000 shares of the stock at 17½ and waited for the stock to increase a little in value so the option premiums would be higher. When the 30-day option premiums for this stock hit $2 per share, he sold 10 call contracts. He receive an immediate cash profit of $2,000. The option expired, unexercised, 30 days later, and he pocketed $2,000, for a one-month gain of 11.4 percent. In the next five months he repeated the process three more times. The profit summary is as follows:

Oct 13, 1995	Sold 10 contracts at $2	$2,000 premium
Nov 18, 1995	Option expired unexercised	
Nov 30, 1995	Sold 10 contracts at $1¼	$1,250 premium
Dec 20, 1995	Options expired unexercised	
Jan 2, 1996	Sold 10 contracts at $1	$1,000 premium
Jan 20, 1996	Options expired unexercised	
April 11, 1996	Sold 10 contracts at $2	$2,000 premium

In May he was called out—the options were exercised at 17½—and he received the full cash of $17,500 for his stock. Therefore, in seven months, covered calls were written four times, for a total of $6,250 in premiums. Before commissions, this amounted to a return of 35.7 percent, or an annualized return of 61.2 percent. Not bad.

At the same time he was rolling with Organogenesis, he purchased 1,000 shares of Iomega at 18¾. On October 4, he sold 10 contracts of Iomega October 20 calls with a premium of 1⁷⁄₁₆. He pocketed the premium of $1,437 and waited for the expiration date. He was called out at $20 before the expiration date and pocketed a stock gain of $1,250. His gross profit with premium and stock was $2,687 less commissions of $194.55. This was a net profit of $2,492.45, or 26.6 percent return in only 17 days. During this same time period, using covered calls on three other stocks, he earned profits of 8.9, 14.0, 22.9, and 18.3 percent.

Now you can see why this strategy can be exciting if done carefully.

The Cooper Covered Call Strategy

Well, it's time for you to learn how to do this. Let me teach you the Cooper covered call strategy. Before we begin, remember that covered calls work best in a rising bull market. If you're in a bear market, don't even think of doing this strategy.

Of the possible 10,000 stocks in the market, only about 2,000 of them are optionable. How do you determine whether a stock is optionable? Three ways:

1. Call your broker.

2. Go to www.cboe.com, which is the web site of the Chicago Board Options Exchange, and click on the Symbol Directory.

3. See a listing of available options in the *Wall Street Journal* or *Investor's Business Daily.* The *Investor's Business Daily* general stock listings also include a tiny "o" at the end of the line if a stock is optionable. For example, see Figure 7.3.

Investor's Business Daily contains some other very useful information, so we will use this newspaper for our once-a-week screening information. If you don't have access to this newspaper, you can obtain a free two-week trial subscription by going to www.investors.com (U.S. residents only).

Because 2,000 companies would be a formidable number to analyze, we need to screen only those stocks that have the probability of either maintaining their price (fluctuating in a narrow trading range) or increasing in value in 30 days. What criteria should we use? Dr. Cooper uses five screens that will filter out such stocks.

Screen 1: We select only those stocks that are within 10 percent of their all-time high. Stocks that have either hit new highs (NH) or are within 10 percent of new highs are displayed in bold type in *Investor's*

IBD *SmartSelect*™ **CORPORATE RATINGS**
— Earnings Per Share
   — Relative Price Strength
     — Industry Group Relative Strength
       — Sales + Profit Margins + R.O.E.
         — Accumulation/Distribution

	52-Week High	Stock	Symbol	Closing Price	Price Chg	Vol.% Chg	Vol. 100s	PE	Day's High	Low
28 68 A B A	64³/32	AT&T	r5T	55¹/4	– ¹/4	– 32	7.5m	25	56¹/16	55³/16
13 86 A E A	**48³/4**	LMGA	rLMGA	47¹/8	– ⁷/8	+ 14	2.6m	..	48³/4	47 0
13 89 A E A	**N H**	**LMGB**	rLMGB	**54⁹/16**	– ⁷/16	+ 73	135	..	55¹/4	54¹/2
59 89 A D A	47³/16	AVX	rAVX	42¹/2	– ¹³/16	– 17	1655	64	43³/8	42³/16 ᵏ₀
89 69 D C B	80¹/4	AXA Ads	AXA	70¹³/16	– 1⁷/16	– 15	440	25	71¹/4	69⁷/8

FIGURE 7.3 *Investor's Business Daily* general stock listings.

Business Daily. As you scan down the columns, they pop out easily.
When you come to a boldface line, notice the column marked 52-
week high. If you find the symbol NH next to the stock price, it
means that this stock hit a new high that day. If only the stock price
number is bold, it means that this stock is within 10 percent of its 52-
week high.

Screen 2: We eliminate all stocks that are priced above $25. Why $25?
When you write covered calls, you need to buy the underlying stock.
To get the best leverage you need to sell at least five contracts.
That's 500 shares. The cost of 500 shares at $50 per share is
$25,000. Ouch! That's a lot of money. However, if you are dealing
with a $10 stock, you can buy 500 shares for only $5,000 . . . a
much more manageable sum. In addition, the premium on a $75
stock for a 30-day option will be very similar to the premium for a
$10 stock. You get more leverage with the cheaper stock. Because
leverage is what we're looking for, stay below $25. Scan to the right
to the Closing Price column. If the stock is higher than $25, elimi-
nate this stock and keep scanning down until you reach the next NH
symbol or bolded 52-week high price.

*Screen 3: Include only those stocks that have an earnings per share rank
of 80+.* You want to find stocks that *over the short term* are exhibiting
a tendency to continue to increase in value. One of the best ways to
predict a company whose stock price will increase is to watch for
increased earnings. If earnings are increasing, the stock price should
at least have some upward pressure (in theory). *Investor's Business
Daily* actually tracks this statistic on the left side of the listing under
the column marked Earnings Per Share. We are looking for stocks
that have high earnings per share, in the 80th percentile. This means
that 80 percent of all of the companies listed have lower EPS growth
than this stock does. This stock is in the top 20 percent. If you have

come this far and the EPS number is not 80, eliminate this stock, keep scanning down for the next NH or bold price, and start all over again at screen 1. (See Figure 7.4.)

Screen 4. Include only those stocks that have a high relative strength figure of 80+. A high figure means that, compared with all the other stocks, this stock price is relatively strong. If you choose stocks with a relative strength of at least 80, you are sure that it is in the top 20 percent of stocks in terms of price performance. Check the current stock to see if it has a number of 80 or more. If so, go to the next screen.

Screen 5. Include only those stocks with a group strength of A. This compares the stock's industry group price performance over the past six months to the other 196 industry groups (oil, retailing, pharmaceuticals, gambling, etc.). If your stock is marked "A" it is in the top 20 percent of all industry groups. A high tide lifts all boats. Make sure that your stock is in a sector with a high tide.

Once you have performed these screens, you will be left with a handful of possible candidates. This is your watch list. On the day in which I performed these screens in the *Investor's Business Daily,* only 3 stocks remained out of a universe of 2,000. These are the stocks that I placed on my watch list, as shown in Table 7.1. How can we tell which of these three is the *best* candidate? On a limited budget, we have money for only one stock. We need to do some more screening.

Just so you know, the first five screens we performed were based on company fundamentals such as earnings, group strength, and so forth. People in the stock world call this *fundamental analysis.* It simply means that you are checking on a company's fundamentals . . . how well it is doing.

The second major form of analysis is called *technical analysis.* Don't be intimidated by the word. . . . It simply means analyzing a chart of the company's stock price to determine its pattern of behavior for the past six months.

Where do you get charts? Depends whether you want to pay for them or not. . . . Okay, free wins. There are two ways to get them for free.

35	95	A B A	136¹/4	TMP Wrldwd	TMPW	130¹/4 + 1¹⁵/16	− 17	4561	99	130⁷/8	128³¹/320
91	73	B A B	14¹⁵/16	TSIIncMinn	TSII	11⁷/8	− 88	21	14	11⁷/8	11³/4
22	92	A B A	55³/8	TSIIntlSoft	TSFW	48¹/16 − 6⁵/16	− 74	1542	..	54⁷/8	47¹/2 0
96	40	A A B	13⁷/8	TSR	rTSRI	7¹⁵/16 − ¹/8	+ 67	437	9	8¹/4	7¹¹/16 k
98	94	A A A NH	84¹¹/32	TTI TeamTel	TTIL	21⁹/16 − 1⁷/16	+ 17	2433	41	24³/8	21¹/4
33	94	A B A	84¹¹/32	TVGuide	cTVGIA	74¹/4 − 3⁹/16	− 23	2655	99	78¹/8	74¹/4 0
85	45	E A D	11¹/8	TacoCabana	rTACO	7⁷/8 − ¹/8	+ 260	4135	7	8¹/8	7³/4 k
77	91	A A A NH		TakeTwoIS	TTWO	16⁵/16 − ¹¹/16	+ 84	8320	30	17¹/2	15¹³/16
17	55	A D A	18¹/2	TalkCity	TCTY	12³/8 − 1⁷/16	− 31	2430	..	13⁹/16	11⁹/16

FIGURE 7.4 *Investor's Business Daily* **general stock listings.**

TABLE 7.1 Stocks That Passed through the *Investor's Business Daily* Screens

Earnings Per Share	Relative Price Strength	Industry Group Relative Strength	Stock	52-Week High	Symbol	Price	Optionable
68	88	A	NFO Worldw	22⅞	NFO	22⅜	o
87	89	A	Bio Technlgy	NH	BTGC	15¼	o
93	83	A	Sapiens Intl	17¼	SPNS	16⅞₆	o

1. If you have a stockbroker, he or she can fax you one in moments.

2. The second way I like best. It involves accessing the Internet and doing my own checking. If you have Internet access, go to www.bigcharts.com. Type in the symbol of the stock you want to research, press Quick Chart, and voilà, a chart showing the stock price immediately appears. With your naked eye you can determine whether this stock is trending up or trending down.

Reproduced in Figure 7.5 are charts for two of the stocks that made it through our filters. In your rough estimation, which of these stocks seems to have the best-looking chart? What do I mean by best-looking?

The most stable-looking chart

The least number of big dips downward

The most steady march upward without huge spikes upward

Now, make your choice: Which chart, in your humble opinion, looks to be the one that would most likely *not* drop dramatically in value in the next 30 days? This is informed guesswork . . . but it can be fun. In the blanks that follow, I want you to choose which chart looks the best.

NFO　　　　　　＿＿＿＿＿＿＿＿＿　　　　　　(check your choice)

BTGC　　　　　　＿＿＿＿＿＿＿＿＿

Now that you've made your decision, let me tell you which stock looks best to me. Notice how the second chart in Figure 7.5 was trading downward and then spiked upward in the middle of December, whereas the first chart shows a steady upward trend. Therefore, the first chart looks the best.

How do we determine how much these options are going to sell for? Two ways:

1. Call your stockbroker.

2. Look it up yourself on the Internet. I think it's much more fun to look it up yourself . . . and then you can check with your broker to

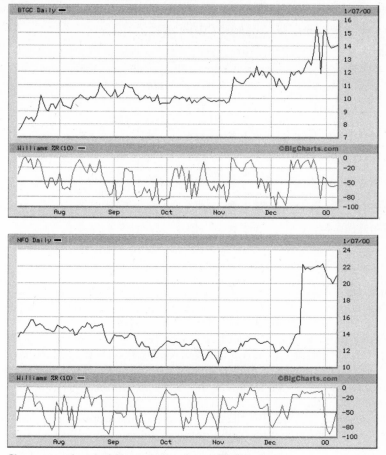

Charts reproduced with permission of www.BigCharts.com.

FIGURE 7.5 BigCharts View of the Stocks on Our Watch List

find out if you've done it right. Go to www.cboe.com. This is the web site for the Chicago Board Options Exchange, the exchange that markets all of the listed options. Click on Delayed Quotes. Then type in the symbol for your first stock choice and get a list of all call options. It will most likely be a bewildering list of numbers and columns that make perfect sense if you know what you're looking for and can give you an instant headache if you don't. Let me show you what we're looking for. (See Table 7.2.)

You'll notice that several months are listed. You want to find the month that is closest to 30 days from the month in which you are selling the option. Let's suppose that today is September 10. You'd be looking for options that expire on the third Friday of October.

Now that you have determined the month, let's determine the strike price. You'll notice that next to each month are various strike prices

TABLE 7.2 Listed Option Prices from www.cboe.com

NFO　Bid 22 1/8　**Ask** 22 5/8　**Size** 1 × 1　**Vol** 21500

Calls	Last Sale	Net	Bid	Ask	Vol	Open Int
00 Jan 10 (NFO AB-X)	10 7/8	pc	11 3/4	12 1/2	0	8
00 Jan 12 1/2 (NFO AV-X)	9 1/4	pc	9 3/8	9 7/8	0	80
00 Jan 15 (NFO AC-X)	6	pc	6 7/8	7 3/8	0	56
00 Jan 17 1/2 (NFO AW-X)	0	pc	4 5/8	5	0	0
00 Jan 20 (NFO AD-X)	1 15/16	pc	2 1/8	2 1/2	0	5
00 Jan 22 1/2 (NFO AX-X)	0	pc	9/16	13/16	0	0
00 Jan 25 (NFO AE-X)	0	pc	1/8	3/8	0	0

(Jan 5, Jan 7½, Jan 10, etc.). You are looking for a strike price that is at or slightly above your current stock price. Suppose you bought 1,000 shares of a $6.50 stock. You would select the Oct 7½ strike price.

Notice that there is a bid and an ask price. The current ask for BTGC Jan 15 is 1¾ ($1.75 a share). The current bid is 1½ ($1.50 a share). If you're the seller of the option, you want the ask price. If you're the buyer, you want the bid price. Table 7.3 shows the bid and ask prices for BTGC stocks in our example.

Because you've already selected one of the two stocks, determine how much you could receive by selling options on your stock if you got your bid price.

$_____ option premium

TABLE 7.3 Bid and Ask Call Option Prices for BTGC

BTGC　Bid 15 3/16　**Ask** 15 3/8　**Size** 10 × 2　**Vol** 3241100

Calls	Last Sale	Net	Bid	Ask	Vol	Open Int
00 Jan 5 (QTG AA-E)	10 1/2	pc	10	10 1/2	0	141
00 Jan 7 1/2 (QTG AU-E)	6 7/8	−1 3/8	7 5/8	8 1/8	1	330
00 Jan 10 (QTG AB-E)	4 7/8	+2 7/16	5 1/4	5 3/4	20	1284
00 Jan 12 1/2 (QTG AV-E)	3 1/4	+2 1/2	3 1/8	3 1/4	440	1774
00 Jan 15 (QTG AC-E)	1 3/4	+1 3/8	1 1/2	1 3/4	481	612
00 Jan 17 1/2 (QTG AW-E)	1/2	+3/16	3/8	5/8	5	30

Now, let me tell you which stock you would probably pick. Look again at Tables 7.2 and 7.3 on the far right column under "open interest." This shows the number of contracts that are currently "open" on this stock. A quick glance at both stock tables reveals that BTGC has substantially more open contracts than NFO. This indicates that there is a much more active options market in BTGC. Dr. Cooper's final decision before writing a covered call is to make sure there are *at least* 50 contracts in the open interest column so that you can have a liquid market for your options. This helps you make the final decision.

Odds are (depending upon the stock you pick) that you will win. If you do this four or five times a year, you'll probably get *called out* (be forced to sell your stock) about one time in four. You win three times; you lose once. Still, you're ahead by the end of the year, perhaps 20 percent, maybe 30 percent or more. You could also break even or even lose a bit. But with study, practice, and dedication you could improve your win/loss ratio.

Dr. Cooper believes that using his unique covered call strategy increases the chances of finding the right option candidates with the lowest risk of failure. Learn more about the latest refinements to this strategy at my web site, www.multiplestreamsofincome.com. Just type in the keyword Cooper System, or call my office at 801-852-8700.

Table 7.4 shows you how the filters screen the universe of stocks to find the right candidates.

TABLE 7.4 Writing Covered Calls: Filtering Process

Stocks that are optionable	Filter 1 10% of High or NH	Filter 2 Below $25	Filter 3 EPS80+	Filter 4 RelStr 80+	Filter 5 Group Str A	Examine Stock Chart
_____	_____	_____	_____	_____	_____	_____
_____	_____	_____	_____	_____	_____	
_____	_____	_____	_____	_____	_____	
_____	_____	_____	_____	_____		
_____	_____	_____	_____			
_____	_____	_____				
_____	_____	_____				
_____	_____					
_____	_____					
_____	_____					
_____						

Profit Multiplier 2: Buying and Selling Call Options

Until now we've concentrated on the selling side of the equation . . . where you own the stock and are selling an option to someone else (writing covered calls). Now it's time to learn the power of being on the other side of the equation . . . the buying side. After I've gotten you accustomed to the advantages of selling options (where 80 percent of options expire without being exercised), then why would you want to risk being on the other side? What makes you think that you can be one of the lucky 20 percent who actually wins?

It all depends on the stocks you select. What if your analysis shows that a stock has an excellent chance of increasing in value? If your research is right, you could double, triple, even quintuple your money. If you're wrong, you can lose 100 percent of your premium.

When you buy an option, it's possible to make money in one of two major ways.

Option profit method 1: You make money from stock appreciation. In our previous example, Tom was the option buyer. He makes money if XYZ stock increases above the strike price. Of course, if the stock doesn't reach the strike price, he loses his entire premium.

Option profit method 2: You make money from the appreciation of the option itself. For example, ABC stock is selling for $17 per share. An option with a strike price of $20 with three months to expiration is selling for $1 per share. You buy one contract (100 shares) and pay $100. As the underlying stock appreciates in value, the option also increases in value. The exciting part is that, because of leverage, any appreciation in the stock price has a magnified effect on the option price. If a $20 stock goes up $1.00 (a 5 percent increase), the option itself might increase in value from $1 to $1.50 (a 50 percent increase). The options for which you paid $100 can now be sold for $150. That's a 50 percent profit. You can do this anytime before the option expires. Just remember than an option is a *wasting* asset. It may increase in value in the short run, but unless exercised it eventually becomes worthless. To make the most appreciation with minimized risk, you want to sell your options to someone else when there are at least 30 days left on the option.

We will be focusing our attention on the second method. Our goal when buying options is to profit from the option itself and not from the underlying stock. We will be out of the option at least 30 days before it expires.

Obviously, the rules for buying options are slightly different than for selling options. When *writing* covered calls, you want the exercise date to be as close to the current date as possible while still carrying a good premium. Thus, the stock is tied up for a shorter time and the annualized gain is larger. On the other hand, when you are *buying* options, you want to extend the time frame to at least 90 days to give your stock time to move up in value.

	Writing Covered Calls	**Buying Call Options**
Time frame	Generally 2 to 8 weeks	90 to 120 days minimum
Strike price	Hope stock doesn't hit strike price	Hope the stock exceeds strike price
Expiration	Let option go full term and expire	Sell option 30 days before expiration date
Filtering	Looser analysis filters	Tighter analysis filters
Entry strategy	Looser entry strategy	Tighter entry strategy
Exit strategy	Don't need exit strategy	Need precise exit strategy

Ironically, the filters we use to write covered calls (sell an option) are many of the same ones we use to buy options. But we're going to add a few extra cautions because we can *make serious money only if the stock increases substantially above the strike price.* If the stock goes nowhere, then our money evaporates. (We don't like *that* thought.)

So the goal is to pick the hottest stocks that have the highest probability of increasing in value *in the short run.* Therefore, our screens must be even more demanding. These tighter standards are reflected in the fundamental analysis chart in Table 7.5.

Once a week, you should run the Table 7.5 screens on all the stocks listed in *Investor's Business Daily.* This will take you about 20 minutes. Some weeks, you will find six stocks and some weeks there will be none. You want only those stocks that are priced above $50 a share. These stocks are more stable on the upside and less volatile on the downside. When you see the charts, you'll see what I mean. On a sample day, I found four stocks that filtered through our screens, and I placed them on my watch list.

TABLE 7.5 Buying Options: The Filtering Process Using Fundamental Analysis

Filter I New High	Filter 2 Above $50	Filter 3 EPS80+	Filter 4 RelStr 90+	Filter 5 Group Str A
_____	_____	_____	_____	_____
_____	_____	_____	_____	_____
_____	_____	_____	_____	_____
_____	_____	_____	_____	_____
_____	_____	_____		
_____	_____			

The question is, which of these stocks on the watch list has the greatest chance of increasing *substantially* in price *in the short term?* Dr. Cooper has tested various methods and determined that out of the hundreds of possibilities, he relies most heavily on two technical indicators. They are the 50-day moving average and the Williams %R technical indicator. Just knowing this information will save you hundreds of hours of trial and error . . . with an emphasis on error.

The 50-Day Moving Average

Let's look at the charts for these stocks and add a 50-day moving average. You do this by going to www.bigcharts.com, entering the symbol of a stock, and clicking on Interactive Charting. You want to configure your chart to show six-month price movement. To this we add a 50-day moving average overlying the stock pattern. In the box below the stock pattern, we want to see the Williams %R indicator as shown in Figure 7.6.

The 50-day simple moving average is calculated by taking the previous 50 days of closing prices, adding them up, and dividing by 50. This gives you an average daily price for the past 50 days. If the stock price is above the 50-day simple moving average (SMA), then there might be a tendency toward continued growth. When a stock price breaks below a 50-day SMA, there might be a tendency for the stock to continue to decline.

A stock with an excellent 50-day SMA (trending nicely upward with few major dips and valleys) is found in Figure 7.6. For a stock on your watch list to be considered further, you need an increasing 50-day moving average.

Chart reproduced with permission of www.BigCharts.com.

FIGURE 7.6 Technical analysis using the 50-day moving average and Williams %R.

$$$	Technical Analysis	$$$

Many technical analysts look at charts like those shown in Figure 7.6 as the bible, while other stock market experts think that technical analysis is like reading tea leaves or having your fortune told. Rather than listening to one or the other, remain neutral and let your own experience prove to you whether or not this method is useful to your stock selections. I strongly recommend that you "paper trade" for at least 90 days before you ever commit a penny to these strategies. If you can't make this work on paper at least three times out of four, then you shouldn't be risking real money until you figure out what you're doing wrong, because playing with real money will be much more difficult and will require more discipline.

The Williams %R Indicator

Williams %R is an indicator that tracks the overbought and oversold status of an individual stock. Notice it in the bottom box below the stock chart in Figure 7.6. You'll also notice a solid line that cuts horizontally through this box. Let's call this line the neutral line. Some of the squiggly lines run above this neutral horizontal line and some drop below it. When the squiggly line is in the upper range above the neutral line, then the stock is overbought, meaning that there are more buyers than sellers. When the Williams %R line drops to the lower range, below neutral, then the stock is oversold, meaning that there are more sellers than buyers. Since things tend to revert to the average, when a stock is in an extremely oversold condition (near the extreme bottom of the chart) there will be a tendency for it to bounce back. During this bounce back, the stock may move up in price.

The Williams %R is the final major screen. Each day, look at the stocks on your watch list and notice the pattern of the Williams %R indicator. When it dips to the 90 percent oversold position, this is your preliminary buy signal. Table 7.6 shows how the filter chart looks.

Dr. Cooper does his analysis each evening after the stock market closes. It takes about 30 minutes to scan through his watch list of about 50 stocks. He looks at the 50-day moving averages and the Williams %R indicator. If this last indicator has dipped to −90 percent oversold, he then checks out the option prices at www.cboe.com. He selects the appropriate call option to buy at least three months and sometimes five months out in the future. He chooses an "at-the-money" strike price that is nearest to the current price that day.* Then he notices the open interest activity on this particular option. *Open interest* refers to the number of contracts that are outstanding, which gives an indication how many people are inter-

---

* Strike prices can either be (1) at the money, (2) in the money, or (3) out of the money. For example, if the current stock price is $10 a share, then a future strike price of $9 would be termed *in the money*. A future strike price of $10 would be termed *at the money*. And a future strike price of $11 would be termed *out of the money*.

TABLE 7.6 Buy Options: Filtering with Fundamental and Technical Analysis

Fundamental Analysis					Technical Analysis			
Filter 1 New High	Filter 2 Above $50	Filter 3 EPS80+	Filter 4 RelStr 90+	Filter 5 Group Str A	Filter 1 ↑ 50-Day MA	Filter 2 Williams %R Dips to −90%	Open Interest	Action List

ested in this particular option. If this number is less than 50, he will not buy. He wants to buy only those options with enough liquidity to allow a quick exit. If the open interest column is low, then there is a probability that he won't be able to sell quickly when he wants to sell. He feels even better if the open interest number is 100 or higher.

All of these screens and filters make the process of trading much more scientific and much less emotional. And much more conservative. Because the screens are so restrictive, he makes only one to two trades per month, but each trade has a much higher probability of success. Having done his homework and being satisfied with his choice, Dr. Cooper waits until the next day before placing his order. He never buys during the first hour of trading. The market is subject to more volatility at the opening bell. He wants to wait until things settle down. Then, if things still look positive, he makes his purchase.

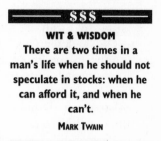

WIT & WISDOM
There are two times in a man's life when he should not speculate in stocks: when he can afford it, and when he can't.

MARK TWAIN

In 1998, Dr. Cooper made 12 such purchases—about one per month. Table 7.7 shows his track record. Since then, he has been constantly refin-

TABLE 7.7 Dr. Cooper's Track Record

Underlying Security	Date Opened	Price	Date Closed	Price	Time Held	% Gain/Loss
Microsoft	2/12/98	7.375	2/12/98	8.375	3 hours	13.56%
Microsoft	2/20/98	7.75	2/23/98	12.00	3 days	54.84%
Maytag	3/10/98	3.75	4/23/98	8.00	43 days	113.33%
Carnival Cruise Lines	3/11/98	3.75	5/20/98	11.00	69 days	193.33%
Fred Myer	3/13/98	5.50	4/9/98	2.25	27 days	(59.09%)
Merrill Lynch	3/13/98	6.375	4/6/98	19.50	24 days	205.88%
Cisco Sys.	6/15/98	7.00	6/17/98	8.00	2 days	14.29%
Wal-Mart	7/10/98	5.00	8/11/98	5.50	32 days	10.00%
Maytag	8/19/98	4.00	11/23/98	10.00	94 days	150.00%
Intel	8/21/98	8.50	9/1/98	3.375	11 days	(60.29%)
Peco Energy	9/22/98	2.00	11/20/98	6.375	58 days	218.75%
Ascend Com.	9/22/98	5.25	11/23/98	5.625	61 days	7.14%

The table header spans: **Options Transaction History 1998**

Total Trades	Number of Profitable Trades	Average Hold Time	Average Gain Per Trade	Total Gain to Account
12	10	35 days	71.81%	228.92%

These numbers are based on actual trades. All trades made in 1998 are represented. The total gain was computed after brokerage fees were deducted and interest gained during 1998 was added. Dr. Cooper's portfolio in 1999 was up over 300%.

Courtesy of Stephen M. Cooper

ing this process even further. If you would like a special report on his most recent refinements, you'll find it at my web site (www.multi-plestreamsofincome.com). Enter the keyword Cooper System, or call my office at 801-852-8700. The report is called The Cooper System: The Latest Strategies for Earning High Profits in Low-Cost Options.

Once you have purchased an option contract, the most important decision still awaits . . . when to sell. Suppose you have taken a position in PQR stock with a strike price of $15 per share in 90 days. You bought 10 contracts at .75 (quoted as ¾) per share or $750. Depending on the movement of the stock, you need to know when to sell your options. All stock options should be sold 30 days prior to expiration, no matter what. Also, if a stock price ever dips below its seven-day moving average, this is a good time to take your profits and run.

Scenario 1: The stock price increases to $18 per share. Because the stock price has increased, the option has most likely also increased in value. It may have gone from ¾ to 1¾, giving you a full $1 in profit. You could sell now and earn $1,000 profit on your 10 contracts, which represents a 133 percent return on your investment of $750, or you could sell some of your contracts at this point to lock in your profit. Or you could let it ride.

One of Dr. Cooper's money management strategies is to let the winners ride as much as possible. This is more difficult than it sounds. For example, during August of 1998, Dr. Cooper bought January options on Maytag (symbol MYG). The cost was $4 per share. Unfortunately, the market took an unexpected dive toward the end of August and the options declined drastically in value. Dr. Cooper felt the underlying stock still had excellent value and, with several months remaining, decided to hang on. In his own words, "I had to ride this one out twice. It declined sharply by August 31, then rallied to a peak on September 17. There was then another steep market decline. It neared my 50 percent stop-loss limit on October 9. One could have given up hope at this point, but at the darkest hour the disciplined trader relies on the trading rules. With uncommon faith and rare courage, I held out, then sold on November 23 at $10 for a profit of 150 percent!" A chart showing these swings in price is shown in Figure 7.7.

Scenario 2: The stock remains below the strike price. If the underlying stock isn't increasing in value, neither will the stock option. Actually, as time expires the stock options begin to lose value. If, at any time before the 30-day automatic selling date, your options lose 50 percent of their value (of what you paid for them), you should sell them, take your losses, and move on.

Some people have likened investing in options to gambling. For those who invest without a proven system and a powerful screening process, this may be accurate. But in one way at least, investing in options is completely unlike gambling. In gambling, if you bet on horse A and it gets a bad start out of the gate, you can't get your money back. But with options, if you select ABC Company and it gets a bad start out of the chute, you can often sell your position and recoup at least part of your losses.

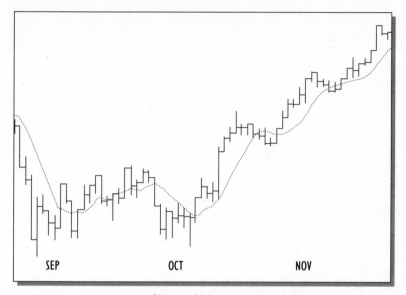

FIGURE 7.7 Chart of Maytag price swings.

With a careful selection process and wise money management, you can often cut your losses short and heighten your winners.

A final word of warning about trading in the options market: Although I've given you enough information to broaden your understanding of a few of the strategies in the exciting but potentially dangerous world of options, you obviously need to do much more study before you commit any of your real dollars to this approach. Here are six rules:

1. *Paper trade first.* You should paper trade for at least three months. Never invest real money without a successful paper-trading track record.

2. *Never invest money you can't afford to lose.* First, establish a survival fund. Then commit 80 percent of your stock market funds to long- and medium-term investment approaches. Consider options only for the short-term/high-risk portion of your portfolio.

3. *Study, study, study.* Your first place for free information about options is the web site of the Chicago Board Options Exchange (www.cboe.com). Click on the Education link, where you'll find plenty of free tutorials and some free software—The Options Toolbox. If you're a beginner, the tutorials here are a bit difficult to follow, but as you learn the lingo, you'll do fine. I also recommend the following:

Getting Started in Options by Michael C. Thomsett
The Options Course by George A. Fontanills
Trading for a Living by Dr. Alexander Elder

4. *Establish a mentoring relationship.* Find someone who not only understands the world of options, but who consistently makes money trading in the real world . . . and pay them to teach you how to do it. The money will be well spent. Just one idea or strategy or money management system could pay for your tuition 100 times over. The best players in the world need coaches. Even the Lone Ranger had Tonto. Don't go it alone. You'll find some coaching options at www.multiplestreamsofincome.com (keyword Cooper coach).

5. *Don't overcommit.* Investing in options can be exciting. But don't get *too* excited. Be prudent. Dr. Cooper's rules for money management will keep your enthusiasm in check: Commit no more than 25 percent of the funds in your high-risk bucket to any single trade if your account is under $25,000. If your account is over $25,000, commit no more than 10 percent on a single trade. Buy five contracts if your account is under $25,000. If your account is over $25,000, buy five or more contracts up to a dollar amount of no more than 10 percent of the account. Other experts insist on even tighter money management rules. Dr. Alexander Elder recommends risking only 2 percent of your available capital on any one trade.

6. *Don't confuse brains for a bull market.* Any system is going to look good during a bull market. When things so south, sit on the sidelines—or return to paper trading. It may be that the system is not broken—perhaps it's just not the right time to be trading with this system.

Good luck in doubling your money.

Recent comments about real trading and paper trading from some of Dr. Cooper's most recent Double Your Money in Options Trading Course:

> *Thanks to 'selling covered calls' option techniques I learned from Dr. Cooper, I just earned $593.75 in one month by selling 30-day calls on my AXA-Financial stock. This is equivalent to earning an annual rate of 25% interest on my money! Had I known of these techniques when I started buying stock over 7 years ago, I would be tens of thousands of dollars richer today.*
> Rubin Wald, New York

> *WOW!! Am I excited or what? My CPN contracts are up 234% in a month. The profits I made and am still earning on this one option have more than paid for your class and we are still making more profits. I sold my GBLX position for a very nice profit as well last Friday.*
> Joseph R. Rabbia, Tampa, FL

*I didn't think I'd ever be able to make any money in the stock market.
My first paper trade made 300%, and I'm averaging 99% overall
on my paper trades. I'm really excited about the prospect of putting
real money behind these trades, but I'm going to paper trade for 90 days,
like Dr. Cooper taught us, before I invest any real money.
Just follow the system, and it will pay off.*
Diane Conklin, Stone Mountain, GA

*"I Made $5,310 (157%) on Comverse Technology October 75 calls
using Dr. Cooper's option system. Thanks Bob, Tom and Dr. Cooper.*
John McGee

CHAPTER 8

The heights by great men reached and kept
Were not attained by sudden flight,
But they, while their companions slept,
Were toiling upward in the night.
HENRY WADSWORTH LONGFELLOW

YOUR FOURTH STREAM
Winning Big in Real Estate

Do you remember the story *Acres of Diamonds,* told so famously by Russell H. Conwell? It's about a man who dreamed of owning a diamond mine. He sold his farm, took the money, and wasted his life in a futile search. Ironically, the man who bought his farm was looking in the stream behind the farmhouse and noticed a brilliant, shiny stone glittering in the water. Yes, it was a diamond. Thus was discovered the famous diamond mine from which came many of the crown jewels of Europe. The farm was sitting atop acres of diamonds! True story.

Many of us are like the man going off in search of diamonds. We waste time, money, and energy in endless moneymaking schemes while the greatest source of wealth is lying right at our feet—real estate.

In Chapter 2 I introduced you to the seven essential money skills (value it; control it; save it; invest it; make it; shield it; and share it). For the last few chapters, we've been practicing money skill 4: *Invest it.* For the rest of the book, we'll take a more active role and learn money skill 5: *Make it.*

Everybody knows that one of the smartest ways to make serious money is in real estate. In the long run, the largest asset most people ever have at retirement is the equity in their own home. According to an article several years ago in *Reader's Digest,* the average net worth of the average North American homeowner was $63,000. The average net worth of the average renter was only $1,921. About 30 times less. Obviously, you've got to get into a home. And if you've already purchased your own home, you've got to learn how to turn it into a cash machine.

Figure 8.1 shows what has happened to the median price of a home in North America over the past 60 years. But even if property values don't continue to increase, I'll show you techniques for buying properties so far below market that you won't care whether prices in your city ever appreciate again.

In this chapter, you'll learn . . .

How you can still build a real estate fortune starting with little or no money down.

Nine ways to find super real estate bargains.

The five most powerful nothing-down techniques.

First, a comment to those readers who are skeptical about whether it's still possible to profit from real estate starting with little or no money down. In the past 20 years, since my groundbreaking best-selling book *Nothing Down* was published, I have talked to thousands of people who have purchased properties with little or nothing down.

Yet when you ask members of the real estate community (mortgage lenders, bankers, real estate agents, etc.) whether they think it's possible to buy property with no money down, these professionals usually reply that this is a fiction of the late-night infomercial. If they'd check their own records, they'd see that nothing-down deals are made every day, in every major city in the world.

For now, all you need to understand is that there is no investment like real estate for versatility and power. The best time to buy real estate is today . . . and this isn't going to change anytime soon. Your home will continue to be not only your castle, but also your bank, your cash

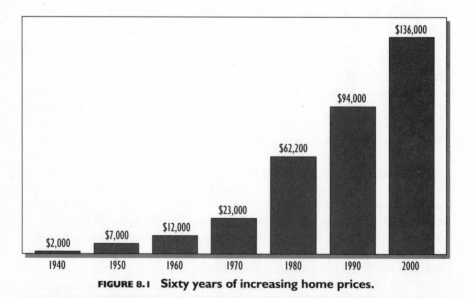

FIGURE 8.1 Sixty years of increasing home prices.

machine, your forced savings account, and your vehicle to rapid retirement and the lifestyle of your dreams.

Owning your own home is the first building block in your empire. It's the largest and most important investment you'll ever make. I'm not talking about buying property the traditional way—big down payments, difficult bank financing, embarrassing credit checks. I'm talking the Robert Allen way. You can learn to use creativity instead of cash and credit—flexibility instead of financial strength.

> ━━━ **$$$** ━━━
> **WIT & WISDOM**
> Never put your money
> in anything that eats
> or needs repainting.
> BILLY ROSE

Obviously, you can't move into your dream home tomorrow. You may be moving through a series of homes, making handsome profits on each one, and parlaying your growing equities into larger and larger properties . . . until the day arrives when you walk out of the closing office with the deed (of course, you'll pay all cash) to the home of your dreams. Don't let the train of prosperity pass you by. Catch the caboose; then work your way to first class.

Nothing down is not only a system of creative techniques, it's an attitude—a way of thinking. It's a belief in the creative spirit in all of us. If you want to own property, there is a way for you to do it—if you just don't let somebody talk you out of it!

While I was preparing this chapter, I received the following letter from one of my seminar graduates, which illustrates the kind of serendipitous events that occur when you're willing to follow your dreams.

Dear Mr. Allen:

I started investing in real estate several years ago after reading your book and attending one of your wealth training seminars. The year we started, the real estate market was hot and getting hotter, prices were moving up at an unprecedented pace. It almost seemed that if you didn't buy something you would eventually be priced out of the market and unable to purchase anything. I was 25 years old, newly married, and committed to buying real estate before the prices went too high.

In May of that year my wife and I, knowing we couldn't afford to purchase a single-family home at these prices, decided to buy an investment property. We put a few thousand dollars down and bought our first property, a three-family house that needed some work, in a not-so-great area (the price was right).

We paid $115,000 for the property. The payment was approximately $1,060 and the rents were $1,435. Not bad, we made approximately $375 per month. We continued to live in our rented apartment because it was in a nicer area than the house we bought. Everybody thought we were nuts, and had no problem telling us this either! Well, after about six months, with some paint, carpet, and minor repairs, the property was appraised at $185,000, which allowed us to get a second mortgage and pull out $30,500. This payment was $382 per month so it was basically covered by the rents as well.

Approximately five months after this, we closed on our second property, a four-family house in a very nice area. We used the cash from the second mortgage on the first property, together with a second mortgage from the sellers of the second property, to put the deal together. We paid $285,000 and our payment on the first was $2,170, payments on the 2nd were $256, making a total of $2,426. We moved into one of the apartments (which was nicer than where we lived before) and rented the other three out for $675 each for a total rent of $2,025.

So exactly one year from our first purchase, our first house was essentially break even, and we used none of our own money to buy the second, much nicer home, which ended up costing us about $401 per month *to live in* our new house!

A few months later we found another property. In January, we closed on a six-family investment property we purchased for $250,000. Using some creativity we closed in the beginning of the month and utilized the credit for rents and security deposits, a second mortgage from the seller, and a credit for repairs to allow us to close on this property with less than $4,500 of our own money. The 1st mortgage payment was $2,394, the 2nd was $219, taxes $280, and insurance of $216/mo, bringing the total payments to $3,109/mo. The monthly rental was $3,700, leaving me a positive cash flow of $591.

Another few months later, in March, the four family (property 2) appraised at a high enough level for us to refinance the second mortgage and pull out an additional $23,400 in capital.

In April we also closed on a nice two-family house that was an estate sale. The cost was $156,000. The value was approx. $170,000. We entered into an equity share agreement with my sister, who was divorced at the time and had limited income. She provided the down payment and I found the property, negotiated the transaction, and agreed to manage the finances, lease the other apartment, and assume the responsibility for any repairs required during the ownership. We shared the tax advantages, and she owned a home that she normally would not have been able to handle on her own.

In June, I was able to buy another estate sale. This was a single-family house that I was able to get for $145,000. My intention was to immediately resell the property. I knew it was worth $170,000 to $175,000 at the time. As a matter of fact, I had a couple of offers in the $170K range even before we closed on the house. However, it was about this time that my wife and I found out that we were going to have our first child. Although I was content in the four family, and didn't really buy the single family to live in it, we ended up renting out our apartment for $1,000/mo and moving into the one family.

Now, in about three years we went from zero to five properties consisting of 14 apartments, with gross rents of over $10,000 per month, and an accumulated mortgage debt of approximately $1 million. Based on appraisals, we had created an equity of approximately $248,500 in our properties. Our positive cash flow was not significant but they were all break even or slightly positive properties.

Then the real estate market came to a screeching halt. Interest rates went up and some property values dropped drastically. It was about this time that many investors found themselves losing their properties because they had financed them to a point where they had huge negative cash flows. Because our properties were all break even or slightly positive, we were able to weather the storm.

The road we have taken has been difficult at times; however, the good news is as follows:

- Even with the loss in values, we have been able to accumulate, through principal reduction, a combined equity of approximately $200,000 in the four investment properties.
- Partly due to the depreciation laws, over the past few years we have been able to generate rental losses of $255,948. These deductions have saved us approximately $50,000 to $70,000 in taxes.
- Our six family mortgage will be paid in ten years and our two family in 15 years, which will generate to us a gross annual income of $64,500. That will give us financial freedom.

One of the most significant side benefits I realized from this whole process came from the fact that I had learned so much about real estate investments and how to finance them. A mortgage banker I was working with explained to me how I could use my knowledge of the industry to help others finance their homes. I started my mortgage loan officer career at that time. I have earned a six figure income for the past 4 years. If it wasn't for my interest and passion in real estate, I never would have found this career!

Six years ago, we sold the one family at about break even to purchase another one family for us to live in. This was a bank foreclosure which needed some repairs. It now has an equity of $160,000, bringing our total real estate equity to approximately $360,000 and climbing.

In addition to our real estate, we have also been developing other streams of income.

Thanks for helping us start on the road to prosperity. I look forward to hearing from you and working with you.

Sincerely,

Adam Wizner
Pequannock, NJ

Would you like to learn how to do deals like this? The bedrock principle underlying creative real estate investing is this:

While the vast majority of sellers are inflexible in their prices and terms, a small percentage of sellers are highly motivated to sell.

I call these highly motivated sellers "don't-wanters." They *don't want* their property . . . and are willing to do seemingly irrational things to get rid of it. The secret to buying property creatively is to look for these don't-wanters—the 1 percent of sellers who are highly motivated. Don't be discouraged by the other 99 percent of sellers who are not flexible. The process is more than mere bargain hunting. . . . It's hunting for *the right kind of seller,* then trying to determine if the property is a good value. This process consists of three critical activities:

1. Finding   2. Funding   3. Farming

Critical Activity 1. *Finding:* How to Find Highly Motivated Sellers

What causes someone to become highly motivated? There are 20 reasons, which conveniently spell the words DON'T-WANTER CONDITIONS.

D   Divorce
O   Obsolescence of property—needs major fix-up
N   Negative cash flow
T   Transfer

W   Wrong management approach
A   Arrears in payments
N   Negative location
T   Taxes
E   Estate situations (deaths)
R   Retirement

C   Competition with neighboring properties
O   Out-of-area owners
N   Neurotic fears
D   Debts
I   Ignorance of investment principles and market conditions
T   Time constraints
I   Investment capital—needs capital for another investment
O   Ornery partner(s)
N   Need for status symbols (a new Lexus beats an old building)
S   Sickness

If you'll scan the preceding list, you'll see that the majority of the reasons for motivation have to do with the seller's personal situation as opposed to problems with the property. Your goal is to find an excellent property in the hands of a seller with personal problems. Then you attempt to help this particular seller come up with creative solutions to solve these personal problems. Hopefully, the solution doesn't require that you come up with a large down payment.

How many people have personal problems? Take a city like Los Angeles. There are well over 1 million individual properties in the five major counties surrounding LA. In any given year, approximately 40,000 of those owners will default on their loan payments and receive a letter from the mortgage company threatening foreclosure.

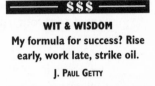

WIT & WISDOM
My formula for success? Rise early, work late, strike oil.

J. Paul Getty

About 5,000 of these properties will actually be foreclosed on, and many more will be sold for substantial discounts just before the foreclosure sale.

And that's just one source of flexible sellers. Every year, about 70,000 people move out of Los Angeles, and many of those people own homes that they have either sold or are still trying to sell. Every year there are almost 50,000 divorces, 10,000 bankruptcies, and 75,000 deaths. In other words, there is a lot of opportunity . . . if you know where to look for it.

Let me say a quick word here about ethics. After I rattle off a list of misfortunes like these, it's possible you might be saying to yourself that you don't want to take advantage of someone's troubles. Actually, it's just the opposite. These people need you. They no longer want their property. It has become a burden to them—an albatross around their neck. They need you to help them get rid of it as quickly as possible, and they will be grateful for any help you can give them.

There's no better feeling in the world than to help someone and, in the process, to help yourself. As the saying goes, "Help thy brother's boat across and, lo, thine own has reached the shore."

Before you become too excited, realize this: Only one in twenty sellers is going to have a problem this severe. Less than half of these will own properties worth buying. So the odds are slim but not impossible.

Most of the ads in the newspaper are not flexible—95 percent won't be interested in your creative deal. Almost all of the properties listed with Realtors in multiple listing books are not flexible—sellers have been told by their real estate agents that they will get top dollar. But there are highly motivated sellers out there—plenty enough for you to find at least one good property per year. Let me show you how to find them.

The Bargain-Finding Funnel

There are actually nine excellent ways of finding once-in-a-lifetime deals. Imagine a real estate money machine. At the top of the machine, chunks of raw ore are being delivered by conveyor belts to the first of several collecting bins. This ore is processed, and the refined ore drops through to the next lower processing bin, where it is again processed and funneled to the next level. Finally, out of the last processing bin comes the final product . . . beautiful polished diamonds. Raw ore at the top. Finished stones at the bottom. Your finding system is a similar process: putting lots of ore (raw leads) into the top of the machine and refining (or qualifying) these leads until you have an accepted offer on a fabulous bargain property. (See Figure 8.2.)

There are nine sources of information for finding highly motivated sellers (or, to use our analogy, nine conveyor belts bringing raw ore to the machine).

1. Newspaper classified ads
2. Realtors and real estate agents
3. Your own sphere of influence
4. Focused wandering around
5. Banks and lending institutions
6. Your own ads
7. Direct mail
8. Investment clubs, associations, and exchange groups
9. Other professionals

Each of these nine sources can provide you with raw ore for your machine to process. And there are four steps to the processing. Let me give you an example.

Step 1: Find the lead. Suppose you are reading the classified section of your newspaper. You spot an ad that seems interesting: "Seller transferred out of state. Need quick sale. Take over payments. Call 555-1212." This is a lead—a piece of raw ore to process.

Step 2: Complete a BargainFinder. Call on that ad and fill out a BargainFinder form—a simple one page, fill-in-the-blanks form that I'll be teaching you how to use in a few minutes. The BargainFinder will give you a property score: If the score is 11 or less, you just walk away. If it's 12 or more, you're interested. Suppose you call on the ad and, sure enough, the seller wants out and is willing to sell below market for a quick sale. It scores a 12. You rush over to inspect the property and it looks good. Now, you're ready for the next step.

Step 3: Write an offer. Prepare an offer to purchase the property on terms that meet your own special needs. The seller may accept your offer, reject it, or counteroffer. Suppose he or she accepts your offer. . . . The lead was processed all the way through your machine and dropped out at the bottom as a diamond.

Step 4: Buy the property. That's it!

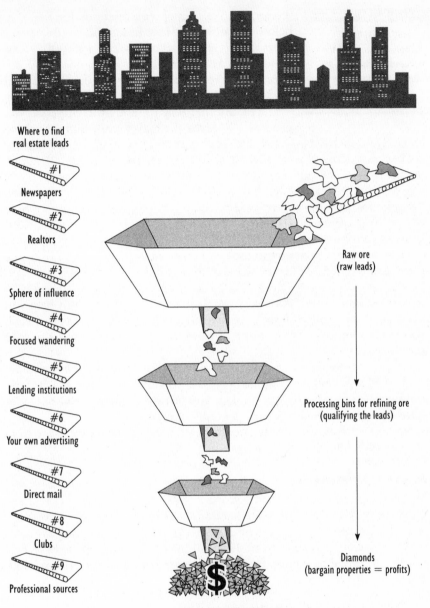

Where to find
real estate leads

#1
Newspapers

#2
Realtors

#3
Sphere of influence

#4
Focused wandering

#5
Lending institutions

#6
Your own advertising

#7
Direct mail

#8
Clubs

#9
Professional sources

Raw ore
(raw leads)

Processing bins for refining ore
(qualifying the leads)

Diamonds
(bargain properties = profits)

FIGURE 8.2 Bargain-finding funnel.

It's pretty simple, actually. But not easy. The difficulty comes in the processing because very few leads turn into diamonds. But as long as you are willing to keep processing leads through your machine, you will eventually win. It's a numbers business—like diamond mining. You run a ton of gravel through your machine in order to find a sparkling diamond.

Some people become discouraged and quit too soon. Here's how I stay motivated. Suppose it takes you 100 hours of searching to find a potential real estate deal, which you then buy for $20,000 below the market. How much did you earn for every hour you worked? Well, $20,000 profit divided by 100 hours of effort equals $200 per hour. If you're too busy to earn $200 an hour, I'd say you're too busy!

Here's another way to look at it. Suppose you process 100 leads through your finding machine and only 10 in 100 pass your test. You write an offer on all 10, looking for the best deal. One of your offers is accepted, resulting in a $20,000 equity profit. How much money did you earn for every offer you wrote? Let's see, $20,000 profit divided by 10 offers equals $2,000 per offer—even though nine of those offers were rejected. Did you get that? Every time one of your offers is rejected a $2,000 check floats out of the sky and lands in your outstretched palm.

Here's still another way to look at it. You make 100 calls to find one good deal worth $20,000. How much money did you earn every time you picked up the phone? A cool $200! You might have a fear of phone calling, but if I gave you $200 every time you made a call, would it help you overcome your fear? If I gave you two $100 bills for every telephone call you made tomorrow from sunup to sundown, how long would you take for lunch?

Of course, the kind of calls I'm talking about involve the complete analysis of a potential real estate deal. And you can't collect your $200 per call until after you've found, funded, and farmed each deal. But now you have a way to motivate yourself to keep looking.

So let's turn on the money machine and start processing these nine sources of highly motivated sellers.

Source 1: Newspapers

When you read the classified section of your local newspaper, you are going to look in three separate sections: (1) houses and/or condos for sale; (2) houses for rent, lease or option; (3) investment property for sale.

As you scan each ad, ignore descriptions of the property. You're primarily interested in finding clues to the seller's flexibility. Here are some examples of words/phrases you're looking for:

"Owner transferred"

"Low down"

"No down"

"OWC" (owner will carry)

"Out-of-state owner"

"Can trade/exchange for equity"

"Take over payments"

"Lease option"

"Rent to own"

"Desperate"

"FSBO" (for sale by owner)

"Must sell—make an offer"

You call on the ads and fill out your BargainFinders until you find a property that scores 12 or more. It takes only one.

Source 2: Realtors

Most licensed real estate agents have access to the Multiple Listing Service (MLS), which is a listing of all available properties for sale in your area. Obviously, this is an extremely good source of information. Searching through this data can be daunting. Narrow your focus to areas of homes priced below the median—bread-and-butter-type homes. Then be on the lookout for the clues in the multiple listings that indicate flexibility. Generally, each listing contains a section called "remarks" or "comments" or "miscellaneous information." You look first to this section to see if the seller has been willing to indicate extra flexibility with comments like, "OWC" (owner will carry), "seller transferred," "price just reduced for quick sale," "will consider trade," "can exchange part equity for down payment," "might consider a lease option."

These clues let you know that the seller is willing to deal—that he or she may not need a conventional transaction with straight cash and a new loan. These clues can also lead you to a creative real estate agent.

Finding a creative agent is almost like trying to find a flexible seller. Most agents do not like creative financing—especially the nothing-down kind—because they falsely assume that no cash means no commissions. Nothing down doesn't mean there is no cash involved. In fact, there may be a lot of cash. . . . It's just not *your* cash.

If you can work with highly creative real estate agents, you will find the process much easier . . . because they will understand what you are looking for—they will be on your side and not resisting you every step of the way. Actually, I find the resistance to creative financing to be largely a matter of ignorance and not philosophy. . . . They simply don't know how to do it, and therefore they claim that it can't be done. So, if you're planning on using a real estate agent, try to find one who is very creative and avoid anyone who seems to resist your desire to find a highly motivated seller.

> ══ **$$$** ══
>
> **WIT & WISDOM**
> I conceive that the great part of the miseries of mankind are brought upon them by false estimates they have made of the value of things.
>
> BENJAMIN FRANKLIN

How do you find creative Realtors? Notice the kinds of ads they are running in the newspaper. If they use motivational clues, then they are more likely to understand the process. Ask for referrals. When you call a real estate office, ask the secretary for the most creative realtor in the office. It takes only one.

Source 3: Sphere of influence

As soon as you begin your process of trying to find your next bargain property, you need to let people know you are in the market for a great deal. Talk to friends, coworkers, family members, total strangers—anyone can be a lead source. It takes only one.

Source 4: Focused wandering around

Pick an area of town in which you'd like to buy your next property. Start driving around this neighborhood on a weekly basis. Stop at every "For Sale" sign and ask what the selling price is and how they arrived at that price. If possible, get a feel for their flexibility. If they seem amenable, you might even try to ask the BargainFinder questions. More than likely, you won't find a lot of flexibility this way, but it's good practice. Don't be shy about asking questions. If they're not anxious to sell, they'll brush you off. That's okay. Ask if they know someone else in the neighborhood who really needs to sell. It takes only one.

Source 5: Banks and lending institutions

When a bank makes a loan using real estate as collateral, it is hoping that the loan will be paid. But from time to time, the loan goes bad, the bank has to foreclose, and the bank ends up with the property—a property it really doesn't want, a property it wants to unload. This is where you come in. Call major banks in your area, ask for the person in charge of foreclosures, property repossessions, or REOs (that's bank lingo for *real estate owned*). This is an excellent source of potential bargain properties.

Source 6: Your own advertising

If you really want to be creative, you can run your own classified ad to attract sellers. There are several benefits. First of all, *time*. If you have more money than time, your ad can attract the kind of seller you are looking for. Have these sellers leave their information on your answering machine and call them back at your leisure. The second benefit is *negotiating leverage*—they are calling you, which puts you in the driver's seat. And third, you may attract people who have not even thought of selling their property yet . . . thus you *avoid competition with other buyers.*

I taught this idea to a group of 100 people in the Los Angeles area recently. One woman took this seriously and ran her ad in her local *Penny Saver* newspaper. It cost her $300 for an ad running several weeks. She received only six responses to her ad. That's $50 per lead. But it was high-grade ore. One seller wanted a quick sale and was willing to sell at 40 percent below market. That single call was worth $50,000. I'd say that was a pretty good investment.

I encourage you to experiment with several local newspapers, with several classified ad placements, and several different ad wordings until you find a combination that seems to produce the greatest number of inquiries from interested sellers. Think cheap at first. Spend extremely frugally. Here are some phrases to put in your ads that have worked for others:

"Willing to close quickly."

"Need flexible seller."

"Excellent references."

"Family has $5,000 down for seller who can carry."

"Close quickly."

"Fair price."

"Need to sell?"

"No commissions."

Perhaps an inexpensive ad like the following will draw a few responses:

"Young couple looking for first home. Fair price for your home if you can be flexible on terms. Principals only. Call 555-1234."

Source 7: County courthouse direct-mail method

Where can you find the highest concentration of highly motivated sellers? Answer: your local courthouse. If you've never been to the courthouse except to pay a traffic ticket, I recommend you take a trip down there on a lunch break and check it out. It is a gold mine of information. Ask the person at the information desk to help you find information about the following:

1. Out-of-state owners
2. Bankruptcies
3. Tax sales
4. Default notices
5. Foreclosure sales
6. Divorces
7. Sheriff's sales
8. Liens filed

Each of these situations is a ripe source of motivation. Case in point, out-of-state owners: A certain percentage of all of the property in your area is owned by people living out of state. Check with the tax assessor to find properties for which tax notices are being mailed to out-of-state owners.

Why might out-of-state owners be more flexible? Three reasons: (1) They may have management problems that are difficult to handle long distance. (2) They don't know property values as well as local owners and may be happy with a below-market price. (3) They are not emotionally involved in the ownership of the property. They are detached. Unlike resident homeowners who need the cash for their next home purchase, the out-of-state owner probably doesn't need the cash and might be more flexible.

There is an eight-step process for tapping into this source of highly motivated sellers:

1. Select the type of situation (divorces, default notices, etc.).

2. Research name and address.

3. Create a form letter similar to the sample that follows.

Dear Mr/Mrs.____,

It has come to my attention that you may be considering selling your property soon. Before you list with a real estate agent, please consider giving me a call. I'm a private individual who would like to make an offer to buy your property. I might just save you thousands of dollars in commissions. Even if you've already listed your property for sale, I'm a serious buyer who can close very quickly if the price and terms are right. If you're interested, please call 555-1212. Leave a message on my answering machine if I'm not home and I'll return your call quickly.

Sincerely,

Your Name

P.S. I will make a written offer to purchase your property within 48 hours of your call.

---

4. Have your letter printed.

5. Sign and mail your letter.

6. Wait for response.

7. Process each lead through a BargainFinder.

8. Do a second mailing with a new letter to the same list.

Let's say you send 100 letters a month—that'll cost you some time for research and about $50 in mailing costs. How many responses might you get? Certainly not more than two or three out of a hundred. Five if you're lucky. How many good responses do you need? One.

So let's be pessimistic for a minute. Suppose you take a full year to find yourself a fabulous bargain property, and you budget $50 a month for mailing costs. You send 100 letters using the sources I mentioned earlier (divorces, default notices, etc), so that after a year you've mailed out 1,200 letters. How many responses will you have generated? My guess: maybe 20 on the low side and 50 on the high side. What is the probability that one of those properties is owned by a highly motivated seller who might be flexible enough give you a good deal? It's a numbers game. It's certainly better than playing the lottery.

Source 8: Investment clubs, apartment associations, exchange groups

All major cities have a combination of clubs, associations, and groups dedicated to people interested in real estate investments. Checking on the Net, I found dozens of listings. The National Apartment Association lists its affiliates' local addresses and phone numbers at www.naahq.org.affiliates.html.

An excellent magazine that lists investment clubs and exchange groups is the *Creative Real Estate Magazine*. It's published monthly by A. D. Kessler, one of the originators of creative real estate education in North America. You can get a sample copy of the magazine by sending $6 to *Creative Real Estate Magazine,* Box L, Rancho Santa Fe, CA 92130.

Mingling and networking with like-minded investors is an excellent source for ideas, tips, investment opportunities, and deals. It takes only one.

Source 9: Other professionals

Certain professionals are aware of their client's problems long before these problems become a matter of public record: attorneys (divorce, estate, probate), tax consultants, accountants, real estate management companies, collection agencies, banks and lending institutions, and so forth. If you know professionals in these areas, let them know that you are an investor looking to buy property. They may just have a client who might be seeking a quick sale. All it takes is one.

By sifting through these nine sources of highly motivated sellers, you can generate some hot leads on excellent bargain properties. But what do you do when you find one? How can you know whether a property is a good deal? You've probably heard that the three most important things to look for in real estate are location, location, and location. Actually there are five things you need to analyze:

1. Seller motivation

2. Good location

3. Good financing—including down payment and long-term financing

4. Good condition

5. Good price

All five of these conditions combine to make a great deal. I have devised a simple scoring system that takes the emotion out of bargain hunting.

I give each of the five areas a score from 1 to 3, where 1 is poor and 3 is excellent. If the property scores less than 12, I pass and keep looking. See the scoring grid in Figure 8.3 and the BargainFinder form in Figure 8.4.

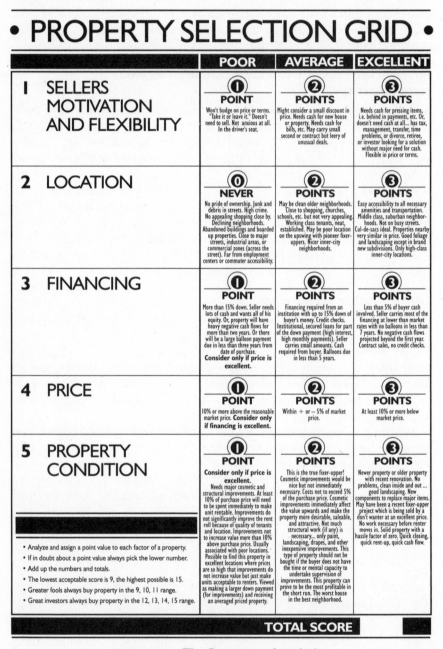

• PROPERTY SELECTION GRID •

		POOR	AVERAGE	EXCELLENT
1	**SELLERS MOTIVATION AND FLEXIBILITY**	**① POINT** Won't budge on price or terms. "Take it or leave it." Doesn't need to sell. Not anxious at all. In the driver's seat.	**② POINTS** Might consider a small discount in price. Needs cash for new house or property. Needs cash for bills, etc. May carry small second or contract but leery of unusual deals.	**③ POINTS** Needs cash for pressing items, i.e. behind in payments, etc. Or, doesn't need cash at all... has tax, management, transfer, time problems, or divorce, retiree, or investor looking for a solution without major need for cash. Flexible in price or terms.
2	**LOCATION**	**⓪ NEVER** No pride of ownership. Junk and debris in streets. High crime. No appealing shopping close by. Declining neighborhoods. Abandoned buildings and boarded up properties. Close to major streets, industrial areas, or commercial zones (across the street). Far from employment centers or commuter accessibility.	**② POINTS** May be clean older neighborhoods. Close to shopping, churches, schools, etc. but not very appealing. Working class tenants, neat, established. May be poor location on the upswing with pioneer fixer-uppers. Nicer inner-city neighborhoods.	**③ POINTS** Easy accessibility to all necessary amenities and transportation. Middle class, suburban neighbor-hoods. Not on busy streets. Cul-de-sacs ideal. Properties nearby very similar in price. Good foliage and landscaping except in brand new subdivisions. Only high-class inner-city locations.
3	**FINANCING**	**① POINT** More than 15% down. Seller needs lots of cash and wants all of his equity. Or, property will have heavy negative cash flows for more than two years. Or there will be a large balloon payment due in less than three years from date of purchase. **Consider only if price is excellent.**	**② POINTS** Financing required from an institution with up to 15% down of buyer's money. Credit checks. Institutional, secured loans for part of the down payment (high interest, high monthly payments). Seller carries small amounts. Cash required from buyer. Balloons due in less than 5 years.	**③ POINTS** Less than 5% of buyer cash involved. Seller carries most of the financing at lower than market rates with no balloons in less than 7 years. No negative cash flows projected beyond the first year. Contract sales, no credit checks.
4	**PRICE**	**① POINT** 10% or more above the reasonable market price. **Consider only if financing is excellent.**	**② POINTS** Within + or – 5% of market price.	**③ POINTS** At least 10% or more below market price.
5	**PROPERTY CONDITION**	**① POINT** **Consider only if price is excellent.** Needs major cosmetic and structural improvements. At least 10% of purchase price will need to be spent immediately to make unit rentable. Improvements do not significantly improve the rent roll because of quality of tenants and location. Improvements not to increase value more than 10% above purchase price. Usually associated with poor locations. Possible to find this property in excellent locations where prices are so high that improvements do not make units acceptable to renters. Viewed as making a larger down payment (for improvements) and receiving an averaged priced property.	**② POINTS** This is the true fixer-upper! Cosmetic improvements would be nice but not immediately necessary. Costs not to exceed 5% of the purchase price. Cosmetic improvements immediately affect the value upwards and make the property more desirable, saleable, and attractive. Not much structural work (if any) is necessary... only paint, landscaping, drapes, and other inexpensive improvements. This type of property should not be bought if the buyer does not have the time or mental capacity to undertake supervision of improvements. This property can prove to be the most profitable in the short run. The worst house in the best neighborhood.	**③ POINTS** Newer property or older property with recent renovation. No problems, clean inside and out ... good landscaping. New components to replace major items. May have been a recent fixer-upper project which is being sold by a don't wanter at an excellent price. No work necessary before renter moves in. Solid property with a hassle factor of zero. Quick closing, quick rent-up, quick cash flow.

- Analyze and assign a point value to each factor of a property.
- If in doubt about a point value always pick the lower number.
- Add up the numbers and totals.
- The lowest acceptable score is 9, the highest possible is 15.
- Greater fools always buy property in the 9, 10, 11 range.
- Great investors always buy property in the 12, 13, 14, 15 range.

TOTAL SCORE

FIGURE 8.3 The five areas of analysis.

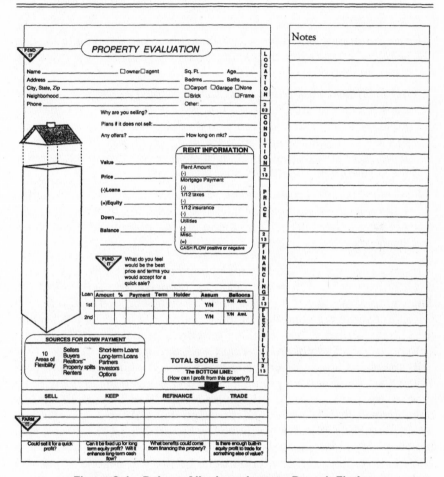

Figure 8.4   Robert Allen's real estate BargainFinder.
Go to www.multiplestreamsofincome.com for a printable copy of this form. Keyword: BargainFinder.

For example, suppose you find a house owned by an out-of-town investor. He is desperate and wants to unload the property ASAP. You call and ask questions about each of your five areas. Let's say this property scores a 3 in seller flexibility, a 2 in location, a 3 in financing (because the seller wants nothing down and is willing to carry the loan himself), a 1 in condition (the property is in a run down condition), and a 2 in price—for a total score of 11. Remember, a property should score at least 12 before you get excited about it. The scoring system also gives you clues on how to negotiate. In this instance, you either need a better price or the seller must fix up the property before he sells it to you.

There are four guidelines to follow when using this system:

Let your fingers do the walking. Never look at a property until you have scored it and believe it has the potential of being a good deal. You don't have time to waste on unmotivated sellers and uncreative real estate agents.

Never fall in love with a property. Remember, you're going to have to sell that property one day. Make it easy on yourself; buy it right on the front end.

Never be afraid to ask sellers questions about their property. Even if the questions seem probing. For example, ask the seller, "If you don't mind me asking, what do you plan on doing with the proceeds from this sale?" In other words, what are you going to do with the money? It would be very helpful to you, as a creative problem solver, to know the answer to this question.

Remember, the first person to mention a number loses. When asking the seller questions on the phone, try not to mention numbers yourself. Always let the seller tell you the numbers. It could save you thousands of dollars.

If a property scores well in your phone analysis, you'll want to do a physical inspection. When you inspect a property, you verify all of the data you took over the phone. You verify the neighborhood. You verify the price. You verify the condition of the property, the financial details, and the seller's flexibility. It's one thing to score a property over the phone, sight unseen, and another to physically walk through the unit.

By the way, I always recommend that before you buy you look in your Yellow Pages and enlist a reputable property inspection company to go through the property to do a thorough report. They'll check things like plumbing, electrical, roof, foundation, and many of the details that you would most likely miss. It's worth the few hundred dollars it will cost you. But always try to have the seller pay for it as part of your negotiation. You don't have to have the inspection done before you negotiate, but you should at least make your offer contingent on or subject to the inspection. If the inspection uncovers a lot of problems, you may decide at that time to back out.

After you've completed your physical inspection, if the property still scores well on your BargainFinder form, then you're ready to go to the next step.

Critical Activity 2. *Funding:* How to Finance Bargain Properties

How do you negotiate the best deal possible? Actually, the negotiation has already begun. It started with your very first contact with the seller and won't stop until the property is yours. You see, negotiation consists of three basic activities:

Gathering information

Building trust

Solving problems

Let me give you three words that describe a master negotiator: friendly, fair, and flexible.

Most people assume that business is just the opposite—that negotiation is a battle in which one person wins and one loses. They believe that you create competitive advantage by using intimidation—that it's "my way or the highway." This may work in the short run, but in the long run, being friendly, fair, and flexible always wins. Even if the seller is still operating from the old philosophy of intimidation, competition, and inflexibility, always be friendly, fair, and flexible.

Perhaps the following tale will help explain my point.

Aesop's Fable

A dispute arose between the North Wind and the Sun, each claiming that he was stronger than the other. At last they agreed to try their powers upon a traveler, to see which could strip him of his cloak. The North Wind had the first try; and, gathering up all his force for the attack, he came whirling furiously down upon the man and caught up his cloak as though he would wrest it from him by one single effort. But the harder the North Wind blew, the more closely the man wrapped his cloak round himself. Then came the turn of the Sun. At first he beamed gently upon the traveler, who soon unclasped his cloak and walked on with it hanging loosely about his shoulders. The Sun then shone forth in his full strength; and the man, before he had gone many steps, was glad to throw off his cloak and complete his journey more lightly clad.

Gentle persuasion is better than force. There's a rule of thumb concerning negotiation. The stronger the tactics, the greater the resistance. The quickest way to lessen the resistance is to develop rapport. Then, and only then, are you able to exert influence. Friends help friends get ahead. Enemies don't. If you want to get ahead, be a friend. Your philosophy is win-win. Both parties should feel that they have achieved a fair settlement.

The Five Most Powerful Nothing-Down Techniques

When I first wrote *Nothing Down,* the number one all-time best-selling real estate book, very few people believed that you could actually buy property for little or no money down. I had to prove it by issuing my now-famous challenge to the *Los Angeles Times:*

> *"Send me to any city. Take away my wallet. Give me $100*
> *for living expenses. And in 72 hours, I'll buy an excellent*
> *piece of property using none of my own money."*

With an *LA Times* reporter by my side, in 57 hours I bought seven properties worth $722,715. And I still had $20 left over. The headline read BUYING HOME WITHOUT CASH: BOASTFUL INVESTOR ACCEPTS TIMES CHALLENGE—AND WINS. Yes, these techniques work. In the next few pages I'll teach you 5 of the 50 most powerful creative financing techniques.

Actually, creative financing didn't start with me. Between 1483 and 1492, Columbus was repeatedly turned down by several different partners and governments in his quest to find someone who would finance his voyage to the New World. King Ferdinand and Queen Isabella of Spain eventually became his lucky investment partners. America herself was a nothing-down deal!

— $$$ —

WIT & WISDOM
I don't think I'll get married again. I'll just find a woman I don't like and give her a house.

LEWIS GRIZZARD

As I said earlier, nothing down doesn't mean there is no cash involved. It just means that it's not *your* cash. Besides, there are other flexible ways to buy property that don't require cash. I want to open your mind to the possibility that solutions exist besides those that the conventional banks and real estate agents espouse. Not every one of the following techniques works every time. They are like notes on a piano. . . . You use them when the circumstances dictate.

First we'll address the mind-set of a creative real estate investor. When I look at a property for sale, I see different things than most buyers do. I'm looking for flexibility. Several players in the purchasing drama might be able to provide pieces of the puzzle:

You and your assets

The property owner and his or her needs and goals

The property itself

The future buyer

The current or future renters

The real estate agent

The current mortgage holders

The future mortgage lenders

The current or future partner(s)

The current or future investor(s)

As I'm walking through a property, I'm asking myself questions, "Where is the flexibility in this deal?" "Which of the players in this drama has an incentive to help me make this transaction?" "Which of the players might be willing to lend me money, or some other asset, to help me solve the seller's problem?"

Nothing-down technique 1: Ultimate paper out

Many sellers own their properties free and clear of mortgages and prefer to act as the bank. By carrying the financing on the property themselves, they earn higher rates of return than a bank would offer on money secured by solid property. Obviously, such "private" lenders are much more lenient than conventional financial institutions, which require detailed financial statements, stable monthly income, and perfect credit. When a seller carries all the financing, I call this the *ultimate-paper-out technique.* No cash changes hands. The buyer starts making monthly payments and the seller starts receiving interest and principal payments just like a bank. How often does a transaction like this happen? Very rarely. One in a hundred. It takes luck, chutzpah, and quick feet. But these types of deals do happen. The story you are about to read is recent and true. It illustrates how some sellers are willing to sell their property with absolutely zero money down . . . and even pay Realtor fees and closing costs.

Hi Bob,

Just before enrolling in your real estate training, I had been out of work for about nine months, with all lifetime savings exhausted. I was forced to accept a job (hate that word anymore) out of the area. We made the move and "settled in." We soon determined that the area had a very high cost of living with subpar wages, so we resigned ourselves to never being able to own a personal residence again (in this area at least). Then we started using the techniques you taught us and found a "textbook" nothing-down property.

This house was on the market less than 2 weeks when I found it listed on Cyberhomes. An immediate drive-by was done, with an immediate phone call to the listing agent attempted. We knew this property was hot. The listing agent was not available so I spoke to the desk agent who proceeded to explain to me how she worked with potential buyers and how we had to come in to the office to be pre-qualified and how she couldn't show the property to just anyone . . . Well, I HUNG UP and called a more accommodating agent with whom I had developed a relationship (ironically from the same listing office). We were shown the property a few hours later. Of all the properties my wife and I had looked at, this was the only one she enjoyed walking through, smiling all the time, giving me a quick thumbs-up. Although she wanted the "perfect" home—one we could move into without any work whatsoever, she still said OK to this one willingly—it did need some work. We thought about it overnight and put the offer in the next day.

> Asking price 104,900 (10k under market).
> It had a new roof, new carpet, a remodeled bath and was owned by a church.
> It was on ⅗ acre (most lots in this area are ¼ acre).
> It also included the stove and dishwasher.

We offered full price at $104,900 with the owner "to assist" on the full amount of closing costs of $5,600. No money down. They accepted. No changes, no counteroffer. We closed in 5 weeks. During the walk-thru prior to closing we noticed 4 additional items, a new refrigerator and wood stove remained as did all the window treatments. We had already prearranged a delivery of oil but to our surprise they had refilled it even though it was still ¼ full and our responsibility. When we mentioned the items at closing they replied "Merry Christmas." Then the closing agent handed us OUR check in the amount of $1,400 Money Back At Closing!

We moved in 4 days later, the day after Christmas. My wife and I did not exchange gifts on Christmas and our son received fewer than he wished for; but it was the merriest Christmas we have ever had.

Thanks Bob! Regards,

Aden W. Curtis

Aden W. Curtis

I read recently that the average couple saves for three years to buy their first home. By saving $250 per month, it would take three years to save just $10,000. In the preceding success story, being "creative" instead of "average" enabled this couple to move into a home with a built-in profit of almost $10,000 *plus* an extra $1,400 in cash at closing. By the time the average couple buys their first property in three years, this creative couple will be into their second or third property, having parlayed their profits into $100,000.* Can you see the difference?

One of the main reasons that sellers won't accept nothing-down deals like this one is fear. They want to feel secure that the buyer will make the payments as promised. If the buyer does not, the seller's equity is truly at risk. They might be forced to repossess a property in a damaged condition with all of the hassles that entails. As a creative investor, your job is to alleviate the seller's anxieties . . . to solve the security issue in ways that don't require cash. Here are three options:

1. *The blanket mortgage.* If the seller objects to your low-money-down deal, it's probably because he or she is concerned that you haven't invested anything and therefore have nothing to lose. In this case, offer to increase the security so that you would have something to lose by defaulting on your agreement. Offer the seller a blanket mortgage that collateralizes the real estate you are purchasing *plus* other collateral. Perhaps you have equity in another property or own a vacant recreational lot in the mountains or even hold the title to your car.

    Make sure that the seller agrees to release your extra collateral items from the mortgage upon certain conditions—such as a perfect payment record for 12 straight months, or a new appraisal showing

---

* If you'd like a special report entitled *How to Save $100,000 on Your Next Home,* go to www.multiplestreamsofincome.com and enter the keyword Save $100,000, or call my office at 801-852-8700. You'll like this one.

substantial equity, or a certain amount of "fix-up" investment on your part.

Often, by offering the blanket mortgage, you'll give the seller confidence to accept your "creative" offer.

2. *Term life insurance with the seller as beneficiary.* Offer to buy a term life insurance policy on your life for the amount of money you owe the seller. This gesture lets the seller realize that you are willing to help resolve the seller's concerns. It will cost you very little . . . and can buy a lot of security for the seller.

3. *The creation of paper.* Sometimes sellers are afraid that if you don't make the payments they might get the home back. And that's the last thing they want. In this case, rather than a blanket mortgage (i.e., security on several properties), offer the sellers security on other properties you own *instead of* the property they are selling. The sellers might prefer collateral on equities other than the property they are trying to sell. For instance, suppose you own a home worth $200,000 with a loan of $160,000. You could offer this equity as collateral for a property you are trying to buy. I call this technique *the creation of paper* because you are creating a note against equity you have in another asset.

After you've alleviated the fears about security, if the seller is still balking at your nothing-down offer, appeal to his or her greed. Here's a technique to raise the price and lower the terms.

Always start your negotiation at a lower price, but be willing to raise your price *if the seller will agree to lower his or her terms.* Here is a sample dialogue:

"Mr. Seller, let me show you how it could be to your advantage to accept my nothing-down offer. Your equity is $10,000. If I gave you $10,000 for a down payment, where would you invest it? Probably in a bank at 5 percent interest or less. Instead of giving you $10,000 in cash, I'll give you an $11,000 note for your equity bearing an interest rate of 10 percent. This means you'll earn an extra $1,000 immediately. It would take two years to earn $1,000 in your bank account. Plus, I'll pay you 10 percent on the note—a full 5 percent higher than any lending institution."

Once sellers are "educated," they are often more willing to be creative.

Nothing-down technique 2: The lease/option

I'm going to show you how to afford almost twice the home on half the money. Sound good?

Where do you start? In the newspaper, under the Houses for Rent section, searching for these clues: "rent to own," "lease to buy," "option to buy," "lease option." What you're looking for is a desperate seller who has purchased another property and is now stuck with two houses . . . and two house payments. By "willing to rent with an option," this seller is announcing that he or she doesn't need cash . . . just a willing renter who might eventually want to buy. That's you. Let's build our example.

It's a $100,000 house with a $60,000 loan and payments on the underlying loan of $600 per month. The seller advertises in the paper, looking for someone to rent the property to help meet the mortgage payment. Why could this be good for you? Three reasons: (1) It's no cash down. (2) The payments are lower than a straight purchase. (3) You can lock in the price today hoping that prices increase rapidly before your option runs out.

There are three things to ask for that can make this even better.

1. Try to lock in the option price at today's price. If the seller wants to make the option at an inflated price in the future, then you are really just renting . . . and that's not good enough. You want to lock in a bargain.

2. Always ask for the longest option term possible—two years minimum, three is better, and five is highly unlikely but worth asking for.

3. Ask that your monthly rent be credited toward the eventual purchase price. "Will you credit $100 of the monthly rent toward the eventual purchase price if I am a model tenant and make my payments to you on a timely and hassle-free basis?"

Lease/option example: Suppose our seller in this example agrees to an $800 monthly rent and a purchase price of $110,000 in three years, with a $100 per month credit from the rent going toward the purchase price. You wait three years, enjoying your lower monthly payments; you do some minor repairs to make the property look real good; you have the property appraised. It comes in at $125,000. Your purchase price is $110,000 less the $100 a month credit you negotiated, which amounts to $3,600. Deduct this from $110,000 and your purchase price is $106,400. Which means you have a built-in equity of $125,000 less $106,400, or $18,600. Not bad for a renter.

Now you have two options: Buy the property yourself or sell it at a profit If you want to buy the property, you obtain a new loan for $112,000—enough to pay off the seller and pay your closing costs—and you're now the owner. If you don't want to own the property, you start advertising to sell the house about six months before the option is due to expire, find a cash buyer for $125,000, and pocket your $18,000 cash profit.

Now, how does this work in real life?

WIT & WISDOM

For an idea which, at first, does not seem absurd, there is no hope.

ALBERT EINSTEIN

One of my students found a very unique home in Palm Springs, California, which had a swimming pool in the shape of a piano. Yes, it had once belonged to the great Liberace. It was available on a two-year lease option for $400,000 with payments of $2,000 a month. The buyer (my student) negotiated a $500 credit of the monthly payment toward the eventual purchase price. She leased the home on a weekly basis to vacationers, and because these weekly rentals generated a monthly total greater than $2,000, she was able to earn a nice positive cash flow. In two years, she sold the home for $425,000. After deducting $12,000 in lease credits, her option price was $388,000, netting a profit of $37,000—not to mention the positive cash flow from rental.

Not too bad for nothing down!

Nothing-down technique 3: ABC (anything but cash)

Often, sellers will exchange their equity for valuable items other than cash.

One of my seminar students used a motorcycle as a down payment. Another traded attorney services. There is no end to the things you can offer as all or part of the down payment. My graduates have successfully offered, at various times, the following:

Carpentry services

A future inheritance

A personal, unsecured note

A vacant recreational lot

A car

Once, when I was speaking to a group in Colorado Springs, a bearded man approached me. He explained that he had purchased a copy of *Nothing Down* at a bargain-basement sale the day after he was fired from his job at a radio station. He got excited and started applying the techniques. His first property was a duplex being sold by a highly motivated military officer who was being transferred to a nearby state. Necessity being the mother of invention, our unemployed, cashless, nothing-down buyer offered to pay moving expenses for the military man in exchange for the down payment to buy the duplex. He borrowed a friend's credit card, rented a U-Haul truck, loaded up the seller's furniture and drove with him to the next city. Oh, by the way, this was the first of 17 more properties he bought in the next 12 months.

Whatever it takes, as long as it's ABC: *anything but cash.*

Nothing-down technique 4: Divide and conquer

Sometimes you don't have a lump sum in cash for a down payment, but using a few little-known techniques, you can accumulate enough credits and cash to equal the money necessary to close.

For example, suppose you are searching through the MLS and find a duplex listed for sale. The sale price is $210,000 but in the remarks section of the listing it indicates that the seller will carry financing, with a small down payment. He is highly motivated. You discover that one side of the duplex is rented for $1,000 a month; the renters have a security deposit for $1,000. You are hoping to live in the other side.

The total loans against the unit are $175,000—an assumable first mortgage of $150,000 and a second mortgage of $25,000 with the previous seller. You discover that the real estate broker is the seller's friend and is charging only a 3 percent commission. The current seller just wants out and is willing to walk away with $10,000 in cash, knowing full well that the unit is worth at least $210,000. If you can find $10,000, you can buy this unit for $25,000 below market. You don't have $10,000 in cash. Let's see if we can figure it out.

Divide and conquer idea 1: Rents and deposits. As part of the purchase, you will receive a credit for the $1,000 security deposit for the existing tenant. Many states and provinces allow the buyer to legally use these deposits as a credit toward the down payment. In this case, it would lower your cash needed at closing by $1,000. When the tenant moves out, you'll be required to return this deposit. By then, you will have found a new tenant with new security deposit.

If you close on the day the rents are due, you can collect $1,000 in rent from the tenant and use this toward your down payment. With the $1,000 credit and $1,000 in collected rent, you have only an $8,000 problem.

Divide and conquer idea 2: Assume sellers obligations. One of the main obligations of the seller at closing is the real estate commission—usually 6 percent of the sale price. In this example, the seller will be obligated to pay a 3 percent commission to his Realtor friend; that's 3 percent of $185,000, or $5,500. Having discovered this, you ask the Realtor if she would consider a $6,500 note in lieu of a $5,500 cash commission. She agrees to accept $2,000 in cash and a $3,500 note. Hmmm . . . it's better than nothing. And you just saved yourself from having to come up with that $3,500 in cash. So, by using the rents and deposits plus the Realtor's commission, you've reduced your $10,000 problem to $4,500. We've still got a ways to go.

You discover that one of the main reasons the seller wants to sell is to get rid of some old debts—a $2,000 bill to a hospital for some emergency surgery. You ask the seller, politely, if he would allow you to assume these debts instead of having to pay cash at closing. The seller says he needs assurance that he will be released from the obligation. You approach the hospital and ask them to release the seller from his obligation and to verify this in writing. Then you arrange for payments to the hospital that meet your needs. In this way, the debt is resolved and you get in with less cash. That just knocked $2,000 more off your cash problem . . . $2,500 to go.

Divide and conquer idea 3: Credit cards. If your credit is good, use a cash advance from your current credit card to obtain the cash. Yes, it stretches your financial limits, but if the property is a great deal, you don't want to end up just a few thousand short. You draw $1,000 from your credit card cash advance line. That leaves you with $1,500 to go.

Divide and conquer idea 4: Get a personal loan from your banker. You could sit down with the branch manager of your bank and ask for a personal loan to help you with the down payment. You explain that you've been a good client for several years and need the extra cash on a short-term basis. Let's suppose your banker says no. This is your clue to find another banker. But this time, *before* you open an account, explain to the branch manager what your long-term goal is—to establish a relationship and to build a track record over time that will allow you to borrow larger and larger amounts to take advantage of short-term moneymaking opportunities. Find a banker who is amenable to this. Then begin to establish this kind of relationship.

> ── **$$$** ──
>
> **WIT & WISDOM**
>
> Life is the only game in which the object of the game is to learn the rules.
>
> ASHLEIGH BRILLIANT

Divide and conquer idea 5: Furniture and property splits. You determine that the vacant unit is furnished with a working fridge, a couch, several beds, and a microwave oven. In the attached garage, there is an old motorcycle that the seller agrees to give you because it doesn't work. You hold your garage sale, with permission of the owner, and raise an extra $750. By the way, another way to raise money is by splitting off pieces of the property you are buying. I once bought a house with money raised by selling off the back portion of a deep lot to one of the neighbors. A friend of mine bought an apartment building by selling off all of the antiques in the furnished units.

After raising $750 from the garage sale, we're still $750 short.

Divide and conquer idea 6: Use discounts of existing privately held mortgages. You have already determined that the $25,000 second mortgage on this property is held by a private individual. You contact this mortgage holder and offer him $15,000 cash for his $25,000 note. It is commonplace for a note holder to accept a deep discount for cash. Suppose he accepts, where do you get the cash? By going to a small finance company, you arrange for a new hard-money second mortgage of $18,000. The new mortgage pays off the underlying $25,000 second mortgage at a discount. After closing costs and points, you have $1,500 left over to complete the down payment.

Here is a summary:

Credit for security deposit	$1,000
Cash from rent collected	$1,000
Credit for Realtor commissions	$3,500
Credit for assuming hospital bill	$2,000
Cash from credit cards	$1,000
Personal loan from banker	$0

Cash from garage sale	$750
Net cash from new 2nd mortgage	$1,500
Net credits and cash	+$10,750
Needed for down payment	−$10,000
Available for closing costs	$750

The closing takes place and everyone leaves happy.

The old second mortgage holder walks out with $15,000 cash. He's happy.

The new second mortgage holder lends $18,000, secured by a property worth $210,000. He's happy.

The Realtor walks out of closing with $2,000 cash and a note for $3,500. She's happy.

The renters still live in the unit next door to you. They're happy.

The credit card company that lent you $1,000 is making 18 percent. They're happy.

The seller of the duplex walks out of the closing with some cash—not a lot—but enough to close this chapter of his life and move forward.

You walk out of closing with a duplex valued at $210,000 with total mortgages of only $168,000—and you have a built-in real estate equity of $42,000 minus the personal obligations to the hospital, the Realtor, and your credit card.

Nothing-down technique 5: OPR

You've heard of OPM—*other people's money.* I like to broaden the concept to OPR—*other people's resources.*

Say this out loud right now: "If I don't have it, somebody does." If you don't have the cash or credit or financial statement or even a job, somebody does—and might be willing to lend it to you under the right circumstances. For example, suppose someone approaches you with the following deal:

> *I've located a great property worth at least $100,000. I can purchase it for $80,000, with only $5,000 down. But I have to close in 72 hours. I'm a bit short of cash for the moment. . . . I need a partner. Would you be my partner for half of the profit? I'll do all of the work, manage the property, and do some minor fix-up to get it into marketable condition. I'll handle the sale and all of the details. I reasonably expect to turn over this property in six months for a full $20,000 profit. You'll get your $5,000 back plus 50 percent of the profit, or $10,000. That's 200 percent on your money in six months. Interested?*

How did you feel as you were reading this proposal? That's how your partner will feel. People love to make money. If you can show them how to do it with you, you'll never lack for people to lend you what you need. Suppose they say, "I don't have $5,000 in cash." You say, "Can you borrow it? How? From your life insurance policy, from a credit card, from your retirement plan, from your banker, from your house—no matter." The deal doesn't care where the money comes from—as long as it's there in 72 hours.

Sometimes you don't need cash. You need someone to help you qualify for the long-term loan. I bought my first major apartment building for nothing down. However, it required a new first mortgage. Because I couldn't qualify for a large loan, I asked a partner to qualify for the new loan—in exchange for half of the profit. He provided only his signature and a financial statement. That's it. And he became a 50 percent partner in a beautiful building. You see, if *you* don't have it, somebody does. The key is to convince that person to lend it to you.

Every state, province, or country has different rules about borrowing money from potential investors. You should definitely check with a local attorney to make sure that your fund-raising activities are within the bounds of the law. If you don't, you could get into serious trouble—and even risk going to prison. It's also a good idea to have a local real estate attorney draw up your partnership agreement.

But in many instances, a partnership is good for both parties. For example, one of my students living in the San Francisco area received a call from his creative Realtor. Here was the deal. Several months earlier, a corporate executive in the Bay area received a transfer to another state. This meant he and his wife would have to sell their home. Because the transfer was sudden, the company offered to buy the executive's home, which was appraised at $322,000. His company paid the full amount and turned the home over to a holding company to prepare it for sale. Six months went by, and because of an extremely poor marketing effort, the home remain unsold. The large corporation made the decision to unload the property.

My student offered $242,000 cash, with the buyer to obtain a new loan and the corporation to pay $5,000 of the buyer's closing costs and loan fees. The company countered with $245,000 and agreed to pay the $5,000. The property was professionally inspected and found to be in immaculate condition.

Now it would need a new loan and a large down payment. The buyers qualified for a 90 percent new loan, but still needed $25,000 for the down payment. They were able to borrow $15,000 from their own retirement plan, but they were still $10,000 short. Time to look for a partner. Luckily, a family member agreed to lend them $10,000

Remember, if you don't have it, somebody does. Most beginners start by borrowing something from someone else. Don't be shy. Isn't your dream worth it?

There are literally dozens of powerful nothing-down techniques—far more than I can share with you in this book. Search my web site at www.multiplestreamsofincome.com under the keyword Nothing Down, or call my office at 801-852-8700, and I'll send you a special report that includes several more of my favorites techniques.

Critical Activity 3. *Farming:* How to Harvest Your Profits

To review, the three critical activities to your real estate success are as follows:

Finding deals

Funding deals

Farming deals

A word about *farming:* This is my term for harvesting your profit. Creative financing should not be used to make a bad deal good . . . only to make a good deal great. If it's a bad deal—if there is no profit potential—don't buy it, even for nothing down.

I once was approached by a man who bragged of purchasing a $150,000 home two years earlier with "not a single penny down." He thought I would be impressed. Then I started to ask him some tough questions.

Q. What is your cash flow situation?

A. Payments, $1,400. Rents $1,000. In the red $400 per month for 24 months. Total out of pocket, about $10,000. Ouch!

Q. Has the property gone up in value?

A. No. He overpaid when he bought it. It was worth less than what he paid.

Q. Where is the profit in this deal?

A. There is no profit. There never was a profit. This property should never have been bought.

He should have asked himself these tough questions *before* he committed himself to the purchase. Before you buy, you should have an idea of how you intend to harvest your profit. There are two basic ways:

1. *Buy and hold:* Is it your intention to buy property and become a landlord?

2. *Flipping:* Is it your intention to buy property below market and resell it quickly for profit?

Buying and holding is about *cash-flow* profits. Flipping is about *equity* profits. I've always advocated that, at a minimum, my students should do both: Buy at least one property per year to hold in your long-term portfolio, and flip at least one property per year for short-term profit. In Chapter 9, we'll talk a lot more about flipping.

Each of these strategies requires different skills:

Strategy	Critical Skill
Buy and hold	Management expertise—finding excellent long-term tenants
Flipping	Buying-right skill and marketing expertise—selling quickly

In Chapter 9, I'll share with you more ways to earn huge profits from real estate bargains.

I have shared the full nothing-down system with hundreds of thousands of people over the past 20 years with incredible success. Here are just a few of the letters I've received:

Dear Robert,

First of all, let me introduce myself. My name is Bernie Worby. I am sure that that does not mean much to you, but last year you were responsible for a very good real estate deal which I made.

Last June I signed up for your training and learned a great deal of very helpful information and techniques. In October I completed a deal which paid for the course many times over. The details are as follows:

There was an apartment for sale for $79K on which I made an offer, but we could not even get close to making a deal. But then my real estate agent, who was also my partner in taking your course went and talked to the seller directly, not his broker. She found out he also had two other apartments which had not been listed yet. It turns out he wanted $300K for the package, so we previewed them, and then the seller, his broker, my agent and myself had a meeting to discuss the properties. That night I went to the office and looked at all the cash flows and property prices and made an offer of $240K with a 10% down payment, the seller carrying back a 10% second and the bank taking an 80% first position, hoping it wasn't too low and insult the seller. The next day he countered with $245K which I quickly accepted. The best part was the appraisal came in at $283,000 and with this the bank based their loan on the appraisal rather than the contract. So at closing the seller carried back his 10% and the bank gave me a 90% first mortgage at 8.14% interest and I walked away with rents and deposits. This was truly a no money down deal and all three properties have a good positive cash flow.

Thank you very much for making this happen for me. My agent also thanks you. Because of the knowledge you have given her, she made a good commission on the sale.

Thanks a million, Bernie Worby

Hi Bob:

When my husband, Kenbob, was 21 he purchased the house next door to his parents, not really knowing what he was doing at all. It was for sale so he decided to look at it. The Realtor said he could get owner financing, so he bought it with $1K down. Years later he found out the owner had 11 others she would have sold for little or no cash. So *now* we always ask the seller, "Do you have any other property you are selling?"

We got involved with each other 11 years later. We decided we wanted to do some type of business together. I was a baker, he was a carpenter. We looked into bakeries, but it seemed like buying into a job. Then we talked real estate. His house had always been very good to him. I'm a "readaholic," and began reading on the subject. Of course, I read your book. I said, "I could do this." So we began looking at houses and learning value. And we heard about your seminar. We were living basically paycheck to paycheck, but living very frugally and saving here and there. We scraped the cash together (like $3,800) and Kenbob went to the class, and I went vicariously through his experience. It was a great motivator and jump-starter!! We bought our first place together 2 months later. In the beginning of 1999 I was updating our financial report (8.5 years since our first purchase together) and we had a net worth of just over $1,000,000!!!

To think back now, 10 years ago we were tenants, 9 years ago bought our own home, and 5 months later bought our first rental. We have sold a few here and there but now have close to 100 rental units!

We have obviously made quite a bit of money on that $3,800 investment. Our best deal was just this past year, from a tidbit learned through your seminar. We had learned to always write "and/or assigns" on all our purchase offers. This past year we got a signed offer for a place for $25K. We flipped the property to another investor for $35K. We basically put about 5 hours into this deal and walked away with $10K.

Thanks so much for the great inspiration you've been and continue to be.

Kenbob and Jill Lee Whiting

Kenbob and Jill Lee Whiting

Bob,

Hello. My name is Todd Ballentine. I feel like I know you from reading all your books. We met briefly on the phone in 1980. I called you one night after hearing about what you did (I was still a student at BYU) and wanted advice on whether I should buy condos or houses. You told me either could work and the techniques were in your new book coming out soon. I moved and got married, went to work for Bank of America and found your book at a store across from work. I read it chapter by chapter standing up at lunch. (Sorry, I was broke. However I did later buy a copy and have bought probably 10 or 15 copies of *Nothing Down* and *Creating Wealth* for relatives and friends.) Anyway, I have used your techniques for years—got my first home for nothing down in Concord, California, in 1981 (yucky time for rates) and the next year using a photocopy of your lease option contract in *Creating Wealth* bought my neighbor's house with a Visa cash advance of $1,000 down. You said to ask for credit on the monthly lease payment so I asked for 100% credit for every payment and . . . they agreed! I sold it in a double escrow 2 years later and made $47,000. I never said thanks. So *thanks!*

I then bought a Subway sandwich franchise (4 actually) and hated it, sold them on contract. My buyer stiffed me and went bankrupt and I was forced to follow about a year later. Anyway now I am in Oregon and am having a wonderful time being creative in buying RE for little or nothing down into the millennium. With my bankruptcy and all that mess still on my credit and with no job for most of this period since I moved here I have bought 22 units (9 properties) all with less than $400 down and most with cash back at escrow (my personal best was a check back for $3,000 and a partitioned lot free and clear worth $35,000). I would be glad to supply additional details if it would be helpful. Anyway, I look forward to being on your *Multiple Streams of Income* conference call tomorrow. Sometime I would enjoy meeting you again.

Sincerely,

Todd Ballentine

Todd Ballentine
Roseburg, Oregon

CHAPTER 9

*The secret of success in life is for a man to be ready
for his opportunity when it comes.*
BENJAMIN DISRAELI

YOUR FIFTH STREAM
A Fortune in Foreclosures
and Flippers

In the Chapter 8 we learned how to *find, fund,* and *farm* real estate bargains. I spent so much time teaching you about creative financing that I didn't make a clear distinction between stream 4 and stream 5. Stream 4 is *buy-and-hold* real estate. In this chapter, I'll teach you about stream 5: *buying and flipping.* The main distinction between these two streams is time: long term versus short term.

Before I launch into the full-blown discussion of short-term flips, I want to remind you of the power of a long-term buy-and-hold approach (stream 4). It's very similar to the Warren Buffett buy-and-hold approach in the stock market.

If you're fully vested in a property through long periods of time, you'll eventually participate in every major move in price appreciation. For example, since my first book was published in 1980, there have been many ups and downs in the real estate market. During these ups and downs, real estate investors tend to make the same mistakes that stock market investors make. They buy when everyone is excited (*buy high*) and sell when blood is running in the streets (*sell low*). Then they have the audacity to say, "I've tried real estate. Didn't work for me." Nobody makes money by buying high and selling low. As in the markets, you need to be buying when the sheep are selling and selling when the sheep are buying.

The statement I made in my first book, still holds true.

"Don't wait to buy real estate. Buy real estate and wait."

In 1982, a 24-year-old young man named Tom Painter came to one of my seminars. This is how he recalls it.

Being a college student in 1982, I didn't have the financial resources such as credit and money to invest in property. With only a dream and desire, I started my investment career. It took me a year to find a property that I could buy with a small down payment.

I was running ads in the paper when I received a call from the owner of a four-unit apartment building. He was an older gentleman who was tired of the management. The value was approximately $75,000. He had purchased it many years earlier, and the property was free and clear of all loans.

We negotiated a price of $60,000, with $5,000 down. Instead of going to the bank and obtaining new financing, he agreed to carry the contract for 15 years at 10 percent interest. I would make payments directly to him of $591.03 a month.

I closed the transaction on the first of the month. At closing, I was credited with the security deposits of $800 and the rents of an additional $800. Since my first mortgage payment wasn't due for 30 days, I was able to use the rents and deposits toward the down payment. Therefore, my actual down payment was approximately $3,400.

Fifteen years later, through the ups and downs of the real estate market, the loan was eventually paid off. Today, it's free and clear of all loans, with a value of $180,000. Better still, it pumps out cash of at least $1,600 every single month.

Same Strategy, Just Add Zeros

In 1997, I came across a similar situation. The seller had purchased an apartment complex 10 years earlier and had experienced a nice profit. He had grown tired of the management. The property consisted of seven buildings with a value of $1.8 million.

We negotiated a purchase price of $1,650,000, with nothing down. He got his price and I got my terms. We have improved the properties and increased the rents.

If all goes well, the properties will be paid for in 22 years.

I've been asked why would I put up with the hassle of rental units. The answer is simple. I have a big "why": My son is 10 years old and is autistic. Maybe you saw the movie *The Rainman,* with Tom Cruise and Dustin Hoffman. Dustin Hoffman plays the part of a man with autism.

My son will need financial help his entire life. In 1993, at the age of 34, I had a heart attack. This was a major wake-up call for me. My son will outlive me by at least 30 to 40 years. I am trying to put systems in place to take care of my family if something happens to me.

If you have a big enough *why,* you will figure out a *how.*

I'm proud to say that Tom came to work for me in the mid-1980s and within five years, through character and persistence, became president and full partner in Challenge Systems, Inc., our nationwide seminar company. Today, he still practices many of the streams of income you'll learn in this book. His long-term real estate strategy (stream 4) has paid off handsomely.

But the short-term strategy has its place as well.

What Creates Short-Term Bargains?

Real estate is illiquid. In other words, it can't be sold quickly. The stock market, by contrast, is liquid—if you buy a stock this minute, you can resell it 30 seconds later. Because real estate is slow to sell, smart real estate investors can earn huge profits by assuming the risk of illiquidity.

We know that, given enough time, a property we buy below the market today can eventually be remarketed for a profit. In the meantime, we may have to make monthly payments, resolve a bad tenant situation, upgrade or renovate the property, resolve a zoning issue—or find a solution to a myriad of other problems. In other words, we make money by solving problems. The more problems we solve, the more money we make.

In Chapter 8, we learned of at least 20 problems that may force people to sell their property. The more desperate people become, the quicker they need a sale and the more flexible they will become. The only way to effect a quick sale is to do one of two things: Lower the price, or come up with attractive financial terms—such as a low down payment. As a real estate bargain hunter, you must have something at wholesale—price or terms and preferably both. If not, don't buy.

More bargains are available in the area of foreclosures than in any other area of real estate.

Bargain Opportunity 1: Foreclosures

Why would individuals walk away from perfectly good property? Why would they be willing to risk ruining their credit rating? Why would they face the embarrassment of having to be forced out of their home?

Well, for whatever reason, according to the Mortgage Bankers Association, over 400,000 homes went into foreclosure last year. . . . That's over 33,500 a month in North America. How many of those do you need to buy to earn enough profit to equal or exceed your current year's salary?

Just one.

One good property bought and sold could support you for a year! In fact, if you persist long enough, I believe you'll find at least one bargain property that's good enough to set you up for life. But you're probably not willing to believe that yet. So let's lower the expectations and assume that sometime in the next five years, with consistent searching, you'll find one excellent property that you can buy at 20 percent below the market. Do you think that's realistic?

Even if real estate is not your "thing," you should at least be willing to learn a few basics so you can buy your personal residence at a substantial discount. If you'd like a free report on "How to Save $100,000 on Your Next Home," go to www.multiplestreamsofincome.com and enter the keyword Save 100K, or call my office at 801-852-8700.

Bargain Hunting in Foreclosures

One of the most effective ways to find a wholesale property is to look for foreclosures. When property owners fail to make the monthly payments on their mortgages, their loans become delinquent. Each lending institution has different guidelines for handling delinquencies.

It usually starts with a nice reminder letter asking the customer to bring his or her payment up-to-date. This is followed by a series of increasingly threatening letters leading up to a formal notice of default. Depending on where you live, the time frame between the notice of default and the actual foreclosure sale can be 90 to 365 days. There may also be a period of redemption after the foreclosure sale. Generally speaking, however, most states have a 90-day foreclosure process with no redemption period. After missing a payment, most homeowners are technically 90 days away from losing their home.

There are four important phases in the foreclosure process:

- Presale, before the lender files the notice of default at the courthouse
- Presale, after the lender files the notice of default
- At the foreclosure sale
- Postsale

Presale: Before notice of default

Each phase has its advantages and its disadvantages. For example, the least competition will occur before the bank files notice of default. In essence, the only people who know of the delinquency are the lender and the property owner. Unfortunately, it is very difficult to find these people. You have to flush them out with your own ads in the newspaper and your own bird-dogging.

Presale: After notice of default

After the notification has been filed at the courthouse, it becomes a matter of public record. There are several foreclosure service companies that search out these notifications and sell a subscription to those who are willing to pay for this information. Generally, the sellers become increasingly flexible as the foreclosure date draws near. Still, there are other buyers to compete with.

At the foreclosure sale

If the property makes it to the foreclosure sale, you have only one option—to pay off the mortgage holder in full. Therefore, it takes a lot of cash to be bidding at a foreclosure sale: If you win the bid, you have only a short time to pay for the property. I encourage you to visit your courthouse, find out when the next foreclosure sale takes place, and show up to watch. You'll find many of the properties due to be sold that day have been withdrawn for various reasons. Of the properties remaining, the vast majority have little equity (the loans and legal fees equal or exceed the value) and therefore no one bids on them and the lending institution takes them back. A small number of properties are really worth bidding on.

Occasionally, there is an exceptional bargain. Sometimes you end up in a bidding war with another investor. One of my beginning students began bidding with a seasoned investor. When the bidding stopped, my young student had won the bid. He was then approached by the seasoned investor, who made him an immediate cash offer of $2,000 to take over his position on the property. He accepted $2,000 in cash for 15 minutes of work. I don't recommend attempting to buy your properties at a foreclosure sale, but it is instructive to watch what goes on.

Postsale

Once lenders have foreclosed on a property, those lenders become remarkably more flexible. Now it's their problem and they want to get rid of it. . . . they actually show many signs of "don't-wanter-itis." They can even be convinced, under the right circumstances, to sell the property to you for less than the mortgage. This is referred to in the industry, as a *short sale.* For instance, suppose a lender foreclosed on a $100,000 house with a $95,000 mortgage. If no one bids at the auction, the lender gets the house back. Many times the lender will consider an offer for less than $95,000 and take a loss to get rid of it.

You can buy foreclosures in any of these stages, pre- and postsale. Let me give you some real examples. (Some of the amounts in these examples have been adjusted for ease of illustration.)

Case Study 1: Preforeclosure/Before Notification of Default

One of my students, Jim, in Florida, located an excellent property by calling on lending institutions and asking if they had any delinquent loans. He found a small lending institution that had a troublesome loan on a small strip center—a few retail stores in a commercial area. The lender's representatives had tried to legally serve the owner of the property with a notice of default but had been unable to find him. They indicated to Jim that if he succeeded in finding the seller, they might be willing to help him purchase the property if it became available. The loan was approximately $375,000 on a property worth about $750,000. The loan payments were delinquent by about $25,000.

Jim began his detective work and finally located the seller in the Cayman Islands. The seller had essentially abandoned the property. Jim asked the seller what he might need for his equity. The seller said he

━━━━━ **$$$** ━━━━━
WIT & WISDOM
A study of economics usually
reveals that the best time to
buy anything is last year.
MARTY ALLEN
━━━━━━━━━━━━━━━━

would be happy with anything—how about $7,000 in cash? Jim explained that the papers would be overnighted to the Cayman islands and, on receipt of the seller's signature, the $7,000 would be wired to the seller's bank to complete the transaction. (See Figure 9.1.)

Therefore, Jim had the potential of acquiring $350,000 in equity for only $7,000 in cash. He approached the lender, who agreed to add the back payments ($25,000) to the original loan ($375,000) and give Jim a new loan in the amount of $400,000. So the bank situation was taken care of.

But the $7,000 down payment was a problem. Jim didn't have it. That's where his understanding of creative financing saved the day: There were dozens of ways to raise the $7,000, and Jim came up with his own extremely creative solution. He discovered in his analysis of the property that the electric company was holding a $7,000 security deposit to secure the tenants' utility bill. He asked the electric company if it might accept a lower security deposit and release some of these funds. The company replied that it would release *all* the funds if Jim would post a *surety bond* for the whole amount. What's a surety bond? A surety bond is like an insurance policy. It bonds (or insures) the electric company in the event tenants default on their utility bills. How much does it cost? In this case, less than $500.

At the closing, here is what transpired: Jim bought a surety bond for $500. This satisfied the electric company, which released $7,000 in cash. This was used as Jim's down payment. The delinquent owner had already signed the papers to sell his building pending the receipt of $7,000. The money from the electric company was sent to the delinquent seller in the

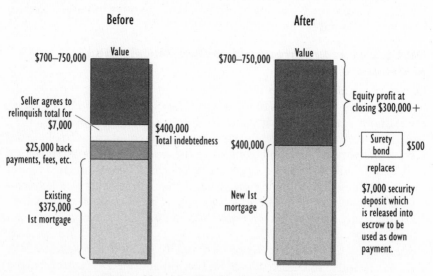

FIGURE 9.1   How the Florida deal came together.

Cayman Islands. Jim walked out of the closing as the proud owner of an excellent property with an instant $350,000 equity profit. He flipped the property a month later for $150,000 in cash profit.

This is an example of buying a bargain property before the notification of default.

Case Study 2: Preforeclosure/After Notification of Default

One of my favorite graduates is a woman from the Los Angeles area. The last time we talked, she and her husband were successfully buying four to five foreclosures a year. One of her most profitable deals was a preforeclosure with an existing loan balance of approximately $17,000. With further checking, she determined that the home was in a neighborhood of homes in the $150,000 to $200,000 range. There was a huge potential for equity profit in this property. She inspected the home and found it in deplorable condition. (Maybe this is why the neighbors never bothered to check it out.) It was inhabited by three teenagers whose parents had recently passed away. When she visited the home, the young boys showed her piles of unopened letters from the bank that they didn't know what to do with. These were the foreclosure notices. She informed the boys that they were within days of the foreclosure. It was almost too late. They needed to act immediately. Because of her trustworthy demeanor, the boys turned their affairs over to her and she proceeded to stop the foreclosure. Then she arranged for enough money to complete a total renovation of the property. (There were holes in the walls, broken windows, motorcycle tracks in the lawn—a mess.) She involved the teenagers in the fix-up process, and several months later the property was sold and the $100,000 profit was divided up among the teenage boys and the Good Samaritan investor. Without her, there is no doubt that these boys would have been thrown into the street with nothing.

——— **$$$** ———
WIT & WISDOM
There are three kinds of people; those who can count and those who can't.

Every time I think of this woman, I am reminded that real estate investors can be not only problem solvers, but saviors as well.

Case Study 3: Buying Properties at the Foreclosure Sale

Several years ago I held a foreclosure seminar in Baltimore. In Maryland, foreclosure sales take place on the steps of the property to be foreclosed (as opposed to the courthouse steps in other states). We arranged to take the entire class to a live foreclosure sale. We arrived at a scheduled foreclosure sale with two minibuses full of people. The only other people there were the auctioneer and a solitary investor, a Mr. Rochkind. Needless to say, he was very disappointed to see us arrive because he assumed we would be bidding against him. He was relieved to learn that we were there only to observe. He proceeded to buy the property for the minimum bid— and a substantial profit. The whole affair lasted only a few minutes.

After the sale, we began to question the investor. After some coaxing, we learned that he was the largest single owner of residential homes in the entire state of Maryland, with over 3,000 single-family homes in his portfolio. For 25 years he had been buying properties at foreclosures and had amassed a huge net worth. Many of the homes were free and clear of mortgages, which generated a massive positive cash flow. To our delight, Mr. Rochkind agreed to attend our class, and he spent several hours sharing his vast experience and wisdom with us. It was an unforgettable demonstration of the power of pursuing a single profitable strategy over a long period of time. I couldn't have scripted it better.

Case Study 4: Buying Properties—Postforeclosure

One of my students, John Burley, was a financial planner in the San Francisco area. After attending my seminar, he moved to Phoenix in the early 1990s. He began to buy VA foreclosures using a unique strategy. Rather than buying and holding each property, he immediately flipped each one.

Here was a typical deal: John purchased a home valued at $80,000 from the government's Veterans Administration (VA) in foreclosure for $60,000 with a small down payment. He then ran an ad in the newspaper offering to resell the home for $80,000 with only $900 down. This attracted many calls. John's profit came in the form of payments made on a wraparound mortgage that John would carry back, as shown in Figure 9.2.

This may not seem like much of a profit until you learn that John was buying and flipping four to five houses *a month!* The last time I talked to him, he had purchased and flipped more than 800 homes in this manner. In each instance, he carried back a wraparound mortgage with

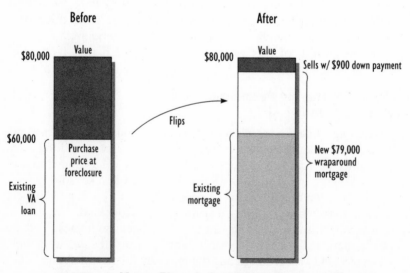

FIGURE 9.2 How a Phoenix foreclosure became a flipper.

monthly payments. His accumulated equities in these wraparound mortgages totaled millions of dollars, with a cash flow of tens of thousands of dollars a month. Admittedly, this took several years of concentrated, dedicated effort, but you can't deny that it was a powerful way to create residual income.

Here's another example from Bob Schumacher in Georgia:

> I specialize in foreclosures and tax deeds. I learned about this house in Macon, Georgia, by attending a foreclosure sale at the county courthouse. The house had sold in 1994 for $108,000. Following the foreclosure, I negotiated a "short sale" purchase from the lender in June 1999 for $91,000, with the lender paying most of the closing costs. After I invest about $8,000 in painting and other repairs, the house should be worth $120,000 or more. By using an existing home equity line of credit for my down payment, I was able to buy the property without any cash outlay.

One Good Property Can Set You Up for Life

One of my students in Chicago, Candice, found an exceptional bargain property as a result of a tip from a friend at church. She immediately drove over to look at the property after church and discovered a completely renovated, older apartment building in excellent condition. She began her research by calling the number on the for-sale sign. She learned that it was a property being liquidated in the collapse of a local savings and loan. After borrowing a large amount of money to renovate these units, the builder had defaulted on his loan. The property had reverted to the S&L through foreclosure. Then the S&L had gone belly-up. A government agency was given the task of liquidating the remaining properties. There was an extensive appraisal on the property indicating a value of $950,000 (although Candice felt that the appraisal was much too conservative). Candice made an immediate offer of $550,000 cash in 30 days—$10,000 in earnest money and no contingencies except the right to inspect the property before closing. Her offer was accepted almost immediately.

> **$$$**
> **WIT & WISDOM**
> Yes, even as you read this the universe is plotting to make you utterly happy, healthy and successful, and there isn't a thing you can do about it.
> STEVE BHAERMAN

With a 30-day closing looming, she arranged for her banker to look at the property. Because of a well-established relationship, he agreed to lend her $650,000 against the property on the strength of the $950,000 appraisal. Figure 9.3 shows how it looked.

At the closing, she walked out with a check for $100,000. The property had a built-in equity of at least $300,000 and a healthy positive cash flow. Imagine that! Excellent property. Cash at closing. Built-in equity. Powerful positive cash flow. It doesn't get any better than this. At a brunch meeting in Chicago, Candice shared with me that this one property was probably going to set her up for life.

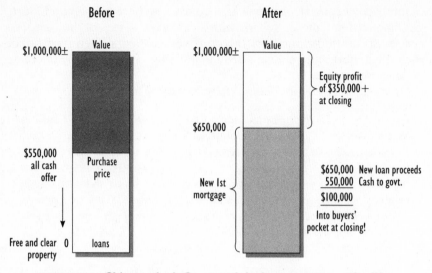

FIGURE 9.3 Chicago deal: One good deal can set you up for life.

I have often told my students that if they'll pursue these strategies for a five-year period of time, they, too, will uncover a property that has the potential to set them up for life. It may happen in the second year or the fifth year . . . but eventually, that once-in-a-lifetime deal will present itself. You just have to be ready when your opportunity arrives. I hope you find yours sooner rather than later. (If you'd like a free report about the latest strategies for profiting from foreclosures, visit www.multiplestreamsofincome.com, keyword Foreclosures, or call my office at 801-852-5700.)

Bargain Opportunity 2: Flippers

In Chapter 7, on options in the stock market, I related an example of a nice profit I earned by buying a one-year option on some raw acreage. In buying this option, I signed an option agreement that was legally binding upon both parties.

Whenever you make an offer to purchase a property at X price in X number of days, you sign a similar legal document. It's called an *offer to purchase.* In essence, an offer to purchase is a short-term option. It is a legally binding agreement that obligates the seller to sell the property to you within a specific time frame. For example, suppose you offered to buy a $100,000 home with a closing date 60 days in the future. In essence, you have a 60-day option on this property with a locked-in price of $100,000. What if someone approached you *during* this 60-day period of time, *before* you had actually taken title to the property, and offered you $110,000 for your position? Could you sell your "position" to this new buyer and pocket the $10,000 profit? The answer is *maybe.* (Of course, these kinds of questions should always be discussed with a competent real estate attorney.)

In theory, and I emphasize "in theory," you should be able to sell your position to another individual, who then completes the purchase in your place. To strengthen your legal position, I recommend that whenever you fill out an offer to purchase any property, you add these words to your contract: "and/or assigns."

For example, when I buy property in my own name, I write my name as follows: "Robert G. Allen and/or assigns." In theory, this enables me to "flip" my contract to someone who may want to buy it. When you sign your name to an offer you should *always* include those three magic words after your name: "and/or assigns." This gives you the right to purchase a property *and/or* to assign your contract to someone else. With this as a backdrop, let's discuss some situations in which you could handsomely profit by flipping these properties to other buyers for profit.

> **$$$**
> **WIT & WISDOM**
> The two most beautiful words in the English language are: "Check Enclosed".
> DOROTHY PARKER

Case Study 1: A Quick $7,000

My first flip was a 12-unit apartment building. The owners were considering selling this choice property at a price that I knew was substantially below the market. Unfortunately, the owners required a substantial down payment, which I did not have. At this point, I could have left disappointed with my inability to take advantage of an obvious bargain. Instead, I immediately pulled out an Offer to Purchase and proceeded to offer the sellers exactly what they wanted—cash with a seven-week closing date. As earnest money, I gave them my personal check for $500. Of course, to give myself a little cushion of protection, I also included the following phrase in my offer, "This offer is subject to the inspection by my partner on or before closing."

By including this "subject to" clause, I had an "out" if my partner wasn't in agreement with the purchase. (Who is my partner? My spouse, my brother—anyone I designate.)

Now, let's analyze this situation. The sellers had given me the right to control the price of their property. I had given them $500 for this right. If I didn't complete the purchase, my $500 would be forfeited. *But,* by including the "subject to the inspection of my partner" clause, I had effectively eliminated my risk of losing even my earnest money. In other words, I was able to tie up this very valuable property for seven weeks with absolutely no risk!

I immediately began to canvas my friends to find someone *with cash* who wanted to take advantage of a fabulous bargain. I found one interested investor and explained my dilemma—I had found a bargain property but I didn't have the cash to close. If this investor would come up with the cash, I would agree to flip the property to him immediately after the closing. Seven weeks later, I

> **$$$**
> **WIT & WISDOM**
> The shortest and best way to make your fortune is to let people see clearly that it is in their interest to promote yours.
> JEAN DE LA BRUYÈRE

closed on the property using my friend's cash and, in the same escrow, flipped the property to my friend, who paid me a $7,000 finder's fee.

Did you get that? I made $7,000 in seven weeks because I had the presence of mind to make an offer to purchase a property I couldn't afford. At the closing, all parties won. The sellers got their cash. My friend bought a nice bargain property. I walked out with a nice finder's fee.

Because this was the first time I had ever done a flip, I didn't know that I could have written those magic words—"and/or assigns"—and I would have eliminated the need to close on the property. I could have simply sold the paper rights and my friend could have legally closed in my place.

Case Study 2: Colorado Ski Cabin

One of my students used the flipping technique to make a huge profit. He and his spouse were on a ski vacation at a famous Colorado ski resort. To be able to get a partial tax deduction for the ski trip, he spent several hours searching through real estate listings and found what I call "the worst house in the best neighborhood." It was priced at $1,250,000, while other properties nearby were priced in the $2 million to $5 million range. My student was actually considering buying this property for his own personal use. He offered $800,000 cash. His offer was countered at $900,000. The offer was signed by both parties with, as I remember, a 60-day closing date.

During this 60-day period, my student let the Realtor know that he might consider reselling the property before the closing date. Shortly thereafter, he received an offer for $1,150,000—a full $250,000 higher than his contracted purchase price.

Because he had included the phrase "and/or assigns" he was able to flip the property to the new buyer and reap a substantial profit after commissions. Note: My student never took title to the property, never had to obtain a new loan, never had his credit checked, never had to verify his income or down payment. He simply assigned his right to buy the property to someone else. He made a substantial amount of money without ever having owned the property. That's the advantage of the flipping technique.

Case Study 3: Ads in the Paper

One of my students advertises in the newspaper for bargain properties. He offers to close quickly with fair prices. He doesn't receive many calls, but when he does, it's usually worth the bother. He once received a phone call from a retiring couple who owned a home free and clear. The sellers wanted a $150,000 purchase price with $15,000 down. They were willing to carry a first mortgage of $135,000 at 8 percent. The numbers appeared as shown in Figure 9.4.

After checking out the property, my student determined that it was worth at least $180,000. This had the making of a great deal. He agreed to all of the sellers' terms, with one exception. . . . He negotiated for a moratorium on interest payments for the first six months after the pur-

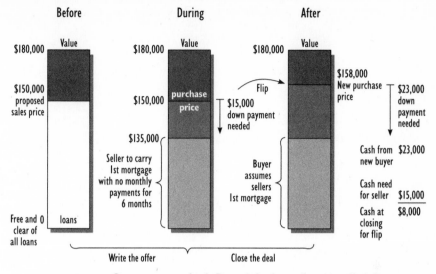

FIGURE 9.4 **Sacramento deal: Buy right in order to sell right.**

chase. The sellers agreed, the Offer to Purchase was signed with a closing date six weeks in the future.

With the offer signed, my student immediately ran an ad in the paper similar to this:

- Must sell this week.
- $20,000 below market!
- 0% interest for 6 mo!
- No qualifying loan for the right buyer.
- Hurry. This won't last.
- $158,000 home in good neighborhood.

As you might have guessed, this investor looks for properties he can buy and flip almost immediately. In this example, he found a buyer within days. The new buyer agreed to make a $23,000 down payment, of which $15,000 was given to the original sellers and $8,000 was kept as the profit for flipping.

Everybody won. The original sellers received a $15,000 down payment and payments on a new first mortgage. The new buyer bought a property substantially below market with excellent terms. The student earned a quick $8,000 profit.

Whether you're flipping for cash (as in the preceding example) or flipping for cash flow (as did our Phoenix investor), flipping can be one way to create substantial profits and extra streams of income.

Join me in the next chapter and I'll share with you another moneymaking idea.

CHAPTER 10

Unless you try to do something beyond what
you have already mastered, you will never grow.
RONALD E. OSBORN

YOUR SIXTH STREAM
OPT: Huge Profits by Paying Other People's Taxes

AMERICA'S BEST-KEPT INVESTMENT SECRET!
Investors Earn 18% to 50% GUARANTEED by the Government

If you saw this headline in the *Wall Street Journal,* you probably wouldn't believe it. You'd think it belonged in the *National Enquirer.* Well, this headline is for real. In this chapter you're going to learn a safe way to double your money in three years . . . and double it again in the next three . . . and so on. For as long as you like.

This is the fascinating story of a whole new way to build wealth, and it's so simple it will astonish you. Once in a great while a program comes along that's so "right" I can hardly wait to tell my friends about it. I call these extraordinary programs *money machines.*

To qualify as a money machine a program must have four crucial elements. It must be easy to do. It must be simple so everyone can do it. It must be fun. But most of all, it must actually work—it must legitimately make money.

My good friend Ted Thomas called me a short while ago and told me about just such a money machine—a low risk way to earn high rates of return. Usually, when you hear of things like this, a little voice goes off in your head, "Yeah, right!" But I've known Ted for many years and I trust his judgment. As he began to share the details with me. . . . Well, rather than retell the story, I'll let Ted tell you himself, just the way he shared it with me—enthusiasm and all. But don't let his exuberance overshadow the seriously legitimate opportunity he's about to share with you. This checks out.

━━━━ **$$$** ━━━━
WIT & WISDOM
Money may not buy
happiness, but it surely
helps one look for it in
more interesting places.

Hello, my name is Ted Thomas. And I have discovered what is undoubtedly the best-kept secret in America: a way you can create an extra stream of income, with low risk and a steady 24 percent interest. It has made fortunes for hundreds and hundreds of people just like yourself. And yet, it was virtually unknown to all but a select few of the nation's wealthiest investors. It is said that the rich are really no different from you or me. Except for what they know. With the knowledge I'm about to give you—you, too, can be "in the know."

We're talking about a virtual no-risk investment that pays you up to 50 percent return . . . and yet is so simple and so rock-solid safe, that you'll wonder why everyone isn't involved in it . . . why anyone would even bother with the roller-coaster ride stock market . . . or why anyone in their right mind would even risk a single penny investing in low-paying CDs, money market funds, or anything else!

But I'm getting a little ahead of myself. You'll have to forgive me, but I get so excited about this exceptionally lucrative investment that I sometimes jump headlong into the amazing details without bothering to give people a few of my credentials.

As I said, my name is Ted Thomas. Like many other movers and shakers, I was heavily invested in real estate in the early eighties. Only to have the bottom fall out. I was left holding the bag . . . and lost millions in the process . . . with bills to pay and a mortgage to meet—just like you.

If it is true that adversity gives us character—then I've got more character than you can shake a stick at! In short, I made and lost a virtual fortune . . . and then made it back all over again using many of the ideas that you're reading in this book—especially the ideas I'll share with you in the next few pages.

A Hard Lesson Learned—
A Fortune Recaptured!

I know what it's like to start all over again from zero and rebuild a fortune. You could say that I have "perspective." I now know that a lot of investments can seem exciting in the heat of the market, but can crash and burn just as quickly. This makes what I'm about to share with you all the more relevant.

Just what is this secret investment? It's called a *tax lien certificate*. Remember the name.

How do tax lien certificates work? In hundreds of counties throughout the United States, local governments have millions of dollars in outstanding and overdue property taxes owed by property owners who will not or cannot pay their property taxes.

To fund daily services like police, fire, hospitals, welfare, and so on, local governments create and sell these tax lien certificates to investors like you and me. The lien is secured by the real estate it is attached to.

You are not actually buying the real estate—you are buying the government's lien on the real estate. In a sense, it's just like a mortgage! When you buy a tax lien, you are paying someone else's property taxes. Best of all, the government actually gives you the right to receive all of the tax money due—including fees, high interest, and penalties. To encourage taxpayers to pay their property taxes, the government charges "punitive," sky-high interest rates, which are passed directly to the tax lien purchaser—that's you.

That's right. State and county governments turn to you and me and say something like this:

> We have thousands of homeowners who are late in paying their property taxes. But we need the money now. So, if you'll pay these back taxes and give us the money, then we'll charge the homeowner a penalty fee. When the homeowner eventually pays the taxes, we'll collect the taxes plus a late fee and give it to you, the investor. That's right. We'll send you a government check to return your investment plus the penalty. And if the property owner doesn't pay the taxes, we'll let you foreclose on the property to recover your invested dollars. This way, we get our tax money now. And you just wait for a period of time to see which way you win. If the taxes don't get paid, you get the property. And if the taxes do get paid, then you get your money back plus a substantial interest penalty.

A substantial penalty. Those are the kinds of phrases that banks like to scare us with. But in this case, *you are the bank.* And *you* get to collect the substantial interest penalty for late payment!

For example, in some counties in Florida the interest rate penalty is 18 percent. In Texas it's 25 percent, even if the homeowner is only one week late! In Michigan it's only 15 percent in the first year, but a whopping 50 percent in the second year. Well, it sounds exciting, but, as with everything, there are a few catches.

First catch: Not every state does it this way. At present, about 30 states use tax lien certificates. The rest don't, so that narrows the field a bit. (Since the number of states that do this is constantly increasing, check at www.multiplestreamsofincome.com, or call my office at 801-852-8700, and I'll e-mail you a current list of the states that participate. Use the keyword TLC.)

Next catch: In the states that do offer tax lien certificates, each individual county handles its own tax lien auction. . . . With about 1,500 different counties holding separate auctions at different times and with slightly different rules, it can take a lot of homework to track down all of the

$$$

WIT & WISDOM

I can give you a six word formula for success: think things through— then follow through.

EDDIE RICKENBACKER

information. But this extra effort keeps most people away . . . which is actually an advantage to you.

Third catch: Let's see, I'm trying to think of a third catch. Hmmmm. Nope. You just show up at the tax lien auction and bid with other people for the right to pay other people's taxes for them. Sometimes very few people show up and the certificates go begging. At a recent auction in Chicago, thousands of tax lien certificates went unsold! At other auctions, hundreds of people are there to do the bidding. (You can be sure that some of your bankers will be in the audience.)

You bid for the certificates that you're interested in, buy them, and wait. The government collects the money for you from the delinquent taxpayer and sends you the check. And you earn, like I said, 10, 20, 30 percent or more.

Hey, wait, it can't be that easy. Well, it is. That's all there is to it.

Government Guaranteed Checks of 16, 18, 25, up to 50 Percent Interest

For safety-first investors like you and me, these government certificates are the premier investment—the absolute best wealth builders of the future. Just imagine receiving continual high-rate income from the government—because tax lien certificates (TLCs) are just like municipal bonds and Treasury bills. You invest your money, and when the government collects the past-due taxes, it sends you a guaranteed government check, returning your investment plus high interest.

Best of all, these government-sponsored certificates are armor-car safe. You no longer have to be stuck with those lousy CD returns from banks and institutions. In my opinion, brokers and bankers who sell certificates of deposit (also known as "certificates of depreciation") and money market funds as primary, long-term investments should be tarred and feathered. Why? Because you can get four to six times as much income from TLCs. If you invested in a 6 percent CD, it would take you 12 long years to double your investment! And during this time you are getting brutalized by taxes and inflation.

You can get tax lien certificates in almost any size, ranging from $10 to over $1 million. And the high interest rates on tax liens are mandated by state law. They don't rise and fall like the stock market—nor are they subject to the whims of bankers who control interest rates.

$$$

WIT & WISDOM
With money in your pocket you are wise, you are handsome and you sing well, too.

YIDDISH PROVERB

If you're worried about diversification, you can buy tax lien certificates secured by different properties and in different locations in the same state—or in several states all over the country. And, because there are many well-secured separate certificates for over $10,000, you can quickly invest substantial amounts of money by buying just a few certificates. In short, you could be making huge profits on small or large investments!

That's what is great about tax lien certificates: It doesn't matter whether you've got tens of thousands to invest or not! It's the most democratic of investments—making everyone rich regardless of where you come from or how much you have to invest! In fact, I get notes and letters from my former students all the time. Just look at some of the amazing— but all true—success stories I hear every day:

> Tax lien buyer Mary Potter of Fort Myers, Florida, purchased a tax lien for just $1,957. She's receiving 17 percent return on her investment!

> A Coral Gables couple purchased a Miami tax lien for $5,000 and are enjoying an 18 percent return.

> Craig Talkington of Tulsa, Oklahoma, sold a 5-acre tract for $20,000. His cost at the tax sale: $300. Then he sold a 10-acre tract, for which he paid $17 at the tax sale, to a neighbor for $4,000! That's $23,700 in two months, working part time.

These people are no different from you—they're just raking in the profits on one of the most lucrative investments of all time! And believe me, if they can do it, you can, too!

Best of All, You Can Test This Out on Paper

As with other important things in life—this, too, can be tried in a dry run to see how you do. All tax liens and tax deeds can be thoroughly reviewed prior to purchase. That means you can see the stated official value and the expected auction price (5 cents on the dollar, for example). By looking before you leap, you can calculate your profit. You go in knowing all the angles—nothing is left to chance. And that's what makes this investment low risk: There are no hidden surprises. Just pure, shear, profitable returns of 16, 18, or even 25 percent without a single element of risk! In fact, you can even purchase tax lien certificates through the mail prior to the auction.

Don't Make These Deadly Mistakes with Your Hard-Earned Dollars!

Just the other day, my friend Dave invested $2,000 in his IRA—and the bank is paying him a whopping 3.75 percent. Big wow. If he leaves that money in the bank for 20 years and doesn't touch it, his $2,000 will have grown to the enormous sum of $4,219 . . . hardly an auspicious start on a retirement plan.

He Could Have Enjoyed 25 Times Greater Earnings Than the Banks Will Ever Pay!

If Dave had invested in Arizona tax lien certificates and reinvested the funds in new certificates each time the government paid him, it would have been a completely different story. Arizona pays certificate holders 16 percent interest. At the end of 20 years, Dave's $2,000 would have grown to more than $30,000! Savvy investors at the Iowa tax lien certificate auction receive 24 percent interest on their investment dollars. Dave's initial $2,000 would have skyrocketed to $120,000 in just 20 years . . . and that's if Dave had never invested another dime. By my calculations, that's 25 times what Dave would have made at his local bank.

Tax lien certificates invested at 24 percent make a lot of sense for tax-deferred earnings. A $10,000 investment today, assuming it could grow tax deferred, could be more than *$1 million* in just 21 years.

The best part is that it takes no experience or special skills whatsoever! It's so simple, so low tech, anyone can do it, even if you've never made an investment in your life. You're probably asking yourself—what are the risks? Glad you asked. In my opinion, the biggest risk is this: The property owner pays you off too early and you have to reinvest the money. At these rates, you hope that the taxes *never* get paid.

According to the county treasurers I've interviewed, 97 percent of all tax lien certificates are paid off in two years. And the other 3 percent? That's your ticket to the ultimate American dream: owning a gorgeous home for just the taxes and a few fees!

The United States is divided into 3,300 separate counties. Approximately half of the counties sell tax liens. The remaining states sell *tax deeds* to properties. Therefore, some states, called *lien states,* sell a piece of paper similar to a mortgage. The other states, the *deed states,* sell a right to ownership. They deed the property owner's real estate to the auction buyer. One opportunity is a cash interest return. The other opportunity is a chance to own real estate for pennies on the dollar.

In most states however, if the property owners don't pay the taxes they forfeit the property to you. Congratulations! You've just won the lottery! In most states, you would now own the property free and clear of all mortgages and liens. However, state laws differ, and a few states allow the property to be sold at auction with the liens remaining on the property.

Many properties that are delinquent in their taxes have existing mortgages. In order to protect these mortgages, at the last minute the mortgage holders usually end up paying the back taxes . . . plus, of course, the hefty interest penalty. So it's very rare that you'll end up owning a property as a result of buying a tax lien certificate. But it does happen from time to time. Therefore, make sure that the amount you invest in back taxes is not more than the value of the property. Maybe the property is on a toxic waste dump. That's why you need to do some due diligence.

A Home to Own or Sell for Just Pennies on the Dollar!

Throughout history, many of the truly great fortunes have been made in real estate. And that's what makes tax lien certificates so ideal. It doesn't matter whether the real estate market rises or falls, drops or skyrockets! You've purchased a magnificent home for a fraction of its original cost— just the back taxes. Whatever you can sell it for is pure profit!

It's a win-win situation, with you on the receiving end of all the good things: 16, 18, up to 50 percent return on your investment; a way to double your money in half the time; and home ownership (for you to use or to sell)—all for just pennies on the dollar!

Here's what one client did: In Texas, Mark Novack purchased a single-family home valued at $75,000 for only $16,000 plus back state taxes of $17,000. That's just 60 cents on the dollar!

Life-Changing Events

The following is a 100 percent verifiable case history.

Danny Smith of Columbus, Ohio, has made a business of purchasing properties at tax deed auctions. Ohio is a *deed state,* which means that the county will deed (transfer) the property to the highest bidder at the auction. (In *lien states,* the auctioneer sells the tax lien and gives the bidder the right to collect the lien. If the homeowner does not pay it, the lien purchaser can then foreclose, ultimately owning the real estate for pennies.)

Danny Smith purchased many properties at the tax deed sales. At this writing, Danny has a positive cash flow of more than $10,000 a month from his tax deed purchases!

He purchases for pennies on the dollar and earns thousands of dollars renting the homes to others. A typical example is a home he purchased on Demorest Road in Franklin County, Ohio, which sold for $2,727. The county treasurer assessed the value at $67,000. Danny paid only 5 cents on the dollar. His total investment of time was less than eight hours, which computes to $8,000 per hour.

> *"I purchased a tax lien in the State of Arizona for $298 and I sold it for $8,450."*
> Joyce Beck, Alameda, California

> *"Ted, my friends gasped when I cashed in my CDs, but their shock turned to envy when they saw my returns on my first tax deed certificate. The tax deed I purchased from the government cost me $264.62. Later I sold that residential lot for $4,900."*
> Lee Lineberger

> *"My research takes six seconds and they (the county) keep my certificates on file and just send me a check! All I have to do is just punch a few things in my computer and cash the check.*
> Louise Wood, Sugarloaf Shores, Florida

Mr. X earns 27 percent cash flow. . . .

A three-million-dollar man, who wishes to remain unnamed, has purchased over $3 million in tax lien certificates in three states. A registered investment advisor, this mystery man regularly purchases tax lien certificates at auctions. He has purchased more than 1,484 certificates—and now performs a service of buying, holding, and managing these certificates for others.

His impeccable record keeping and his systematic tracking of purchases and redemptions are very impressive. The mystery man has received 22 percent interest on certificates below $500 and 27 percent interest on certificates from $501 to $1,500. The wealthy have been doing this for years and years. Now it's your turn!

Ron Hibbard of Columbus, Ohio, purchased a single-family house valued at $55,000. His purchase price was only 5 cents on the dollar—$2,163!

Craig Talkington of Tulsa, Oklahoma, purchased a tax lien for only $44.99 and resold the property for $3,500. On Arrowhead Lake in Tulsa, he purchased a lakefront lot for $298 and sold it for $5,000.

Ron Starr of Oakland, California, turned a $65,595 investment into $262,349 by purchasing four commercial acres from the tax assessor. Amazingly, no other bidders showed up.

In Navajo County, Arizona, John Beck purchased a 40-acre parcel of land for only $550. According to the tax collector, the 40 acres were worth (assessed at) $18,600 just after the auction. The real estate brokers estimated the value to be $22,500. The previous owner paid $20,000.

What do the professionals have to say?

When I decided to get serious about tax lien investing, I traveled all over the country, visiting dozens of tax lien auctions in state after state. (By the way, all of this travel was tax deductible.) I was amazed that many sales had only a handful of bidders. I interviewed many of the professionals and employees who were involved in the tax lien process. Here are some of their comments:

> *"The reason we do this tax lien auction is to allow a greater opportunity for the small investor to participate. We have several people from our own county who may come in and place perhaps only $2,000 on deposit for the tax lien certificates."*
> Dorothy Vogt, Treasurer, Arapohe County

> *"A guy with $200 can be an investor."*
> Dave Browning, Assistant Treasurer

> *"Under state law, the county sets their own interest rate. It's 20 percent here in Prince Georges County. The City of Baltimore pays 24 percent. We are allowed to set our own rate to encourage people to bid on tax lien certificates."*
> Porter Venn, Chief of Treasury, Prince Georges County, Maryland

"It's a safe investment or the government wouldn't let you invest your retirement funds. If you've got $5,000 to invest or $100,000, there is no place you can put your money and guarantee a 14 percent return. This is probably the best-kept secret in America."
Dave Welton, Tax Sale Auctioneer, Littleton, Colorado

In summary, there are so many benefits to being involved in tax lien certificates:

Getting started with a small amount of money

Being successful no matter what the condition of your credit rating

Earning passive interest that rivals the returns of Warren Buffett, world's richest investor

Sleeping at night knowing that your money is as safe as your state government

Having at least a 3 percent chance of buying real estate for pennies on the dollar

Taking tax-deductible trips to tax lien certificate auctions in exotic vacation spots

Speaking of travel, I hope we get a chance to see each other at a tax lien auction sometime in the near future. If you want to get in touch with me or learn how to join me on my next trip to some of the most lucrative tax lien auctions, just visit www.multiplestreamsofincome.com and enter the keyword Ted Thomas, or call my office at 801-852-8700.

Good luck and happy investing.

CHAPTER 11

*I'd rather have 1% of the efforts of 100 people
than 100% of my own efforts.*

J. PAUL GETTY

YOUR SEVENTH STREAM
Network Marketing:
The Ultimate Money Machine

Welcome to the marketing mountain. On this mountain we'll discuss four powerful twenty-first-century streams of income. It's hard to imagine four more representative businesses for the new millennium than *network marketing, information marketing, Internet marketing,* and *licensing.* They all embody revolutions in marketing that have changed and will change the face of the business world forever. Each will impact your life in a major way. That's why you need to participate in each of these massive trends, to sense the different dynamics of each stream, to experience for yourself the unique profits pulsing through each one.

Let's start with network marketing (also known as *multilevel marketing,* or MLM) . . . being an intrapreneur . . . an independent distributor for a company in the burgeoning network marketing industry. *Network marketing.* Just saying the words conjures up lots of emotions for most people. You either love it or you hate it. Sometimes both. But just what is it?

Have you ever been to a great movie or a great restaurant and told a friend about it? That's called *word-of-mouth advertising.* Businesses love word-of-mouth advertising because it's much more effective than all the money they spend on any other form of advertising, promotion, or marketing. Network marketing is a way for businesses to leverage the power of word-of-mouth advertising.

Let me give you a hypothetical example. Suppose you recommend a great restaurant (let's call it *Chez Bob*) to your sister. Your sister and her husband make a reservation for dinner and, during the meal, the waiter asks them how they heard about Chez Bob. They mention your name. How would you feel if the owner of the restaurant sent you a thank-you letter and a coupon for a free meal in appreciation for your recommending his restaurant? It would probably make you feel wonderful. The restaurant owner also explains in the letter that because of your recommendation, Chez Bob has gained a new long-term customer. This customer didn't result from Chez Bob's Yellow Pages ad or its radio and newspaper campaign. Therefore, the owner wants to reward you for this new word-of-mouth customer. Anytime your sister visits his restaurant in the future, he will send you a check for 10 percent of the value of the meal as a continuing thank-you. Sure enough, every several months you receive a small thank-you check. You're so impressed that you encourage others to visit Chez Bob. This generates more free-meal coupons plus more 10 percent word-of-mouth checks. After a year, you are receiving several small checks each month. After several years, you've help to create dozens of monthly customers, which generates hundreds of dollars of extra, no-hassle income to you. That would be nice, wouldn't it?

This is the theory behind network marketing, as it is now called. I prefer to call it *relationship marketing* because the word-of-mouth concept derives its power as a result of the relationship. Businesses these days spend up to 50 percent of the price of their goods on advertising and marketing expenses. Instead of sending these advertising dollars to wealthy newspapers, magazines, and television stations, several smart businesses have begun to share this money with their best customers. Every time one of their best customers influences someone to buy one of their products, they send this loyal customer a check—sort of a referral fee.

One of the most recent success stories in the power of relationship marketing is Amazon.com. Soon after launching this groundbreaking Internet web site, the folks at Amazon.com came up with a bright idea.

Why not pay a referral fee to anybody on the Internet who sends customers to Amazon.com? They launched an "affiliate program" encouraging millions of Web page owners to provide links to the Amazon.com site. If a Web surfer visits an affiliate site, clicks on the Amazon.com link, and eventually buys a product, Amazon pays a small 3 to 7 percent referral fee to the affiliate. This created tens of thousands of satellite minipartners who have a self-interest in the ongoing success of the Amazon mother ship. This strategic marketing move was one of the major reasons for the explosive success of Amazon.com. Now this model is rampant on the Internet. Even my own web site, www.multiplestreams-ofincome.com, has an affiliate program. Network or relationship marketing works! Its time has arrived. It's the cool thing to do.

However, the first time I heard about network marketing I didn't think it was very cool. I'm embarrassed to say that the first time I heard about it, I turned it down flat. Here's what happened. . . .

The Awesome Power of Leverage

It all started with my wife's best friend Collette Van Reusen. She had just gone through a bitter divorce, which left her with five kids, a huge attorney bill, and no money. She needed work, so I hired her as my executive assistant. After a few months, she came to ask my advice.

"Bob," she said, "I've been talking to my brother about a company he's involved with. He's been showing me how I could make some extra income. I think I'm going to do it."

"What kind of company is it?"

"It's a company that markets nutritional supplements through a network of distributors."

Well, that's all she had to say. . . . My mind snapped shut and I told her, "Don't do it!" Despite my objections, she went ahead. She said she had a "good feeling" about it. And sure enough, in a few weeks, she'd earned her first $100 check. Then her weekly check increased to $500 or $600. Then $1,000 a week. Of course, I still thought she was crazy, but I wondered, "How is she doing this?" Then she informed me that she was resigning from my company: "Bob, my check was $2,000 this week."

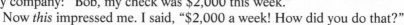

——— $$$ ———

WIT & WISDOM

A single conversation across the table with a wise man is worth a month's study of books.

CHINESE PROVERB

Now *this* impressed me. I said, "$2,000 a week! How did you do that?"

"I keep telling you, Bob, this really works."

I said, "Maybe it works for you, but I can't see myself peddling little bottles of supplements from door-to-door. Dingdong, your pills are here."

And she answered, "It's not like that at all. In fact, I just share my story about how these products have changed our lives. People get curious and want to try them. They call a toll-free number and order products, which the company ships to their front door. I don't deliver a single product to anyone. The company does it all and I get a check."

She continued, "Now, here's the best part. This product is powerful. People fall in love with it and keep ordering it every month. And every time they do, I get more checks. But that's not all. These same people just can't help sharing how much better they feel. And when they do, I get a small sliver of profit from those transactions, too. And so on. And so on. Now there are thousands of people all over the world using these products—people I've never even met—and every Monday, I receive thousands of dollars as a result of my efforts and the efforts of hundreds of other people."

Now this *really* got my attention. I understood the power of leverage from my experience in real estate, where a small amount of money can put you in control of a large amount of real estate. But this was even more powerful. Collette was leveraging herself through the efforts of hundreds of other people. Since these people are located all around the world, she's earning income 24 hours a day—even while she's sleeping.

In a previous chapter, I shared the following quote by David George, M.D.:

> *"Poverty is when large efforts produce small results.*
> *Wealth is when small efforts produce large results."*

That's a perfect description of what Collette was doing—small efforts, huge results. Earning $2,000 a week amounts to about $100,000 a year. Only a small percentage of the families in North America earn that kind of money. It usually takes decades of full-time effort to reach that level of income. Yet Collette had done it in less than 18 months. And it was going higher: $3,000 a week, $4,000 a week, $5,000 a week. More impressive still, this income was residual.

"Bob, I'm telling you, this company is different!" One day Collette left a video at our house, and my wife and I popped it in the VCR and started watching. I'll never forget what happened. As I watched, my intuition kicked in, whispering, "This is the one!"

Have you ever had a hunch? When part of you knows that something is right even though another part is still skeptical? Well, I usually listen to my intuition. It was a hunch just like this one that inspired me to start investing in real estate in the 1970s just before the huge boom. Remember those days? I made a fortune. It was another hunch that inspired me to leave my career as an investment counselor and write my first book, *Nothing Down*. The odds of a new author getting a book published are 10,000 to 1. Part of me just knew that if I followed my hunches something good was going to happen. How could I have known that *Nothing Down* would become a number one *New York Times* best-seller. My second book, *Creating Wealth,* was also a number one best-seller. Then I had a hunch to start several seminar companies. . . . They grossed over $100 million in the next 15 years.

So you see, when I have a hunch it's usually a good one. And when it came to that video, my intuition was screaming, "This is the one!"

Collette phoned the next day and asked, "What'd you think of the video?" Despite my strong intuitive hunch, I replied, "Sorry, Collette, I just don't think I'm interested."

To her credit, she didn't let my negativity stop her. She took my wife to lunch, and they decided to go ahead without me. I was so close-minded, I wouldn't even sign the application. But before long, the checks started to flow in, just as Collette had said they would.

Now, several years later, a very, very large check is automatically deposited into my wife's bank account every Friday, but it doesn't have *my* name on it. It's my wife's check. Mr. Skeptical here didn't want anything to do with it! So she gets the check and occasionally shares some of it with me.

In the next few pages, I'm going to show you how to get your name on a check like the ones my wife gets every week. But only if you're more open-minded than I was.

Blinded by False Information

Why do you think I voted against my own intuition? Perhaps it was because I had heard some negative things about network marketing . . . and without checking things out for myself, I made some snap judgments that turned out to be completely wrong.

My first mistake was to assume that Collette's company was like some of the old-style multilevel companies from the 1960s and 1970s. In these earlier and ancient forms of network marketing, distributors had to stockpile their garages full of products and then try to peddle them to friends and relatives. To recruit new people, they were encouraged to drag everybody they knew to endless weeknight pep rallies. Needless to say, very few people made any money, and almost everyone else quit in frustration, their garages full of stuff that they couldn't give away. It left a bad taste in a lot of people's mouths. Collette assured me that this new company was *nothing* like that.

> ━━━━ **$$$** ━━━━
> **WIT & WISDOM**
> Most folks' financial problems are really quite simple—they simply don't have any money.

Around this time, I learned of a book by a former editor at *Success* magazine, Richard Poe. It's called *Wave Three: The New Era in Network Marketing.* He writes,

> . . . The Wave-Three Revolution . . . began over 50 years ago, when Carl Rehnborg invented network marketing—a business system designed to make it easy for anyone to become an entrepreneur. MLM's rough-and-ready days lasted 40 years, a formative period that I have named Wave One. Wave Two took hold in the 1980s, when PC technology made it feasible to start an MLM company from your garage. That created a groundswell of new companies. But Wave-Two network marketing still tended to work best for those who needed it least—aggressive, sales-oriented entrepreneurs. It is only Wave Three, now making its entrance, that finally offers the masses a realistic promise of financial freedom. Through new systems and technology, Wave Three enables average men and women—not just super sales people— to enjoy the fruits of entrepreneurship while avoiding many of its hardships.

Obviously, Collette had stumbled across one of these Wave-Three companies.

Based on the impressive research in this book, I reluctantly allowed Collette and my wife to introduce the concept at one my smaller seminars.

I was still very skeptical, but within weeks, some of these same people were calling back to tell me how much better they were feeling.

I was amazed. You see, I hadn't been taking any nutritional supplements myself. I felt I was in pretty good health and didn't need anything. Only later did I learn that our health really is in danger and that every one of us should consider daily nutritional supplementation.

When it came to making money through network marketing, my seminar graduates were calling me and saying,

"Bob, this is the best moneymaking idea you've ever recommended."

"I made $1,000 dollars this week."

"I've tried network marketing before, but this is so much easier."

And I'm thinking to myself, "Hmmmm! Maybe there really is something to this."

It all clicked for me when I watched a quadriplegic in a wheelchair earn his first $1,000 network marketing check. I thought to myself, if he can do this, anybody can. That's when I decided to focus more attention on "our" nutritional business and to definitely add it to our portfolio of income streams.

$$$

WIT & WISDOM
Obstacles cannot crush me.
Every obstacle yields
to stern resolve.

LEONARDO DA VINCI

We've been involved in a lot of businesses over the years, and network marketing has been one of the most rewarding things we've ever done. We have no overhead. No debt. We maintain this powerful stream of income with zero employees. We don't even have a secretary. And it's completely portable, which means I can run this business from my own home in my bathrobe . . . from my car phone in my jeans . . . or from a mailbox in Tahiti. It has very little downside. And the income is residual.

When people ask me today if I'm involved in network marketing, I reply with a resounding *absolutely!*

I don't know what your experience with other network marketing companies has been, but my experience has been *fantastic!* Once the income starts to flow, it's like an oil well in your backyard. It just keeps pumping out profits. Looking back, I wonder how I could have overlooked such a powerful moneymaking idea for so many years. And I'm saddened because those same misconceptions are holding back so many other smart, reasonable, intelligent people.

Put Yourself on Neutral Ground

Well, let's suppose that you aren't as skeptical as I was at first. Suppose you take me at my word and at least put yourself on neutral ground to consider adding another stream of income like this to your life. Let's discuss answers to the three most common questions that people ask:

Question 1. Is this really legitimate?

Question 2. Why should I consider this type of business versus a traditional franchise?

Question 3. What do I really have to do to make this work?

Question 1: Is this industry really legitimate?

Frankly, this was one of *my* first questions. I didn't want to get myself, or my loyal readers, involved in some pyramid scheme. I checked out the industry and found it had combined sales of tens of billions of dollars and more than 10 million active distrib-

utors worldwide. Yes, it is not only legitimate, but it's being recognized as the growth industry of the future. It has attracted the attention of many Fortune 500 companies, including Colgate-Palmolive, Gillette, Avon, Coca-Cola, and MCI. Just recently, AT&T, the worldwide telecommunications giant, also began marketing its long-distance services through network marketing.

Do you remember the days when Japan had the reputation of making inferior products? When I was a kid, a product marked "Made in Japan" was usually cheap, inferior junk—a joke. Today the perception of Japanese products is 180 degrees opposite—only the finest products come out of Japan. This same shift in perception is happening to the network marketing industry. The public is quickly finding out that some of the finest and most reasonably priced products are marketed through the vehicle of network marketing. If this weren't the case, do you think AT&T would even have considered it?

If AT&T is willing to bet its reputation on it, then so am I. And so are a lot of other smart, intelligent, successful people: Doctors, teachers, astronauts, Fortune 500 executives, famous actors, best-selling authors, health professionals, university professors, coaches, Olympic athletes, world record holders, chiropractors, nurses, scientists, bankers, and attorneys, along with tens of thousands of other reasonable, intelligent people from all walks of life, are flocking to this industry. Many of us who wouldn't even have considered network marketing in the past are now wholeheartedly embracing the Third-Wave companies that are emerging.

Timing Is Everything

The timing is perfect for the future growth of this industry. It coincides with the massive layoffs and downsizing of the early 1990s and the huge explosion of home-based businesses throughout the decade. Over 77 million baby boomers are searching for ways to earn income to supplement their upcoming retirement needs.

Question 2: Why should I consider this type of business versus a traditional franchise?

Your goal in launching streams of income from the marketing mountain is to select businesses that market products that you can get excited about. Suppose you love nutrition and health. You like the thought of earning money helping people get and stay healthy. You decide to check out several business models.

You see an ad in *Entrepreneur* magazine for a top nutrition franchise. For only $58,500, you can own your own business with the support of a worldwide company using a proven business system. The odds for success are high. However, there are some disadvantages. It will require that you sign your name to a lease, hire and train employees, purchase inventory, equipment, shelving, and so forth. However, after a short, intense training period you can open for business and be your own boss. It sounds irresistible . . . if you have $58,500. Should you mortgage your home?

In the same magazine, you notice an ad for a company that markets quality nutritional products through network marketing. You check out the company, the products, the people you will be working with. You find out that for less than $1,000 (usually a lot less) you can become a distributor and be up and earning income in a matter of days, not months.

Perhaps the most compelling advantage is the fact that this has the potential of creating residual income . . . multiple streams of income from your growing group of downline distributors. It's feasible that with a few short years, you could even retire with a substantial, recurring stream of income that takes minimal involvement on your part. You have none of the hassles of taking inventory, doing books, and managing employees. But there are some disadvantages. You'll be operating out of your own home, so you have to be self-motivated and disciplined. It might get lonely. But that's okay. You can occupy yourself by counting all the money you've saved by not mortgaging your house.

Franchising	Third-Wave Network Marketing
Large up-front franchising fees	Small initial distributor fee
Leasing office/retail space	Work from home
Hiring, training, managing employees	Recruiting, training other distributors
Stockpiling and inventorying products	Little or no inventory
Shipping and/or delivering products	Company ships products directly to customers
Locked into retail business hours	Flexible hours
Linear income (you must be present)	Potential for residual income
High overhead	Low overhead

When I compare my network marketing income to the businesses I've owned and operated during the past 20 years, our network marketing business is the hands-down winner. I've owned restaurants, clothing stores, a chocolate factory, apartment buildings, commercial buildings, seminar companies, newsletter businesses, and direct-mail, multimedia,

$$$ Start-Up Costs for 25 Well-Known Franchises $$$		
	Low	High
AAMCO Transmissions	$151,000	$166,000
Baskin-Robbins Ice Cream	$78,000	$447,000
Blockbuster Video	$245,000	$823,000
Budget Rent a Car	$166,000	$449,000
Dairy Queen	$181,000	$585,000
Denny's Restaurant	$392,000	$711,000
Dunkin' Donuts	$46,000	$287,000
GNC (General Nutrition Center)	$112,000	$197,000
Gold's Gym	$434,000	$1,800,000
Great Earth Vitamins	$92,000	$111,000
Jenny Craig Weight Loss	$159,000	$314,000
Jiffy Lube	$174,000	$194,000
Kentucky Fried Chicken	$1,000,000	$1,700,000
Kwik Copy	$216,000	$357,000
Mail Boxes Etc.	$115,000	$178,000
Manhattan Bagels	$150,000	$337,000
McDonald's	$413,000	$1,300,000
Mrs. Fields Cookies	$45,000	$412,000
One Hour Martinizing Dry Cleaners	$180,000	$260,000
Rent a Wreck	$15,000	$207,000
Stanley Steemer Carpet Cleaner	$80,000	$340,000
Subway Sandwich	$61,000	$170,000
SuperCuts	$90,000	$164,000
Terminix Termite Pest Control	$42,000	$75,000
The Athletes Foot	$175,000	$325,000

Source: *Entrepreneur* magazine, January 1999

and software businesses. I've invested in Broadway plays. I've even owned a piece of a professional basketball team, the Utah Jazz. Network marketing beats them all. My overhead is minuscule compared to my former company that had 250 employees. Just the thought of going back to managing employees makes me cringe. I no longer need to pay salaries, benefits, social security taxes, workers' comp, health care, retirement plans. To an ex-employer like myself, it seems like a miracle.

But, you say, "I don't want to end up with a garage full of unwanted products." Neither would I. And frankly, this used to be a problem with some Wave-One and Wave-Two companies that used high-pressure tactics to induce new distributors to buy thousands of dollars' worth of product to get started.

$$$

WIT & WISDOM

Discontent is the first necessity of progress.

THOMAS EDISON

That's what makes Wave-Three network marketing companies different. Gone are the days when distributors needed to stockpile products in their garages, deliver products door-to-door, fill out endless paperwork, and package and ship products nationwide. All of this drudgery is handled by the company. All you need to do is find customers, fill out some minimal paperwork, answer questions, and do some training. And you're in business.

But, you say, it seems like everybody is into this. Won't I run out of people? Don't be silly. There are 300 million people in North America alone, of which less than 10 percent have ever been involved in network marketing. Plus hundreds of millions, even billions, of people in other countries. Although network marketing was invented in America, it's even bigger and more popular in Japan and is booming in the Far East.

In fact, that's the exciting thing about network marketing. You will be personally involved in the recruiting, sponsoring, and training of the first few dozen distributors in your organization . . . but then it starts to take on a life of its own. These first few people recruit others, who then recruit others . . . until it spreads to other parts of the country and even to other countries. If you persist, your organization soon consists of hundreds, even thousands, of people all over the world who are buying products— people whom you have never met, whom you never will meet, but people who nonetheless are helping to build for you a nice residual income of hundreds of even thousands of dollars a month. This is what I call leverage. It's truly amazing.

Question 3. What do I have to do to really make this work?

First let me tell you what you *won't* have to do.

You won't be delivering many products to anyone. If you were looking forward to delivering products to your neighbors door-to-door, you'll be very disappointed. Third-Wave network marketing companies don't work that way. What will you do? You'll just tell a few people about how much the products have improved your life, and, after some simple paperwork, they'll order the products directly from the company over a toll-free line. The company even handles the delivery for you.

You won't have to attend a lot of boring weeknight meetings. If you were looking forward to donating two or three nights of your week to attending a bunch of boring meetings, you'll probably not like this business. What will you do? You'll just share one of your chosen company's powerful audio- or videocassettes with people who show an interest, and these tools do all of the work for you.

You won't be doing a lot of face-to-face selling. If you love to sell, if you like to handle tough objections, if you live for the thrill of the close, then I'm sorry but I have some bad news. You'll probably do very well in one of those ancient network marketing companies where you have to find 50 or 100 customers to make any decent money. But in many of the new Third-Wave companies, you need only a few new customers a month to start on your road to success. There are 5 billion people on this planet. Do you think you could find two people a month who are interested in adding extra streams of income to their life?

Here is how it will probably work at first. You'll share an audiocassette with someone you meet, who will listen to it and say, "I'm interested. Tell me more." You'll set an appointment for your prospect to have lunch with you and your sponsor. The three of you show up at the appointed time. Your prospect listens while your sponsor does all the talking. You just observe. (This is your on-the-job training.) Your prospect signs up and starts ordering the product. You get a check.

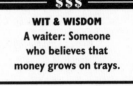

$$$

WIT & WISDOM
A waiter: Someone
who believes that
money grows on trays.

Does this sound too hard? This is the exact model Collette used to sponsor my wife. She showed us a video. My wife said, "Tell me more." Collette said, "Let's have lunch." And my wife said, "If that grumpy husband of mine isn't interested, we'll go ahead without him." And that's what they did.

Using this model, Collette makes more money during her lunch hour than most people earn in a month. And she continues to be paid over and over again for that same effort. Wouldn't it be nice to get paid over and over again for time you spent at lunch six months ago?

What if you don't have time for lunch? Easy. Do it over the phone. It's actually faster and cheaper. Be sure to involve your sponsor in the phone call (a three-way call, to include you, your sponsor, and the prospect). Your sponsor does the presentation while you "observe" (on-the-job training). The prospect joins your team, orders some products, and you start to earn a small stream of income.

Does this sound too hard to you? You listen. Your sponsor talks. People order products. You get checks.

With just a few hours a week on the phone, you can create a wonderful stream of residual income. Would you donate a few hours of your flexible time each week if you knew you could be earning $2,000 to $3,000 a week in residual income in two to three years?

Are You Crazy?

When I explain how simple this can be, some people look at me as though I'm crazy. So I give them the financial-freedom test:

"Do you have multiple streams of income flowing into your life?"
    (They usually answer no.)

"Do you get paid multiple times for every hour you work?" (Again no.)

"Are your hourly earnings potentially unlimited?" (Still no.)

"Do your income streams flow 24 hours a day with or without you?" (No.)

"Do you own or control these streams of income?" (No.)

"Will your income streams continue to flow after you die?" (No.)

"Can you give yourself a raise any time you want?" (No.)

"If your main income stream dries up, could you survive for a year without income?" (No.)

Then I say, "Because of network marketing, I can answer yes to each of the preceding questions." I wonder which of us is the crazy one?

> *This is my definition of crazy:* **Crazy,** n. Work for peanuts at various jobs you hate for 50 years. Then die poor.

> *This is my definition of smart:* **Smart,** n. Work hard for a much shorter period of time. Retire with multiple streams of residual income.

We've been earning regular, residual streams of income from network marketing income for years now. This is smart. This is intelligent. This works! As you can tell, I'm not a skeptic anymore. Sometimes I get so excited I can't sleep at night. Not because of the money I make, but because of the good that is done, the lives that are influenced, the personal growth that I see. This is fun. Yes, fun!

But it's not without its sadness, too. Here's the hardest part for me. I see people struggling financially in their lives. I see people in poor health. I see people whose lives are not working. I say to them, "I've got an answer for you that works!" But because they've tried other forms of network marketing that didn't work, or because they know someone who tried and failed, their minds snap shut. I can't blame them. That's exactly what I did. Still, I wish I had the power to persuade them to take a closer look. They might just like what they find.

Sometimes You Need Someone to Show You the Way

Most people live their lives unaware of the incredible opportunities that exist all around them. I'm reminded of the story of a woman in the early days of this century. She saved for many years to come to America, and she finally had enough money to afford passage on a large ocean liner. Because money was so tight, she stayed in her cabin most of the time, rationing the food she'd brought on board with her. With one day left on her journey, she decided to splurge on a meal. She showed up for the final banquet buffet, and, bracing herself for the bad news, she timidly asked the maître d' how much a meal like this would cost. "But madam, didn't you know? All of the meals are included with your ticket. You can eat as much as you like—for free."

Life is like that. You don't want to get to the end of your life and realize that you could have had anything you wanted if someone had just shown you the way. With the same effort you're now expending, you can be enjoying the banquet of prosperity that life has to offer. *Well, enough motivation. Let's get started.*

Let me show you a specific system for building a lifetime stream of income in network marketing.

First the bad news. It's been reported that as many as 90 percent of the people who get involved in network marketing fail at it. Here's why. . . .

The vast majority of people who get started are not committed. Because they had little to risk in starting (a $50 distributor kit and a few hundred dollars' worth of products), they also have little to risk in quitting. (They eat up their personal inventory and they're out of business.) At the first sign of resistance, they quit. Easy in, easy out.

Because of the ease of entry, the industry tends to attract a get-rich-quick crowd. They play the network marketing game like they play the lottery. Buy a cheap ticket and, if it doesn't work out, no big deal. Some people bounce from company to company like MLM junkies.

In my experience, once you weed out the flakes, the people who stick with network marketing as a serious business endeavor are among the most dedicated, hardworking, wonderful people I've ever associated with.

Still, there are many who work hard at network marketing and can't seem to find the right combination. After five years of studying this industry, I've figured out what works and what doesn't work. Just as I did with real estate, I reduced the entire business to three basic principles. If you'll follow these basic steps, you, too, can be successful at this:

Principle 1: Select the right company.

Principle 2: Use the right marketing system.

Principle 3: Use the right leadership system.

Principle 1: Select the Right Company

There are between 200 and 300 legitimate, long-term, viable companies involved in the network marketing business today—marketing everything from toys to skin care to long-distance telephone services to financial services to legal services to nutrition. When choosing the right company for you, you should examine the following three criteria*:

---

* I can cover these items only briefly in this chapter. My favorite in-depth analysis of how to choose a network marketing company is by Daren Falter. It's called *How to Select a Network Marketing Company.* It's excellent. He has exhaustively researched over 200 companies and analyzes the top 50. If you'll go to my web site at www.multiplestreamsofincome.com, I'll tell you how to obtain your own free copy (keyword Free Falter Book), or call my office at 801-852-8700.

1. The products or services of the business

2. The compensation plan: How will you get paid?

3. The company and its management

Choosing the Right Products or Services

Pick a product you are passionate about or would like to become passionate about. If you do, it will be easy for you to talk to other people about it. . . . It will become your hobby, not just your livelihood. Personally, I picked the health industry. Whether your passion is health, cosmetics, or jewelry, there is most likely a company that markets products you could get excited about.

The most important consideration when selecting a network marketing company is the type of products that the company markets. By "type" I mean the frequency of consumption. Does your customer use the product daily, weekly, monthly, or infrequently? You want a product with high-frequency consumption. Why? Because it generates frequent reorders . . . usually on a monthly basis. Frequent reorders mean constant, residual business. Therefore, and this is extremely important, your business can grow with fewer customers. If, however, the product is used infrequently, orders will be sporadic and infrequent. Therefore, it will mean that you will have to attract more new customers to be able to build enough residual monthly orders to earn regular checks.

The growth of any business is dependent upon an influx of new customers and continuing orders from a base of existing customers. If your base of existing customers reorders your product only on an infrequent basis, then the major source of growth will have to be in attracting large numbers of new customers. Any businessperson will tell you that attracting new customers is the most difficult and most expensive way to build a business. If, however, your existing customer base must reorder frequently, you will be able to build a stable foundation for your business.

To earn residual income, you want a product that lends itself easily to residual reorders. That's the main reason I love nutritional products. People consume them on a daily basis and reorder them every single month to replenish their supply. I also like nutritional products because people can feel the difference in their health—which is one of the most important areas of life.

To illustrate, let me share with you the ancient Arabic formula for wealth, shown in Figure 11.1. In this formula, 1 represents your health, and all the zeros represent everything else in your life . . . cars, houses, stocks, jewelry, real estate, and so forth. As you can see, if you take away the 1 at the beginning (your health), then everything else is truly just a bunch of zeros!

$$1,000,000,000,000$$

When you select products to represent, try to choose those that are

```
                        e
                        t
                        a
                        t
         h    s   s
         t    e   k e
         l    s   s c  l
         a    r u o a
         e    a o t e
         h    c h s r
```

$X,000,000,000,000$

FIGURE 11.1   The ancient formula for wealth.

more like 1s and less like 0s. It fits the money tree formula you learned in Chapter 3: *essential to everybody every day.*

Choosing the Right Compensation Plan

There are five or six different and competing systems that network marketing companies use to reward their intrapreneurs/distributors/associates/affiliates. They are the *breakaway,* the *unilevel,* the *matrix,* the *two-up,* the *binary,* and various hybrid or combination plans. Sounds confusing already, doesn't it?

Let me make it simple for you. Over 75 percent of the companies in the industry use a breakaway or stair-step breakaway plan made popular by such industry giants as Amway, Shaklee, and Nu Skin. In my opinion, they represent old-style network marketing. Recently, these older plans have been losing ground to newer, more equitable, simpler pay plans . . . like the unilevel and the binary used by such rising stars as FreeLife and USANA. Older companies have a challenge keeping up with innovations in compensation plans because their huge distributor base is locked into a single-pay plan.

The most important consideration when choosing a pay plan is the number of people that the average person needs to enroll to begin earning income. Here is the question you would ask before you join a company:

> *How many customers do I need to enroll to be able*
> *to earn $500 a month in extra income?*

The lower the number, the better. If it's relatively easy for the average person to earn a steady income, it will be easier for you to grow your business.

Choosing the Right Company and Management Team

As in any industry, the majority of network marketing businesses fail in the first five years. Therefore, you need to be extremely careful in selecting a company that is going to stand the test of time. The easiest way to do this is to select only a company that has a track record of increasing sales and profits for at least five years. This narrows the field drastically.

On the plus side, if the company you're researching is publicly traded, so much the better. It will be easy to scan the financial statements and quarterly earnings reports. You're looking for a company that is well managed, solvent, with little or no debt, that has reached a critical mass of distributors to sustain growth and that has been around long enough to have worked out the beginning bugs.

WIT & WISDOM

You will become . . . "as small as your controlling desire, as great as your dominant aspiration."

JAMES ALLEN

Check your local Better Business Bureau to see if any complaints have been filed against the company either in your state or nationwide. It will be an indication of the ability of the company to keep out of trouble. If you find problems, you might also check with your state attorney general's office to see if there are any legal actions pending that might affect the ability of the company to do business in your state.

If you are so inclined, you might even make a visit to the headquarters of the company to check things out. Because your income relies on the ability of the company to survive long term, you might even visit with members of top management.

Once you've selected a product, a company, and a compensation plan, you're ready to launch your business.

Principle 2: Use the Right Marketing System

By *marketing system,* I mean how you will attract your customers. Here is the system that most people use to get started in traditional network marketing:

- Make a list of at least 100 names, including everyone you know.
- Call each of them and try to sell them your product or opportunity.

What a formula! It's simple. It's cheap. It's duplicable. But 90 percent of the people who follow that system fail!

Why? Because, the odds of finding a truly qualified customer in any average group of 100 people is very low. Maybe only 1 to 2 percent are actually seeking your product or opportunity *at this moment*—5 percent if you're lucky. Zig Ziglar himself couldn't find more than five good customers in this group. Ninety-five people would turn him down. That's a 95 percent rejection rate—and he's the best salesperson in the world! What's going to happen when our untrained beginner calls this same list? Massive rejection followed by failure.

It's not necessarily because the product is bad or the opportunity is not good or even because the beginner doesn't know how to sell. It's because the odds of finding two good customers in *any list* of 100 average people is very low. But the beginner doesn't know this. Armed with unrealistic expectations, novices call everyone they know, and after only a few calls, it *appears* as if *nobody* is interested. Because these people are supposed to be their friends, beginners take these rejections *personally.* It's painful. And that's why they quit. It sounded so easy when they signed up. But in reality, finding those first two good customers was much harder than they expected.

But here's the good news. Although a beginner feels defeated with only a 5 percent success rate, any mail-order marketer will tell you that a 5 percent response rate is fantastic! It's the stuff fortunes are made of. Mail-order marketers are ecstatic with a 1 or 2 percent response rate!

For example, suppose I'm trying to market a two-day seminar about network marketing. The cost is $295. I write a direct-mail letter and rent a target mailing list of 20,000 prospective buyers. The cost of the letter, the list, and the postage are about $15,000. If I get a 1 percent response rate—which is 200 people—I'm thrilled. It generates $59,000 ($295 × 200) in revenue. After all costs, a substantial profit remains.

Here is the fundamental principle behind any successful network marketing business:

> *If you can find just one or two customers in*
> *every 100 contacts, you can build a fortune.*

Collette, my ex-secretary, invited 44 people to her first meeting. Four people showed up and two people left early. But the two who remained were excited and signed up. From the genesis of those first two people, Collette earns today an income in excess of *$1 million* per year.

How can you find two good people like this? The problem is that most people are not good at selling. . . . In fact, they hate selling. It's not the actual selling they hate, it's the rejection.

To be successful in network marketing you need a system that . . .

Dramatically lowers the probability of rejection.

Sifts through the 100 people to automatically find the five who are most interested.

Gets those five prospects to call you on the phone and tell you they're interested.

Automatically trains the two hottest prospects to sell themselves and give you the money.

Even if you hate to sell, suppose people *asked you* to sell them a product, would you turn them down? I don't think so. Let me show you how to get people to call you and almost beg you to sell them something. In order to do that, we have to take the old *selling* paradigm and turn it around 180 degrees into a *marketing* paradigm. Here are the paradigm shifts:

Traditional Network Sales Model	**High-Tech Network Marketing Model**
Outbound:	*Inbound:*
You call people and try to sell them stuff.	They call us and want to buy.
Massive rejection:	*No rejection:*
You make 10 calls and suffer 9 rejections to find one hot prospect.	Only the hot prospect responds. The 9 cold ones don't respond. Good. We don't want to talk to them anyway. Who wants unnecessary rejection?
Sales model:	*Interview model:*
You try to convince them that you have the best product.	We "interview" them to determine if they are the right fit for our product and opportunity. We decide whether *we* want *them* on our team . . . not the other way around.

In other words, we don't do sales, we do marketing. We talk to only those who "raise their hands."

Well, enough theory. Let me show you how the system works. Study the funnel diagram in Figure 11.2. Then I'll walk you through a system to fill up that funnel with hot prospects.

Let's assume it's an ordinary Monday, the first day of the month. You've chosen your company, and your distributor kit has just arrived along with a small supply of your company's products and some marketing materials (tapes, brochures, etc.). Let's assume your goal is to earn your first networking check within 21 to 30 days from the moment you launch.

Just a reminder about the kind of income we're going to be earning: If all you want is to earn some extra money, you could always go into the working world and get a part-time job ($10 an hour and 20 hours a week gives you a quick $200). From that, of course, you have to deduct the hard costs: taxes, gas, insurance, and child care if necessary. Then you add the emotional cost of this part-time work . . . dressing up, getting stuck in commuter traffic, dealing with a grouchy boss and office politics, sacrificing your freedom. When you add it all up and subtract the negatives, there's not much left over. And all you have to look forward to is another week just like the last one—week after miserable week as far into the future as you can see.

The kind of income I want to show you how to earn is a recurring stream of income, one that can possibly continue to flow for years to come. Most people who toil in the working world have difficulty imagin-

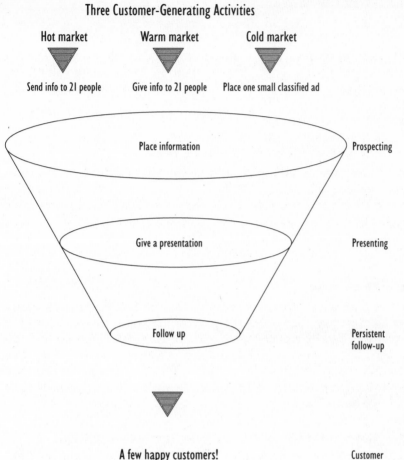

Three Customer-Generating Activities

Hot market — Send info to 21 people

Warm market — Give info to 21 people

Cold market — Place one small classified ad

Place information — Prospecting

Give a presentation — Presenting

Follow up — Persistent follow-up

A few happy customers! — Customer retention

FIGURE 11.2 **The marketing funnel.**

ing this kind of income flowing into their lives. But those of us in the networking world see it happening every single day. And the best part of this world is the lifestyle.

For me, it's not about the money. It's all about lifestyle. For example, my commute time from my bed in the morning to my office is 26 seconds (I know because I just timed it). This saves me an hour a day in commute time. That's an extra hour I can spend with my family. That's something you can't put a price tag on. When you're the boss, you get to choose the dress code. For me, it's my exercise outfit. And I rarely shave before noon. When I'm on the phone (where I do most of my business) people can't tell what I look like. And I like it that way. There are no office politics in my home office. And here's the exciting part: In contrast to the working world, there is no limit to the amount you can earn in the networking world. Low downside, huge upside potential. That's a good combination.

The 21-Day Challenge

What quality of lifestyle do you want, and what price are you willing to pay to get it? It takes a special kind of person, a person with vision, to step back from the pressures of life and say, "I don't want to live like this anymore," and then to do something about it. Even though you may be earning good money, it can't be all that good if it's attached to a bad lifestyle.

Here's the seven-step plan. Let's call it the 21-day challenge.

Step 1: Set aside at least 5 to 10 hours a week.

That's about an hour a day. For most people, that's difficult, because our lives are already full. Luckily, I'll show you how to earn this extra income by using a golden minute here, a spare moment there. You'd be surprised how, just by reshuffling some of your time and refocusing your priorities, you can grow a wonderful stream of extra income. Are you willing to do that?

Step 2: Think small.

You heard me right. Most opportunities boast of how you can earn huge amounts of money . . . $100,000 a year for life—in three weeks! It's just not realistic. So, let's chunk down. Shoot for a few hundred to a few thousands dollars a month. When the checks have started to flow and you have proven to yourself that this is realistic for you—given your personality, your time, and your circumstances—then you can decide whether you want to go for the big bucks.

Step 3: Make a list of 21 sharp, opportunity-oriented people.

Twenty-one. No more, no less. Choose people you know who might be interested in earning an extra stream of income. Let me say that again: Don't put anyone on that list unless you think that person might be interested in earning some extra income. I call these people *hot market contacts* because they are people you know—friends, coworkers, relatives, members of groups you belong to. You're going to be sending these people a very nonthreatening package of information that is designed to find one person . . . only one in twenty-one . . . who might be interested in what we have. Let me repeat, we expect to find only *one* person from this list.

When you join your selected company, ask your sponsor to help you gather a package of the company's top prospecting materials* . . . audiocassettes, videos, special reports, or brochures. You can also obtain excellent generic prospecting tools from a company called Sound Concepts.

* For my own team, I have created a special starter kit complete with 42 audiocassettes, 21 special mailing envelopes, and 21 specially designed marketing letters in box with a handle . . . like a business in a box. It's called "21 Days to Freedom."

You can find a link to them at www.successfulpeople.com. Your job is to organize 42 sets of these materials. Using your list of 21 people, address and stuff the mailers, affix the proper postage, seal them, and set the mailers aside. Don't mail them yet.

Step 4: Prepare 21 sets of prospecting materials to hand out.

As you go about your normal day, there will be opportunities to meet new people, people you may not know but who might be interested in earning an extra stream of income. I call these people *warm market contacts* because they are people you meet on a daily basis. I'm going to show you a very nonthreatening way to hand out these 21 tapes to 21 interested people over the next 21 days. This activity is designed to find one person . . . only one in twenty-one . . . who might be interested.

Step 5: It's time for action. Drop the 21 mailers in the mail.

As soon as you've dropped them in the mail, you now focus on handing out one tape a day. That should be your habit . . . one tape a day, no matter what. Do you think you could do that? For 21 straight days?

Here's how. Notice how many people you interface with each day. At lunch, while shopping, at the gym, at a school meeting, in a mall, at work. There are dozens of possibilities. Your assignment is to hand out one of these tapes to an interested person each day. How will you know they're interested? After breaking the ice, ask them, "Have you ever thought about adding an extra stream of income to your life?"

If you get a yes, say, "So have I. In fact, I've decided to do something about it. For the next 21 days, I'm going to hand out one tape a day to help me find someone who would like to create extra streams of income. I've got an incredible tape that I'd like to give you . . . Will you listen to it?"

Get their name and number and set an appointment to call them back. Just before you leave, say this: "Whether you want to do this or not is not important. I'm just looking for one person who wants to improve his or her life dramatically. My goal is to help that one person start earning income within 30 days. When I call, I'm not going to try to get you to do this. . . . If the tape doesn't get you excited then, this isn't for you. I'm calling only to ask you what you thought. Just tell me frankly what you thought, negative or positive. . . . It makes no difference to me. The only thing that will really offend me is if you won't return my calls. When I call, just tell me straight, "This sounds good, let's do it," or, "You know, this just doesn't sound like me."

Step 6: Follow up.

This is the most important step. It is the razor's edge between success and failure. You can't expect to just mail out or hand out some tapes and then have people start throwing money at you. We all are busy. Most of us need multiple exposures to a new idea for it to sink in. Here's how to follow up.

As soon as you've dropped the information in the mail to your top 21 people, call them all on the phone the same day, tell them you've sent them a package of information, and ask them to be looking for it. This will ensure that when they get it, they won't throw it away. Ask if it would be okay for you to call them after they've reviewed it to get their reaction. If you can't reach a live voice, just leave a message on their answering machine.

Some people hate to communicate with their hot market. Why? Perhaps they've already approached these same people with previous opportunities that didn't pan out. In short, they're embarrassed to contact them again. That is why sending letters is so nonthreatening. If they're not interested, they won't respond. If they are interested, they will respond. Let them make that decision, not you. It's been my experience that in *any* group of 100 people, there are *always* a few who will respond to an opportunity—if only out of curiosity. Since the last time you contacted your list, a few of them may now *need* an opportunity. Your letter might just be a godsend. Don't you want to be the answer to someone's prayers?

In 21 days, you'll be talking to a total of 42 people. Here's the question to ask when you make the follow-up call, "Well, what did you think?" And just let them talk. Don't be defensive, just listen. Listen as if you were an employer trying to hire a new employee. See if you can select the best person for the job. If you wouldn't hire the person for a real job, maybe you wouldn't want to work with them in your new business. I want you to cycle through those 42 people until you get a no, a maybe or a yes, from every single one of them. This may take several calls. I've included a sample follow-up chart to track your contacts (see Figure 11.3). Marketing executives have long quoted the statistic that 80 percent of the sales take place after the fifth contact. Why is this? Because nobody follows up! Those who persist get the gold.

Once again, it all boils down to finding two people *and* helping them to find two people. Do you think you could do this? Let me show you how to dramatically improve your odds of finding those two people *fast*.

Step 7: Increase the probability that one person in twenty-one will say yes.

1. *Do a three-way call.* I highly recommend that you ask your sponsor, the person who enrolled you in your company, to be with you during the initial call—not only for moral support but to add credibility to the process. (In networking, we call this a *three-way call.*) Also include your sponsor in the follow-up call. Believe me, it will dramatically improve your success rate. Something magical happens when the two of you work together.

2. *If you can, meet with them face-to-face.* Better yet, try to meet with your hottest prospects face-to-face if possible, perhaps over lunch. If you can, get them to a local meeting where they can rub shoulders with the kind of people your company attracts.

Our Three Main Customer-Generating Activities

| Hot market | Warm market | Cold market |

Goal: To fill up your follow-up funnel with 21 interested people as fast as you can.

Name of Prospect	1st Follow-up	2nd Follow-up	3rd Follow-up	4th Follow-up	5th Follow-up
1.					
2.					
3.					
4.					
5.					
6.					
7.					
8.					
9.					
10.					
11.					
12.					
13.					
14.					
15.					
16.					
17.					
18.					
19.					
20.					
21.					

FIGURE 11.3 The follow-up funnel.

3. *Use high-tech recruiting systems.* You can also build credibility by directing interested prospects to any of your company web sites, hot lines, weekly or daily conference calls, and so on. If you would like to experience how a system like this might work, check out the hot line at 1-801-235-0600 and/or the web site at www.successfulpeople .com.

All told, you'll be distributing sets of materials to 42 people in your first 21 days. This is designed to find two sharp, interested people—let's call them Bob and Sue. When Bob and Sue become part of your team and buy a supply of products for their personal use, you will most likely earn your first small check. This may not seem like much to you now, but remember, this could be the start of recurring streams of income.

In your next 21 days of activity, you will be working with your first two people to help them find *their* first two people using the same 21-day system.

Let's assume they do it. In your second month, there would be six people on your team in addition to yourself. Every time anyone on your team buys one of the company products, you earn a small referral fee. As the weeks roll forward, you continue to work with Bob and Sue to help each of their two people find two more people. At the end of the third month, your team potentially consists of 14 people. Bob and Sue below you, four people below them, and eight people below them $(2 + 4 + 8 = 14)$.

In this third month, if everything goes according to plan, everyone on your team is consuming products and your checks are getting larger and larger . . . large enough to catch your attention. Bob and Sue's checks could be growing as well. And many of the people below them are starting to earn their very first checks. Your top people are starting to see that if they just follow the plan, consume these wonderful products on a daily basis, and find a few others who consume these products, then everyone can earn income.

By this time, you'll most likely have a product success story to tell. When you meet people you know, you'll be able to say with conviction that your part-time, home-based business is starting to work. Your enthusiasm will be contagious.

In the ideal situation, after six months your team could consist of over 100 people, of whom you have personally sponsored only a handful. The other people on the team have brought in the rest. Now you're starting to see the power of leverage. Then the magic begins as people below you start bringing in customers from other parts of the country and, eventually, from other parts of the world. Your influence is spreading all over the planet, and small streams of income are flowing from the four corners of the earth. And you didn't even have to leave home!

Placing Small, Classified Ads

When you're ready to accelerate your business building, I encourage you to attract new prospects by using inexpensive classified advertising. This is the most exciting but least effective of the three approaches. For every 50 prospects who enter the top of your funnel, there may be only one or two who come through for you. It's hard to warm up these people, and they cool down very quickly. But they are an important part of the system.

The fastest, cheapest way to get your phone to ring is to place an inexpensive classified ad. Returning calls to these prospects is excellent practice. After all, these are total strangers—if they reject you, who cares? Knowing that there is a low probability of success with these cold leads helps remind us that this is a numbers game. Some will join your team. Some won't. So what? Next! But there can be gold in the gravel, so even if the odds are low, you should run ads regularly.

Here are some guidelines:

1. *Keep your budget small.* Don't spend more than $50 to $100 a month on this activity.

2. *Don't run your ad longer than a week at a time.* I prefer the ads to run for three to five days. Even though you might get a better rate by running an ad for a longer period of time, opt instead for the short-term ads. Your job is to test which ads and which newspapers pull the best leads. Change ads often. Try different combinations of headlines and body copy. Try putting the headline in bold type. Put your ads in the income-opportunity section of the paper. Keep track of the number of calls that come from each ad and each paper. You will generally find a combination that outpulls the rest by a wide margin.

3. *Run your ad in the cheapest local paper possible.* Every city has dozens of inexpensive daily and weekly newspapers. Some are by subscription and others are free local rags found at gas stations and convenience stores. Start with the cheapest paper possible. This is not because the leads are better (they're not), but it's just a good, cheap way to get your feet wet. The quality of the prospect generally mirrors the quality of the newspaper—the cheaper the paper, the poorer the lead. But we're just testing and practicing.

Don't run your ads in nationwide magazines or newspapers until you have honed your skills. Stay local at first. It's easier to develop rapport with people in your geographic area. It's also easier to build a local support group. Once you've perfected your system locally, you can expand your horizons. There are over 7,000 newspapers in the United States alone.

Here is an example of a classified ad that works:

Perfect part-time home business!
2 hours/day earns you financial freedom.
24-hr. msg. 800-668-7262

If you'd like a list of ads that have worked well in the past, including our latest winning ads, call my office at 801-852-8700.

The best format is for your ad to contain a 24-hour recorded message so that a prospect can "taste" what you have to offer without having to

$$$ Sample Three-Minute Script for a $$$
24-Hour Recorded Message

Thanks for calling. Would you like to *add an extra stream of income* to your life this year? My associate and I are looking for a few people who really want to be financially free. Does this describe you? First, let me tell you who I am and why we're *selecting* people for a brand-new moneymaking program.

My name is Robert Allen. I'm the author of two of the largest-selling financial books of all time, *Nothing Down* and *Creating Wealth*, published by Simon and Schuster. Both were number one *New York Times* mega-best-sellers. My current best-selling audio program is called *Multiple Streams of Income: How to Generate a Lifetime of Unlimited Wealth.* For the past 20 years, I've been helping people just like you to create financial success, and many of today's millionaires credit their success to the secrets that I taught them. And now it's your turn.

I'd like to send you some *free* information about a brand-new way of making money that has me more excited than anything I have ever seen. It's simple, it's powerful, and, more important, it really works. We'd like to show you how you can *start earning streams of extra income* almost immediately. And the best part is, my associate and I are willing to coach you for free. But we want to work with only the few who are ready to *take action now.*

How about you? Are you ready? Is this your year? Do you really want to be financially free? If you're the kind of person we're looking for, this could really change your life. I'm going to ask my associate to send you some more information. Included with the information is my latest special report containing the most important financial concepts I've ever learned. I know you'll enjoy it. But I only want to send it to those who can answer yes to the following three questions.

Question 1. Would you be willing to *spend 5 to 10 hours a week* working with me and my team using this revolutionary new system if you knew you could really be successful at this? If you answered yes, please continue. As you know, it can sometimes take thousands of dollars to start a new business from scratch. However, this new system can be launched for only a few hundred dollars. Fully guaranteed, of course.

Question 2. Is your financial future important enough that you'd be willing to *commit such a small amount of money* if you were convinced *that this could really take you to financial freedom?* If you answered yes, please continue.

Question 3. On a scale of 1 to 10, with 1 meaning, "I'm just window-shopping," and 10 meaning, "*I'm extremely interested and ready to act immediately,*" how would rate your interest level at this time?

If your interest level is 5 or less, you can hang up now. We hope you have success in some other venture. If your level of interest is 6, 7, or 8 we invite you to *leave your name, address, and phone number* so we can send you valuable *free* information. Remember, no information will be sent without a telephone number. If your interest level is high, a 9 or 10, make sure you *say this when you leave your name, address, and phone number* so we can rush this powerful information to you ASAP. The only thing we ask is that you *review it within 24 hours.* Then let's talk again.

Oh, by the way, how does it feel to be one phone call away from having everything you've ever wanted? Please leave your name and number at the sound of the beep, *now.*

commit. This type of toll-free ad will generate many more calls than one that gives a local number with the possibility of a live person. The script you record on the three-minute message should be compelling enough to encourage serious prospects to leave their name and number but strong enough to discourage curiosity seekers. The sample script starting on page 203 has worked extremely well for me.

Principle 3: Use the Right Leadership System

Earlier I told you that your success depends upon three basic principles: (1) selecting the right company, (2) using the right marketing system, and (3) using the right leadership system. It's now time to talk about leadership.

Each of the streams of income in this book emphasizes a different aspect of business. Stock market investing is about managing numbers. Real estate is about managing properties. The Internet is about managing technology. Infopreneuring is about managing communication. Network marketing is about managing people and developing leaders.

As your group starts to grow, you will begin to experience a whole new set of challenges. The real secret to creating residual income is to develop leaders in your downline who, because of their own self-interest, will have an incentive to grow your business as well. To develop leaders in your group, you will need to focus on training, support, and recognition. The leadership funnel is illustrated in Figure 11.4. This chart may not mean much to you now, but when you have a large organization, as I have, you quickly learn why each part of this chart is critical to growing a vibrant and long-lasting team. Therefore, I encourage you do to the following:

1. *Hold weekly training sessions with your key leaders.* These meetings can be held over the phone using inexpensive conference-calling technology. My own training calls are held each Monday in the later afternoon. This keeps us focused for the week.

2. *Hold weekly training meetings for all new members of your team.* You'll be amazed at how a 30-minute weekly teleconference with your group can sustain enthusiasm and teach critical skills. The only cost to link up team members is the long-distance phone bill. In this way, I am able to train hundreds of people simultaneously from any telephone in the world. I call this the *PowerTrain.* I've conducted conference training calls from Singapore, Sydney, Auckland, London, Winnipeg, Toronto, Chicago, and from a cell phone on a halibut fishing boat in Homer, Alaska.

3. *Hold weekly recruiting conference calls to support your team.* For the first several weeks, new distributors are uncomfortable talking about either the products or the opportunity. That's why I hold a weekly recruiting call—a 30-minute, live discussion via teleconference— during which I discuss our products and our opportunity with my new team members and their invited guests. This serves two impor-

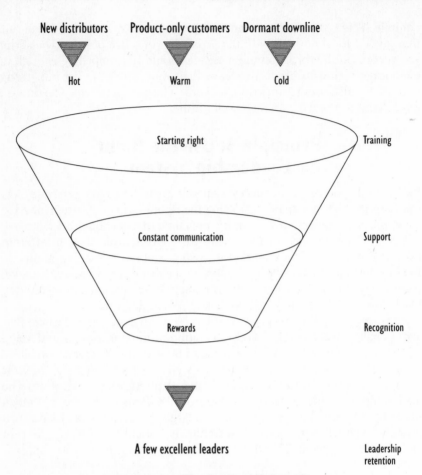

FIGURE 11.4 The leadership funnel.

tant purposes: (1) The new members of the team are trained in how a presentation should done; (2) their guests receive a presentation from the person who is the most qualified to give it. It is very effec-tive.

If you've read this far and still aren't convinced (as I was not at first), then I encourage you to reserve judgment for a few more pages. I have two more surprises for you. The first surprise I've hidden on my web site at www.multiplestreamsofincome.com (use the keywords: Still skeptical). If that doesn't convince you to be more open-minded, then perhaps the last surprise will. Hidden in Chapter 14 is a marketing idea that I've held back especially for those who are still skeptical about launching a network marketing business.

For the rest of you, it's off to the next chapter.

CHAPTER 12

At this moment, you are one classified ad away from a fortune.
ROBERT ALLEN

YOUR EIGHTH STREAM
Infopreneuring: How to Turn a Tiny Classified Ad into a Fortune

In Chapters 8 and 9 I told you about the huge potential in *real* property. Well, there is substantially more money to be made in *intellectual* property. The money can be made faster and can result in lifetime streams of cash flow.

You say, "Show me the money!" I say, "Bring your wheelbarrow!"

In this chapter, I'll share with you what I believe is the most exciting opportunity of the new millennium: *information marketing.* An entrepreneur whose main product is information is called an "infopreneur." And information is a very hot topic.

Intellectual property is the real wealth of the new millennium. For proof, I offer you the name of William Gates III. Wealthiest person on the planet. Infopreneur extraordinaire. I rest my case.

Marketing Information

Don't let the term *intellectual property* confuse you. You don't need to be intellectual or have a high IQ to do extremely well in the information business. The information you market doesn't even have to be your information. Let me offer you two prime examples.

Case Study 1: Money for Nothing

Cindy Cashman took an old idea, added a twist to it, and made a fortune in the information business. Cindy now lives in a huge mansion on a lake in Texas. She made over $1 million from marketing her specialty book—all by herself, without a publisher. You might have seen her book, *Everything Men Know about Women* by Dr. Richard Harrison (her pseudonym). Here's the amazing part: *Cindy's book is totally blank!* There isn't a single word printed on any of the 96 pages of this paperback! Yet women bought this book by the caseload—100 books at a time to give to their friends! Cindy made enough to retire. She doesn't have to work another day in her life.

This is a true story. Cindy has been a guest lecturer at several of my intensive, hands-on infopreneur training sessions. She's now back in Texas working on a video version of her best-selling book . . . also blank.

Case Study 2: Secretary's Mistake Turns into $1 Million Income Stream!

Stan Miller loved to collect quotes. He started when he was 16 and continued until after he was married. For Christmas, he and his new wife Sharon decided that a compiled collection of all his quotes and stories would be a good Christmas gift. He went to a printer and asked how much it would cost to have 100 copies printed and bound. She said it would be cheaper to have 1,000 copies made. She quoted him $1,000 for 1,000 copies. Stan thought that sounded like a good price, so he ordered 1,000 copies. Unfortunately, when the bill came, it was $10,000 instead of $1,000! The secretary had misplaced a *zero!*

Stan and Sharon were devastated. In desperation, Stan took a few copies to the local university bookstore, but the bookstore didn't want them. The manager did agree to let him leave a few dozen copies on consignment. When Stan came back a week later, the books were all gone . . . much to everyone's surprise. The book took off like hotcakes, and now more than 1 million copies of several versions of this book have been sold. That was over 25 years ago, and the checks are still flowing. That secretary's silly mistake had turned into a $1 million godsend. By the way, the name of Stan's book is *Especially for Mormons.* There are now six volumes of quotes, stories, and thoughts designed to inspire and warm the heart.

------ **$$$** ------
WIT & WISDOM
I got what no millionaire's got. I got no money.

I've told Stan many times that there are still unmined millions in this idea: He could take the exact same thoughts, quotes, and stories and repackage them for dozens of other specialty groups. How about *Especially for Episcopalians,* or *Especially for Catholics,* or *Especially for Agnostics?*

Does this idea sound familiar? Yes, my two great friends, Jack Canfield and Mark Victor Hansen, have already capitalized on this idea in their incredibly popular book series, *Chicken Soup for the Soul.* Each book is a

compilation of 101 heartwarming stories contributed for free.* Jack and Mark don't have to
write a single word, and yet, as infopreneurs, they
will now earn lifetime streams of income. There
are now dozens of separate Chicken Soup books
(*Chicken Soup for the Pet Lover's Soul, Chicken
Soup for the Teenager's Soul,* etc.) with dozens
more on the drawing board. The authors have a
goal to have 1 billion books in print worldwide. Knowing them, I have no
doubt they'll pull it off.

━━━━ **$$$** ━━━━
WIT & WISDOM
The universe is full of magical things patiently waiting for our wits to grow sharper.
EDEN PHILLPOTTS

Turn Your Expertise/Passion/Hobby into Lifetime Cash-Flow Streams

You might wonder how little old you can sell your ideas when so many
other people seem to have beaten you to the punch. Fact is, anyone with a
good idea, a good plan, persistence, and some savvy can earn lifetime
streams of income selling information.

The Book Within: Everyone Has at Least One

It is my firm belief that everyone—including you—has a least one good
book in them. You have enough information and experience in your head
right now to turn into a lifetime stream of income. With some proper positioning, your book can become the cornerstone of an information empire.
An information empire? Well, at the very least, a modest stream of income
that could support you and your family.

Case Study 3: The One-Book Bookstore

When he was in his 70s, Walter Swann wrote a book about growing up in
Arizona with his brother Henry. He called his book *Me and Henry.* (Now,
there's a moneymaking title!) But no publisher would publish it. So he
published it himself. But no bookstore would buy it. Undaunted, he
rented a small vacant space right next to another major bookstore in his
city and opened his own bookstore. But his bookstore was unique. It carried only one title. He called it the One Book Bookstore. The only book
you can buy in his bookstore is *Me and Henry.*

Dumb idea, right? Wrong. He has sold thousands of books worldwide
and earned thousands of dollars a month from this one simple idea. Business
was so good he was even invited to be on *Late Night with David Letterman.*

All this success has prompted him to write another book. This one is
called *Me and Mama.* It was sold in a special room inside the One Book
Bookstore. It's called The Other Book Bookstore.

If Walter can do it, why can't you? Your life story or your life's exper-

---

* I contributed a story for *Chicken Soup II,* which I've posted at www.robertallen.com. Enter
the keyword Chicken Soup.

tise has market value if presented in a unique way. It may have enough market value to support you for life.

Turn Your Life Story into Money... Even If You've Been a Miserable Failure

Almost all successful books are based on personal failures. The author tells how he or she used to be fat, poor, ugly, unhappy, lonely, addicted, or dead—and through some miracle, willpower, or newfound knowledge was able to overcome failure and rise to the heights of success. Let me give you some pretty impressive examples,

Author	Title	Subject
Tony Robbins	*Unlimited Power*	Success
Susan Powter	*Stop the Insanity!*	Diet
John Bradshaw	*Homeward Bound*	Self-esteem
Betty J. Eadie	*Embraced by the Light*	Near-death experiences

The list could go on and on. Each of these infopreneurs used the story of their rise from the ashes of failure (even death) to create, if not an information empire, at least a powerful stream of extra income. Many of them now produce books, seminars, newsletters, tape programs, video courses, speeches, consulting relationships, and infomercials. They turned their failure-to-success stories into a fortune.

Do you ever wonder how those famous stars on those diet commercials are able to take the weight off and keep it off? How did they do it? Think! If someone offered you $500,000 to lose 50 pounds, wouldn't you be able to find the motivation somehow?

Now take this to the next logical conclusion. What if someone offered you $10 million to turn your life around right now. How much would it take for you to be motivated to perfect your relationships, to get in shape, or to get your financial act together? What if you decided that *you* are the before-and-after story?

$$$
WIT & WISDOM
Everything that has happened to you, good or bad, has cash value.

The truth is, where you are right now is your "before" picture. The worse your "before" picture is, the better your "after" picture will look. Once you find the motivation to fix yourself, then you, too, will be able to market your newfound know-how.

Case Study 4: Fat, Depressed, and Drunk— Surefire Formula for Success

As an example, let me offer you Susan Powter, who appeared out of nowhere in the early 1990s with her bleached crew cut, offering a hugely popular infomercial and best-selling book, *Stop the Insanity!* This is the marketing blurb about her book:

Susan tells how depression led to her 260-pound "fat coma" and how she overcame "the insanity" of the diet and fitness industry to develop her own wellness plan.

These failures, rather than being embarrassing, actually gave her credibility. It was the seed of her success. Ironically, she used this same formula in 1997 to produce another best-selling book— *Sober . . . And Staying That Way: The Missing Link in the Cure for Alcoholism.* Here is the marketing blurb for this book:

> **———— $$$ ————**
> **WIT & WISDOM**
> **If a book about failures doesn't sell, is it a success?**

With the same fierce determination that took her on a journey to understand and cure her own obesity, she set out to find the answers to her own alcoholism. For the first time, Susan Powter tells the story of her search for answers. What she found was the missing link in a cure for alcoholism— Powter devised a program that cured her and will work for millions of others.

Can you see the same failure-to-success formula from the previous story? Maybe the only thing you need to turn your life around right now is the realization that people might be willing to pay you plenty to teach them how to do what you did.

Let's look at another success expert, Tony Robbins. According to Tony, he started out as a loser, living in a studio apartment washing his dishes in a bathtub (his "before" picture). Then he discovered a new science of personal achievement, Neuro-Linguistic Programming, and applied it to himself. Soon he had raised himself from the ashes

> **———— $$$ ————**
> **WIT & WISDOM**
> **The chief cause of failure and unhappiness is trading what you want most for what you want at the moment.**

of failure to confidence and success (his "after" picture). He began marketing his ideas through a popular fire-walking seminar, *Fear into Power.* (Yes, I myself went and walked on fire in 1986. Powerful stuff.) Then came the hugely successful book, *Unlimited Power.* Then the groundbreaking infomercial with Guthy/Renker, which has sold millions of audio programs by the same name. Now he coaches presidents, gold medal–winning athletes, and corporate leaders.

You don't have to do it on such a grand scale. I've met small-time infopreneurs all over the world. At one speech in Florida, a woman shared with me how she has earned hundreds of thousands of dollars marketing her own self-published work to health food stores nationwide. It's called *I Cured My Arthritis. So Can You,* by Margie Garrison.

If she can do it, so can you. Everything in your life has value: the failures, the successes. It's all part of the equation. One mediocre idea with some good marketing power can generate a lifetime stream of cash. With some luck, it might even turn into millions of dollars. So, figure out how to turn your life around now and then tell the rest of us how you did it.

Case Study 5: You're One Classified Ad away from a Fortune!

I graduated in 1974 from Brigham Young University with a Master of Business Administration (MBA) degree. Don't let that impress you. I graduated in the one-third of my class that made the top two-thirds possible. It was during a major recession, and jobs were scarce. I sent resumes to 30 of the top companies in America: General Foods, General Electric, General Motors (generally, anybody I could think of). I received 30 rejection letters. I was running out of money. I had no job prospects. I was desperate. (Hint: This is my "before" picture.)

I had had an interest in real estate investment ever since reading Nickerson's classic book, *How I Turned $1000 into $1,000,000 in Real Estate in My Spare Time.* Rather than going for the secure paycheck (actually, nobody was offering me one), I asked a local multimillionaire real estate developer to take me under his wing and teach me the ropes. I was single. My financial needs were minimal. I would do anything he asked. He gave me a commission job selling recreational property (i.e., land in southern Utah good only for holding the world together). Working for him, I found and bought my first property, a small duplex apartment in Provo, Utah. The down payment of $1,500 took everything I had. This led to other successful purchases and a few notable failures. Within a few short years and some massaging of the numbers, I was a paper millionaire.

I decided to share my systems with a few of my close associates, who also profited. I wondered if anyone else might be interested and ran a small classified ad in my local newspaper. It offered to teach people "How to Buy Real Estate with Little or No Money Down." The next day my phone almost rang off the hook. With weeks, I was making up to $10,000 a day in the information business. Within months, I was pulling down up to *six figures a month.* It was crazy!

Then I licensed my name and ideas to a national seminar company who agreed to train people to use my systems and to pay me a nice royalty for every student. The timing was perfect. Within a year, my royalty checks had grown to between $25,000 and $50,000 a week! This went on for six years! These residual streams gave me the time to write and promote two best-selling books. When my licensing royalties dried up in 1985, I launched a new training business that took in another $100 million *for the same information* from many of *the same people!*

The concept of real estate investing was as old as the hills. What I added to the equation was to take old techniques and to repackage them under the banner of a single, sexy concept: "nothing down." Here is the result:

2.5 million book buyers at $20	$50,000,000
100,000 seminar attendees at $500	$50,000,000
20,000 Wealth Training graduates at $5,000	<u>$100,000,000</u>
	$200,000,000

Of course, these are gross dollars, not net profits, but it still amounts to over $200 million from one silly idea! This doesn't include additional millions from audio programs, newsletters, ancillary products. Add to this all of the knockoffs of *Nothing Down* from Dave Del Dotto, Tommy Vu, Carlton Sheets, and dozens of other copycats, and the tally goes even higher.

During my lifetime, over $1 billion is going to be dug out of the mine shaft called *Nothing Down* real estate. It was a *billion-dollar idea!*

In this chapter I will share with you the blueprint for how I did this. Once you uncover a mother lode of ore, you can spend the rest of your lifetime digging it out . . . as I have done. I want to share with you a shortcut to making money fast in the information business. I hope to help you avoid the many mistakes I have made in my career. This can save you hundreds of thousands of dollars and years of frustrating wasted effort.

As I've tried to illustrate by these few case studies, there are at least 12 ways you can personally profit from the information business. They are outlined in Table 12.1.

Best Business in the World: Selling Information

Just think of all of the advantages of the information business compared to almost any other business:

Unlimited worldwide market

Easy to research

Easy to create

Easy and cheap to test

Easy and cheap to produce, inventory, and correct

Low start-up costs

High perceived value

High markup

Mobility (can operate from any mailbox or telephone in the world)

Copyright protection from competitors

Prestigious, impressive career ("I'm an author")

Satisfying (permanent record for future generations)

I can't think of a more satisfying career than producing information products. I get success letters from happy, satisfied customers each year who share their gratitude for having used my ideas to improve their lives. I keep pinching myself. For example, while writing the very words you are reading right now, I paused to check my e-mail. Here is an exact copy of what I found (grammatical mistakes included):

TABLE 12.1 Infopreneur's Opportunity Chart

Passion	
Do you have a current passion/hobby/interest/talent (P/H/I/T)? (History, making money, relationships, pets, collecting, selling, etc.) Write it here_____	How many people have same passion/hobby/interest/talent? How have other infopreneurs successfully reached this group? What is your USP (unique selling proposition)? How will you deliver your promised benefits quickly?
Do you want to develop a dormant passion/hobby/interest/talent? Write it here _____	Where can you learn to develop your P/H/I/T? How long will it take you to develop you P/H/I/T? While you're learning, keep in mind the questions in item 1.
Do you know someone with a current passion/hobby/interest/talent? Write the names here _____ _____ _____	Are they willing to share this with you and others? Is their P/H/I/T marketable? Is their P/H/I/T organized into a presentable info product? Can you obtain the rights to market their P/H/I/T?
Can you find someone with a passion/hobby/interest/talent? When found, write the names here _____	Are they willing to share this with you and others? Is their P/H/I/T marketable? Is their P/H/I/T organized into a presentable info product? Can you obtain the rights to market their P/H/I/T?
Expertise	
Do you have a current knowledge base, expertise, or skill (K/E/S)? (Managing people, accounting, teaching, nutrition, etc.) Write it here _____	How many people have the same knowledge/expertise/skill? How have other infopreneurs successfully reached this group? What is your USP (unique selling proposition)? How will you deliver your promised benefits quickly?
Do you want to acquire a certain knowledge base, expertise, or skill? Write it here_____	Where can you learn to develop your K/E/S? How long will it take you to develop you K/E/S? While you're learning, keep in mind the preceding questions.

Do you know someone with a knowledge base, expertise, or skill? **Write the names here** _____ _____ _____	**Are they willing to share this with you and others?** **Is their K/E/S marketable?** **Is their K/E/S organized into a presentable info product?** **Can you obtain the rights to market their K/E/S?**
Do you want to find a person with knowledge, expertise, or skill? **When found, write the names here** _____	**Are they willing to share this with you and others?** **Is their K/E/S marketable?** **Is their K/E/S organized into a presentable info product?** **Can you obtain the rights to market their K/E/S?**

Story

Do you have a unique failure-to-success story? **(Losing weight, overcoming fear, overcoming addiction, etc.)** **Write it here**_____	**Which groups of people would benefit from your story?** **How have other infopreneurs successfully reached this group?** **What is your USP (unique selling proposition)?** **How will you deliver your promised benefits quickly?**
Do you want to create a unique failure-to-success story? **Write it here**_____	**Where can you learn how to go from failure to success?** **How long will it take you to do it?** **While you're doing it, keep in mind the preceding questions.**
Do you know someone with a unique failure-to-success story? **Write the names here** _____ _____ _____	**Are they willing to share this with you and others?** **Is their failure to success story marketable?** **Is their system organized into a presentable info product?** **Can you obtain the rights to market their system?**
Do you want to find someone with a unique failure-to-success story? **When found, write the names here** _____	**Are they willing to share this with you and others?** **Is their failure to success story marketable?** **Is their system organized into a presentable info product?** **Can you obtain the rights to market their system?**

*Hi, Bob: I have been looking for you for a while. Let me introduce my self.
My name is Paul T. Huynh. I was one of your students in your Wealth
Training in 1990. The reason I am looking for you because I like to write a
book about my success. I have achieved my goal of having $1,000,000.00
net worth in ten years. Because my English expression is limited I need
your help or even working together with you to share my story. I think
it is worth it. I am a Vietnamese refugee who had no education and
no English when I came to this country in 1979. Please let me know
what you think. I love to hear from you. God bless.*

Can you believe I get paid for helping people create stories like this?

People Will Pay for Expert Advice

It all starts with a core expertise. What do you know that we don't? Do
you know someone who knows something that the rest of us need or want
to know? You don't have to spend years learning a core expertise. You can
find some expert who is undermarketed and take his or her idea to the
marketplace.

For instance, suppose you go to a local church meeting on parenting
because you are having trouble with your teenagers. You find the room is
filled to overflowing. You realize that you are not alone . . . that there are
hundreds of other parents in the same predicament. A lightbulb comes on
in your head: *Aha!* Here is a hungry marketplace. You listen to the
speaker and see that his material is perfectly organized for the communication age. . . . It appears to be fun, fast, simple. It promises swift results
and is easy to learn. You go home and try a few of the techniques on your
own teenagers, and voilà, you have them cheerfully cleaning up their own
rooms in no time. Hmmmm!

There might be something here. You call the parenting seminar leader
and find he is just a small-time operator with a
passion for helping people. He doesn't have a clue
about marketing, packaging, or promoting. You
ask him if he would be willing to let you market
some of his ideas . . . on a nonexclusive basis. It
could mean a few extra thousand in his pocket. He
agrees, and you draw up an agreement. Then you
create a simple classified ad to test the
waters . . . to see if anyone would want what you
have to offer. The ads start to pull responses. You realize that you've got a
"live one." You create your product—tapes, books, seminars—and roll
out your marketing blitz. You make money, your expert makes money,
and your information empire is launched.

> **$$$**
>
> **WIT & WISDOM**
> Father to son: Get a job.
> Work. Save your money. Soon,
> you'll have enough to stop
> working. Son: But, I'm not
> working now.

What made all of this possible? You recognized a great idea. You got
the rights to market it. You organized a team of people to help you capitalize on it, and all of you took buckets of money to the bank. Most
experts out there have no idea how to create, package, and market their
expertise. There are literally thousands them out there waiting to be discovered. You might be one of them.

Let's learn how to do this together. Remember the 80/20 principle? That is, 20 percent of the things you do give you 80 percent of your results. The successful infopreneur has three essential skills:

1. *Targeting:* Finding schools of hungry fish
2. *Baiting:* Creating irresistible bait
3. *Lifetiming:* Landing lifetime customers

No matter what your expertise, if nobody is interested, your business is dead before it begins. You are looking for an area of expertise that meets the needs of a large and growing body of interested people . . .

✔ who can be *easily identified*

✔ who have an immediate *need/want/problem*

✔ who are *highly motivated* to find a solution

✔ who have the *money* to spend

✔ who are *willing to spend* it

✔ in an *economic climate* that encourages spending

Think of your market as a school of fish. Does your market contain enough fish? Is it a growing or declining school of fish? Is it easy to find where they are and what their feeding pattern is? Are they really hungry? Is the weather cooperating for the ideal fishing conditions? Is there a certain bait that sends them into a feeding frenzy? Are they willing to come out of the safe, dark depths of the bottom to fight for this new bait? Can you catch them?

Cracking the Code

Once you have decided on your area of expertise and identified your market, the process of cracking the code begins. What I mean by *cracking the code* is finding a way to offer your expertise such that the fish "rise to bite in a feeding frenzy."

Before I came along, there were hundreds of books on real estate investing. However, showing people how to buy property with little or no money down was just the right bait at the right time. There was a large and growing pool of baby boomers who were moving into their prime home-buying age in the late 1970s. Inflation forced house prices upward, creating increased incentive to "buy now." The climate was right, the school of fish was hungry and wanted to buy. My information was perfect.

Later in the decade, the climate changed: Inflation died, government tax laws discouraged investment, a steep recession dampened the feeding frenzy, and the baby boomers moved on to other interests. This doesn't mean there aren't still millions to be made in real estate or in real estate information. Every economic cycle brings a renewed feeding frenzy in real estate.

Finding the right combination of hungry fish and irresistible bait can be tricky. Basically, there are no totally new or unique human needs or wants. They have been the same for millennia. Sex, money, self-esteem, health, God, relationships, beauty. Your information should tap into one of these universal wants/needs with just the right bait at just the right time. (See Figure 12.1.)

Case Study 6: A Great Idea That Went Right into the Toilet

I know of an infopreneur who spent years and several hundred thousand dollars creating a product called *Compact Classics.* He had researched all of the great classic books, fiction and nonfiction, and condensed each book into a two-page format. Instead of taking weeks to read the original, you get the meat of the book in only two pages. Great idea. Only one problem: No one would buy it. And lot of money went right into the toilet.

Then somebody had a bright idea. Why not repackage all of these powerful two-page summaries under a different title and remarket them to a totally different audience? The new title? *The Great American Bathroom Book.*

It worked, and millions of dollars later, the idea is still pumping out cash. By the way, you can buy the same book with either title. If you are the highbrow type, you order *Compact Classics.* If you prefer lowbrow, it's the *Bathroom Book.* Same information, different title. Guess which title outsells the other by about 100 to 1? But neither market would have enjoyed success if some savvy marketer hadn't "cracked the code."

Cracking the code is the process of figuring out how to reach your school of fish in a unique way. A student at one of my infopreneuring seminars shared how he had cracked the code and turned his failing personal-development training business into a raging success. He discovered, after months of testing, that the people he attracted to his seminars were motivated to action by a single word in his ads. Once he had isolated this key "power word," he began to feature this word more prominently in all of his ads . . . and went from empty seminar rooms to packed, sold-out seminars a year in advance. He had cracked the code. He had found the bait that his fish were hungry for. Want to know what the one word was? I

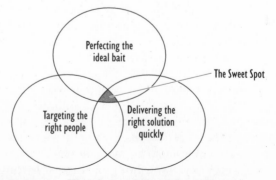

FIGURE 12.1   The three skills of the infopreneur.

can guarantee you won't be able to guess it. Come to my web site at www.multiplestreamsofincome.com and I'll share it with you. Enter the keyword Cracking the Code, or call my office at 801-852-8700.

Each industry has its "hot topic du jour." This hot topic seizes the attention of the entire industry until a near feeding frenzy develops. Until the feeding frenzy subsides (or is killed off by negative press), almost any information about the subject is snapped up by legions of voracious infomaniacs.

Case in point: *Day trading*. These two words seized the entire investment industry in the late 1990s. For several years, every investment book containing those key code-cracking words in its title became a best-seller. The bloom is a little off the rose these days, but savvy infopreneurs will be hauling fortunes from this mine shaft for many years to come. If you can't crack the code yourself, then notice who's pulling in the most fish and drop your hook into the feeding frenzy.

Case Study 7: Success or Failure Can Hinge on Changing One Digit

Sometimes cracking the code involves only a minuscule adjustment. About 30 years ago, you might have seen full-page ads in newspapers nationwide touting a book called the *Lazy Man's Way to Riches* by Joe Karbo. It was 156 pages of self-published information for $10. I'm told that the first full-page ad to test the sale of this book was a complete flop. Zero results. Imagine buying a full-page ad in the *Los Angeles Times* and not getting one single order! Joe Karbo, who was a master at marketing, intuitively knew that his idea would fly if he could just crack the code. He decided to risk running the ad again, unchanged except for one number in the subtitle. Instead of "How to earn $50,000 a year the lazy way," he changed it to read, "How to make $20,000 a year the lazy way." It worked. The orders poured in. And this minuscule adjustment produced one of the classic marketing campaigns of all time. Joe pulled hundreds of thousands of dollars from his ads, year after year.

Why did this one change make such a huge difference? Because people can only "see" what they believe. Back then, earning $5,000 a year was an excellent salary. Earning 10 times that amount—$50,000 a year—was such an enormous amount of money that it wasn't believable. Therefore, nobody responded. When he lowered the amount to a more believable number, suddenly millions of people began to "see" it. The title you select, the words you use to market your information, the benefits your information offers, the way it is packaged will cause this to happen.

Five Rings of Riches: Vast Opportunities Await All Infopreneurs

One of the least-understood concepts, even by successful infopreneurs, is how vast the opportunities are for making money from just one good idea. I'll explain this to you by teaching you what I call the five rings of information riches.

Think of your infobusiness as a series of five concentric circles. At the center is the bull's-eye, or the first ring. (See Figure 12.2 and Table 12.2.)

Ring 1: Succeeding in Your Core Expertise

You must have a core expertise that is either a revolutionary new technology or is an old expertise that has a new marketing strategy. My core expertise was real estate investing. I became very good at it. Therefore, I could teach it to others. Then I expanded my core expertise to include infopreneuring, investing, marketing, and the Internet, to name a few. As I said earlier, you don't have to be the expert yourself. But you do need to borrow, license, or otherwise acquire the expertise from someone. Once you have discovered the right combination of message and media, you have cracked the code. Then you are ready to move to the next ring.

Ring 2: Teaching Others Specific Know-How to Succeed in Your Core Expertise

First I made money by investing in real estate (ring 1). Then I taught others how to succeed in real estate just as I had (ring 2). There are about 20 ways to sell this ring 2 information. In other words, there are 20 sepa-

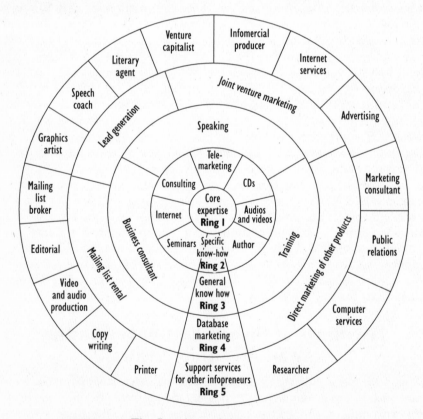

FIGURE 12.2 **The five rings of riches in infopreneuring.**

TABLE 12.2 The Five Rings of Riches Infopreneuring Chart

Ring 1 Achieving Success in a Core Expertise	Ring 2 Specific Know-how (Teaching Others Core Expertise)	Ring 3 General Know-how (Teaching Others Success Skills)	Ring 4 Database Marketing to Your Core List	Ring 5 Support Services to Infopreneurs
Being an expert	Author	Success speaker/ trainer	Mailing-list rental	Printer
Finding an expert	Desktop publisher	Leadership	Lead generator	Copywriter
Being a distributor	Seminar promoter	Goal setting	Joint venture partner	Audio producer
Licensee	Public speaker	Time management	Direct marketer	Editorial services
Franchisee	900 numbers	Sales training		Mailing-list broker
Co-owner	Teleconferencing	Team building		Graphics artist
	Newsletters	Stress		Ghostwriter
	Computer programs	Success		Speech coach
	CD-ROMs	Motivation		Literary agent
	Infomercials	Management		Venture capitalist
	One-on-one consulting	Business consultant		Infomercial producer
	Licensing	Entrepreneurship		Infomarketing coach
	Professor / teacher	Marketing		Cassette duplication
	Freelance writer	Advertising		Advertising agency
	Syndicated columnist	Strategy		Public relations
	Talk-show host	Financial analysis		Book reviewer
	Media expert	Computers		Researcher
	Magazine publisher			Information broker
	Internet expert			Computer services
	Game designer			Video reproduction
	Calendar creator			Internet Web master
	Specialty products (T-shirts, etc.)			
	Audiocassettes			
	Videocassettes			

rate $100,000-plus-a-year businesses that result from having cracked the code. Here is an incomplete list:

Ring 2: Businesses Growing from Your Core Expertise

1. *Author:* Selling information to other publishers
2. *Desktop publisher:* Self-publishing for yourself or others
3. *Seminar promoter:* Selling information in seminars
4. *Public speaker:* Selling information from the platform
5. *Telecommunicator:* Selling info via 900 numbers and teleconferences
6. *Newsletter editor:* Selling info in periodic format
7. *Computer programmer:* Selling info via disks and CDs
8. *TV producer:* Selling info via TV infomercials/shows
9. *Personal consulting:* Selling personalized, one-on-one info
10. *Professor/teacher/trainer:* Education, corporate, public
11. *Freelance writer:* Selling info in magazine articles
12. *Syndicated columnist:* Selling info in newspapers
13. *Media expert:* Informing those who inform others
14. *Talk show/info host:* Becoming a radio or TV host or producer
15. *Magazine publisher:* Packaging info in magazine format
16. *Game designer:* Selling info packaged as a game
17. *Calendar creator:* Selling info packaged as a calendar
18. *Product designer:* Selling info on T-shirts, mugs, posters
19. *Licenser:* Licensing others to sell your ideas
20. *Online expert:* Producing online services and products
21. *Audio/video producer:* Selling info on audio- and videocassettes

Most successful infopreneurs have tapped into only a handful of the preceding businesses. They leave massive amounts of money on the table. A major misconception people make is assuming that their customers will want information in only one format. I made this mistake in the late 1980s and it cost me millions of dollars. I made the foolish assumption that the best way to learn about real estate investing was in a live seminar. Therefore, I refused to sell my ideas on audiocassettes in a home-study format. Competitors came into the marketplace (some of my former graduates and employees) and started offering a more convenient and less expensive way to get the same information. It was a costly mistake . . . one I want to help you avoid.

The truth is that a loyal fan of your information will want it in multiple formats. Talk about multiple streams of income! If they like the book, they'll want the video. If they like the video, they'll be ripe for the calendar. If they like the calendar, they want the live seminar. If they like the live seminar, they'll love the private, exclusive retreat. Not all of your customers act this way, but those who are in feeding frenzy are insatiable. They want all of you. Have you ever bought information from someone in more than one format? I do it all the time. I want the whole enchilada—and I want it *now!* Once you understand the big picture, you'll be able to capitalize on the opportunities around you. Then you will be ready to expand into the third concentric circle, or what I call the third ring.

Ring 3: Using Your Specific Experience to Teach General Success Skills

For example, famous sales trainer Zig Ziglar honed his sales skills by selling pots and pans door-to-door. There wasn't exactly a large and growing market of hungry pots and pans salespeople to which to market his expertise. Therefore, he became a *general* expert in the broad field of sales training. Then he wrote the best-seller, *See You at the Top.* He went from a specific expertise to a general expertise and made millions of dollars. Mary Lou Retton won gold medals in the 1984 Olympics for gymnastics. There wasn't a big market for her information among gymnasts, so now she delivers general success and motivation speeches to corporate audiences worldwide—on the subject of how to be a gold medal performer. She earns speaking fees and enjoys a steady infopreneuring income from her third ring. Other third-ring opportunities are as follows:

Success Trainer—General Subjects

Success and motivation

Leadership

Goal setting

Time management

Sales training

Management

Team building

Stress

Business Consultant—General Subjects

Running a successful business

Entrepreneurship

Advertising

Marketing

Strategy

Financial analysis

Computer services

There are literally thousands of successful third-ring infopreneurs nationwide. Harvey MacKay, author of the best-selling book *How to Swim with the Sharks,* is another example. He made his fortune running a successful envelope business in Minnesota. What do envelopes have to do with you? Nothing. But he claims that his great success in the envelope business has given him the right to teach us all kinds of general success principles in the areas of sales, management, and positive attitudes. He's made millions turning his specific know-how into general how-to information.

Ring 4: Marketing Other Products to Your Database

Once you have attracted a growing, satisfied customer database, you may approach your customers with other products and services. For example, my original database is made up of people who have attended my real estate seminars. But in reality, these people are entrepreneurs who like to explore other moneymaking opportunities. That's why many of them welcome learning about new ways to earn extra income. My current list consists of over 250,000 active investors and entrepreneurs.

Suppose you launch an infopreneuring business and are successful in building a database of 10,000 customers over a period of years. Here are four extra ways of mining more money from your customer list:

1. *Mailing-list rental agency.* You could rent out your list to other similar but noncompeting businesses to try to sell their products. For example, suppose someone wants to use your mailing list for a seminar to improve relationships. This person is willing to pay 10 cents per name to test 1,000 names from your list. If the results are positive, the buyer agrees to pay 25 cents a name for your entire list. Your customers do not know that you are involved. They simply receive a piece of mail announcing a seminar and choose whether to sign up or not. Renting your mailing list generates $2,500 net profit, with no time or hassle on your part. Some lists generate hundreds of thousands of dollars in list-rental fees to the primary infopreneur. There's a gold mine in those names! That's why it's so important to gather and retain the name of every customer.

2. *Lead generator for other businesses.* You can earn even higher profits by sending an endorsement letter to your customers encouraging them to buy other products or services. Because the seller of a product is much more likely to sell to your database with your endorsement, you can charge an even higher fee—sometimes as high as $1 per name. That's an extra $10,000 in pure profit.

3. *Joint venture partner.* In some instances, you may even choose to split profits on the sale of a product to your database. In one such arrangement, I split the profits 50-50 with a seminar promoter who sold a seminar using my database. I appeared at the seminar and gave it a hearty endorsement. In this case, the profit generated was much higher than for a list rental.

4. *Direct marketer.* If you have built up a great relationship with people on your database, you may even influence them to buy products other than the ones you are known for . . . perhaps even totally unrelated products. In this instance, you would buy the products wholesale and sell them to your database for a profit. If they trust you, they will buy. Just make sure that you never do anything to violate that trust.

Ring 5: Support Services to Infopreneurs in the Other Four Rings

Sometimes there is more money in selling bait to other fishermen than to go fishing yourself. Some infopreneurs don't service the general market. They focus on selling information to other infopreneurs. For example, Web designers' primary income is generated from helping other entrepreneurs make money on the Net.

Once you become a successful infopreneur, you have earned the right to share your expertise with other infopreneurs. One of the most successful infopreneurs of the past 20 years is Ted Nicholas. He's retired now and lives in Switzerland, but during his heyday you could see his full-page ads in dozens of nationwide magazines offering to show you how to form your own corporation for under $50. He sold hundreds of thousands of these books at $75 apiece. Drawing upon years of successful experience, Ted launched another successful business . . . teaching other infopreneurs how to successfully self-publish their own books. He held a series of sold-out $5,000 seminars teaching how to be a successful writer and self-publisher. Then he sold the audiocassettes from the seminar for additional profits. My favorite Ted Nicholas information product is a $300 three-ring binder containing copies of each of the ads he ran in his long career . . . the ones that worked and the ones that bombed . . . with notes on why they worked or didn't work. Once again, everything an infopreneur does has value—the successes *and* the failures.

The following is a listing of potential support businesses for infopreneurs:

Printer

Copywriter

Audio producer

Editorial services

Mailing-list broker

Graphics artist

Ghostwriter

Speech coach

Literary agent

Venture capitalist

Infomercial producer

Infomarketing coach

Video reproduction

Cassette duplication

Advertising agency

Public relations

Book reviewer

Researcher

Information broker

Computer strategist

Web site designer

The Info-Funnel: Attracting Lifelong Customers into Your Inner Circle

Now that brings us to probably the most important concept in all of information marketing: the *funnel*.

At the top of the funnel are people who sample your product or service for free. Most of these people are only curious, but a certain percentage of the lookers are seriously searching for an immediate solution. They vote with their wallets by purchasing a product at the most reasonable price to check out your information. Suppose they buy a book. You can be fairly certain that if your information is solid, a fixed percentage of these book buyers will want even more information. Perhaps they will want a more in-depth home study course or even a live seminar. Once again, you can be fairly certain that a fixed percentage of these people will want to become part of your inner circle and receive more in-depth, hands-on, personalized experience or training. These are your lifetime customers—your groupies. They like what you do and they'll be lifelong fans. These are your most valuable customers. (See Figure 12.3.)

Determining the LTV of a Customer in Your Funnel

Just what is the value of a customer who enters your funnel and stays in there for a long time? Tom Peters says that every time a Federal Express courier comes into his office, the driver should see $180,000 stamped on the head of the secretary. His small firm of 30 people has a $1,500 a month courier bill. That's $18,000 a year times 10 years, for a total *long-term value* (LTV) of $180,000. And, if the secretary convinces just one other customer to start using the service, the value doubles. But most mail couriers think the value of the customer is just the $13.95 he or she spends today.

Each of your customers is worth thousands of dollars if you'll take care of them . . . much more than the initial $20 book or $500 seminar. The ultimate goal is to keep that customer loyal to you and your products for 10 years or more. By offering great service and value, customers can be enticed to remain forever. The longer they stay, the deeper they go into the funnel, and the more money you make.

Sometimes you can afford to lose money on the front end by offering a free seminar or a free report to entice a customer into your funnel, where you can then offer more profitable services. So, the funnel starts out with your least-expensive items at the open end of the funnel and ends with your most-expensive item at the other end.

Table 12.3 shows the logical progression through the funnel. The least-expensive items are on the left side. The most-expensive, back-end products are on the far right. Study this chart. It cost me several million dollars to learn what I've summarized on this chart.

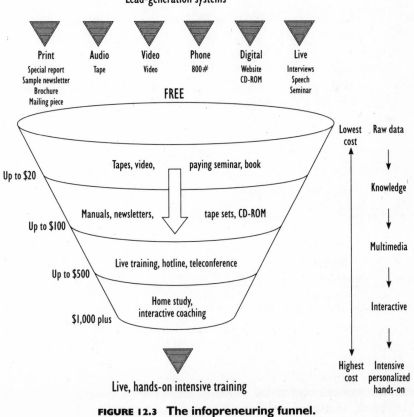

FIGURE 12.3 The infopreneuring funnel.

TABLE 12.3 The Information Marketing Funnel Chart

The Infofunnel: How to Entice Your Customers into Profitable and Long-term Relationships				
Free	Up to $20	Up to $100	Up to $500	$1,000-plus
Print Special report	Special report	Manuals	Home study course	Interactive system
Sample newsletter	Book	Newsletter		
Newspaper column	Calendar			
Magalogue	Poster			
Brochure	Game			
Mailing piece	T-shirt, mug, etc.			
Audio Free tape	Single tape	Six-tape set	Home study course	Interactive system
	Double tape set		Taped seminar	
Video Free video	Video	Three-video set	Seminar videos	Interactive system
Telephone 800 number, live	900 number, live		Consulting hotline	Conference call
800 number, taped	900 number, taped			
Digital Sample diskette	Online databases	CD-ROM	Applications	Interactive system
		Books on disk	Software	
		Laser disc		
Live Free interviews	Evening seminar	One-day seminar	Weekend seminar	Hands-on training
Free speech			Client consultation	
Free seminar				
Free consultation				

The Back End: Publishing versus Infopreneuring

People often ask me, "What is the difference between the traditional publisher and the modern infopreneur?" I respond, "Publishers don't understand the back end." They produce information products that cost between $10 and $50—books, tapes, videos—but they ignore the part of the funnel where most of the money is made: the back-end products.

Imagine the typical publisher trying to make a profit. She publishes a book and sells 10,000 copies. Although the retail price of the book is $25, the publisher gets only the wholesale price, or about 50 percent. With the remaining 50 percent she needs to pay author royalties (I like that part!), bookbinding, staff, editing, office space, publicity, inventory—until there are, at best, only a few dollars profit per book. A profit of $2 per book on 10,000 books gives a net profit of maybe $20,000.

Not much for all of that effort. The traditional publisher publishes many books a year, loses money on most of them, and hopes for a few big winners to make a nice profit. The next year it's the same scenario. Publishing is a tough business. You don't want to go there.

> **$$$**
> **WIT & WISDOM**
> Money talks—
> mine only stutters.

Now, let's look at the same process when viewed through the eyes of an infopreneur. The goal of an infopreneur is to sell information in as *many formats as possible as deep in the funnel as possible* to squeeze out the most profit from a single idea.

Suppose we start with the sale of the same 10,000 books and collect the same revenues as the traditional publisher. After marketing and overhead, you make a few dollars' profit, at best, from each book. Hardly worth the trouble. But, you're not a publisher. You're an infopreneur. As you will soon learn, the most important task of an infopreneur is to capture the names and addresses of your readers. In fact, the primary purpose of a book is to attract customers into your funnel.

With this in mind, you send a carefully worded mailing piece to your 10,000 book buyers inviting them to come to a two-day seminar. The cost is $300.

With repeated mailings and some follow-up with telemarketers, about 10 percent of your book buyers will either attend one of your seminars or buy the audio/video recording of the seminar. That's 1,000 people at $300, or total gross revenues of $300,000. Sales costs and mailing costs will be high, but you still should have $100,000 left over as profit.

> **$$$**
> **WIT & WISDOM**
> When the product is
> right, you don't have to
> be a great marketer.
> LEE IACOCCA

But that's not all. Of these 1,000 attendees, between 5 and 10 percent will want to come to your advanced, hands-on, intensive training, costing perhaps $2,995 to $4,995. That's 50 to 100 people at $3,000 to $5,000, producing additional revenues of $150,000 to $500,000. Most of this is pure profit, because the hotel you choose for your program will often give you a free training room if most of the attendees stay in the hotel.

Add this to the previous $100,000 from the two-day seminar, and the total net infopreneuring profit from the sale of 10,000 books is between $250,000 and $600,000. Compare this to $20,000 from traditional publishing and you get the picture.

Still skeptical? Okay, suppose I've been too optimistic. Cut the lowest numbers in half. That still leaves $125,000. Could you live on that? And we haven't added in the profits you could earn by selling other products such as software, one-on-one consulting, and additional books and videos. This could add another $50,000 to $100,000 to the bottom line.

Now you understand why I'm not a publisher. Don't misunderstand. I love my publisher. I'm thrilled that the company will earn a small profit from every one of my books. I hope it sells a million of them. But my heart is not in the sale of a pile of single books. My heart is in the long-term relationship that I build with my readers. Let me explain.

How to Find and Keep Customers

Remember what my friend Mark Victor Hansen taught me:

"The sole purpose for your business is to find customers and keep them."

The key to keeping customers in your funnel is to develop a long-term relationship with them. Customers in your database are not just names in a computer. They are real people, with changing and evolving needs and wants. They don't exist in a static world where nothing changes. They are being constantly bombarded with a hundred other options. You need to do whatever it takes to keep them loyal to you . . . and to keep them out of your competitors' funnels, because the long-term payout is so great.

Any marketer will tell you that the hardest and most expensive sale is to a cold (meaning a new) customer who has never heard of you before and has never tried your product. The cheapest, easiest sale is from a satisfied customer. If you want to have a real tough time in business, if you want each sale to be difficult and expensive, then play the old game of "Find the New Customer." You cannot survive in this competitive environment by constantly being forced to find new customers. You must take care of the ones you have—and make it easy for them to tell their friends.

How Quickly Can You Turn an Idea into Cash?

Let's review the three critical skills of an infopreneur:

Find hungry fish.

Create irresistible bait.

Establish long-term relationships.

Seven-Step Getting-Started Action Plan

With these three skills in mind, let's explore a seven-step action plan to get you earning up to $1,000 a day in the information business ASAP.

Step 1: Select a subject that matches your passion/expertise.

If you want to prosper in the information business for a long time, you should be marketing information that matches your passion and your expertise. It is possible to market information that you are not passionate about. But at the very least you should be an expert in that subject. Conversely, it is possible to market information that you are not an expert in, but at the very least you should be passionate about it. Better, of course, to be a passionate expert.

Sometimes a specific passion/expertise doesn't lend itself to making lots of money. Suppose you are passionate about helping homeless people. Sorry. You'll probably have to collect your riches in the next life. If you want to make serious money now, you have to choose subjects that lend themselves to the right kind of economics.

Luckily, there are dozens of subjects to choose from. Here is just a partial list:

Weight loss

Nutrition

Relationships

Sports

Investments (stocks, real estate, home businesses, asset protection)

Business (management, sales, marketing, advertising, employees)

Personal development

Organization and time management

Addictions of all kinds

Hobbies and collecting

Martial arts

Public speaking

Languages

Computers

Fear and other emotional issues

The Internet

Entertainment

Your first task is to decide on a passion or expertise that has high profit potential.

Step 2: Find the hungriest fish in the lake.

There are two main ways to find out if people have been willing to pay for your chosen kind of information:

1. Call a mailing-list broker. List brokers make a living by renting out mailing lists. If you tell them which product or service you are trying to market, they can tell you which lists to rent to market your information. They act as paid consultants. Their fees are paid by the list owner, so you have no out-of-pocket costs prior to selecting a list to rent.

2. Obtain a copy of the *Standard Rate and Data Survey*. If you've never heard of this publication, this one tip will be worth the price of this entire book. In the reference section of most major public libraries, you can find a copy of the *Standard Rate and Data Survey*. The SRDS directories list all business publications, consumer magazines, newspapers, direct-marketing mailing lists, and broadcast media in North America and internationally. It is a gold mine of information if you know how to spot the nuggets. If you plan to be a major player, you'll want to visit the SRDS web site and see what a $500 subscription will buy you. You'll find it at www.srds.com.

Suppose you want to run a classified ad in a magazine devoted to your passion/expertise. The SRDS *Business Publications and Consumer Magazine* directory lists the names of all of the publications that deal with your subject, complete with contact names and numbers.

Suppose you want to send a direct-mail letter to people who are interested in your subject. The *SRDS Direct Marketing Directory* contains mailing lists of potential purchasers, by subject, complete with the total number of names on the lists and the list brokers to contact.

By consulting a list broker or studying the SRDS directories, you try to identify a large audience of potential customers for your information. The characteristics of this mailing list should match those we discussed earlier: Your audience should be a large and growing school of fish who are hungry and ready to be whipped into a feeding frenzy.

If you have an existing database of your own previous customers, you should probably test your new idea on them first. But if you are starting from scratch, then you'll have to either build a database of potential customers or rent a list. (Other than finding and keeping customers, the most important function you must perform as an infopreneur is to constantly maintain and update your database.)

Step 3: Discover the kind of bait your fish have been biting on.

There are two ways to do this:

1. *Indirect:* Determine which bait others have used successfully.

2. *Direct:* Talk to the fish yourself.

Let's talk about the last option first. This is called *market research.* Just what do your potential customers want? Have you ever asked them— called them up on the phone? Are you trying to sell them what they want or what *you think* they need? Ask. Ask. Ask. Find out what information is vital to them and how they want that information.

There are many levels of information. You must determine at which level your customers want to be informed.

Do they want raw data? (Examples: the number of foreclosures in Los Angeles or the number of cars on the freeway at rush hour)

Do they want preliminary information? (Example: a special report on the main causes of cancer in females over 50 and how to prevent it)

Do they want in-depth know-how? (Example: a complete home study system on how to raise happy and healthy children)

Do they want skills training? (Example: a hands-on, experiential, five-day training program on how to be a successful public speaker)

Do they want personal consulting? (Example: online, live, or face-to-face coaching on how to invest your personal money in stocks)

How much information do they want? How much are they willing to pay? The deeper the level of information, the more expensive the product. These are all important questions, and you would do well to ask these questions to 100 people before you launch.

For the indirect approach, here is a critical question: *What have the fish been biting on?* Where has your school of fish been buying their information? Which other infopreneurs have been able to "crack the code"? Your objective is to discover the top information providers in your subject. Who are the best? They must be doing something right. Make a list of the top three information providers. These people will be your competitors.

Call up each of your top three information competitors. Pretend to be a potential customer. Ask them to send you their sales literature. Visit with their top salespeople and notice how they try to sell. Which hot buttons do they push? Which benefits do they emphasize? Which features do they brag about? Gather information. Buy their product. Rip it apart. What makes it so special? Is it a matter of design? Is it a matter of marketing? Find out their strengths. Probe for weaknesses. Sleuth where they are advertising and how they get their leads. Notice how other upstart competitors are making inroads into the market share of the top three companies. How are these smaller companies surviving? What do they say to draw away customers from the major players? What niche are they exploiting? Let this information simmer in your psyche.

A word about competition. Sometimes beginners start with what they feel is a unique idea and naively rush off to start a business. Soon they discover that someone else is already marketing this idea—sometimes with a very similar title—and they become discouraged.

Understand that there is a huge market for information and that, with the Internet, it is expanding exponentially. You don't need to reach 10 million people. You just need to attract 10,000 hot people into your funnel and you'll be set for life! If each of these 10,000 customers sends you on average just $1,000 over the next 10 years, that's *$10 million!* When you read Chapter 14 (about the Internet), you'll learn just how quickly you can attract these 10,000 customers.

━━ $$$ ━━

WIT & WISDOM

Writing is turning one's worst moments into money.

J.P. DONLEAVY

Step 4: Design your own unique bait.

Ask your target database what they don't like about your competitor's product. Ask them what they would add to your competitor's product to make it perfect. Ask them what they would delete from your competitor's product that is not necessary. Ask them to design it *exactly* the way they want it.

From this research, you will try to create a competitive advantage, or what Jay Abraham calls the *unique selling proposition* (USP).

Probably the best USP in the past 50 years belonged to Domino's Pizza.

Fresh, hot pizza delivered to your door in 30 minutes or less—Guaranteed.

The second-best USP was created by Federal Express:

When you absolutely, positively have to have it overnight.

People were willing to pay *50 times* the price of a first-class stamp just to receive their mail three times faster. Think about that!

The USP is a specific promise that you make to your customer. What can you promise your customer that your competitors aren't promising?

For my real estate seminars, my USP was "Nothing Down." My promise was as follows:

Send me to any city. Take away my wallet. Give me $100. And in 72 hours I'll buy an excellent piece of real estate using none of my own money.

Today my USP has expanded:

A stream of checks in your mailbox—in 21 days from today.

At our training sessions, we show people how to be up and earning several streams of income within days, not months or years.

When it comes to a USP, you can't go wrong by emphasizing and delivering fast results. Remember, people are lazy. If they have a choice between easy and hard, they'll take easy *every single time!* If they have a choice between fast and slow, they'll take fast every single time. If they have a choice between simple and complicated, they'll take simple every single time.

Time is the scarcest currency of the new millennium. We don't need more data. We are already on information overload. We are all data drunk. We need information that is time-friendly. This is your most important competitive advantage: *the ease and speed of results.*

You should read the classic book, *Positioning: The Battle for Your Mind*, by Trout and Ries. Great book. It will teach you how to position your "David" infoproduct against a "Goliath" competitor.

Step 5: Test your bait.

As I said before, marketing is the key. Having determined your USP, you have to create advertising that causes people to *act!*

Your ad should emphasize the *ultimate* benefit your product promises. What is the amazing miracle cure your information can provide? In his book, Dr. Jeffrey Lant shares a list of ultimate benefits:*

Financial stability

Health

Love

Security

Salvation

Self-regard

Community and peer recognition

Independence

Sexual fulfillment

Beauty/desirability/personal attractiveness

The headline of your ad should promise an ultimate benefit as well as your competitive advantage. The body of your ad should include as many other benefits as you have space to describe. Of secondary importance in your ad are the features of your product.

What is the difference between *benefits* and *features?* Features describe your product. Benefits are what your customers get when they use your product. When you talk about your product, you are doing "features" selling. When you talk about results, you are doing "benefits" selling.

For example, when airlines want to sell you airline tickets to Hawaii, do they describe the kind of aircraft you'll be flying in? Do they brag about the airline meals? Do they describe the amount of legroom? Or do they show you pictures of palm trees, sand, and sun? Palm trees are benefits. Legroom is a feature. You'll get more people to Hawaii with palm trees.

Features speak to the head. Benefits speak to the heart. Features are about logic. Benefits are about emotion. Emotion will outsell logic 10 to 1. Logic may be an important part of the sale . . . but only after you have engaged the customer's emotion.

Write your classified ad. Your bait should be reduced to a single classified ad of 25 words or less. It should start with a bold headline followed by a few lines of text. It's best to offer free information from a short-form classified ad. You're just trying to gauge interest. You will generate more responses if you include a 24-hour recorded message for people to listen

---

* This list comes from Lant's excellent book about information marketing, *How to Make a Whole Lot More Than $1,000,000: Writing, Commissioning, Publishing and Selling "How-To" Information.* The jacket blurb reads, "This is what you want when you're serious about making big money from books, booklets, audiocassettes and special reports." Over 500 pages of exhaustingly detailed rantings and ravings from a serious infopreneur. But it's not cheap. I offer it in my online bookstore for $50 (www.multiplestreamsofincome.com), or call my office at 801-852-8700.

to. If you would like to listen to the type of three-minute message that can compel someone to ask for more information, go to my web site and search for the words: Samples of 24-Hour recorded messages. Here is an example of a typical classified ad that works:

Earn $1,000 a day!
Famous author reveals simple way
to make unlimited income working
from home. 24-hr. msg.
Toll free 800-97MONEY
www.multiplestreamsofincome.com

Run your classified ad. Using the SRDS, select a magazine, newspaper, or publication that's read by the kind of people you are trying to reach. Place your ad and wait for the responses. The people who respond are your marketing guinea pigs. Offer to send them more free information if they will answer your marketing test questions. Use their responses to refine your ad and your offer.

Test other classifieds until you find one that outpulls any other ad by a factor of 3 to 1. This may be your code-cracking ad. You're looking for an ad that costs the least to run and pulls the greatest number of responses. All of this testing is done *before* you create your information product. What you learn from testing may change the focus of your final product. It doesn't do any good to offer customers peanut butter if they're really hungry for honey. Find out what they want and give it to them.

In Chapter 14, I'll show you how you can do all of this testing for free.

Step 6: Roll out your marketing campaign in a major way.

Once you have found a bait that works, you can roll it out to hundreds of publications and thousands of newspapers all over the world. Each publication will vary in its results. You can then test larger versions of your ads . . . all the way up to full-page ads. But first start small. If the small format doesn't work, the large format probably won't work, either.

For example, my first ads were classified. They cost me about $25 a day. Then I graduated to a small display ad (about 3 by 5 inches), which included my photo. It cost about $300 in my local newspaper. I still remember how worried I was about spending so much money on a single ad. But the results far outstripped the less-expensive classifieds. Next I grew to quarter-page ads. Then to half-page ads. And finally, to full-page ads, each costing thousands of dollars. These ads attracted hundreds of people to our seminars . . . and into our funnel. Soon there were hundreds of people attending my weekend seminars at $395 and $495 apiece. But it all started with a simple, inexpensive classified ad.

$$$

WIT & WISDOM
The future never just happened. It was created.

WILL AND ARIEL DURANT,
THE LESSONS OF HISTORY

Simultaneous to your testing classifieds should be a direct-mail letter campaign. Direct mail is more expensive but far more effective than almost any other medium because it is so focused—you can narrow down your audience to street and zip code. This will lead to other forms of advertising: the 30-minute TV infomercial (I have created nine infomercials in the past 20 years, including the very first infomercial recorded, in the early 1980s); the 30-minute long-form radio-mercial (used so successfully by Wade Cook for his stock market seminars); Card Decks; and, of course, the Internet.

Step 7: Add other ring 2 versions of your winning info-product.

Once you have a winning ad for a winning product and you have rolled out your marketing campaign, it is time to start strategizing the next versions of your information. If you'll look back to the five rings of riches chart in Table 12.2, you will see that there are over 20 ways to sell your information in ring 2. Ironically, each different version of your product will have a different price range and will reach totally different audiences. Just as hardcover book buyers differ from paperback book buyers, so do CD-ROM buyers differ from audiocassette buyers. Happily, some of your regular customers may want to have your information in several different formats—one for the car, one for their CD player, one on their computer, one for their nightstand, one in their library, one by the telephone, and so on. If they love you and your information, they're going to want all of you.

> **═══ $$$ ═══**
>
> **WIT & WISDOM**
> What an author likes to write most is his signature on the back of a cheque.
>
> BRENDAN FRANCIS

There is a lot more about information marketing than I can cover in this book. It is, in fact, a lifelong study. There are shortcuts, however. Tricks that we pros have learned. Words that can double sales. Phrases that can cause your phone to ring off the hook. Strategies that can cause people to beg to do business with you (as impossible as that might sound to you now). And there are snake pits of mistakes to avoid. As we get to know each other better, I hope to have a chance to share this information with you personally.

One last word of advice. On my office wall hangs a sign that reads:

> *I make money by writing words.*
> *The more I write, the more I make.*
> *Therefore, Write 1,000 words today!*

I have calculated that whenever I write a word on a page . . . like this one . . . and get it in front of a reader, I eventually make $20 per word. One. Two. Three. Four. Five. There, that was $100. If I want to make $1,000, I just write 50 words (500 words equals $10,000, and so on).

Why do I make so much money for every word I write? Because every time I write a best-selling book, it is placed into thousands of bookstores.

Every time a book sells, I not only make a nice royalty (usually about $4 per book), but many of these book buyers become part of my infopreneuring funnel. They are so impressed with the results that they tell many others, who also buy books and become part of the funnel. And so on. Therefore, every word I write *eventually* results in somebody's gladly sending me more money—at least $20 for every, single word.

So you see, I don't get writer's block. *Ever!* Whenever I have to make a decision about whether to watch some worthless TV show or to sit down at my computer and write my daily 1,000 words, my computer always wins.

If you knew that you could make $20 a word, wouldn't you be motivated to write 1,000 words right now? Why are you still reading? Start writing!

(P.S. My computer just did a word count in this chapter. There are over 11,000 words. Let's see . . . 11,000 multiplied by 20 . . . hmmmm. . . . This is good. Very good.)

CHAPTER 13

*A good book is the precious lifeblood of a master spirit,
embalmed and treasur'd up on purpose to a life beyond life.*

**QUOTE OVER DOOR TO MAIN READING ROOM OF THE
NEW YORK PUBLIC LIBRARY**

YOUR NINTH STREAM
Licensing: Intellectual Property at Warp Speed

In Chapter 12 you learned about infopreneurs—people who make money from selling intellectual property. The information I'm about to share with you is the most powerful and yet least understood form of intellectual property in the world. It's called *licensing.*

Licensing. Just saying the word brings blank stares from most people. Real estate, they understand. Network marketing, they've heard of that. But just what is licensing? Well, as soon as I make you aware of it, you're going to notice it everywhere. I must thank my good friend Ken Kerr for teaching me the real secrets of licensing. Ken was Director of Design for the Walt Disney theme parks worldwide, where he was one of the major forces behind the successful launch of Disney's Epcot center and Tokyo Disney. In addition, he was instrumental in the creation and successful marketing of such household names as Smurfs, Gummi Bears, the California Dancing Raisins, and Raggedy Ann and Andy, to name just a few. These products have generated hundreds of millions of dollars in licensing revenues.

Licensing is the ultimate form of leverage. It's the fastest, simplest, and shortest distance between an idea in your head and a lifetime stream of income in your mailbox. . . . So just what is it?

History of Licensing

It started as almost an afterthought more than 60 years ago. Today, it accounts for tens of *billions* of dollars of sales every year. At this very instant, your home probably contains dozens of licensed items that have enriched dozens of companies and individuals. For the most part, licensing is the bailiwick of extremely large, wealthy organizations—not for ordinary folk like you and me. But most of these organizations had very small beginnings. . . . Who's to say that either you or I couldn't do the same? Perhaps it's time you got on the receiving end of the cash flow instead of the sending end.

Let's go back to the beginning. It's 1928. A train from New York to Los Angeles carries Walt Disney and his wife home from a meeting in which they have learned that they have lost the rights to Walt's cartoon creation, Oswald the Rabbit. The news is devastating. In effect, they are out of business. But a stray mouse on the train inspires Walt to come up with a new idea. Walt wants to call his cartoon creation Mortimer Mouse, but his wife prevails. Mickey Mouse it is.

With this idea, Walt and his brother Roy started in a one-car garage on the wrong side of the tracks in east LA and grew the largest entertainment organization in the world. Walt and his brother Roy wanted to be moviemakers, but moviemaking is not the biggest moneymaker for Disney these days.

Licensing began as an accident, really. An afterthought. An enterprising businessman, trying to ride the coattails of the Mickey Mouse phenomenon, approached the Disney brothers and asked permission to silk-screen the image of Mickey on 10,000 wooden pencil boxes. Permission was granted, and thus was launched the modern concept of licensing. Disney Licensing and Merchandising Division eventually became the most profitable division of Disney. At first, the checks were small, but licensing soon grew into major streams as Mickey began appearing on Lionel trains and Hallmark cards and in Little Golden Books. It wasn't long before the brothers Disney recognized their gold mine. With little effort or risk on their part, they could generate huge streams of income. Talk about leverage!

———— **$$$** ————

WIT & WISDOM
Proof carefully to see if you
any words out.

In effect, the Disneys had sold that original businessman only the right, or license, to attach an image to one of his products to enhance its sales potential. The businessman did all of the manufacturing, marketing, and the movement of product from seller to buyer. He took all of the risk, managed all the money, and simply sent Walt Disney a fee for each product sold that carried the image of Mickey. Think of it: no manufacturing, no setup costs, no inventory, no sales costs, no sales force, no distribution costs, no employees, no risk, no money, and little or no investment of time or energy. And yet always maintaining control of product quality. Today, billions of dollars' worth of Disney merchandise is marketed throughout the world . . . all from the genesis of that idea. It's the ultimate form of leverage.

Using this same concept, in the 1960s a local San Diego surfer came up with the idea to manufacture swimming trunks for surfers—trunks made of a sturdier material than the flimsy swim-suit material popular at that time. He started with a prototype sewn from rough canvas. His logo showed 10 toes hanging over the edge of a surf-board. He called his new brand Hang Ten. For many years, the company grew larger and larger as it manufactured surf-related clothing. At its peak, Hang Ten had thousands of employees in various plants throughout Southern California. Today, the manufacturing plants no longer exist. Hang Ten is down to only one building with a fraction of the number of employees compared to the old days. It might sound like things are not going so well. *Not so.* This year, Hang Ten will collect over $300 million in licensing revenues worldwide! And what do they license? Just that silly 10-toed logo. Clothing manufacturers all over the world pay Hang Ten millions upon millions of dollars just to attach the Hang Ten logo to T-shirts and surfwear of all kinds. Hang Ten employees no longer focus on making clothing. They focus instead on making sure that copy-cats don't knock off their designs. And all of this is a result of licensing.

> ━━━ **$$$** ━━━
> **WIT & WISDOM**
> **Warren Buffett's Two rules of investing:**
> **Rule #1. Never lose money.**
> **Rule #2. Never forget rule #1.**

Using this same concept, a geeky computer nerd named Bill Gates and his fledgling company Microsoft paid $50,000 to buy the exclusive rights to a new computer program called DOS, the disk operating system for minicomputers. The year was 1979. It would turn out to be the deal of the millennium. Gates then licensed the nonexclusive rights for DOS to IBM to use in its very first minicomputer, the PC. Note, he didn't *sell* it to IBM, he *licensed* it to IBM. He also licensed it to manufacturers of IBM clones. That simple, shrewd decision is the reason that the market value of Microsoft is greater than the market value of IBM, General Motors, and most of the Fortune 500. From zero to billions in about 10 years. Bill Gates is the richest human being on the planet.

If he had sold his idea to IBM, he would have make a nice chunk of cash. But Bill Gates wasn't interested in *chunks* of cash. . . . He wanted *streams* of income. The only way to do that was through licensing. He doesn't have to manufacture any of those complex computing machines that use his software. He just sells the right to install his operating soft-ware on every computer built—and then he gets to sell upgrades to all of these computer owners. Little wonder he's the richest person in the world. Smart. Real smart.

Using a variation of this concept, an inventor approached a large cor-poration in the 1990s with a crazy idea to enhance company sales. The inventor wanted only a few pennies per item sold. It sounded reasonable. But the first company he approached turned him down flat. Undaunted, he gathered up his idea—his intellectual property, his thin-air concept—and went down the street in New York City to present the idea to the next-largest competitor. After some brief research, the executives of the second com-pany caught the vision and signed a licensing

> ━━━ **$$$** ━━━
> **WIT & WISDOM**
> **The first man gets the oyster, the second man gets the shell.**
> **ANDREW CARNEGIE**

agreement with the inventor. In exchange for his idea, they would pay him a few pennies per package.

The result? In the first year, the company increased its total sales by $100 million. And the inventor has since put several million dollars into his own pocket. Lifetime streams of income.

What was the idea that made both company and inventor so much money? Have you ever bought a package of batteries? Did you notice that Duracell batteries come with a small battery tester built right on the side of the battery? Duracell was the first battery company to introduce this concept. It was an idea worth hundreds of millions of dollars. I'm told that the inventor of this idea was the same person who created the popular Mood Rings of the 1960s and 1970s. Do you remember those plastic rings that would change colors based upon a person's body heat? Decades later, this same person used the same thermogenics technology to create a huge extra stream of licensing revenue.

Old idea + new application + the power of licensing = multiple streams of lifetime income

Applications of Licensing

So what if you're not Disney or Gates. Maybe you don't even own a garage to start from. How does all this relate to you? Hold on, let's get the concept down and let the theory soak into your psyche. Disney and Gates were once little guys. Why *not* you? Come to think of it, I, too, was a little guy. And it wasn't that long ago. About the time that Gates started tinkering with computers, I started buying real estate. A few years later, I started teaching other people how to buy property with nothing down. My seminars, started in a small hotel room in Provo, Utah, were soon playing to packed houses in major cities. Without my knowledge, I was being watched. I was the "kid on the rise," and my seminar competitors wanted to know how I was doing it.

One of these competitors called me on the phone and made me an offer I couldn't refuse: "Let us license your name and your idea. Let us market your seminar for you. Your presence won't be required at the seminars. We'll train and teach the seminar instructors. Once it's up and running all you'll need to do is cash the royalty checks." Wouldn't you say yes? Over the next six years, with little or no effort on my part, this company sent myself and my family millions of dollars in royalties.

I didn't realize it at the time, but I had become a licensor, granting the rights to my ideas in exchange for a small royalty. Although I had done well investing in real property, my *intellectual property* was the real gold mine.

Wealth was in my thoughts, not in my things. In the future, so will it be for you. Every day, your mind processes thousands of thoughts. Some of those thoughts are million-dollar ideas. How many million-dollar ideas do you need? Disney's idea was Mickey. Gates's was DOS. Mine was Nothing Down. What is your idea? How do you turn that idea, that thought, into a licensing stream of cash?

First, you've got to believe that your idea is just as good as the thoughts flashing through the person standing next to you. There is a thought in you, a big one, waiting to be clothed in action. If you only believe it can. Break free from the belief that these kinds of things happen only to other people.

WIT & WISDOM
Never give in. Never give in.
Never give in.
Sir Winston Churchill

The first step is to expand your awareness so that you begin to see the possibilities everywhere. And soon, maybe not this year, but eventually, the opportunity to spin off a licensing deal will drop into your lap as it did into mine.

Intellectual Property Is Protected by Law

I don't claim to be an attorney, and this explanation may not be technically correct, but here goes. Ideas, images, information, names, and all forms of intellectual property are protected by patents, copyrights, service marks, and trademarks.

If your ideas are legally copyrighted, patented, or trademarked, then you own the rights to them and no one else can use them without your permission. In order for others to use your ideas, you need to grant them permission, or *license,* for an agreed-upon fee, commission, or royalty.

Licensing is not very complicated. It all starts with a simple agreement between two people who want to do business together: "I, Robert G. Allen, hereby grant the rights to John Smith to market XYZ product for X period of time in exchange for a royalty of X based upon the following restrictions . . . yada, yada, yada." Then, under the watchful eye of a knowledgeable attorney who adds a lot of boilerplate, your licensing agreement takes shape.

And that brings us to the many ways of licensing products.

Celebrity licensing

Well-known celebrities lend their names to various projects for royalties and fees. I once paid television talk-show host Gary Collins $50,000 plus a percentage of gross sales to host one of my infomercials. The day we shot the show was a long day of work. (Fifty grand for one day's effort! Celebrity pays.) Gary was superb, a true professional, and a wonderful human being. He left with a hefty fee plus additional streams of income from the sale of the products. We both won. I bought the needed credibility and he traded his celebrity status for extra streams of income.

Every time you see a celebrity endorsing a product, you'll know it has something to do with licensing. And it's everywhere. Listen to the voices of famous actors in almost any television or radio commercial. Notice the rich and famous who have created their own lines of products—from Johnny Carson suits to Rush Limbaugh's colorful ties to Michael Jordan's cologne. Celebrity sells. And there are hundreds of celebrities available to help you sell your product for a fee.

Character licensing

Mickey Mouse, Power Rangers, Gummi bears, and the California Dancing Raisins are all good examples.

Ken Kerr, our licensing guru, spotted some strange, blue plastic figures at a toy show in Germany many years ago. He brought home a few samples and kids went wild for them. He knew he had a winner on his hands. He and his partners flew back to Europe and finally tracked down the creator in Belgium. A deal was struck to license and market these characters in America . . . and the rest is history. You know them as Smurfs. In addition to cartoons, the image of Smurfs can be found on dozens of products, all produced under license. The list is endless: bedsheets, pillowcases, lunch pails, thermoses, toys, school supplies, pencil boxes, erasers, pencils, pens, schoolbooks, T-shirts, sweatshirts, other articles of clothing, hats, bumper stickers, calendars, planners, ties, buttons, figurines, dolls, mugs, greeting cards, and comic books.

> **$$$**
> **WIT & WISDOM**
> If only God would give me some clear sign! Like making a deposit in my name in a Swiss bank account.
> **WOODY ALLEN**

Ken Kerr's company didn't produce any of these items. They simply relicensed the Smurfs to dozens of North American companies who wanted to use the Smurf logo to enhance the sales of their products. The result was hundreds of millions of dollars in sales and millions of dollars in licensing fees.

Where do you find ideas like this? Whenever you travel, keep your eyes open. Suppose you spot a soon-to-be-discovered Pet Rock idea. What is to prevent you from acquiring worldwide merchandising rights? You'd be surprised how many foreign successes are dying to get to the big top and are willing to almost give away marketing rights for the privilege. The Smurfs had been successful in Europe for over 20 years before they appeared in America. Someone just needed to recognize the idea and bring it here.

Speaking of character licensing, I wonder how much the Metropolitan Life Insurance Company pays for the rights to use the cartoon character Snoopy in its advertising. You've seen it in magazines everywhere. "Get Met. It pays." Yes, I'll bet Met pays a bundle.

Information Licensing

I've already referred to how I earned income licensing Robert Allen seminars. Any idea, concept, or specialized information is licensable. Most creators of information leave millions of dollars on the table because they simply don't know how to package and market their information into dozens of information products. Take the infopreneuring ideas I taught you in Chapter 12 and license the ideas of rising-star authors. Watch the best-seller lists and be there early. Catch the comet and hang on.

There is clothing licensing, as in the Nike swoosh.

There is sports licensing, as in Michael Jordan, Tiger Woods, and Jack Nicklaus.

There is invention licensing, as in the Duracell battery deal.

Profiting from Licensing

Here are four basic ways to profit from the field of licensing.

Method 1: Start from scratch with your own idea.

Disney created Mickey out of thin air. Grab an idea out of the air and get started. Using this concept, two guys working out of their garage in 1988 put their ideas (their intellectual property) down on paper in the form of some roughly drawn black-and-white sketches. By 1991, this simple concept had been turned into reality and had generated $400 million in worldwide licensing revenues. The idea, which doesn't seem all that intellectual but was certainly profitable, is called Teenage Mutant Ninja Turtles. Ever heard of them? Your teenager has.

Method 2: Use licensing to add multiple streams of income to your existing business.

As with the Hang Ten logo, you might find that sticking logos on other people's products is even more profitable than building the products yourself. Using this concept, sports licensing has added huge streams of income to the bottom line of all major sports. Money is made not just by selling tickets to sporting events or by selling rights to see these events on television, but by licensing football, baseball, basketball, hockey, and soccer logos for clothing, equipment, and product endorsements. This is a multi-billion-dollar industry. The teams don't manufacture the clothing or equipment themselves. They just license others to do so.

Think about the Olympics. The Olympic Committee doesn't manufacture, market, and move products that bear the Olympic logo. It just licenses others to do it . . . and collects royalties. As an independent businessperson, you could acquire the rights to use the Olympic logo to enhance the sale of your products. But the preferred position is to be the *licensor,* not the *licensee.*

Method 3: Acquire the license to someone else's idea and grow it from scratch.

Look at Bill Gates. DOS was actually someone else's program, which Gates acquired for the sum of $50,000 and parlayed into a company that made him the richest man in the world. You see, your multi-million-dollar idea doesn't even have to originate in your own head.

**Method 4: Use licensing to add multiple streams of income
to someone else's existing business.**

There are thousands of businesses in every country in the world that need
to be educated on the benefits of licensing. Either they need to license
their own products for sale (like the European creator of the Smurfs) or
they need to license other people's ideas to enhance the sale of their own
products (like Duracell). *You* could be the person to educate these business and earn a stream of income as a result.

This kind of approach was used by an enterprising infopreneur who
turned a tip into millions of dollars of revenue for himself and his client.
According to the story, this man noticed in a trade journal that a New
York symphony orchestra was planning to present an evening of music
entitled *Marilyn,* devoted to the life and career of the famous actress.

This was the spark that he needed. He contacted the estate of a photog-
rapher that contained a rare collection of Marilyn Monroe photographs,
acquired the merchandising rights to Marilyn Monroe's name, and
licensed the creation of products to coincide with the evening of the symphony. Then he contacted the symphony and asked if it would allow a
special exhibition of Marilyn's rare photos in conjunction with the symphony performances. The symphony, of course, was delighted. The pre-
publicity also attracted other owners of rare photographs, who were also
allowed to display their photographs in this special showing. Vendors
were contacted to create Marilyn merchandise especially for the
show . . . calendars of photos, scarves, sweaters, T-shirts, pens, and a host
of related merchandise—all of which were produced under license from
the promoter. The publicity greatly increased public awareness, millions
of dollars of Marilyn merchandise was sold, and the bottom line was huge
streams of licensing royalties.

How to Get There from Here

Let's explore a five-step plan for cashing in on licensing.

Step 1: Saturate your mind with tollgate thinking.

Start thinking like Bill Gates. Every moment of his business life seems to
be spent thinking of ways he can become the tollgate through which
people have to pass (for a small fee) to access specific information.
Maybe that's why his name is Gates. He has effectively become the tollgate to the minicomputer world. Using this same thinking, Gates is now
acquiring vast libraries of photo archives of famous art from all over the
world. These photographs are being digitized, and people who use them
will have to pay Bill a small royalty for the privilege. Once again, he's the
tollgate. He's lining up strategic alliances with businesses all over the
world. He wants just a little piece of practically everything that is sold.
He wants to be the tollgate. You and I should start thinking more like
Bill. I'd be happy with just one one-thousandth of his net worth,
wouldn't you?

Step 2: Pretend you're a licensing mogul.

Make a game out of noticing at least one licensing possibility each and every day. Watch for hot trends and hot people. Read newspapers and trade journals. When you spot a promising idea or concept, ask yourself, "I wonder if they've given up the worldwide rights?" "Would that idea look good on a T-shirt?" "What does this business need in the form of a licensable idea that could make us both a fortune?" "How could they squeeze more profit out of their successful business?" "Would kids like this?" "How could I help someone become famous and make us both rich in the process?" "How could I market this idea to the rest of the world?"

Step 3: Spend a day at the local library or bookstore.

Perhaps you remember my famous outrageous public claim:

"Send me to any city. Take away my wallet.
Give me a $100 bill. And in 72 hours I'll buy an excellent
piece of real estate using none of my own money.

The *LA Times* challenged me to prove it. With a reporter by my side, I bought seven properties in 57 hours. It was a great learning experience.

I challenged Ken Kerr, the licensing guru, to a similar dare: to be dropped in a strange city without prior contacts or resources and find, negotiate, and sign a profitable licensing deal within 72 hours. He accepted and told me exactly how he would do it. Before I reveal his solution, let me ask you, how would you do it?

Here's what he would do: He would go directly to the main branch of the local public library and ask one of the librarians to show him the patents on microfiche. There are thousands of patent filings, with more being added daily. Next he would scan through the microfiches, making a list of the those products, ideas, or inventions that he felt had major potential. Then, using the inventor's phone number or address listed on the patent form, he would contact at least 10 whose ideas he had selected as worthy. In Ken's experience, 9 out of 10 of these inventors do not have marketing or licensing agents and are very open to discussing such an arrangement. He would pick the best alternative, arrange for worldwide licensing rights, and sign the agreement.

> **$$$**
> **WIT & WISDOM**
> The shortest way to do many things is to do only one thing at once.
> SAMUEL SMILES

If the patent section didn't yield fruits fast enough, Ken would scan the how-to section of the library. Or back issues of the *New York Times* bestseller list. There always seem to be authors and experts who have not capitalized on their value and who are willing to grant licensing rights to the information products not covered in their publishing royalty agreement. If the library isn't current enough, any major bookstore could provide plenty of fodder for a challenge. One way or another, he felt that 72 hours would be more than adequate.

In one such experience, Ken was able to acquire the direct-mail marketing rights to a famous author and his work. In a short time, he paid this author over a half a million dollars in licensing fees. To the benefit of both parties.

Step 4: Find a manufacturer or end licensee.

Once Ken had acquired licensing rights to a patent, he would look through the *American Registry of Manufacturers*, which lists all major manufacturers by subject. Depending on the idea, he would contact manufacturers and try to interest them in a licensing arrangement.

For example, suppose his concept included the marketing of a baseball cap with a specialized logo. The *Registry* lists dozens of baseball cap manufacturers . . . each with its own distribution channels already in place. If the idea is right, the manufacturer provides seed capital, inventory, rollout, and distribution, with instant access to hundreds of outlets.

Step 5: Enjoy lifetime streams of royalty checks.

Yes, this discussion is an oversimplification of a very complex subject. My purpose has been to open your mind to it, to increase your awareness about it, to plant the seeds of possibility that at least once in your life you'll be able to profit from the ideas I've shared with you here. If you'd like a free special report, "The Little-Known Secrets to the World of Licensing" by Ken Kerr, just visit my web site at www.multiplestreamsofincome.com and I'll e-mail a copy of it to you. Enter the keyword Ken Kerr.

Here are answers to some of the questions you're probably thinking right now.

Q. When is the best time to acquire a license to market someone else's product?

A. When they don't want an arm and a leg for it. Disney today charges about $500,000 up front for a specific-use license to Mickey Mouse, plus about 15 percent of gross wholesale revenues. This is one of the highest rates in the industry. If a T-shirt is sold for $20, the wholesale cost is about $10. Disney receives 15 percent of the $10 wholesale cost, or $1.50, every time a T-shirt is sold. That's today. But years ago, the businessman who first acquired the rights to do this probably paid nothing.

The licensing rights to the entire Cabbage Patch Kids doll concept were offered to Ken Kerr for free. At that time, the inventor would have been happy for any help to get the dolls into the marketplace. Ken passed on the offer, like most everyone else in the industry. Live and learn. A few short years later he paid $380,000 for the licensing rights for just one small part of Cabbage Patch doll license.

So, it's a good idea to watch the rising stars. They usually don't know the value of what they have and are anxious for any extra revenue. In many cases, the licensing rights can be acquired for next to nothing. And the ongoing royalties can be 3 percent on the low end up to 10 percent.

Nonetheless, it is possible to make nice streams of money from an expensive, hot property like Power Rangers or an established property like the Muppets—if you've got the cash. But remember the money tree formula: The N in MONEY stands for Nothing down. It's there for a reason. Keep your risks low. There's got to be one good, inexpensive licensing idea still out there . . . with your name on it.

Q. What are some other ways that an existing business can earn an extra stream of income from licensing?

A. Let's take the unlikely example of the LA coroner's office. Some smart licensor has convinced this government office to license merchandise—T-shirts, sweatshirts, bumper stickers, and body chalk for drawing the outline of dead bodies on the floor, to name just a few. These items are becoming very popular. Who would have guessed that such a morbid government agency could be converted into a wildly successful entrepreneurial source of money?

Could *you* capitalize on this idea? Are there other coroner's offices in the world? Change the name, copy the idea, and perhaps the resulting streams of income could be yours. There's nothing wrong with copying—as long as you don't cross legal boundaries. After all, how many hamburger restaurants are there?

Let's take another example: the Hollywood Chamber of Commerce. Did you know that the famous Hollywood sign in the hills of Hollywood is trademarked. Whenever an image of that sign is shown anywhere, a fee must be paid to the Hollywood Chamber of Commerce. The same holds true for the stars on the Hollywood Walk of Fame. Bet you didn't know that, did you?

Finally, let's explore the example of Gold's Gym, where you'll find muscle-bound men and women in major cities nationwide. It is my understanding that almost any gym can become a Gold's Gym for a very nominal fee. However, each licensed Gold's Gym must sell the Gold's Gym T-shirts and other bodybuilding paraphernalia, thus providing huge licensing and merchandising revenue to Mr. Gold from his nationwide network.

Q. How about franchising? Is franchising a form of licensing?

A. Yes, but there's too much work involved for my taste. With a franchise, you license your successful business in exchange for a lump-sum franchise fee plus a percentage of the gross profits. Residual streams? Yes. Lots of work, risk, effort, management, employees? Yup. Is this a money tree? Nope. Got to be an easier way.

Q. What if someone hasn't protected him- or herself with the appropriate copyrights, trademarks, or patents?

A. Did you know that the "Happy Birthday" song was not copyrighted until a smart woman did the research and discovered it was in the public domain? She was granted a copyright, and each time you hear this song being played on the air, a royalty is paid to that smart woman. Or so they tell me.

Did you know that in the 1960s some of the major American car companies had failed to properly copyright and trademark their logos in Europe? It was a multi-million-dollar mistake. One enterprising young college student discovered the oversight and went from country to country in Europe doing the necessary legal work to "capture" the names. In order to sell their cars in Europe, these careless U.S. car companies ended up paying him millions in licensing fees.

Well, there you have licensing in a nutshell. As I said earlier, a licensing idea is bound to fall out of the sky and hit you some day. Let's hope your mind is open and the timing is right.

CHAPTER 14

*There is a tide in the affairs of men, which, taken at the flood,
leads on to fortune. Omitted, all the voyage of their life is
bound in shallows and in miseries.*
WILLIAM SHAKESPEARE, *JULIUS CAESAR,* **IV, III**

YOUR TENTH STREAM
The Internet: Your Next Fortune Is Only a Click Away

The Internet. How many times have you heard that word this week? What is all the excitement about? Is the Internet for real, or is it doomed to a high-tech graveyard?

The Internet *is* for real. It's not a fad. It's the most influential business innovation in history. I could quote you numbers about how many hundreds of millions of people are online or coming online, but this thing is moving so fast that by the time you read this page any numbers will be embarrassingly obsolete. The Internet is not just another minor blip on the radar screen of the business cycle. The Internet is a tidal wave. You can ride this wave to fortune or be churned under by it.

Are you on the Net yet? If not, stop reading right now and get hooked up. It's that important. Go. I don't want you to be left behind. When you get back, I'll show you how to make money from digital 0s and 1s.

If you're already hooked up, fire up your computer right now. We're going for a drive on the information superhighway.

First, let's compare traditional marketing tools with Internet marketing and see what all the fuss is about.

Traditional Marketing	Internet Marketing
Snail mail (slow, expensive, unreliable, wasteful)	E-mail (fast, cheap, reliable, efficient)
High mailing costs	Zero mailing costs

Traditional Marketing	Internet Marketing
Long delivery time	Instantaneous delivery time
Business week/business hours	24/7/365
Local/limited geographic area	Entire world
Limited, shrinking customer base	Unlimited, expanding customer base
High overhead	Almost zero overhead
Real time, real contact	Store-and-forward time (asynchronous)
Average customers	Upscale, wealthy, intelligent customers
Long inquiry time	Instant response time
Dress up/go to the office	Stay home in your T-shirt
Mass marketing	Intimate, one-on-one marketing
Impulse/wait	Impulse/instant gratification
Old, traditional	New, exciting, mysterious
Intrusive marketing (interrupts)	Noninvasive (customer-launched searching)
One-dimensional marketing	Interactive and multimedia marketing
Ads disappear quickly	Ads are as permanent as you want
High entry costs	Low entry costs/level playing field
High cost of failure	Low cost of failure
Launched from a fixed location	Launched from any computer in the world
Need to be a big player with big money	Can be a nobody with little or no money
High barriers to entry	No barriers
Highly visible/public	Private, anonymity between buyer and seller
Judged by your age, sex, $, looks, race	Judged by the quality of your ideas
Uncool	Cool

As I said in Chapter 4, marketing is the oxygen of any business. Without it, you won't be in business very long. In the regular world, marketing is expensive . . . one of your largest business expenses, in fact. Therefore, if you make a mistake in your marketing, it can jeopardize the existence of your entire business. The Internet has revolutionized the concept of marketing. First of all, it has dramatically lowered the cost of marketing. It makes it possible for you to reach new customers for pennies per thousand versus hundreds of dollars per thousand. More important, the Internet lets you reconnect and interact with these new customers over and over again with almost zero cost. The advantages are staggering.

Because of the cost advantages, new businesses are going online by the millions. It seems as if the status symbol for the new millennium is to have your own Web page. But if you want to make money on the Net, having your own Web page is just the beginning. It's like having a billboard in the middle of the Nevada desert. . . . If nobody sees it, it may as well not even exist. It's worthless.

If the three key passwords in real estate are *location, location, location,* then on the Internet, they're *traffic, traffic, traffic.* Your most important task is to drive traffic to your site. If you have no traffic, your site has no value. I repeat: A Web page in and of itself is nothing. Traffic is everything. By *traffic,* I mean visits by people. The more visits, the more valuable your space.

Think of it this way: Before Las Vegas became the "hot spot," it was nothing but a few lonely buildings in the middle of the desert. Along came gambling and attracted a few people. The casinos needed to attract more people, so they added famous entertainers and glitzy dancing girls. Traffic increased. They offered cheap airfares and inexpensive food. Traffic increased even more. They staged major boxing bouts, and people flew in from all over the world. Traffic increased again. They added a major convention center. Traffic zoomed. Then they added attractions for kids and families. Traffic exploded. With traffic flowing (people circulating) throughout the city, everything else in the city became more valuable . . . the commercial street corners, the office space, the restaurants, the retail stores. Newspaper ads, magazine space, billboards, television and radio spots—all increased in value. However, if the traffic were to stop flowing, the buildings would stand empty, the stores would have no customers, the population would leave. Las Vegas would become a ghost town.

Your web site is like an imaginary city in the middle of the desert. If you can attract people to it—traffic—and encourage them to come back again and again and bring their friends, then everything on your site will

The Cost of Reaching 1,000 Potential Customers One Time	
Direct mail	$330
Big-city newspaper	$31
Television	$16
Radio	$7
National magazine	$7
Internet	$.03 for an entire month

Source: *How to Make a Fortune on the Information Super Highway,* Canter and Canter.

increase dramatically in value. *You* own all the real estate—the digital property. *You* own the commercial corners, the malls and shopping centers, the residential apartment buildings. *You* own the television stations, the radio stations, the newspapers, and all the billboards on every street corner. Without traffic, all of these assets are worthless. With traffic, *you* can rent out these assets for a fortune! It's all about traffic.

With the goal of building traffic in mind, let me show you how to build an Internet marketing machine—a machine that not only drives traffic to your site but gets people to leave money as they're passing through. Interested?

At this point, I'm going to introduce you to one of my favorite Internet gurus, Daren Falter. I myself turned to Daren and his inner circle of Internet experts to coach me in launching my own web site, www .robertallen.com. I consider Daren eminently qualified to be your Internet coach for the rest of this chapter. . . . Daren, they're all yours. Take it away. . . .

Thanks, Bob.

My name is Daren Falter, and I'll be your Internet coach for the rest of this chapter. The Internet is not as complicated as it might seem. If I were to describe the function of the Internet in the simplest terms possible, I would say this: "People go on the Internet and look for stuff . . . specific stuff. Your first job is to find the ones looking for *your* stuff and get them to visit your web site in order to buy your stuff—over and over again."

How can this be done? Robert Allen, or Bob as he likes to be called, is very big on condensing each stream of income into three key points. The three keys to Internet success spell the word SAM:

S   Strategizing your launch

A   Automating everything

M   Marketing for traffic

First Key to Internet Success: Strategizing Your Launch

Before you can turn on your Internet marketing machine, you need to carefully strategize what products or services you intend to market. People make several common mistakes when trying to decide what product or service to promote on the Internet. Most people end up selecting a product or service for the wrong reasons.

Let me give you a short quiz. Pretend that you are selecting a product you'd like to market on the Internet. What should be your number one concern? Choose from the list that follows. Be sure to choose well, because if you make the wrong choice, your chances for success on the Internet will be virtually eliminated.

In choosing a product or service to market on the internet, my number one concern should be:

1. ____ Marketing my offline business online.

2. ____ Turning my favorite hobby into a booming business.

3. ____ Marketing products that give me and my family fantastic results.

4. ____ Marketing products and services that benefit as many people as possible.

5. ____ Marketing products and services that appeal to a specific online niche.

6. ____ Marketing products that are proven winners for marketing online.

7. ____ All of the above.

Although none of these answers will guarantee success, if you selected numbers 4, 5, or 6, you're on the right track. Discover what your passion is. If it fits one of these categories, you might have a good product.

Bringing Your Offline Product or Service Online

I've consulted with many people who have tried to take an existing, traditional, offline company or product and bring it online. Most of these people simply create an online catalog of their products or services and expect it to be a big hit online. Most of the time, they are disappointed. Then there are those who want to turn a favorite hobby or an expertise into a raging online business success without doing any marketing research to determine if the product will sell online.

Although I would never discourage you from testing your idea, it's hard to force a square peg into a round hole. For example, take the case of a successful chiropractor who would like to promote his business online. Instead of spending thousands of dollars on TV, radio, newspaper, and the Yellow Pages, he decides to find customers on the Internet. Without any strategic planning, he spends the next three months' advertising budget on developing a beautiful, high-tech web site with all of the bells and whistles only to find that most of his leads come from out of state or out of the country!

Or take the example of a bagpipe enthusiast whose 20-year hobby has been playing bagpipes with the Seattle Scotts. He decides to invest his savings into an Internet site that sells bagpipes. Even though he needs to sell only four sets of bagpipes to cover his full-time salary, he just can't seem to find enough qualified buyers to make it fly.

There are tens of thousands of failure stories like this for every successful eBay or Buy.com. And it simply isn't necessary! My job as an Internet marketing coach is to help you find an idea that *will* fly on the Internet and will still match up with your expertise and your passion. For example, if our chiropractor had come to me *before* he launched, I might have saved him a lot of money by refocusing his efforts. I might have suggested that he market an online book targeted toward all those millions of aging

baby boomers with aching backs. Or that he develop a Chiropractic
Business Success Kit to teach other chiropractors how to create a successful practice. Or better still, that he develop a national referral network
for other chiropractors. Then he could earn money from sore backs
worldwide.

By focusing on the strengths of the Internet, this chiropractor could
strategize a powerful Internet business to supplement his successful
hands-on business (pun intended). It might generate enough money to
completely replace his existing income. But in order to do that, he needs
to discover a totally different clientele—one with a broad national, and
eventually international, appeal.

To my Scottish brother, I would recommend that he simply change his
product offering to include items that might be more suited for the
masses: Scottish music, books, and collectibles. He can still sell the pipes
as a back-end bonus product. You don't ever need to give up your
dream. . . . You might just need to modify and enhance your vision to
include more potential buyers.

Mass Market versus Niche Market on the Net

I've heard motivational speaker Zig Ziglar say, "You can have anything
you want in this life if you'll just help enough other people get what they
want." Do you want to help a few people, many people, or millions of
people? It may be fun and exciting to work with products that are interesting to *you,* but there just isn't any profit in marketing products that do
not also appeal to large segments of the population. If your potential customers include almost everyone on the entire planet, you have a distinct
advantage over companies that appeal only to a select group of customers.

If you don't like the mass-marketing model, that's okay. Many savvy
online marketers are having unbelievable success marketing to niches that
are 2 inches wide and 100 miles deep. This is still mass marketing, but
with a specific focus. As your focus becomes more narrow, you will have
fewer potential customers. You must apply your most effective, laser-
focused, targeted marketing techniques to win this game, and your niche
must have sufficient depth. In other words, you can either go wide or you
can go deep. But it's extremely difficult to make money with a narrow,
shallow product line.

The best test, however, is to determine whether the product or service
you wish to offer is doing well online right now and whether trends sug-
gest that it will continue to do well for the next 20 years. Why pay twice
for expensive market-testing information that can be yours for free? A
fool learns from his or her own mistakes, while the wise person learns by
observing the mistakes of others. This wisdom applies on the Net. Find
several successful business models related to what you want to do, and try
to duplicate their success. Make sure you get some expert advice before
settling on a theme. After all, you will be living with this decision for the
rest of your life.

Successful Web Business Models

Over the past year I have examined thousands of successful online business models. However, I have discovered three business models that are particularly easy to launch and can yield fantastic results. If I were starting from scratch, I would make sure to select a business that most closely matched one of these three concepts: *information marketing, network marketing,* or *affiliate programs.*

Successful web business model 1: information marketing

Take everything you learned about infopreneuring in Chapter 12 and apply it to the Internet. Many people are having tremendous success marketing information online. This business is particularly suited to the strengths of the Internet.

$$$ Going Digital $$$

In his excellent book, *Being Digital,* Nicholas Negroponte argues convincingly that the world is rapidly changing from moving things or atoms to moving digital bits or thoughts. You no doubt remember how long it took to send a book via regular mail. Then someone had the brilliant idea that you should absolutely, positively be able to get that book overnight. Thus Federal Express was born. But now even Federal Express has a growing problem. A book is made of atoms in the form of paper, which takes up space, has weight, is visible, and consumes time and money to transfer from one place to another. What happens when you convert that book from atoms of paper to bits in a computer and then transmit those bits via a phone line? Those bits take up no space, have no weight, are invisible, and can be transported in seconds at almost zero cost! The advantages of being digital are incredible. Music, video, audio, television, movies, information, magazines, newspapers, photos, mail. The world is going digital at mind-boggling speed.

There are no borders in a digital world. You can do things the old way by sending a book via snail mail: Package it, travel to the post office to affix expensive postage, and physically drop it in a box to be picked up by a truck—from whence it's handled (or mishandled) by dozens of human hands, finally getting held up at some international border and ransomed for a hefty custom's duty before being dropped into your customer's box in a faraway land. Or you can simply push a button on your computer and whisk away the e-mail file of your book, which alights in seconds ready to be downloaded to your customer across the globe. No fuss. No muss. The barriers of time, space, and money are obliterated. In a digital world, the individual has power that was once wielded only by Fortune 500 companies. Are you ready to wield that kind of power?

It used to be very difficult for a beginning infopreneur to break into the world of publishing. The odds of getting a book published through a traditional publisher are very slim. But on the Internet the advantages are incredible. You can get started with no publisher, no agent, no printer, no inventory, no PR person, no bookstore, no warehouse, no sales staff, no distribution vehicles, no office space, no employees. It's a no-brainer.

Let's examine a hypothetical case study. Let's suppose you're already in the information business—an infopreneur—selling advice on how to invest money in the stock market. You have a home-study course consisting of a manual and six audiocassettes compiled from your experience and study. From time to time, you teach an in-depth seminar. This leads to some private consulting. You have three employees operating out of a small office space near your home. Like most businesses, advertising and marketing expenses account for 40 to 50 percent of your gross revenue. You advertise in some trade journals and do some selective direct-mail drops. You've tried television and radio but found the results spotty. You work hard, but after expenses you wonder if it's worth it. From time to time, you long for the security of a salary. *Whoa! Stop that thought right now!* You use the Internet for e-mail, investment research, and online brokerage. But you wonder if you could use the Net to increase your business. Is this Net for real? Or just a flash of excitement and back to business as usual? Here's a better question:

> *Would your business be more profitable if you had*
> *no mailing costs, no product costs, and no shipping costs?*
> *Would you make more money if you could be open 24 hours a day,*
> *365 days a year, with no office space and no employees?*

Yes? Well, that's a description of the Internet.

Back to our hypothetical case study. As you examine the Net's advantages, you determine that you want to start marketing on the Internet. You've had good success marketing your home-study course in the real world. It has been your primary tool to attract customers into your funnel—your lead generator. Once people study your material, about 20 percent of them request more-expensive and more-profitable services from you.

With the costs of printing the manual, copying the tapes, overhead, marketing, and shipping, you can't afford to sell your materials for less than about $50. But if you could figure out a way for more people to read your manual or listen to your tapes it would definitely put more money in your pocket.

With this in mind, you decide you'd like to try marketing on the Internet. A friend of yours who works for a company that builds Web pages agrees to help you develop an inexpensive home page. He helps you register a domain name by taking you to one of the domain registration pages: www.networksolutions.com, www.register.com, or www.internet-crusade.com. You spend $70 to lock up your Internet name for two years. Then you spend a couple of weekends and evenings browsing the Net to observe how other people are doing it. You scan the big guns, General Motors, *USA Today,* CBS. You visit the IBM site, download some free software for accessing audio broadcasts, and listen to the president of IBM give a speech at a major trade show. You are amazed to hear the guy speaking in his own voice as if you were there yourself. "Wow!" you think, "Could I put my tapes online and let people listen to me as I'm now listening to the president of IBM?"

You wonder what it would cost to digitize your tapes . . . probably thousands. Then you pass by the CNN Web page and download small video images of current news stories . . . a war somewhere, a presidential debate, a tornado in the South. Wow! Video right on your computer . . . not nearly as clear as on television . . . but you wonder how you could get a video of *you* sharing some of your most powerful moneymaking advice. You wonder what it would cost to turn *your* video into digital data. Probably thousands. And you don't even know whether it'll work. But your techie friend assures you that a simple Web page with a few screens of data is relatively inexpensive. He can digitize both your audiocassettes and a short snippet of video for a few hundred dollars. After your techie scans in a photo of you and photos of your information products, you'll have an immediate Internet presence, and you can put the rest "under construction" for later.

Now he asks you what you are offering as a product. What are you trying to sell, and what are you willing to give away to attract people to your web site? Give away? You're not used to giving away your information—your least-expensive product is $50 and you barely break even on that. But wait, your $50 home-study course is your lead generator. . . . It attracts people into your information funnel. You make your real money on back-end products and seminars. You charge only $50 for your material because that's what it costs you to advertise, print, produce, and mail it. If your costs were somehow reduced, you could lower your price. You review some of the numbers in your mind. . . .

Let's see, the information in the manual wouldn't be difficult to load onto the web site—it's already in digital format on a computer at the office. It's 75 pages of great information, organized into neat charts and graphs. Your customers have always told you how valuable it is to them. The audiocassettes, according to your techie friend, can be digitized and stored on the web site (just like the message from the president of IBM) and can include a short video of you introducing some of your hottest moneymaking ideas.

And the cost? Let's see, no printing costs for the manual. The potential customer on the Internet would simply download the entire manual into his or her computer and print it out on a laser printer if needed. No shipping costs. Little or no marketing costs. Your entire $50 introductory package would cost you almost nothing to deliver instantly to anyone who wanted it. Wow. You're beginning to see the possibilities.

You and your friend decide to offer the first chapter of your manual and the first audiocassette of your course absolutely free to anyone who drives by on the information superhighway. To get the rest of the material, they need only to register with you by leaving their name, snail mail address, e-mail address, and telephone number, which will allow them into your private, members-only area. You e-mail a secret code to registrants that allows them access to your best material. The ones who go through this extra bit of hassle to get your secret password have qualified themselves as those who are very interested in your subject. And that's who you're looking for—hot prospects. And just because these hot prospects have access to free stuff doesn't mean that some of them won't want a hard copy of your manual, professionally published and autographed by you, along with the cassette tapes to listen to in the car. Because your costs of marketing are so low, you can afford to give them your Internet discount . . . only $29.95 plus shipping and handling.

With these plans in place, you launch your Web page. You can now boast that you, too, are online. But, remember, having a web site is not the goal. The goal is to drive traffic to your site. More on this later.

First, let me share with the second successful model for launching a business online.

Successful Web business model 2: Network marketing

Take everything you learned about network marketing in Chapter 11 and apply it to the Internet. Many people are having tremendous success building powerful network marketing businesses online. This business is particularly suited to the strengths of the Internet.

It used to be very difficult for beginning network marketers to get off the ground. The first thing they were encouraged to do was to make a list of 200 of their closest friends, neighbors, and acquaintances and then hound them until they bought some products. It wasn't long before these network marketers became neighborhood pariahs—members of the NFL club, No Friends Left.

It's time we put the marketing back into network marketing. It's time we stopped harassing our friends and started finding people who are truly seeking the kinds of products and opportunities we have to offer. I firmly believe that the future of network marketing is on the Internet, and those who learn to develop a successful online network marketing strategy now are going to be light-years ahead of the competition.

Here's a quick case study showing how this is working online right now.

Suppose you have a floundering network marketing business. You love the products—in fact you're passionate about them, but you just can't seem to find anyone else who is as excited about them as you are. Your parents take the products, more out of loyalty to you than anything else.

You've approached everyone you know. But after people show interest and sign up, they just seem to dwindle away after a while. Your attrition rate is faster than the growth in your downline. You seem to be getting nowhere fast. You need an infusion of hot, excited customers.

Then you hear about some people having great success building their network marketing businesses online. You decide to try your hand at it. You contact your techie friend, and before long you are doing business online at www.successfulpeople.com. By using some of the marketing ideas that I'll outline in the rest of this chapter, you start to drive traffic to your site. People are coming—total strangers from all parts of the world—who are looking for a product and an opportunity that meshes with what you are offering. You've been accustomed to chasing people down for so long, it's refreshing to have them come to you for a change. You've been accustomed to dealing with people who are broke, but these Internet contacts are sharp and they have money! It's as though you've tapped into a vein of pure gold.

But that's not the best part. Using the automated features of the Internet (which I'll be sharing with you in this chapter), you find it almost effortless to do your marketing. For example, when people are attracted to your site and ask for more information, you can send it to them instantly and for *free*. No more sending tapes and videos via snail mail. As soon as they click the button requesting more information, your autoresponder automatically sends an e-mail

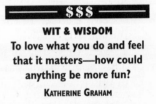

message with the information they are seeking. But that's still not all. Your autoresponder automatically sends a series of value-laden e-mail messages every day for the next week. Now *this* is marketing.

All of these contacts take place automatically—you're not even aware they are happening. Your customers are encouraged to check out the audio and video clips that are available at your site 24 hours a day. They read success stories from others whom you have helped to create successful network marketing businesses on the Net. They check out your company web site and become even more impressed.

These customers don't need you—they are selling themselves. All of this can happen online, without any physical contact whatsoever. If you don't like rejection, then you should be loving this.

Here's the clincher. You offer to help them build an Internet network marketing business using the exact same tools that *you* used to convince *them*. You offer to share all of your powerful recruiting strategies that have the potential to create a never-ending supply of qualified leads. These leads can flow daily from the Internet for a lifetime *for free*. They don't need to harass anyone ever again. They can build a massive business automatically, working with total strangers—a growing network of happy customers in far-flung countries around the globe.

The company ships all of the products directly to your customers' new-found customers. They don't have to deal with any of the hassles of running a traditional business—inventory, accounting, warehousing, research, product development, employees, overhead, shipping.

There's still more. All of the ongoing communication—training, support, recognition—can take place right online. Fast, cheap, powerful.

Now, that's my idea of an exciting business model.

Before I share with you how to set up the automated systems to create such a business, there's another exciting business model for you to consider.

Successful Web business model 3: Affiliate programs

What if you could have your own personal online supermall that allowed you to sell any and all of the hottest products on the Internet for a significant commission without the headaches of setting up your own web site? What if your site were set up for you complete with pictures of the products and an online order form? What if your credit card approval system were already in place? What if you had to provide only limited customer service and training and could spend most of your time finding more business? What if you could have the freedom to *just market products* and receive a check in the mail a few weeks later for the products that were purchased?

Well, this program does exist . . . and its called an *affiliate program.* The money being generated on the Internet today through affiliate programs is astronomical, and experts tell us that this trend will continue to explode over the next several years.

So what is an affiliate program, and why would you want to get involved with one? *Affiliate program* is the name given to a company that allows independent affiliates, associates, or distributors to refer business to a company in exchange for a commission. As you learned in Chapter 11, the most well-known affiliate program on the Net is the world's largest online bookstore, Amazon.com. One of the reasons Amazon has been so successful is that they pioneered the first megasuccessful affiliate program. Let's review how it works.

Suppose you want to become affiliated with Amazon.com. You register with Amazon as an affiliate or associate by going to www.amazon.com. Then, with the help of Amazon, you set up your own personal Amazon.com bookstore. As you start promoting the book titles on your web site, your visitors purchase these books based on your recommendation. In return for your referral business, Amazon sends you a 5 percent commission each month for your cumulative referral business. Pretty slick, eh?

$$$
WIT & WISDOM
I'd like to live like a poor man—only with lots of money.
PABLO PICASSO

Well, if you think the Amazon model is powerful, wait until you see some of the other new affiliate programs on the market. And you don't have to limit yourself to just one program. There are thousands of similar programs on the Net offering even more dynamic benefits and the opportunity to earn hundreds if not thousands of dollars a month.

Orders per Day	Estimated Weekly Income	Estimated Monthly Income	Estimated Annual Income	Estimated Annual Income with Two Affiliate Programs	Estimated Annual Income with Five Affiliate Programs
1	$140	$600	$7,300	$14,600	$36,500
2	$280	$1,200	$14,600	$21,900	$73,000
3	$420	$1,800	$21,900	$21,900	$109,500
5	$700	$3,000	$36,500	$73,000	$182,500
10	$1,400	$6,000	$73,000	$146,000	$365,000
20	$2,800	$12,000	$146,000	$292,000	$730,000

How much can you earn? Imagine that you are marketing an affiliate product on the Internet and netting $20 per product unit sold. The chart at the top of this page estimates hypothetical incomes based on number of sales per day, week, month, and year.*

New affiliate programs are popping up all the time. It's tempting to get involved with dozens of programs. One distinct advantage of affiliate programs is your ability to successfully manage multiple affiliate programs simultaneously. Also, because most affiliate programs pay commissions only on products sold, there is generally no conflict with other business opportunities that you may be marketing on your site (e.g., network marketing and direct sales programs).

Many web site owners put affiliate programs on their site as a kind of "by the way" offer: "By the way, this service is available if you should need it . . . and here is a convenient link." Most people are not going to be able to quit their day job by sponsoring one or two affiliate programs, no matter how well they do.

Some people may be able to manage more, but it's best to build only one or two streams of income at a time and then add additional programs as you are able. Make sure the affiliate programs you choose complement your existing business rather than detract from it or distract site visitors.

One of the best examples of an exciting affiliate program is one I helped Robert Allen design for his own site at www.multiplestreamsofincome.com. The best part is that it's free. Robert's site specializes in wealth-building strategies, books, audio training programs, and especially Robert Allen's new four-week Multiple Streams of Income Tele-Seminar program. Rather than developing your own web site, creating your own information products, setting up credit card merchant accounts, and all of the other

* The chart simply gives sample commissions based on criteria in the chart itself. Although the $20 payout per sale is typical of some affiliate programs currently on the market, many pay more or less than $20 per sale. This chart should *not* be used to project actual earnings. The scenarios are purely hypothetical. Affiliate programs, like any commission-based direct sales, are based on performance. Affiliate commissions are limited by the affiliate's ability or inability to effectively market affiliate products.

hassles of launching an Internet business, you can simply become a partner with Robert Allen and let him handle the details. Wouldn't it be nice to have a famous millionaire maker send you checks every month?

Affiliate programs on the Net are just in their infancy. When you turn loose the creative juices of the smartest minds in the world, you have access to opportunities that people in the "real" world can only dream about.

But remember, none of these three business models work without automation and marketing. Let's continue examining the three keys to Internet success. The first was to strategize your launch. Here's the second key.

Second Key to Internet Success: Automating Everything

In Chapter 2 of this book you learned the money tree formula—nine characteristics of a high-profit, hassle-free stream of income. One characteristic is to find an *employee-resistant* business.

Let me tell you about your own Internet marketing robot. I call him SAM.

Instead of hiring a bunch of employees to do the inventory, shipping and receiving, customer service, data entry, and all of the other tedious tasks of owning a successful business—SAM, your Internet marketing robot, is going to take care of all of those details for you.

SAM needs no sleep, no food, and no baby-sitting. He never complains, never calls in sick, never goes on strike. SAM works for you around the clock, allowing you to spend more time with your family, friends, church, community, and hobbies.

SAM is empowered to operate your entire web site marketing system. A constant flow of qualified leads is directed into his response-gathering database brain. He collects critical information about potential customers and then automatically offers customized products or services to each individual customer.

All of this happens behind the scenes, outside of your awareness. At precisely the right moment, when the customer is most ready, you are prompted to personally step in and add the human element so you can cultivate your contacts into long-term relationships of trust.

Sounds far-fetched, doesn't it? But that's what's happening right now on the Internet.

The Internet is the most powerful and efficient direct-response marketing machine in the history of marketing. With the aid of ordinary computers, direct marketers can create an online marketing machine not unlike SAM the robot. When you can learn to harness the power of this system, you will move years ahead of your competition.

There are three absolutely critical automation tools that enable SAM to perform his robotic marketing miracles: (1) an advanced Web stats program, (2) automatic e-mail templates and autoresponders, and (3) a list server.

Advanced Web Stats Programs

Think about those million-dollar spots aired during the Super Bowl in January each year. In 60 seconds, $1 million evaporates into thin air. There is no mechanism for fast, easy follow-up contact with any of the potential customers. These advertisers just lay down their million bucks with the *hope* that somebody notices. Do you think that the company who bought those million-dollar Super Bowl spots would be interested in having the addresses of all of the people who watched the ad and were interested in the product? Absolutely! The company could then refocus all of its advertising budget on precisely these few, highly qualified prospects and quit wasting money on uninterested or unqualified viewers (like the other 500 million people who watched the Super Bowl).

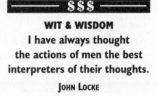

WIT & WISDOM
I have always thought the actions of men the best interpreters of their thoughts.
JOHN LOCKE

This kind of marketing sophistication is available on the Internet right now. When people enter your cyberspace, they leave an indelible trail that lets you know exactly when they arrived, where they came from, how long they stayed, where they browsed, what they bought, where they went when they left, and how often they returned.

What is this kind of information worth to a savvy marketer? It's worth a fortune! Not just in the money you can make—but in the money you save in wasted advertising.

When you host your web site with a Web hosting service or Internet service provider (ISP) one of your first questions should be, "How sophisticated are your Web stats?"

Whichever consultant you choose to guide you in launching your site, make sure you have access to a superior Web stats package. For example, you should be able to automatically track the results of any promotion you do on the Net—not only the amount of traffic it generates but, more important, the amount of sales it generates.

Automatic E-mail Templates and Autoresponders

One of the strengths of online marketing is your ability to use an e-mail-based contact management system for following up on customers. Every routine contact with a customer can and should be automated and systematized. When you receive a similar request from other customers, you can send them a templated response almost immediately.

According to one author, "With templates, I become an astonishing one-man dispatch center, able to do in minutes what would take the traditional office days, even weeks, to accomplish. Such productivity leads to increased profits, and increased profits makes me a very happy camper indeed."*

Many routine requests for information can be handled by autoresponder—a computer program that sends any e-mail response (or series of

* *E-Mail El Dorado*, Dr. Jeffrey Lant, p. 64.

responses) you specify. For example, when people ask us for information about network marketing opportunities, our autoresponder sends them a series of seven specially written, value-laden e-mails, spaced out over a seven-day period of time. The first of these e-mails is sent immediately after the request is received. This has the effect of "getting them while they're hot."

In fact, one of the main benefits of the Net is that it shortens the time frame between the initial contact and the eventual sale. In the real world, this gap may be two or three weeks. For example, notice the sales gap in a network marketing lead from a real-world classified ad:

Day 1, A.M.   Prospect calls on your classified ad. Leaves message on answering machine.

Day 1, P.M.   You retrieve the message and place a return call to prospect's answering machine.

Day 2, P.M.   No response from prospect, so you place another call.

Day 3, P.M.   Still no response from prospect, so you place a third call.

Day 4, A.M.   Prospect returns your call. Leaves message on your answering machine. Phone tag!

Day 5, P.M.   You finally connect with prospect and offer to send information.

Day 6, A.M.   You send information via two-day priority mail packet.

Day 8, P.M.   You call prospect to confirm information received and reviewed. Prospect is too busy. Promises to review it over the weekend. You make appointment for three days from now.

Day 11, P.M.   Prospect still hasn't reviewed information.

Day 12, P.M.   Prospect likes the information but requests additional information.

Day 13, A.M.   You send more information by two-day priority mail.

This goes on for another two weeks. Eventually, the prospect decides against your program. It took you almost 30 days, 10 phone calls, two mailed info packages, and many lost evenings of follow-up to get a rejection. I say, if you're going to get rejected, let's find out *now*. Saves everybody a lot of time and money.

Here is the process on the Internet.

Day 1, 9:00 A.M.   Prospect requests information.

Day 1, 9:01 A.M.   Information sent by e-mail autoresponder.

Day 1, 10:37 A.M.   Prospect checks e-mail. Likes information. Sends e-mail with several specific questions.

Day 1, 12:19 P.M.   You check your e-mail. Send a FAQ template specifically designed with marketing in mind.

Day 1, 4:12 P.M.	Prospect checks e-mail. Too busy to respond.
Day 2, 9:00 A.M.	Autoresponder sends first of follow-up templates designed to motivate prospect to action.
Day 2, 9:45 A.M.	Prospect checks e-mail. Decides to check out your web site and do some research. Spends 25 minutes of private, focused research roaming around your site. Watches video clips, listens to Real Audio, reads testimonials, checks out the company web site. Sells self.
Day 2, 10:00 A.M.	Sends e-mail requesting a telephone conference.
Day 2, 11:15 A.M.	You check your e-mail. You call the prospect, who likes your message but needs to discuss it with spouse. You get spouse's e-mail address and send spouse an e-mail introducing yourself.
Day 3, 9:00 A.M.	Autoresponder sends second follow-up message to prospect, who is impressed with the content of the message and the constant reminder of your marketing prowess. Prospect sends you an e-mail confirming discussion with spouse (who also researched your site and approves). They are ready to go.

In the real-world example, the process was a turnoff—playing phone tag, evening phone calls, who wants that? In the Internet example, the process is so effortless, it actually sells the prospect. Even if it the prospect decides against your product, the rejection is fast, easy, and cheap.

As Bill Gates says in *Business at the Speed of Thought:* "Insist that communication flow through e-mail, and convert every paper process to a digital process." The faster you follow this advice, the richer you're going to become. Templates and autoresponders will help you get there.

List Servers

In Chapter 12 you saw the following statement:

You don't need to reach 10 million people. You just need to attract 10,000 hot prospects into your funnel and you'll be set for life!

This might sound like hype—but let me prove its validity by relating a true story. Recently, a skeptical business man (let's call him Bob) was shown the power of the Internet. One of Bob's friends (let's call him David) came to visit Bob at his office. Using Bob's computer, David logged on to the Net. Then he typed a short e-mail message offering to sell one of Bob's audio programs at a 40 percent discount to the first three people who responded to the e-mail. As an additional bonus, David offered several free classified ads in "David's Internet Mall." The e-mail was sent to about 1,500 subscribers of a free Internet newsletter that had been formed only 90 days earlier. As Bob and David watched the computer screen, the first e-mail order came in less than one minute later. Before David left Bob's office there were 14 more orders.

All of this was done without spending a penny in marketing costs. David assured Bob that this was a regular occurrence. The best response he had received to a similar offer generated $11,000 in one day.

What makes this type of marketing possible? A list server. A list server is a computer database program that captures the names of every person on your e-mail database. Each person on this list has requested to receive more e-mail communications from you (as opposed to unsolicited spam). Therefore, when you send e-mail to the names on your list server, it broadcasts the message instantly to everyone simultaneously.

I've encouraged you to build a list of 10,000 names. Marketing is a numbers game. A certain, albeit tiny, percentage of *any* compiled group of people will be interested in a given targeted marketing message. Suppose you offer a $100 information product. What percentage of responses do you need from a general list of 10,000 names to put a smile on your face? Your product is digital, so your cost is close to zero.

If only one person in 1,000 responds, you'll have 10 customers. And 10 times $100 is $1,000. Can you see how making $1,000 a day is totally realistic? The key is your list, and the larger your list the easier it will be for you to make at least $1,000 . . . with just the push of a button.

Does this make sense? Here's your question: "How can I build a list server with thousands of names?" I thought you'd never ask. . . .

Third Key to Internet Success: Marketing to Build Traffic

You can always hire someone to design your web site and offer technical support. But marketing is the key ingredient that will make or break your web site. Some people are born with marketing in their blood. You can tell when people "get it" and when they don't. If it is not in your blood, then you must *learn* to be an expert marketer if you want to have fantastic results.

To exercise your marketing muscles, I encourage you to do the following:

- Become your own customer for a day and go shopping . . . using search engines.

- Interview like-minded Webmasters and site owners to probe for marketing information.

- Immerse yourself in information related to your target customers and products.

1. *Become your own customer for a day and go shopping . . . using search engines.* One of the best ways to start collecting information about

where your customers like to shop is to do keyword searches on the most popular search engines. The top search engines on the Internet are AltaVista, Excite, WebCrawler, Lycos, HotBot, GoTo, Northern Lights, Infoseek, and Yahoo, which is a search directory. Simply put an "http://www." in front of each of these names and ".com" at the end, paste it into your Web browser (usually Internet Explorer or Netscape), and hit Enter to go to any of these search engines.

Next, select five keywords or phrases that best represent the products or services you are marketing online, especially any keywords that your target customers would likely be using in a search. For example, if you were selling electronic keyboards (the musical kind), you might choose words like *electric pianos, keyboards,* and *musical instruments* (most search engines prefer the plural form of the keyword). I can't stress enough how important it is to know which keywords and phrases will motivate and inspire your customers.

Type these keywords or phrases into the search bar at the top of the search engine and click the search button or hit Enter. The search engine will bring up a list of 10 to 20 sites related to that keyword. Pretend that you are your customer and explore these sites thoroughly. Select other keywords, explore the sites that come up, and then repeat the process with the various search engines. Make sure you take notes on things you like and dislike about the sites you visit. This information will help you develop a site that has all of the good elements of your competitors sites but none of the bad.

2. *Interview like-minded Webmasters and site owners to probe for marketing information.* When visiting sites that relate to your industry and customers, don't hesitate to ask questions of the Webmasters of these sites. Some site owners love to brag about their accomplishments, so they are very open and generous with their information. After all, there is enough business to go around for everyone on the Net!

3. *Immerse yourself in information related to your target customers and products.* Another way to really get to know your target customers better is to join newsgroups and subscribe to newsletters related to your customers' interests. Your ISP (Internet service provider, the company that gives you access to the Internet) can give you the help you need to get into the newsgroups. Also, don't forget the offline world when it comes to gathering marketing information. Subscribe to and read the magazines your customers read, watch the shows they watch, and constantly ask for their feedback.

Launching Your Site

With this homework under your belt, you're ready to launch your site. The purpose of your site is to be a valuable source of information to anyone who is interested in your subject/product. The three most important elements of your site should be the following:

1. Free special reports
2. Free audio/video clips
3. Free newsletter

Everyone who visits your site should feel like they've just stumbled across a gold mine of valuable information for free. Even if you're marketing a physical object (like bagpipes), your site should still offer free information (e.g., free special report on the care and cleaning your bagpipes, free bagpipe music sheets available for download, free newsletter for bagpipe enthusiasts).

Your objective is to capture the e-mail addresses of all visitors to your site by offering so many wonderful benefits that they'll want to subscribe to your free newsletter. When people subscribe to your free newsletter (or *e-zine* as it is sometimes called), they give you permission to contact them. Therefore, your ongoing communications are not spam, or unsolicited junk mail. Your newsletter becomes a privileged communication.

Your goal is to build this newsletter list as fast as possible. Your newsletter list is your gold mine. It becomes your list server of all of your most interested prospects.

Eight-Step Plan to Increase Traffic to Your Site

If your ultimate goal is to expand subscriptions to your newsletter, then you must increase traffic to your site so that more people will have the opportunity to subscribe. I'll show you eight ways to do this.

Use your e-mail and web site in all of your real-world advertising.

Affix your e-mail and web site address to everything you do—your business cards, stationery, letterhead, fax sheets, flyers, brochures, and all forms of traditional advertising, such as direct mail, classified ads, magazine space ads—even when you sign your name. This should start a trickle of hits on your home page. Now let's turn this trickle into a small rivulet.

Register your web site everywhere.

Register your web site with as many search engines as possible. A search engine is a giant Yellow Pages . . . a listing of every Web page in the world by subject. For example, one of the most popular search engines is Yahoo (www.yahoo.com). When you get there it asks you to search its entire listing of Web pages by subject and keywords, as you would an encyclopedia. When potential customers search Yahoo, you want your web site to be listed along with the thousands of others. Your subject is money. Therefore, when visitors to Yahoo scan down the possible places to get information about money (*Money* magazine for instance), you want them to know that they can get free money information just by visiting your site. You can register inexpensively on all the major search engines by using services such as Post it or Announce it. It will take several weeks for your posting to actually take effect, but at least now you're listed. People can actually find you!

Although space doesn't permit a detailed explanation of the other methods of turning a trickle of Web page visits into a torrent, let me briefly discuss a few.

Join and post messages with newsgroups.

There are thousands of newsgroups devoted to every subject under the sun. Find people who share a common interest with you . . . such as money . . . and join in discussions about it. Read messages left by other daring infopreneurs and see how they are gathering their leads and attracting people to their Web pages. On most newsgroups it is considered bad form to post commercial messages, but there are also many that find nothing wrong with it. You'll get the hang of it in time. Newsgroups have been called the "poor man's Web page" because you can leave your e-mail address and have people contact you directly instead of sending them to your web site.

Rent e-mail lists.

There are hundreds of e-mail mailing lists consisting of dozens of subject interests. Just as with unsolicited snail mail, unsolicited e-mail is not as welcome as information that you personally request. One of the beauties of the Internet is that when people visit your Web page, it's usually because they sought you out and therefore are in a more receptive frame of mind. E-mail steps outside this cozy relationship, but there is still a use for posting e-mail messages to the right lists to invite people to visit your site.

Take advantage of free advertising.

There are hundreds of places on the Net where you can post a free classified advertisement. These sources are changing constantly. If you'd like a current listing of sites that accept free advertising, go to www.multiplestreamsofincome.com and enter the keyword Free Advertising. I'll e-mail a list to you immediately.

Use free links, link swaps, banner exchanges, cross promotions.

Sometimes you will find web sites that offer products complementary to your own. Using our earlier product example, if you're selling musical keyboards, you might find a site that sells popular sheet music for piano and keyboard. If you feel these sites are successful and receiving many visits, it might be in your best interest to try to get them to link to your site. Some Webmasters will voluntarily give you a link or banner ad on their site at no charge. Most Webmasters will want to swap links. In other words, "If you put my link on your site, I will put your link on my site." However, don't swap links with just anyone. Treat your links as bartering credits and give them to those who will treat you right and give you something valuable in return.

One of the most effective marketing strategies on the Internet is called *cross promotion,* whereby you endorse each other's sites. For example, you might find that you enjoy working with Shelly's Sheet Music and that you're getting some referral business from her site. You might post a letter of endorsement at your site telling visitors how much you use and recommend her products and services. She does the same for you at her site. You can even take this a step further and send a letter of endorsement to your entire newsletter list. Shelly does the same, and soon you have both doubled your traffic with no investment whatsoever! What would happen if you did this with 10 site owners? What would happen if you did one endorsement swap per week for two years? Catch my drift?

Develop a daily link acquisition strategy and stick to it. One of the most effective and 100 percent *free* techniques that online marketers are using today is a daily link gathering strategy. It would be foolish to spend all day every day acquiring free links and doing link and banner swaps with other web sites. However, if you were to budget, say, 10 percent of your online business time every day to acquiring links, swapping banners, and placing free ads all over the Internet, imagine the kind of exposure you could have at the end of one year. How about after five years? This long-term strategy can have a compounding effect on the traffic coming to your site. Also, many search engines will give you priority placement based on the number of other sites to which you are linked.

Make use of paid advertising online.

Do not underestimate the power of paid advertising on the Internet. If you have done any kind of research about Internet advertising, you probably know that it can be very unpredictable. If you do not know what you are doing, you can lose a lot of money. The key to effective paid advertising campaigns is to *target* your advertising. Again, seek out sites that your customers are visiting. You may even want to do a customer survey on your site to find out where they are spending their time online. Once you have located 5 to 10 top sites, start contacting their Webmasters to see if they have any paid advertising opportunities. You will find a wide range of options. Go with the deals that will give you the most bang for the buck. In other words, find the sites and ads that will be seen by the largest number of qualified prospects for the least amount of money. Then test, test, test. Soon you will know which ads to reinvest in and which ones to drop. A web site "stats package" can help you track the responses to each ad.

Use traditional offline direct-marketing techniques to drive customers online.

You won't believe the results you can get from a hot direct-mail marketing campaign designed to boost the traffic on your site. Some of my most successful months online have been the result of combining hot online advertising with a direct-mail drop or card deck advertisement (bulk direct-mail postcard advertising). Direct mail can be a great way to expose to your site potential customers who may not normally find you through online sources.

Summary

The preceding eight strategies can help you drive traffic to your site. Let's review the three keys to Internet success:

You need to strategize the launch of your web site.

You need to automate everything on your site.

You need to market constantly to build traffic.

As you build traffic, a small percentage of your visitors will leave their e-mail addresses and subscribe to your ongoing newsletter. A small percentage of your newsletter subscribers will buy something from you every time you broadcast your newsletter. Obviously, the more people on your regular e-mail newsletter list, the more money you will make with every mailing.

Each site will be different. What will be your ratio of visitors to subscribers? What will be your ratio of subscribers to sales? These are numbers you will be developing as you build your online business. As you develop your skills as an online marketer, your ratios will improve. With dedication, you can join the list of those who earn at least $1,000 a day on the Internet.

The information in this chapter is intended to not only inform you but motivate you to action. You must not wait one second longer to become part of the Internet revolution! If you haven't registered your own domain name yet, go to www.multiplestreamsofincome.com and click on the link "Get your own domain name." This will take you to a special page where you can try out various names to see if they have already been registered. Is your own name still available? That's a good place to start.

I wish you well in the online world.

CHAPTER 15

There is nothing sinister in arranging one's affairs as to keep taxes as low as possible . . . for nobody owes any public duty to pay more than the law demands.

JUDGE LEARNED HAND

Tax Cut: Plugging Your Biggest Leak

Tax planning is for everyone, not just the wealthy. In fact, one of the main reasons wealthy people become wealthy is because they understand how to plug the tax leak. If these techniques work for the wealthy, they can work for you.

Remember, the IRS Tax Code is the most difficult and complex set of laws our country has to offer. The key is to learn what those laws are and how they can be used for your particular situation.

Perhaps in no other area of financial planning is the potential for tax savings and accumulation of wealth greater than in retirement plans. Retirement plans, such as your employer's 401(k) plan, are almost as common a part of an employer's benefit package as health insurance. The opportunity for building wealth through a retirement plan is greater now than at any time in history. Let's first look at the benefits that retirement plans offer, and then we will look at some specific types of retirement plans available today.

Benefits of Retirement Plans

Retirement plans offer four main benefits:

- Immediate tax savings
- Deferred tax growth

- Employer matching contributions
- Peace of mind regarding your financial future

In simple terms, retirement plans provide a vehicle in which money can be set aside for retirement without having to pay taxes on that money in the current year. Do you remember the power of compound interest from Chapter 1? Do you realize how powerful compounding interest can be? Essentially, retirement plans give you two avenues for using this compounding factor to your advantage:

1. Compounding of tax savings and tax-deferred growth
2. Compounding of investment dollars

Let's look at each of these a little closer.

Compounding of Tax Savings

A big problem with taxpayers today is that they simply do not know exactly how they are taxed. Even the most educated tax professionals have to refer to resources to determine how certain items will be taxed. The two types of taxes that hammer every one of us are income taxes and FICA taxes.

Income taxes are the most basic of all taxes. Income taxes are progressive: The more you make, the larger percentage you pay. Following are the Federal Income Tax Tables for single and married individuals for the 1998 tax year.

Single		Married	
$0–$25,350	15%	$0–$42,350	15%
$25,352–$61,400	28%	$42,351–$102,300	28%
$61,401–$128,100	31%	$102,301–$155,950	31%
$128,101–$278,450	36%	$155,951–$278,450	36%
$278,451 and over	39.6%	$278,451 and over	39.6%

The dollar values listed in the table represent taxable income amounts, not gross income amounts. *Taxable income* is gross income minus the standard deduction or itemized deductions (but not both) minus personal exemptions. As you can see, the biggest tax jump comes at the 15 to 28 percent border. Your tax basically doubles once you graduate into a 28 percent bracket. Most two-income families find themselves in this bracket. Social Security and Medicare (FICA) taxes are paid on our earned income. This includes W-2 wages, self-employment income, and earnings from partnerships. Social Security taxes are 6.2 percent and Medicare taxes are 1.45 percent. These taxes are imposed on both the employee and the employer. Thus, the total FICA tax paid by an employee is 7.65 percent. Self-employed individuals pay 15.3 percent.

If we look closely at these two avenues of taxation, we see that the absolute lowest tax rate someone could pay would be 22.65 percent (15 percent income tax and 7.65 percent FICA tax). This does not include state income taxes that would come into play. Taxpayers in the next bracket (28 percent) would pay a minimum of 35.65 percent. As you can see, it would not be uncommon for taxpaying individuals to pay anywhere from 30 to 50 percent of their hard-earned money in taxes. Self-employed individuals would pay even more due to the employer-matching aspect of FICA taxes.

Retirement plans give us the ability to set money aside for our retirement years while at the same time reducing our current year's tax obligation. If, say, roughly 30 percent of your hard-earned dollars were to disappear in taxes, any retirement plan contribution would give you back some of those tax dollars. If you were in a 28 percent federal income tax bracket and 7 percent state income tax bracket, a retirement plan contribution of $10,000 would save you $3,500 in current-year tax dollars. That is a remarkable savings. You can plug a leak and create an extra stream all in one move. Look at it another way: If you could invest $10,000 and earn an immediate $3,500 profit on your investment, your rate of return would be 35 percent. Where else in the world can you get an immediate, guaranteed 35 percent return on your money? Although taxes would be due when those funds are pulled out of the plan, having an interest-free loan for 30 to 40 years is not a bad deal. And don't forget to factor in inflation—the future taxes are paid with inflated dollars.

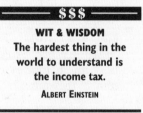

WIT & WISDOM
The hardest thing in the world to understand is the income tax.
ALBERT EINSTEIN

Obviously, figuring out this tax monster will enhance your wealth-accumulation arsenal. In the next few pages, as we discuss various retirement options, don't nod off or let your eyes glaze over. This is the normal reaction from the average (broke) taxpayer. But wealthy people get excited about these deadly dull details—to them it's exactly the same as buying a hot stock that goes up 35 percent in one day. Wealthy people *get excited* any time they can easily, simply, instantly, and *without risk* earn 35 percent on their money. As long as your bank account grows each day, you shouldn't care where the money comes from—tax savings or a bargain real estate property.

Compounding of Investment Dollars

Let's look at an example of the power of compound interest in a retirement plan.

Assume Harry is 50 years old. Harry has recently started his own business and is interested in starting a retirement plan. Harry believes he has the resources to contribute $5,000 to his retirement plan every year.

Let's assume Harry put in $5,000 at age 50. If he did not contribute again, the retirement plan would have around $23,000 in it by age 65 (assuming a 10 percent rate of return). If Harry contributes $5,000 *every year* between the ages of 50 and 65, his total investment of $80,000 would be worth almost $200,000 by age 65. Another great component of this arrangement is that the retirement plan pays zero taxes on the growth. This is incredible!

This example makes three assumptions that can all be improved upon:

1. Investment starts at age 50.
2. Contributions of only $5,000 per year are made.
3. The retirement plan earns only 10 percent per year.

What would happen if Harry were only 30 years old and decided to put away $5,000 per year until age 65? His $180,000 investment over 36 years would be worth about $1,650,000. What if Harry put in more? What if Harry could have his money growing tax-free at a higher rate of interest? There are many variables, but the key is to sock away this money in a tax-sheltered vehicle ASAP.

Types of Retirement Plans

Today, working taxpayers have many choices when it comes to establishing a retirement plan. Let's look at the benefits of a few of the more commonly used retirement plans. There are individual plans, such as IRAs and Roth IRAs. There are also company plans, such as 401(k)s, SIMPLEs, and SEPs. The main differences between these plans relate to how much money can be set aside. The principal benefits, however, remain the same:

- Immediate tax savings (except Roth IRA)
- Deferred tax growth
- Employer matching contributions
- Peace of mind regarding your financial future

In the following paragraphs we will take a brief look at some of the more common types of individual and business retirement plans.

Basic IRAs

The most basic type of a retirement plan is an *individual retirement account* (IRA). An IRA is an individual plan (it is not started through a business). A taxpayer and his or her spouse can contribute up to $2,000 per year in an IRA. This contribution is a deduction from gross income, thus reducing your personal income taxes. The growth (interest and dividends) of this account is not taxed until an individual withdraws this money at retirement. Employees who are "active participants" in an employer-sponsored pension plan are limited in their ability to set up an IRA. Once their gross income surpasses $60,000 they are no longer eligible to set up an IRA.

Roth IRAs

A new type of retirement plan option is a Roth IRA. This has become a very popular tool for retirement planning. A Roth IRA is similar to a traditional IRA except that the original contribution ($2,000) is not deductible. However, the growth of the account is not taxed when money is pulled out at retirement. That means the compounded earnings of this account will not be taxed. The ability to contribute to a Roth IRA phases out when single taxpayers reach $110,000 and married taxpayers reach $160,000.

401(k) Plans

Other forms of retirement plans can be set up through an employer or your own business. The most common type of employer plan today is the *401(k) plan.* This plan allows the employee to elect not to receive a portion of his or her salary but instead to have the employer contribute to the plan on behalf of the employees. This is done with before-tax dollars. This means that the amount you set aside in the plan is not subject to income tax, although it is still subject to FICA taxes. Contributions made by the employee are 100 percent vested, which means these benefits cannot be lost if the employee terminates employment with the employer. Oftentimes, an employer will match the contribution of an employee to the 401(k) plan up to a certain percentage. This matching contribution is not taxed to the employee until it is withdrawn from the plan. The maximum amount any qualified employee can personally contribute to a 401(k) is $10,000 per year.

SIMPLE Plans

A new type of business retirement plan is called a *savings incentive match plan for employees,* or SIMPLE. SIMPLE plans can be started by self-employed individuals or employers with 100 or fewer employees. It works similarly to a 401(k) plan. Salary is deferred by the employee and contributed to the retirement plan. Income taxes are deferred on the contributions until they are withdrawn. The maximum amount any qualified employee can personally contribute to a SIMPLE plan is $6,000 per year. The employer can make matching contributions of up to 3 percent of employee wages, but no more than $6,000. Once again, the matching contributions are not subject to income tax to the employee. SIMPLE plans are relatively easy to set up, and there are few restrictions.

SEPs

A *simplified employee pension* (SEP) is a very common retirement plan for self-employed individuals and small businesses. A SEP is basically a group of IRAs. All eligible employees set up an IRA, to which the employer makes contributions. These contributions are not deferrals of salary. They are made at a rate of 15 percent of wages, with a maximum contribution of $24,000. The main advantage of a SEP is its simplicity. Very little paperwork is involved.

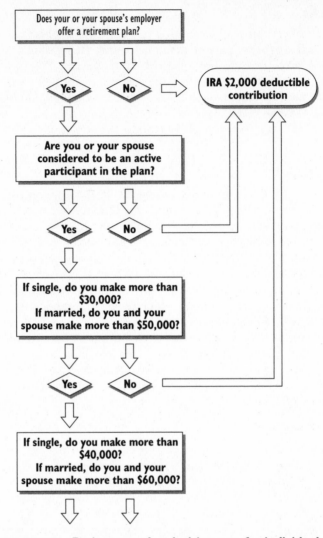

FIGURE 15.1   **Retirement plan decision tree for individuals.**

Whether you are an employee, employer, or both, retirement plans can become an invaluable tool in reducing your income taxes and preparing you and your family for retirement. Retirement plans offer a tremendous opportunity for people in all walks of life. They will definitely help to plug the leaks in your financial situation.

Figures 15.1 and 15.2 (decision trees for individuals and business owners, respectively) will help you determine which pension plan you might qualify for.

Tax Planning Techniques Anyone Can Use

How can you implement proper tax planning? I often hear people say, "My spouse and I are both working. We're living from paycheck to paycheck. We

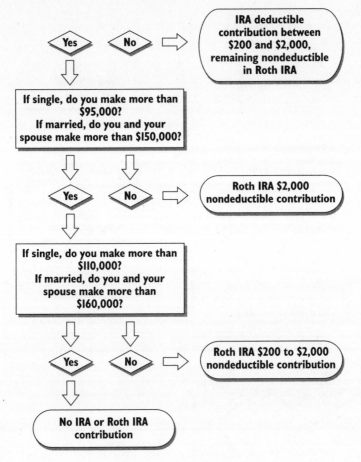

FIGURE 15.1 *(Continued)*

just don't have the money to start tax planning!" Does this sound familiar?
An important point for you to understand is that virtually anyone can obtain
some tax relief through proper tax planning. To illustrate, let's plug in some
numbers in a case study involving Jack and Jane and see if we can help.

	Taxpayer	**Spouse**
Name	Jack	Jane
Occupation	Computer programmer	Dental assistant
Salary	$40,000	$30,000

Jack and Jane have one son, Joe, age 10. Jack and Jane itemize their
deductions with the following expenses:

Mortgage interest	$5,000
Taxes	$3,000
Church contributions	$2,000

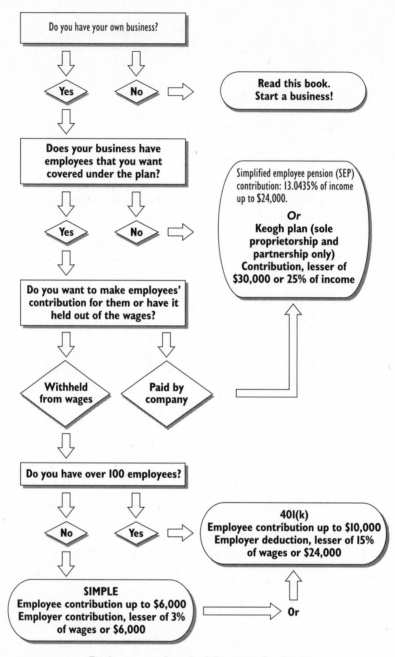

FIGURE 15.2 Retirement plan decision tree for business owners.

Additional information is as follows:

Child care costs	$100 per week	
Credit card debt	$4,000 @ 18%	($100 monthly payment)
Auto loan	$10,000 @ 10%	($350 monthly payment)
Student loans	$8,000 @ 8%	($250 monthly payment)
Mortgage	$70,000 @ 7%	($800 monthly payment)
Market value of home	$100,000	
Original price of home	$90,000	

Jack and Jane are contemplating having another child, but are concerned about the increased monthly expenses that come with children. They are comfortable in their home and are not planning on moving in the near future.

Let's look closer. Jack and Jane's current tax liability can be computed as follows.

Gross income	$70,000
Itemized deductions	($10,000)
Personal exemptions	($8100)
Taxable income	$51,900
Income tax	$9,034
Child care credit	($480)
Net taxes for year	$8,554

Let's remember this scenario. Jack and Jane's tax liability is $8,554. They also have monthly payments totaling $1,500.

Tax Planning Technique 1

Jack and Jane pay child care expenses of $5,200 per year. They received a credit for child care costs of $480 dollars on their tax return. What would happen if Jack elects to be covered under his employer's dependent care benefit plan? If he does, Jack can elect to exclude as much as $5,000 from his taxable income. From our income tax lesson earlier, we know that Jack and Jane are in the 28 percent tax bracket. Five thousand dollars in a 28 percent bracket results in a tax savings of $1,400. Remember also in our tax discussion that earned income is subject to FICA. The employee's share of FICA is 7.65 percent, or another $383 in tax savings. The combination of these two events gives them a tax savings of $1,783. Compared to the $480 credit they would have received if they had accepted the IRS default judgment, electing this type of tax treatment put $1,303 in their bank account. Through a simple process, we have just eliminated $1,303 in leaks!

Tax Planning Technique 2

Jack and Jane have been married for 15 years and have accumulated quite a few household goods over time. It would be no problem at all for them to give $500 worth of goods a year to charities such as the Salvation Army or Goodwill. This $500 donation is an itemized deduction in the 28 percent tax bracket. Thus, add another tax savings of $140 to our financial basin.

Tax Planning Technique 3

Jack and Jane currently have two types of interest: mortgage interest and personal interest. Mortgage interest is tax deductible. Personal interest is not deductible at all. They have personal debt of $22,000 (credit cards, auto loan, and student loans). They have plenty of equity in their home ($30,000) and can get the same interest rate they currently have. Raising their mortgage to $92,000 would increase their mortgage interest to $7,500 per year, or $2,500 more than it was before. In a 28 percent tax bracket, this is a tax savings of $700. What's more, their monthly payment went up only $50 per month. By converting personal debt to mortgage debt, Jack and Jane's monthly personal debt service, which was $700 per month, has now been reduced to zero. With an increase on their mortgage of only $50, they now have added $650 to their monthly cash flow.

   If we look at the tax savings we have created with these three simple techniques, Jack and Jane have accomplished the following:

Technique 1	Tax savings of $1,303 per year
Technique 2	Tax savings of $140 per year
Technique 3	Tax savings of $700 per year
Total tax savings	*$2,143*

That's right, by implementing three simple strategies, Jack and Jane have plugged a $2,143 hole in their financial basin in just one year. If we look at the larger picture, the $2,143 tax savings breaks down to $179 per month. Add that to the additional $650 per month gained by debt service reduction, and Jack and Jane have increased their monthly cash flow by $829. This will go a long way in helping to support a second child.

   Jack and Jane could also choose to fund a 401(k) plan at work or start an IRA with the increased amount of money now available. This would, once again, reduce the tax obligation Jack and Jane currently have to pay. Remember, this does not even take into consideration the amount of state income taxes these techniques would save. I would say that Jack and Jane have begun to defend themselves quite nicely against the IRS. All this was accomplished by making some simple adjustments and implementing some basic strategies that are far too often overlooked.

   Actually, there are dozens of tax-saving strategies. They seem to change from year to year like swirling winds in the desert. If you'd like a free report on the top 10 tax-saving strategies for the current year, go to www.multiplestreamsofincome.com and enter the keyword Tax Cut.

Taxes are a fact of life. Whether you are on the high, middle, or low end of the income stream, you've got to find ways to lower your taxes. Your financial future is at risk if you don't. Plug those gaping tax holes in your financial reservoir and you'll have more time and money to enjoy life.

A Revolutionary Way to Shield Your Investment Profits from Taxes

The first part of this chapter focused on a few ways to help you shelter your ordinary income from taxes. The balance of this chapter will deal with how to shelter some of your investment profits from taxes. Let me ask you a question: Would you rather pay taxes on your investment profits now, later, or never?

I think I know your answer. The balance of this chapter is devoted to showing you how to do this. In Chapter 6, I introduced you to mutual fund guru Bill Donoghue, who shared his secrets on how to earn high rates of return using enhanced index funds and selected sector funds. Bill has always been on the cutting edge of the latest strategies to earn profits for his clients.

Remember the early 1980s, when interest rates soared as high as 20 percent and banks were paying only 5.5 percent on passbook savings accounts? About this time, millions of investors turned to the money fund yield charts in *Barron's,* the *New York Times,* and the *Chicago Tribune.* Guess where this data came from? Bill Donoghue's office! *Donoghue's Money Fund Report* (now *IBC's Money Fund Report*) was the source of that information.

Donoghue was one of the first to teach investors to shift their money from federally insured banks and S&Ls to uninsured, but ultimately safer, money market mutual funds to earn higher returns. The press criticized him for recommending uninsured money funds. Yet, in the decades since, no individual investor has lost money in uninsured money funds, but hundreds of billions of our tax dollars were wasted bailing out bankrupt S&Ls.

Then Bill began educating a generation of baby boomers about the exciting power of stock market mutual funds long before they were popular. For almost two decades, financially savvy investors have listened to Donoghue and profited.

Now Donoghue has done it again. For the balance of this chapter, I'll let Bill himself tell you about his latest investment secret. Unless you are extremely astute, I'll bet that you have never heard of (or never fully understood) what you are about to learn.

It all started when Bill Donoghue began seeking a better way for his investor clients to shelter the high profits they were earning in some of his managed investment accounts. The problem with earn-

═══ $$$ ═══

WIT & WISDOM
The rich aren't like us, they pay less taxes.

PETER DE VRIES

ing these high rates of return is that active trading tends to create greater current tax liabilities and fewer tax deferrals. Of course, if after taxes you have greater profits, the income taxes are a bargain. But Bill wondered whether you could protect those profits by choosing *when* you paid the income taxes—or even *if* you paid those taxes. He wanted to be able to say to his clients, "When it comes to income taxes, do you want to pay now, later, or never?"

Here, in Bill Donoghue's own words, is his latest, revolutionary tax-saving strategy.

The secret to being able to defer taxes on your investment profits is to keep an open mind about where you do your investing. Sometimes it's not *which* investment you choose but *where* (i.e., through which financial institution) you invest that is most important.

I want to tell you that the *new* "best financial deal in town" is not at your bank, your stockbroker, your discount broker, your mutual fund family, or through most financial planners. It's available only through specialized *insurance* brokers and enlightened financial planners. It's called *variable insurance.*

You won't be bored with this *type of insurance!*

Don't run for the door. I used to turn off my mind when I heard the word *insurance.* In fact, even today, when I want to sit alone on an airplane, I tell the person next to me that I am a "born-again insurance agent." They are gone in no time, and I don't see them until the baggage arrives.

Sit back, take a deep breath, and I will tell you why I believe that variable insurance is the one of the most powerful investment vehicles I have ever seen. It's like having all the advantages of the best retirement plan with very few of its limitations.

What is variable insurance? Well, you know what life insurance is. *Variable* means that the buildup of the cash value of the insurance policy will vary depending upon how and where you choose to invest the money. You have the choice to invest in any combination of separate accounts (mutual fund–like investments) offered within your chosen insurance policy. Variable life insurance is cash value life insurance that allows you to choose among several ways your cash value can be invested.

Here is the exciting part: All of the profits accrued in these separate accounts are 100 percent tax deferred (sheltered from current income taxes)—just like in an IRA or 401(k) plan—but there is no deadline for when these funds must start to be withdrawn. Within your policy's rules, you can withdraw your principal (basis) 100 percent income tax free, borrow up to 90 percent of your profits 100 percent income tax free (at very low interest rates), or you can simply enjoy 100 percent income tax–free wealth building. If done properly, your accumu-

───── **$$$** ─────

WIT & WISDOM
Bumper sticker: The buck doesn't even slow down here.

lated investment profits are never taxed, and the insured person's heir receives more than the remaining balance—100 percent income tax free. Variable insurance combines the time-tested and IRS-approved benefits of life insurance (tax-deferred buildup of cash value) and income tax–free policy loans. Consider variable life insurance a viable way to invest in the stock, bond, or money markets without ever having to worry about income taxes! Have I got your attention?

As a side benefit, should the insurance company fail, your money does not reside in the general account that is available to the insurance company's creditors. These separate accounts are truly separate. Wise investors are shifting from general account insurance to separate account variable insurance to avoid possible life insurance failures like those we saw in the early 1990s.

$$$
WIT & WISDOM
Insecurity is the result of trying to be secure.
ALAN WATTS

Variable insurance policies can be purchased only from a small (but rapidly growing) number of specially licensed professionals. Most life insurance agents and stockbrokers have not bothered to become licensed to offer variable life insurance, hence they cannot offer you these attractive services. They are usually the ones who criticize it the most. Their biggest criticism is the "extra cost." Folks, the biggest extra cost in most investment programs is income taxes and brokers' commissions. The commissions and administrative costs of variable life insurance will never be as high as taxes and brokers' commissions—plus, they buy real value. Will your broker guarantee that you and your beneficiaries will receive more than the amount that is in your investment account? Only life insurance can guarantee that benefit and avoid income taxes at the same time. (Note: When I make this claim, I assume that you will invest prudently in your separate account portfolio, never surrender the variable life insurance policy, withdraw your basis or principal first, borrow (not withdraw) from the profits, and leave enough in the cash value account to keep the insurance policy in force. Following these simple rules will avoid the risks of high tax penalties.)

But beware, variable insurance is *not* the same as its more well known and popular cousin, the *variable annuity.* Selected variable *annuities* are attractive for deferring income taxes; it takes variable life *insurance* to avoid income taxes entirely. You want to make sure that you specify *variable life insurance.*

Actually, variable life insurance comes in two flavors:

1. *Single premium variable life* (SPVL), which allows you to economically invest lump sums of cash (such as your entire investment portfolio, an entire inheritance, or lottery winnings) into a 100 percent income tax–free portfolio

2. *Variable universal life insurance* (VUL as it is called in the trade), which allows you to open a budget account to make regular annual, quarterly, or monthly installments

Depending on your circumstances, either of these variable life insurance options can become what, in my humble opinion, is the ultimate tax shelter, allowing you to do four things:

1. *Defer taxes on 100 percent of your investment profits.*

2. First, withdraw your basis, or principal, 100 percent income tax free.

3. Second, borrow (remember, never withdraw, or the withdrawal will be taxed) retirement cash flow in the form of policy loans, which are *100 percent income tax free.* (There is no income tax on a loan.)

4. Leave your heirs *more* money (the death benefit, net of loans) than is in your account. (After all, this is life insurance.)

Some policies even offer the opportunity to buy, at additional cost, a disability rider to pay your monthly contributions if you are disabled and/or a long-term care rider that will allow you to draw on your death benefit (over and above your cash value) *while you are still alive* to pay for long-term care, if required!

In addition to these benefits, there are dozens of creative ways to invest more money at a lower insurance cost. The two most popular are (1) buying a second-to-die policy on you and your spouse and (2) insuring the life of an adult child. The *second-to-die* clause simply means that the policy pays off when the second spouse dies and, presumably, the greatest estate taxes are due. If you choose to insure, for example, your adult child, you might make your grandchildren the beneficiaries, therefore skipping a generation's estate taxes. Because VUL is such a great deal and you can own and control it only during your life, why should you care (except for financial planning purposes) who is insured? What you really want is the tax-free nature of the loans, which gives you spendable cash during your life. That is why I call variable life insurance "lifestyle insurance" instead of "death insurance." Most of the greatest benefits accrue to you during your lifetime.

"Why haven't I heard more about this?" Once you understand even the most obvious advantages of variable life insurance, you will be asking, "Why was I not told?" Although this type of life insurance policy has been around for nearly two decades, only recently has the word started to get out to people like you and me.

---- **$$$** ----
WIT & WISDOM
There is nothing wrong when men possess riches but the wrong comes when riches possess men.
BILLY GRAHAM

Why hasn't your stockbroker told you about this? Your stockbroker understands that if he or she sells you variable insurance, he or she makes only one commission. But, if he or she sells you stocks, there is a new commission paid every time you trade.

Why hasn't your insurance agent told you about this? Your insurance agent probably doesn't want to get those phone calls asking, "Why did the stock market go down yesterday?"

Why haven't you read about this in the financial press? That answer is simple: No one is more afraid of stock market risk than an underpaid reporter with no money to invest! So if *they* won't tell you, *I* will. That's what I've been doing for the past 20 years.

And here's the best part: A few of the most innovative variable life insurance companies have set up special separate accounts that allow you to invest in the type of underlying enhanced index funds and sector funds that I told you about in Chapter 6. These potentially high profits can be immediately sheltered from income taxes. Better yet, these profits can be sheltered indefinitely. I'm proud to say that I now use this opportunity to manage some of my power portfolios using separate accounts within selected variable insurance policies. For a list of what is currently available, visit www.donoghue.com.

There is a lot more you need to know before investing in any variable insurance program. I can help. My next book will go into detail about this exciting opportunity, but I'm so excited about it that I decided to give Robert's readers a solid preview. There has actually been so much demand for my next book that I have, to date, sold over 20,000 copies of the first chapter, which deals specifically with variable life insurance. It names no insurance company names, but does explain what you need to know about this exciting program. I highly recommend you read it before talking with your advisors.

To order your own copy of the preview chapter of *The Millennium Advantage: 100% Income Tax-Free WealthBuilding,* send $5.00 for shipping and handling to Donoghue's Power Portfolios, Box 309, Milford MA 01757, or call 1-800-982-2455. I will include, as a special thank-you, a copy of the latest edition of *Donoghue's Power Portfolios* newsletter so you will know which variable insurance policies we are featuring. Remember, this newsletter is not written by an insurance agent but by an independent, opinionated, investment advisor—me.

There you have it. At the very least, I hope this has helped you see a new way to build a prosperous financial future.

CHAPTER 16

Optimism means expecting the best, but confidence means knowing how to handle the worst. Never make a move if you are merely optimistic.
THE ZURICH AXIOMS

Financial Fortress Stategies: Shielding Your Multiple Streams of Income

Creating multiple streams of income can yield benefits that most people only dream about. But the most important things in life are not the material riches that you can and will create. The most important things in life all revolve around people: your family and friends. Many people learn this lesson the hard way, by accumulating large amounts of assets and then losing them all. While this can be a powerful way to learn that lesson, it's extremely expensive.

Yes, at any moment in your life, you could lose it all. I've lost everything twice in my life. Each time was embarrassing, painful, and just plain "not smart." Thankfully, through each devastating crisis, I had my family there to help me weather the storm. They each deserve a medal—my wife and my three wonderful children—for standing by me.

I've learned a lot from these experiences, and I'd like to share some of it with you in this chapter. One of the most important lessons was how much easier it is to make money than to keep it. I now have an enormous respect for those who are able to accumulate. Another lesson was how a seemingly simple mistake can put everything you've worked for at risk.

That's why I've said that you must structure your life to live like a millionaire but be a pauper on paper. In other words, you must create a financial fortress around your family so that nothing can penetrate it. As I have learned from personal experience, there are a lot of enemies to your wealth. You need to know what these enemies are and how to protect yourself and your assets from them.

And that brings us to what this chapter is all about. This chapter is designed to teach you exactly how you can implement an overall asset protection plan for protecting your hard-earned assets in today's litigious society.

Most of the concerns people have about their family's financial future fall within three main categories:

Tax planning

Asset protection

Estate planning

We talked about tax planning in the last chapter. In this chapter we'll focus on asset protection and estate planning.

Asset Protection

In the area of asset protection, it is really important for you to understand what a litigious society we live in. That means, in plain language, that a lot of folks are suing a lot of other folks, often for very frivolous reasons.

Studies show that a new lawsuit is filed in America every 30 seconds on average. That's two lawsuits every minute of every day. In the short time that it's taken you to read these few words, several lawsuits have already been filed somewhere against somebody. Lives have been changed forever! Financial pictures have been altered irrevocably. Entire family futures have been put in jeopardy. The worst part of this is that it could often be avoided by taking a few simple steps.

One out of four people will be sued this year. Even worse, the average number of lawsuits over an individual's lifetime is five, and of these five, one will be what is known as a "devastating" lawsuit. The term *devastating* means that it wipes people out completely, costing them everything they own. It's a horrible sight to see somebody ruined by this kind of litigation, but it *does* happen. By implementing the information presented to you in this chapter, you can go a long way toward making sure it does not happen to you.

Of all the lawsuits filed in the entire world, 94 percent are filed right here in the good old United States. Yes, 94 percent! The United States is the world's leader in filing lawsuits—a dubious honor.

Combine these statistics with the fact that there are currently more students in law school than there are practicing attorneys, and it becomes downright scary, doesn't it? Why is that? Why are law degrees in such high demand these days? Is it because we have a shortage of lawyers in this country? I don't think so! Flip through your telephone book and see how many attorneys are in your area alone. With this in mind, which way do you think the number of lawsuits is heading in this country, up or down? Up, up, up, of course! Now more than ever, asset protection needs to become a central concern in your financial planning. You absolutely must have a plan to protect your assets, and the use of financial fortress strategies is an essential element in that plan.

Estate Planning

A consideration of equal importance to asset protection is estate planning. Too often, families unexpectedly discover that enormous amounts of their wealth are being consumed by estate taxes, fees, and other expenses upon the death of a loved one. The worst part of these tragedies is that many of these situations could have been avoided by implementing simple estate plans using the tools you are about to learn.

Unfortunately, people fail to utilize these tools because they do not believe the tools are necessary. It is sad but true that most people spend more time planning their vacations than they do planning their estates. Studies indicate that the average person will spend over 90,000 hours working to accumulate wealth (40 hours a week times 50 weeks a year for 45 years), but less than three hours learning how to preserve that wealth. These people simply fail to plan their estates. It is a well known axiom that *if you fail to plan, you plan to fail.*

Part of the reason for this failure to plan is that, historically, estate planning has been an area reserved for only the truly wealthy. If your bank account and assets didn't total to seven figures, the traditional line of thinking was that you need not worry about estate planning. That is certainly not the case anymore. *Everyone needs an estate plan.* You need to ask yourself a question. Would you like to have the estate plan of the average person or the estate plan used by many of today's millionaires?

Even if you are living paycheck to paycheck, the simple truth is that you need to be concerned about planning your estate. You are dealing with forces at this very moment that can destroy everything you have worked all your life to accumulate. And it can happen in the blink of an eye! You simply must plug your leaks before they drain your financial reservoir dry!

The key is knowledge. But where do you find this knowledge? Sure, you could go to law school, but do you really want to do that? Who has the time? You're too busy building up your multiple streams of income.

As a creator of wealth you will need to assemble around you a cadre of experts to help you maintain and preserve your financial fortress. These experts will include a competent accountant, an honest attorney, and an excellent tax strategist. These experts will not come cheap. As for me, I look at these fees as cheap insurance to protect me from the catastrophic dangers in our society.

In preparing this chapter, I turned to my own financial fortress strategist, J. J. Childers. J.J. is an attorney and the owner of Profit Publishing Group, Inc., through which he shares the message of sound asset protection strategies. He teaches what he calls the strategies of the Secret Millionaire. You can learn more about J.J. at www.multiplestreamsofincome.com using the keyword Secret Millionaire. Let's take a look a few of the key strategies of the Secret Millionaire.

Legal Strategies

In structuring a solid plan for protecting your assets, you must combine the use of various legal entities:

1. The Nevada corporation
2. The family limited partnership
3. The limited liability company
4. The retirement plan
5. The living trust

This is not a complete list but, when properly combined, these vehicles can provide the type of protection that you need to safeguard your hard-earned assets.

Let's look at each of these entities individually first. Then we'll see how they can be combined to provide a shield for your multiple streams of income. At the end of this chapter, we will look at a case study of the financial situation and the financial fortress plan of the Wilsons, a fictional family.

The Nevada Corporation

If you're in business, odds are you'll need a Nevada corporation. It is the cornerstone of your financial fortress. Essentially, it is the hub of activity for everything you do, both in business and personally. Because it plays such an essential role in the overall scheme of things, let's explore exactly how the Nevada corporation works.

The first question people often ask is, "What is a corporation?" Perhaps the best way to answer that question is to take a look at the legal definition of a corporation as defined by a legal dictionary. *Black's Law Dictionary** defines the *corporation* as follows:

> An artificial person or legal entity created by or under authority of the laws of a state or nation, composed, in some rare instances, of a single person and his successors, being the incumbents of a particular office, but ordinarily consisting of an association of numerous individuals, who subsist as a body politic under a special denomination, which is regarded in law as having a personality and existence distinct from that of its several members, and which is by the same authority, vested with the capacity of continuous succession, irrespective of changes in its membership, either in perpetuity or for a limited term of years, and of acting as a unit or single individual in matters relating to the common purpose of the association, within the scope of the powers and authorities conferred upon such bodies by law.

---

* *Dartmouth College v. Woodward,* 17 U.S. (4 Wheat.) 518, 636, 657, 4 L.Ed. 629; *U.S. v. Trinidad Coal Co.,* 137 U.S. 160, 11 S.Ct. 57, 34 L.Ed. 640.

There it is. Now, does that clear everything up for you? That is the official definition of what it means to be a corporation straight from the Supreme Court. Now that you've read this definition, I have a question for you: What is a corporation? (Now you know why you sometimes leave your attorney's office more confused than when you entered.)

While this may be the legal definition of a corporation, it does little to shed light on the issue of what a corporation means to the average person. This chapter is not meant to prepare you for the bar exam. It's meant to teach you how to think conceptually about your asset protection plan. With this in mind, let's try to clarify the meaning of a corporation in lay terms.

> **$$$**
> **WIT & WISDOM**
> Learn how to fail intelligently, for failing is one of the greatest arts in the world.
> CHARLES KETTERING

A corporation is a separate legal entity. It is an entity separate and apart from its members, stockholders, directors, and officers. While it is indeed a separate entity, it is still dependent on people to take any action. This is the best news of all.

You control this entity in the same way that parents control their children (ideally). The difference is that the corporation always minds you, no matter what the situation. Wouldn't that be nice? Do you understand the power in that? Let's take a closer look.

The corporation is like an artificial person. Its rights, duties, and liabilities do not differ from those of a natural person under like conditions. The only difference between a corporation and those directing it is that a corporation lacks the ability to think for itself. That is the purpose of the officers and directors. These individuals do the thinking for the corporation, as evidenced by the fact that all decisions made on behalf of the corporation are documented in the form of minutes and/or corporate resolutions. This distinction between the entity and those who control it is important.

What does a corporation do, and why should you have one? If someone asked you to define a *car,* you would be hard pressed to do so without telling them what it *does.* So it is with a corporation. With this in mind, let's take a look at our next question: *Why do people incorporate?*

> **$$$**
> **WIT & WISDOM**
> Wall Street: the din of inequity.

Why incorporate?

I prefer to think of a corporation as functioning like a twin brother or sister. Have you ever had a day when you wished that you could send someone to work in your place so that you could stay home and do as you pleased? Really, wouldn't it be nice to have someone step into your shoes and deal with undesirable situations that you often find yourself in? What if you could designate another person to fill in for you? Wouldn't that be ideal? That is exactly what a corporation does.

It would be great in today's litigious society to be able to associate assets with your phantom twin rather than with yourself personally. Then that person could be sued rather than you, right? Would that be amazing or what? That is exactly how a corporation works when you begin to understand it more fully.

As I explain the benefits of corporations to groups, I often hear, "Too bad I can't send this artificial person to court to risk his assets instead of mine. If only I really did have a person who would

━━━━━ **$$$** ━━━━━
WIT & WISDOM
Surplus wealth is a sacred trust which its possessor is bound to administer in his lifetime for the good of the community.
ANDREW CARNEGIE

do anything I told him, I could have him hold title to those assets so that I could significantly limit my vulnerability to lawsuits in connection with those assets, giving me tremendous asset protection. In the event that the other person lost that lawsuit and a judgment was rendered against him, the worst that could possibly happen is that he would lose his assets, not mine. Best of all, my personal assets would not be attached." Sound pretty incredible? Actually, this is exactly what a corporation is all about.

Basically, a corporation is a business entity that is created based on the laws of a specific state or country. All corporations must be set up under the authority of the government of the jurisdiction in which they are created. Where you establish your corporation is a matter of great significance. Let's take a look at why it is important to establish your corporation in the state of Nevada.

Why Nevada?

The state of Nevada has become the nation's leader in establishing small corporate businesses. The reason for this is that the state has created an environment that is absolutely phenomenal for those interested in implementing tremendous protection for their assets. To demonstrate the significance of this environment, let's take a look at some of the many benefits available in Nevada.

Top Ten Reasons for Nevada Corporations

1. One-person corporations are allowed.

2. No state tax (no state income tax, no state corporate taxes, no franchise tax, no tax on corporate shares, no state tax!).

3. Total privacy for shareholders; officer and director names are a matter of public record, but no other information, listings, or minutes of meetings are filed with the state.

4. No formal information-sharing agreement with the IRS.

5. Low annual fees.

6. Case law that prevents easy piercing of the corporate veil.

7. Corporate officers and directors protected from any personal liability for lawful acts they perform for the corporation.

8. Stockholders, directors, and officers not required to live or hold meetings in Nevada, or even to be a U.S. citizen.

9. Corporation may issue stock for capital, services, personal property, or real estate. Directors determine the value of any such transactions, and their decision is final.

10. Allows for issuance of bearer shares.

The benefits of incorporating in Nevada are absolutely unbelievable. Obviously, I could spend a lot more time going into the benefits of Nevada corporations, but that would be outside the scope of this chapter and this book. The point I want to make is that Nevada corporations are an absolute necessity to surviving in today's society. If you are interested in gaining a greater understanding of Nevada corporations, I highly recommend that you get a copy of *The Secret Millionaire Guide to Nevada Corporations* by J. J. Childers. It is the definitive guide to understanding the intricate nuances of this powerful entity. To order your copy and to learn more about Nevada corporations, check my web site at www.multiplestreamsofincome.com and enter the keyword Nevada, or call my office at 801-852-8700.

The Family Limited Partnership

The next tool you must learn to master is the limited partnership. These entities have long been a much-used tool when it comes to asset protection, estate planning, and tax reduction. A limited partnership, or *family limited partnership* (FLP) as it is commonly referred to, is a business entity that contains two or more partners. These partners are the key players in the business arrangement. As such, it is important to understand the role of each in the workings of this entity.

The partners will fall into one of two classifications: *general* or *limited.* At least one of these partners must be classified as a general partner, while the others may be treated as limited partners. This becomes a crucial distinction as you begin learning about the intricacies of this entity. Let's take a look at some of the distinctions.

The first type of partner, the *general partner,* is in complete control over all aspects of the business. The *limited partner(s)*, on the other hand, has absolutely no say-so in the control of the business. When most people hear this, which role do you suppose they prefer? Why, of course, they want to be the general partner. However, there is another factor to take into consideration: *liability,* or the exposure to lawsuits. The limited partners are given limited liability, whereas the general partner is subject to personal liability. *Now* which one do you want to be? This is where proper planning can be so important.

Far too often, people will hear from their professionals that they do not want a limited partnership because of the problems I've just outlined. If you want control, you have to be the general partner. The problem however, is that now you are subject to personal liability. The key then becomes to find a way to avoid the liability. Obviously, with our focus on lawsuits and asset protection, the limited partner aspect is the most attractive feature of this business entity because of the limited liability associated with this status. But who then calls the shots? The answer to this question can mean a lot of money to you and your business.

The key here is to combine legal entities in order to maximize the benefits while minimizing any perceived downside. The perceived downside in this instance is the lack of control with limited liability. With the limited partnership alone, this is not possible. However, if you realize that another legal entity can function as the general partner, things begin to change a little bit. When we stop thinking as individuals and start thinking as legal entities, better options appear. Individuals are subject to personal liability—but is there an entity that is not subject to personal liability? The answer, as you learned earlier in the chapter, is an overwhelming *yes!* That entity is the Nevada corporation. Now you can see why the Nevada corporation is the cornerstone of the overall asset protection plan. In the fictional case study at the end of this chapter, the Wilson family financial fortress will plan two limited partnerships with the Nevada corporation as the general partner. The two types of legal entities are layered to complement each other and actually increase asset protection.

You might ask, why use the family limited partnership when you could simply use the corporation? Corporations are indeed the most common form of business entity, so what does a limited partnership provide that makes it more attractive than a corporation? Let's look at some of the advantages of limited partnerships:

- *Low start-up costs.* The costs of forming a corporation or LLC can be significantly greater than those of forming a partnership. The initial drafting will cost essentially the same, but follow-up work is significantly less with a partnership.

- *Low annual filing fees.* Corporations and LLCs are usually subject to some type of franchise or similar tax in the states in which they do business. Generally, partnership fees are much lower, if they exist at all.

- *Flexibility in management.* A limited partnership is less structured and easier to operate than a corporation. In a corporation, shareholders own the company, the board of directors manages the company, and the officers oversee the day-to-day operations of the company. Even if the same person or persons operates in all three capacities, corporate records must still be reported in a way that shows how the three groups work together. In a limited partnership, there is no layered tier of control. The only rule is that the limited partner(s) cannot participate in the company's management.

- *Pass-through taxation.* Partnerships themselves do not pay taxes. Partnership income and loss is passed through to the individual partners. Corporation profits are often subject to double taxation: once at the corporate level and again at the personal level. This pass-through taxation feature enables the partnership to avoid double taxation. For the limited partners, there can be additional savings through the avoidance of FICA taxes.

- *Ownership interest protected.* Ownership interests in the limited partnership are usually protected from personal creditors, as opposed to corporate stock, which can be extremely vulnerable if not properly structured.

- *No restrictions on who can be a partner.* S corporations put restrictions on who can and cannot be a shareholder. Partnerships have no such restrictions.

- *Limited partners are not liable for partnership debts.* Limited partners (unlike general partners) are not personally liable for debts incurred on behalf of the partnership.

- *Availability of additional sources of capital.* Because limited partners exercise no control over the partnership, additional limited partners can be added without diluting control.

The limited partnership and its characteristics provide a tremendous mechanism to help structure your overall financial fortress strategy. Structured properly, a limited partnership can help in the areas of asset protection, estate planning, and tax reduction. Used in conjunction with other entities, a limited partnership can help shield your hard-earned assets from creditors.

The Limited Liability Company

The next legal entity to be considered in developing any type of financial fortress strategy is the limited liability company. It is absolutely taking the nation by storm, but why? Let's take a look at why a limited liability company is so attractive and how it can be used to "turn on the faucets while plugging the leaks."

First, a brief history lesson. When our Founding Fathers were laying the foundation for U.S. government, there was a very heated debate between the large and small states. Large states wanted representation in Congress to be based on population. Small states wanted each state to be represented equally. The resulting compromise (called the Great Compromise) still guides our government today. Congress was created with two separate bodies, the Senate and the House of Representatives. House membership is based on state population. Senate membership is equal for all states.

Two hundred and one years after the founding of our great nation, in 1977, Wyoming was the first state to pass what it referred to as a *limited liability company,* or LLC, statute. Since that time, all 50 states and the District of Columbia have authorized the organization of LLCs in their jurisdiction.

Two hundred and one years from now, business students and entrepreneurs might just be reading about this event as the "Great Compromise" relating to business. For years, attorneys preferred the corporate structure because of the unlimited liability protection it provides. Accountants have consistently advised clients that partnerships provided stronger long-term tax advantages than corporations. Americans were left to choose what meant most to them, asset protection or tax reduction. The formation of the limited liability company has combined the limited liability feature of the corporation with the tax advantages of the partnership. As a result, the LLC is the fastest-growing business entity in existence today.

You often see the letters *Inc.* at the end of a business name. That's because, for years, the corporation has been the dominant form of conducting business. Do you remember seeing the letters *LLC* at the end of a business name? Probably not as often. While the limited liability company has existed for decades in Europe and other parts of the world, it is still fairly new in the United States.

To understand the power of the LLC, we need to take a closer look at the many benefits it provides. Let's look specifically at the advantages of limited liability companies in comparison to corporations—namely, S corporations.

- *An LLC is not limited to one class of stock.* In an S corporation, each share of stock must have the same rights as every other share of stock when it comes to corporate profits and corporate assets. An LLC is extremely flexible in its profit and loss allocation.

- *Any individual or entity can be a member of an LLC.* An S corporation's shareholders are limited to individuals, estates, certain trusts, and other S corporations. Shareholders must also be citizens or residents of the United States. Thus, a nonresident alien cannot be a shareholder of an S corporation. C corporations, partnerships, and IRAs cannot be shareholders of an S corporation.

- *An LLC is not limited in the number of members it can have.* An S corporation is limited to 75 shareholders.

- *The tax treatment of a properly formed LLC is automatic.* In contrast, a corporation must in a timely fashion file a proper S election in order to receive preferential tax treatment.

- *The liquidation of an LLC is generally a tax-free event.* In the liquidation of an S corporation, taxes accrue as though the corporation were selling the liquidated assets to the shareholder at their fair market value. This advantage makes the LLC a particularly ideal entity for holding real estate.

- *An LLC is not required to maintain corporate formalities.* An S corporation must comply with the same record-keeping and bookkeeping formalities of traditional corporations.

Now let's look specifically at the advantages of limited liability companies in comparison with partnerships.

- *All members of an LLC maintain limited liability.* A limited partnership is required to have at least one general partner who is personally liable for the debts of the partnership. This is not the case with an LLC.

- *Members of an LLC can participate in management without losing their limited liability status.* Remember, if a limited partner participates in the management of the partnership, he or she is exposed to personal liability. One can only limit his or her liability in a limited partnership by giving up control. In the LLC, there is no such requirement.

When you consider the benefits, it is no surprise that the LLC is becoming such a popular business structure. Limited liability companies are the single fastest-growing business entity in the country today. Not having knowledge of the tremendous benefits these entities provide can leave you far behind in the race to protect yourself and your financial future. When properly blended with other legal entities, they can be invaluable.

The Retirement Plan

We discussed retirement plans fairly thoroughly in Chapter 15. As I stated, perhaps in no other area of financial planning is the potential for accumulation of wealth greater than in retirement plans. Remember, the four main benefits of retirement plans are as follows:

- Immediate tax savings
- Deferred tax growth
- Employer matching contributions
- Peace of mind regarding your financial future

There are few other ways in which your wealth can grow as rapidly. In the case of the Wilsons at the end of this chapter, you'll see how their corporations—both the Nevada corporation and their home state corporation—have established pension plans.

The Living Trust

Another entity that should be implemented by anyone who has any sort of asset base is the living trust. A trust has long been viewed as an entity reserved solely for the superrich—Rockefellers, Kennedys, Vanderbilts. Nothing could be further from the truth!

The most common type of trust is known as the *living trust*. A living trust is perhaps one of the most effective tools to help you avoid the burdensome and expensive costs of probate. Probate is a problem we all must deal with at some point in our lives unless we implement a plan to avoid it.

Probate is a legal term that most people do not understand. In fact, most people choose to ignore this concept because it deals with death, which is not a subject most people like to dwell on. Probate is the legal process used to wind up an individual's legal and financial affairs after their death. Assets and liabilities of the estate are identified. Debts are paid. Taxes are filed. Administrative (attorneys') fees are paid. The remaining assets, if any, are distributed to the beneficiaries of the estate as provided by a will or, without a will, in accordance with state law. In short, it's a tedious and expensive process. Your leak quickly becomes a gusher. Probate costs alone can easily amount to 10 percent or more of the total assets in the estate. An average probate period is about 14 months. Do you want your heirs to wait this long? If you are an heir, do you want to wait this long?

Another big problem with probate is the matter of privacy. Probate is open to public scrutiny. Anyone—your coworker, your preacher, your next-door neighbor, even your ex-spouse—can find out what assets, property, and money are part of the estate you stand to inherit. In order to maintain your privacy, you must avoid probate. To avoid probate, you need a living trust.

A living trust is a very simple concept that can have enormous value. Assets are transferred into a trust. A trustee is named to oversee the operations of the trust. This trustee can be the same person that set up the trust (i.e., you). When a specific event occurs, such as the death of the creator of the trust, the assets of the trust pass to another party, thus effectively avoiding probate. While probate avoidance is the primary reason to establish a living trust, there are many other benefits as well. For example, a living trust . . .

- Helps avoid the headache and costs of probate.
- Provides privacy for your estate.
- Provides some estate planning.
- Saves on estate taxes.
- Avoids capital gains taxes by allowing for stepped-up basis.
- Provides for an uninterrupted transition of business enterprises.
- Allows you to provide for your heir(s) and/or beneficiary(ies) in the manner in which you see fit.

A living trust is a tool that appears to be a commonsense answer to the nightmare of probate. However, only a very small percentage of us have taken advantage of the tremendous benefits it offers. To obtain a free living trust kit, go to www.multiplestreamsofincome.com and enter the keyword Living Trust Kit.

A trust is an essential ingredient in a well-thought-out estate plan. To see how a living trust fits into the overall plan, look at how we used the living trust in the Wilsons' overall plan in the following example. The included figures clearly show how the living trust is used to cocoon the Wilsons' assets and protect the vulnerable ones from the nightmare of probate.

Case Study

Let's take a look at an example of how a hypothetical family might utilize the benefits of proper entity structuring. Let's call them the Wilsons, a typical family of four. Steve is the father. Liz is the mother. There are two children: Josh, age 11, and Beth, age 8.

The Wilsons are a two-income family. Steve runs his own computer software business. His business is doing well. It earned a gross profit last year of $480,000 and has the same potential for this year. From this gross profit, Steve nets $150,000 a year in income. Liz has taken one of my courses on the stock market and operates a home business as a stock trader. Liz maintains a trading account of $100,000 with an annual income of $25,000.

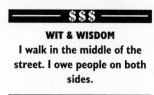

$$$

WIT & WISDOM
I walk in the middle of the street. I owe people on both sides.

Steve's company, Wilson's Computer Concepts, is a sole proprietorship. In addition to the $480,000 per year gross profit, Steve's company has $100,000 worth of equipment and inventory and three full-time employees.

The Wilsons took my real estate investment home-study course several years ago, and they now own two rental houses with an estimated value of approximately $50,000 each. Their own home has a value of $275,000.

Now that we have looked at their assets, let's look at their annual income streams. We'll start with what we already know—that Steve brings home $150,000 in income after his company pays expenses and that Liz earns about $25,000 from her trading.

The rental homes that the Wilsons maintain bring them an additional annual income of $10,000 per year. Obviously, the Wilsons have the proper structure for multiple streams of income already in place.

The flip side of the income coin is, of course, expenses. The Wilsons have created a comfortable income for themselves as long as their expenses remain in check. We've established that Steve's business grosses $480,000 annually, but Steve has equipment and employee expenses to maintain. Due to the large amount of space his technicians require and the expensive security he must maintain for his inventory, Steve's storefront and warehouse lease are costing him $40,000 per year. His security system and insurance, both property and liability, add an additional $12,000, with utility costs for the large space an additional $16,000. Steve must maintain expensive technical equipment as well as a parts and retail inventory, which cost him about $50,000 annually. Salary totals for his three highly trained employees are $135,000 with the additional expenses of FICA, workman's compensation, and medical/life insurance of approximately $30,000 per year. Steve takes a personal salary of $150,000 a year, which leaves an operating fund for the business of $47,000.

$$$

WIT & WISDOM
If people knew how hard I worked to get my mastery, it wouldn't seem so wonderful after all.

MICHELANGELO

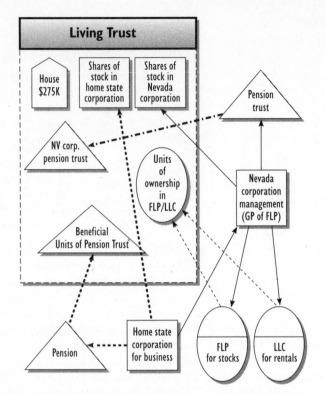

FIGURE 16.1   The Wilson family's big-picture financial fortress strategy.

Liz's expenses are much simpler, as an at-home trader, her costs are limited to her computer, Internet service for online trading, two additional phone lines, a fax machine, and brokerage expenses. The cumulative annual cost for these items is not quite $6,000.

Expenses from the rental property include the mortgage on one house of $6,000 per year, insurance costs of $3,000 per year, and repair and general upkeep of $1,000 per year.

The expenses that the Wilsons incur as a family are similar to those of most families: mortgage costs, home and auto insurance, utilities, auto loan payments, gasoline and auto maintenance, medical and dental expenses, entertainment expenses, dining-out expenses, groceries and household supplies, clothing, and furnishings—typical expenses with which we can all identify.

The Wilsons already have multiple streams of income in place. Now we need to structure them for the three areas of asset protection, estate planning, and tax reduction. We can illustrate a good, solid financial fortress structure for the Wilson's through the use of the big-picture diagram in Figure 16.1. At first glance, this may look complex and confusing, but by following the step-by-step planning process over the next few pages, everything should begin to make sense. You'll see how you, too, could begin to build a financial fortress around your family, piece by piece.

FIGURE 16.2   The living trust.

Step-by-Step Planning of the Wilsons' Financial Fortress

1. Set up initial entities.

   A. *Living trust:* Place home and personal property (represented by ⌂) into a living trust for asset protection from probate and for the stepped-up basis. The living trust will be represented as a rectangle with a dotted line, as in Figure 16.2.

   B. *Home state corporation:* Next we set up a home state corporation for the computer company to limit liability for the company and provide a corporate veil to separate personal and business assets. Place stock into a living trust to avoid probate and reduce estate taxes. Now our entity plan looks like Figure 16.3.

   C. *Nevada corporation:* Set up to act as a management corporation over your home state corporation and to move income exposed to state corporate taxes into a nontax state. Privacy of ownership of the stock is another benefit. Place stock into living trust. (See Figure 16.4.)

2. Set up a limited liability company for the rental properties in order to provide asset protection and income shifting to other family members, and place the units of ownership into the living trust for liability protection and estate planning. The Nevada corporation can serve as a management corporation for the LLC if necessary. Units from a limited partnership and limited liability company are shown by ovals (◯) in Figure 16.5.

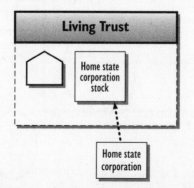

FIGURE 16.3   The home state corporation.

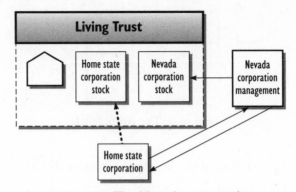

FIGURE 16.4 The Nevada corporation.

3. Set up a family limited partnership for the stock from the Nevada corporation and place into the living trust for liability protection and estate planning. The Nevada corporation will serve as the general partner for the FLP for asset protection purposes. (See Figure 16.6.)

4. Set up pension trust under the Nevada corporation, shown as a △ in Figure 16.7, for the benefit of the Wilsons. Add units from the pension plan shown as a △ to the living trust.

5. Set up pension trust under the home state corporation for the corporation's employees. (See Figure 16.8.)

6. Set up optional entities if needed for protection of income or assets.
   A. Irrevocable life insurance trusts (ILITs)
   B. Charitable remainder trust

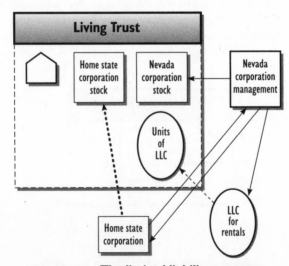

FIGURE 16.5 The limited liability company.

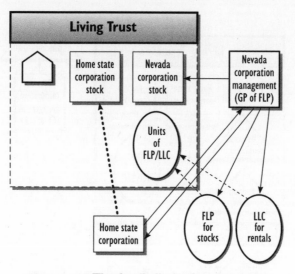

FIGURE 16.6 The family limited partnership.

This is essentially everything the Wilsons will need in order to shield their multiple streams of income. While this may seem overly complex or sophisticated, once you learn how to do it, you'll wonder why you didn't do it sooner. Of course, you can and should always rely on a skilled professional to assist you with this type of a structure. That's why I have entrusted J. J. Childers and his top-notch team to enhance my own financial fortress. If you want to learn more about creating your own financial

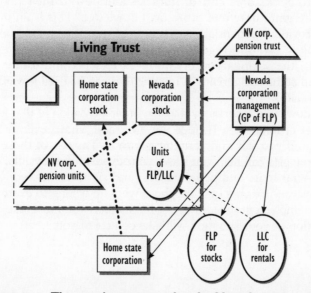

FIGURE 16.7 The pension trust under the Nevada corporation.

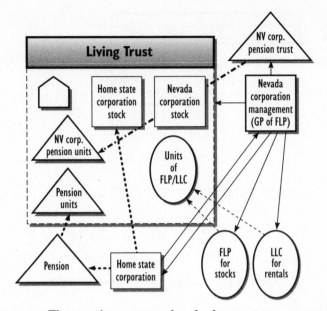

FIGURE 16.8 The pension trust under the home state corporation.

fortress, go to www.multiplestreamsofincome.com and use the keyword Financial Fortress, or call my office at 801-852-8700.

As I stated earlier in this chapter, the key is knowledge. You must accumulate as much knowledge as you can about understanding your tax situation. Read tax newsletters, books, the Tax Code, IRS publications, and anything else that you can get your hands on to increase your knowledge base. Go to bookstores and/or libraries and devour their tax material. Continue to gain more and more tax knowledge. This is an investment that can provide exponential returns in the form of increased tax savings. It can result in savings for generations to come as well. When it gets right down to it, the savings you create in careful tax and estate planning becomes an additional stream of income that can be used toward building up more wealth!

While knowledge is certainly the key, implementation of that knowledge is the most crucial step. It does you no good whatsoever to learn the information if you fail to do anything with it. The use of these financial fortress strategies can help you lower your exposure to lawsuits, plan your estate for your heirs and beneficiaries, and significantly reduce certain taxes. However, it works only for those who are willing to exert the effort required to implement the strategies. Remember, you must take control of your situation or your situation will take control of you.

CHAPTER 17

You may ask me for anything you like except time.
NAPOLEON I

Balancing Act:
Getting Your Act Together

Multiple streams? Multiple tasks? Multiple headaches!

How can you possibly juggle all of the details of your personal life—family, fun, friends—*plus* handle the myriad details of your multiple streams of income? It can be overwhelming.

Reminds me of the plate spinner. Remember him? He starts by spinning one plate on the top of a stationary stick. Then he spins another plate on second stick. Then a third plate. By this time, the first plate has started to wobble, so he returns to respin it—then the second and the third. He adds a fourth spinning plate. And a fifth. Then he returns to respin any plate that is about to fall. He adds a sixth plate. You get breathless just watching him running from wobbling plate to wobbling plate, respinning each just a split second before catastrophe. Does this sound like your life?

Life didn't used to be this complicated. Makes you nostalgic for the 1950s with one-income families and the security of lifetime employment. Sorry. Somebody opened Pandora's box, and out stampeded four horsemen: global competition, the computer chip, the Internet, and instant worldwide communication. It's a different world than the one our parents raised us in. We must adapt.

Remember the old Chinese saying? *Man who chases two rabbits loses both.* If Confucius were alive today, he'd probably say: *Man must chase ten rabbits in order to catch three.*

Just remember, the money-tree businesses you've learned about in this book are different than most businesses. These businesses are designed to eventually operate with little or none of your presence! Therefore, although they may take time to get up and spinning, they spin much easier and much longer by themselves. This gives you time to get another stream of income up and spinning.

Twenty-one Time Tips for the Twenty-first Century

But you still have to be more efficient than ever before. If you expect to be a one-person home-based business, every second has to count. Let me share with you how to squeeze the most amount of activity into the shortest period of time so that you can have as much free time as possible. Let's set as our goal managing at least six streams of income simultaneously on as little as one hour per day. You can spend the rest of your time shopping, golfing, whatever.

Strategy 1: Remember That Time Is Money

Have you ever heard the saying, "Time is money"? Do you know what that means? It obviously doesn't mean that time equals money. If that were the case, we'd all be millionaires. But it does mean that time is *like* money. It's a scarce resource that, like money, has to be managed.

I learned of a concept in a college economics class that I've never forgotten. It's called *opportunity cost.* Suppose a person only has $1,000 to invest. She can buy either investment A or investment B. She has to make a choice. By choosing A, she has to forfeit the opportunity of investing in B. And vice versa. Each decision requires a sacrifice.

It's the same with time. You don't *spend* time. You *invest* it. You can invest your time in actions that bring you closer to your life's objectives or that take you further away. Each investment of your time carries an opportunity cost. Choosing one activity means you forfeit the opportunity to do something else.

Time is the ultimate scarce resource. An hour spent in front of the TV takes away from time you could have spent in front of a computer writing your book or in front of your son or daughter building a better relationship.

There is one area in which time is *not* like money. You can save money, but you can't save time. When time passes, it is gone forever. Your only choice is to invest your time more wisely in the future. Time wisely invested is like compound interest: Small daily deposits can multiply into a magnificent life.

Benjamin Franklin believed in practicing 13 daily virtues. His first two virtues were *industry* and *frugality.** He said,

---

* The other 11 virtues were temperance, silence, order, resolution, sincerity, justice, moderation, cleanliness, tranquility, chastity, and humility.

The way to wealth, if you desire it, is as plain as the way to market.
It depends chiefly on 2 words. Industry and Frugality. That is,
waste neither time nor money, but make the best use of both.

Good advice.

Strategy 2: Focus on the Critical Few

In Chapter 3 I briefly introduced you to the 80/20 principle. Now, let's go into more depth. To get right to the heart of your life, 80 percent of the things you do account for only 20 percent of your results. Conversely, 20 percent of the things you do account for 80 percent of your results. This is called the *Pareto principle* after the Italian sociologist who postulated it over 100 years ago. It seems so simple but has profound implications. One writer referred to this as "the critical few versus the trivial many" because 80 percent of the things we do each day are trivial (almost a waste of time because they produce so few results) and 20 percent are critical (i.e., vital to our progress).

Let's compare time to money. Suppose you only have $100 to invest— no more, no less. You buy two investments, putting $20 into investment A and 80$ into investment B. A year later, you find that your $20 in investment A has earned a profit of $80, while your $80 investment in B has earned only $20. The results are as follows:

Investment A: $80 profit ÷ $20 investment = 400% return

Investment B: $20 profit ÷ $80 investment = 25% return

In other words, each dollar invested in A earned *16 times more money* than a similar dollar invested in B (400 ÷ 25 = 16). One was a high-leverage investment; the other, by comparison, was a low-leverage investment. Is there any question about where your dollars should be concentrated?

The same is true for time. Brian Tracy writes of a study in which an insurance company discovered that, in fact, 20 percent of its salespeople actually did account for 80 percent of the company sales. Moreover, the average salesperson in the top 20 percent—those critical few—earned *16 times more money* than the average salesperson in the bottom 80 percent.

What were they doing differently? The employees in both groups started each day with exactly the same amount of time to spend (or invest): 24 hours, or 1,440 minutes, or 86,400 seconds. Ticktock. Ticktock. How they invested this time had *enormous implications* in the results they produced. One group concentrated on high-leverage activities (those critical few tasks that yield rich dividends), while the other group got bogged down in the trivial (those time-sapping activities that produce few or no results).

Knowing this, the key to your success is to practice the next strategy. . . .

Strategy 3: You Must Learn How to Procrastinate!

I'm not joking! Procrastination is absolutely essential to your success. You may have assumed that only the losers in this life procrastinate. On the contrary, the most successful people on this planet are also master procrastinators. Losers work on the 80 percent and procrastinate on the 20 percent. Winners do just the opposite: They immediately tackle the high-leverage 20 percent and procrastinate on the trivial 80 percent.

It's said that Napoleon opened his mail only once a month. Why? Because if it was still important after a month, he attended to it; if not, it was just junk mail. He focused his time and energy on only those things that would take him more quickly and more surely toward his objectives, his purpose. And he procrastinated doing everything else. This is important enough to illustrate:

	20% Critical Few	80% Trivial Many
Winners	Do it now.	Do it later.
Losers	Do it later.	Do it now.

Did you get that? Focusing on the critical few is a high-leverage activity. It gives you 16 times faster results!

Strategy 4: Throw Away Your To-Do List

If you're like most people you start your day with a to-do list, which you create the same way every day. You try to make a comprehensive listing of everything you have to do. Then you start crossing things off as quickly as you can accomplish them. There's such an endorphin rush whenever you cross something off. It's almost orgasmic.

But getting things done is not the same as getting the right things done. Very few people sit down to examine the nature of the tasks on their to-do lists. By definition, 80 percent of the items on your to-do list are trivial.

Trivial activities are generally fun, fast and frivolous.

Call Bill to set up tennis match.

Get tickets to the play.

Buy book at the bookstore.

Have lunch with old high school chum.

Critical activities are generally more difficult, take longer, are more important, and involve more risk of failure.

Talk to boss about the new project.

Write my book.

Take spouse to lunch to discuss how to make our average marriage great.

One day, in preparing my own to-do list, I actually wrote the following items *in this order:*

✔ *Call publisher about the new manuscript.*

✔ *Write newsletter article.*

✔ *Check on tenant in unit #3D.*

✔ *Make my wife feel like the most important person in the world.*

That's how out-of-balance my life had gotten!

The truth be told, the most important aspects of our lives rarely make an appearance on our to-do lists!

Discover my purpose in life.

Develop a deeper relationship with God.

Love my children.

Learn how to love everyone unconditionally.

Don't succumb to the tyranny of the traditional to-do list. Turn it into a *power list.* Draw a line through the top portion of your page as in Figure 17.1.*

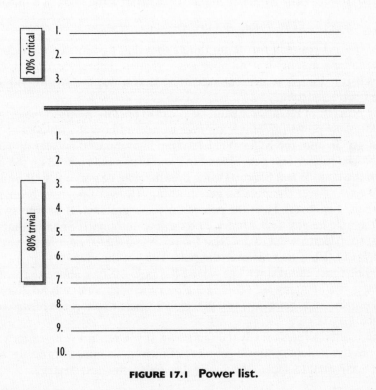

FIGURE 17.1 Power list.

* Let me send you a free printable copy of a power list for your daily activities. Go to www.multiplestreamsofincome.com and enter the keyword PowerList. While you're there, don't forget to sign up for my free Internet newsletter, *Multiple Streams Strategy of the Week,* so you and I can continue to communicate regularly.

Before you write something on your list, ask yourself: Is this a 20? Or is this is an 80? Write your critical activities at the top and your trivial activities at the bottom. This forces you to constantly focus on your critical few activities. Work on the top of the list most of the time. Drop down to the bottom only when you want to take a break. Don't expect to get everything done every day. A little improvement every day—that's your goal. Better to work on only three critical items, even if you don't complete them, than to cross off 20 trivial things.

Strategy 5: Reward Yourself for Doing the Right Things

Tell the truth: It feels good to cross things off your to-do list, doesn't it? Have you ever gotten to the end of your day and remembered that you accomplished something that wasn't on your to-do list . . . so you stopped, added it to your list, and then crossed it off? What a rush! A hit of pure pleasure. Only one problem—you've been rewarding yourself for doing the wrong thing. Like a laboratory rat, you've been training yourself to do the *least important things first*. Oops.

There's a great book by Michael LeBoeuf, Ph.D., called *GMP: The Greatest Management Principle in the World.* Here's the book in a nutshell:

The things that get rewarded get done.

If you reward yourself for doing things that don't count, your to-do list will become a magnet for unimportant activities. Therefore, only reward yourself for doing the critical activities. If you do, the world will also reward you handsomely.

The process of rewarding yourself is called *positive reinforcement.* And it's extremely powerful. Have you ever wondered how the trainers at Sea World get Shamu, the Killer Whale, to leap high out of the water on command? The trainer first gets Shamu to swim over a pole placed on the bottom of the tank. When Shamu swims over the pole he gets a fish. If Shamu doesn't swim over the pole he gets nothing. (Reward positive behavior. Ignore the negative.) Then the pole is raised several feet. If Shamu swims over the pole he gets fish. Under, and he gets nothing. If Shamu wants to eat, he soon learns what to do. Next the pole is raised to water level. Shamu gets a lot of fish if he rolls over the pole. You get the idea. Within a short period of time, the trainer has raised the pole 10 feet above the water. Shamu gets a huge reward for jumping over the pole. Shamu is no dummy. He likes fish. And that's how you get a killer whale to jump out of water on command.

Your brain operates exactly the same way. If you reward yourself for your most positive actions, you will get more of them . . . almost effortlessly. And if you really want to supercharge your day, follow the next strategy.

Strategy 6: Do Your FTF: Feared Things First

Which activity on your list do you fear the most? That's your FTF. When you start your day, ask yourself, "What's my FTF today?" Start your day with that activity.

Most people do just the opposite. They scan their to-list to find something that they can cross off quickly. They do their fast things first. Or the fun things first. Sometimes, they even do first things first. But I believe you should tackle the *feared things first*. If you get that out of the way, the burden will be lifted and you will feel a surge of energy that will propel you through the rest of the day. Why is this?

Generally, whenever you hesitate or resist doing something, there is a reason. Often, it is fear. People are simply afraid to fail. Fear blocks us from doing our highly leveraged activities. . . . Fear blocks our success. Some people would rather do nothing successfully than do what really counts and risk failing. Fear is too expensive a habit. So let's learn to recognize it, face it, tackle it, and move through it. Then reward yourself. Give yourself a verbal pat on the back. Take a short break. Notice how good it feels. Give Shamu a fish. By training yourself to do your FTF, you unconsciously urge yourself to tackle tougher tasks.

Strategy 7: Do a Daily Power Hour

Eisenhower said, "Plans are nothing. Planning is everything." Therefore, take a few minutes every day for planning. Although this planning session may take only 15 minutes, I call it a *power hour.*

In Chapter 2, I talked about the importance of extending your planning horizon every day. Remember, the future doesn't just happen. You *make it* happen. If you don't plan your own future, you are at the mercy of other peoples' plans. Therefore, when you get up tomorrow, plan your next 90 days. If tomorrow is January 1, you should be planning what should happen on April 1. This gives you 90 days to make sure that things go as planned.

Planning is like a rehearsal. Every great actor rehearses many, many times before stepping on the stage. Yet we often step on the stage of life without rehearsing our performance beforehand. During your power hour, rehearse in your mind and visualize yourself performing your daily activities—the way you would like to see it done. Plan your day in your mind and then go out and make your life conform to your vision.

Most people get up in the morning with no idea what to do. They just merge into the flow of life and get carried along with the mass of humanity who have no goals, no plans, no future. Rise above all that. Let the wind of planning fill your wings and lift you up where you belong.

Strategy 8: Exercise

Exercise is a high-leverage activity. It helps you work harder and longer and think more clearly. It increases your health span and your life span. While I exercise, I also listen to my tapes—thus layering those two activities together. Therefore, I'm exercising not only my body, but my brain at the same time. Speaking of which . . .

Strategy 9: Layer Your Activities

Use your waiting time productively. I call this *layering*. If you're riding up an elevator, plan what you're going to say when you arrive at your appointment. If you're driving in your car, plug in an audiocassette instead of listening to music or mindless talk radio. Read while you're riding on the bus or in a taxicab. Use every second as productively as you can and you'll squeeze more into your life. Constantly ask yourself this question, "Is this the most productive use of my time?"

Strategy 10: Set Specific Goals for Each Income Stream

One day, as I was aimlessly driving along the freeway with the flow of traffic, I suddenly remembered that I had an appointment. I glanced at my watch. I was late. Immediately, I began to focus. I stepped on the gas and found the fastest passing lanes. I made the freeway conform to me instead of me conforming to the flow of traffic.

Goals are like that. It's easy to get caught up in the flow of traffic. If you know where you are going and when you need to be there, your brain automatically and unconsciously sorts through the confusing detail of life and notices the fastest passing lanes, the shortcuts, the routes that will advance you faster and more efficiently toward what you want. You don't have to agonize over every decision. This one habit will simplify your life and automatically make you more organized.

The Hindus believe the mind is a very scattered organ that needs to be disciplined. The analogy they use is of an elephant going through a bazaar. An undisciplined elephant moves through the bazaar, its trunk swinging back and forth among the many shops and vendors, picking up apples and bananas and other interesting things, creating all kinds of havoc. A wise elephant trainer has the elephant carry a log with its trunk so that when it walks through the bazaar of life, it does not pick up things as it goes along, but essentially focuses on its main goal, which is getting through the marketplace. Goals help you to focus—to keep your trunk occupied—as you walk through life so that you don't get distracted by a million other options.

Set specific goals for each of your income streams this year. Give your goals a deadline and review them daily. Suppose you have three current income streams in your family and you want to enhance those three streams and add three more. This is what those goals might look like:

> By January 1 next year we plan on having
> six streams of income flowing into our life.

Income stream 1: *My job. Increase income by 10 percent by January 1.* I will make myself more valuable to my company. I will position myself so that I am perceived as a stream and not a leak, as a source of revenue and not an expense item. I will increase my income by 10 percent over last year. This increase will come from either salary, bonuses, stock options, or other rewards.

Income stream 2: *My spouse's job. The same as above.*

Income stream 3: *Maximize company pension plans and/or individual pension plans.* We will have the maximum allowable pension amounts deducted automatically from our bank account. We will administer these investments as much as possible to invest our money in the wisest places.

Income stream 4: Network marketing. Add an extra $500 per month by January 1. We will investigate and find one Wave-Three company in the network marketing industry with a product that we are absolutely convinced will be beneficial to ourselves and our circle of influence. This product or service will be of such exceptional quality and value that we will be proud to introduce it to 12 associates this year. These 12 will be so impressed that they find it almost impossible not to share it with others. This will generate an extra stream of at least $500 per month.

Income stream 5: Buy at least one tax lien certificate at 20 percent interest by January 1. We will save an additional 5 percent from each of our salaries with the specific intent of buying at least one tax lien certificate so that we can begin earning much higher rates of return on our money.

Income stream 6: Decide on the next stream of income before January 1. We will read, study, research, attend seminars, and draw up a specific action plan to enable us to launch at least one more income stream next year.

Strategy 11: Engage in Scattered Focus

Since you have multiple streams you're trying to manage at one time, don't make the mistake of thinking of them all at the same time. The plate spinner focuses intently on getting each plate up and spinning, one at a time. Focused . . . until the plate is securely spinning. And then scattered . . . while he looks for the next wobbly plate. Focused and then scattered.

Don't become overwhelmed by all of your tasks. Select one task. Focus. Give 100 percent attention to your task at hand. Push everything else to the background. Accomplish the task at hand. Then scatter: Scan your list of critical activities and pull up the next item for action.

Strategy 12: Delegate

Delegation is to time what leverage is to money. When you give someone else a job to do, you are using the principle of leverage, just as you would in real estate or any other money investment. You're letting someone else multiply your time. So delegate as much as you can.

What should you delegate? Your 80 percent activities.

Some people have difficulty delegating their 80 percent low-payoff tasks because they are perfectionists. They are afraid of failure. This attitude sets them up for ultimate failure . . . not having enough time for the most important tasks. The key to delegation is to give only lower-leverage activities to subordinates. Even if the job is not done perfectly, the damage is minimal. . . . After all, it is a low-leverage activity.

You might remember Moses' dilemma in the Bible. The children of Israel brought all of their problems to Moses personally until his father-in-law Jethro wisely counseled:

> . . . Choose able men, such as fear God, men of truth . . . to be rulers of thousands, and rulers of hundreds, rulers of fifties, and rulers of tens: and let them judge the people. . . . every great matter they shall bring unto thee, but every small matter they shall judge: so shall it be easier for thyself, and they shall bear the burden with thee.
>
> *Exodus 18*

Like Moses, learn to delegate the low-payoff activities so you can have time to devote to the high-payoff activities. You'll never be great without doing this.

But what if you don't have anyone to delegate to? Then delegate your tasks to specific time slots in your day or week. I call this *20 percent time* and *80 percent time. Critical time* versus *trivial time.* Look at your normal day. Isn't there a time when you are naturally more productive, when your creative juices flow, when your energy is high? For some, it is in the morning. Others are more productive late at night. When is your high-energy time? My low time is generally between 3 and 6 P.M. During this time, when my energies are at a low ebb, I schedule my low-leverage activities—the fun, fast, and frivolous activities. During my most productive hours, my critical time, I work only on critical tasks. The key, then, is to bunch critical tasks into critical time and to bunch trivial tasks into trivial time. To say it differently, 20 percent tasks during 20 percent time and 80 percent tasks during 80 percent time.

$$$

WIT & WISDOM
An ounce of morning is worth a pound of afternoon.
OLD PROVERB

As your income increases, you simply won't have time to do it all. Therefore, delegate responsibility of each project to a separate project manager. Ask for a daily summary sheet from each income stream, listing the critical activities for the day and the progress achieved in the previous day. Demand daily accountability. The longer you go between reviews, the further off track your project can drift before you get it back on course.

Strategy 13: Do It Now

Get in the habit of doing it now. Procrastination is suicide on the installment plan. I've found in teaching hundreds of thousands of people that it's not the knowledge that's lacking. What is really lacking is courage. You see, you can have all the knowledge in the world, and if you're afraid to act on it, it's worthless, isn't it? Do it now.

Strategy 14: Do a Four-Quadrant Test at Least Once a Month

Here's something I learned from Stephen Covey. At the end of one day, take a blank piece of paper and dissect it into four quadrants. Write down everything you did during that entire day and classify each activity under one of four broad categories, or quadrants. Quadrant 1 is for routine things. Quadrant 2 is for things that happen unexpectedly. Quadrant 3 is for things that other people delegate to you. (I call these OPMs . . . *other people's monkeys*.) The fourth quadrant is for your dreams or goals.

Do this exercise and you'll be surprised. If you're not careful, the routine things, emergencies, and other people's monkeys will take up most of your time. This will leave you no time for working on your dreams. You must work on your dreams every day. You've got to make a daily deposit into your dream bank account; otherwise, there will be nothing there to compound.

Strategy 15: Learn to Love the Word *No*

The best time management tool is the word *no.* Be careful about taking on other people's monkeys.

Strategy 16: Handle Paper Only Once

Either delegate it, do it, file it, or throw it away.

Strategy 17: Do It Wrong the First Time

Have you ever heard this saying? "If it's worth doing, it's worth doing right." Trout and Ries in their excellent book, *Positioning,* turn that logic upside down. They say, "If it's worth doing, it's worth doing lousy." If you wait until the time is right—until your ducks are all in a row—it will never get done. If it's important enough, you should be willing to act on it now, warts and all, and sculpt excellence out of the clay of imperfection. You must be willing to fail your way to success.

Peters and Waterman, authors of *In Search of Excellence,* say the same thing in a different way: Instead of "Ready, aim, fire," they prefer "Ready, *fire,* aim."

Strategy 18: Blitzing

Every hour on the hour, when you hear your watch beep or the chime of a distant clock tower, let that be your signal to focus intensely for a 10-minute period of time. You'll find that you get as much done in that 10-minute period of time as you've done in the previous hour. I call this *blitzing.* The beep is your cue to step on the gas and sprint for 10 minutes.

Strategy 19: Return and Review

Take five minutes at the end of your day to review what has transpired. Notice the things you did of which you are proud. Give yourself a mental pat on the back. Notice the things you did that needed improvement. Instead of beating yourself up, imagine what you could have done differently to change the outcome. Visualize yourself doing it the right way.

Strategy 20: Challenge Yourself Daily

What makes you most productive? For me, it's deadlines and challenges. Studies show that creativity dramatically improves immediately before a deadline is reached. Maybe that's why I sometimes put things off . . .

because I'm just sooooo good the day before the project is due. When I challenge myself, my creativity soars. I love challenges so much that I even arranged to have my own name hidden inside the word *challenge!* Challenge yourself, and your creativity will begin to soar.

Strategy 21: Practice the Speed of Going Slow

Finally, with all the talk of getting things done, I've saved the most important strategy for last. In his excellent book, *LifeBalance,* Richard Eyre uses a catchy phrase to describe the necessity for balance in our lives. He calls it the "speed of going slow." It's the conscious decision to work on all areas of your life constantly so that nothing is out of balance. There are six major resources in your life that need to be kept in constant balance (as shown in Figure 17.2):

Being

Brain

Body

Time

People

Money

Let's take a brief look at these six areas of our lives.

Your brain

The brain is the most powerful computer in the universe. They say that we use only a fraction of our potential, maybe 5 percent. If you could just improve the use of your brain by a tiny fraction, you would make massive improvements in your life.

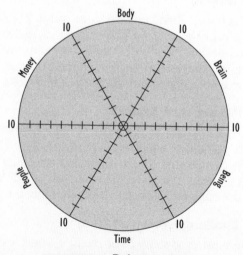

FIGURE 17.2 Balance wheel.

Your body

What an incredible tool it is. Your heart beats over 100,000 times a day without a single conscious thought on your part. Amazing, isn't it? Not to mention your eyes, ears, taste, and smell. What an incredible sensory apparatus. How is your body? Could you squeeze a decade or two more out of yourself by taking better care of body now? Could you be more productive today by treating your body with more care? Could this lead to more money in your pocket? I think so.

Your being

Some people call it *spirit*. Others call it *soul*. I call it *being*. It's your essence, your *be*-ing. It's the part of you that's unique and eternal. Spending time on your spiritual side gives you perspective on the daily pressures of life. With perspective, you can be more grounded, more tranquil, more at peace. This is a very important part of my life. Life would be meaningless without it.

According to a Gallup poll, about 95 percent of North Americans believe in a higher power. We just use different names: God, Universe, Higher Power, Allah, Nature, the Spirit, and so forth. Many of our beliefs are very similar at the wholesale level. It's only at the retail level that the confusion sets in. But that's not the point I'm trying to make.

If there is a higher power—an all-knowing intelligence or being—then what better partner could you have as you create multiple streams of income? This was Rockefeller's belief, and he gave away fully 10 percent of his income all his life.

As I look back over my life, I realize that many of my most powerful income streams were almost impossible to plan. . . . They just seemed to drop out of the sky. That's why I think it's important to work on your spiritual side. Perhaps you will be the conduit through whom the higher power will direct a special stream of income to bless the lives of many others.

Time

Can you imagine anyone at the top of his or her profession who isn't organized? Kind of ridiculous, isn't it? How organized are you? If you'll practice the strategies in this chapter, you will be amazed at how much more effective you can become.

People

What is life without people? People are the bottom line. How are your relationships? Could they be better? Which relationships do you want to improve? What small thing could you do in the next hour to improve that relationship?

Money

Finally, what about money? Who ever has enough? We all know that money doesn't buy happiness, but we'd like to find out for ourselves, right?

What happens when one area of your life gets out of balance? Ever known someone who was strong in one area but neglected the other areas? Look at Howard Hughes. A giant in money but a pygmy everywhere else. That's not success. Ever known someone who focused so intently on success outside the home that the marriage suffered and maybe even died? Ever known someone with a lot of great ideas that never got off the ground because he or she was disorganized? Ever heard of someone who neglected his or her body in pursuit of money and died of a premature heart attack? And then there's the person who seems to have it together in all the other areas but just can't seem to make any money.

You can be strong in one area—but a chain is no stronger than its weakest link. Sooner or later, unless you get your total act together, your Achilles' heel will prevent you from reaching the top. Can you think of any examples of this? Marilyn Monroe. Elvis Presley. John Belushi. Can you think of any politicians with an Achilles' heel? What about television evangelists? The list is endless.

So what's your weak link, your Achilles' heel? If you don't strengthen that weak link, life will exploit it. In tennis, the first thing your opponent does is to size you up, looking for your weak spot—maybe it's your backhand. It doesn't matter how good your forehand is, or your lob or your approach to the net. You opponent plays to that weak spot until you're blown off the court. Game. Set. Match. You're history! Until you improve your backhand, you're never going to rise in the rankings.

You'll notice the people you really admire—the ones who make it big and keep it big—are those who have it together in all six areas of their life. There's such a temptation to jump in and pursue our goals with single-minded determination. We tell ourselves, "Well, once I make my first million, I'll have plenty of time for relationships," or, "As soon as my material side is taken care of I'll focus on my physical side or my spiritual side." In the race between the tortoise and the hare, it's very frustrating to watch your competition speed off up ahead while you take time to balance your life. But the hare is going to have a flat tire up ahead and waste a lot of energy trying to fix it. Then you'll pass him up and leave him forever in your dust.

It's a proven fact that balanced individuals have only 10 percent as many serious illnesses as those who are maladjusted. So slow down, strengthen your weaknesses, regain your balance, and work on all six areas of your life daily. Sink your pylons deep into the earth so that the skyscraper of your life will be built on a firm foundation.

This is my hope for you . . . a life overflowing with abundance of all kinds—multiple streams of income, joyful relationships, boundless energy and health, a quick mind, and a strong spirit.

CHAPTER 18

*When the greatest King of France, Louis XIV, died, a magnificent
state funeral was held in Notre Dame Cathedral in Paris.
The Bishop of Paris mounted the pulpit to preach the eulogy
and uttered only four words "Only God is great."*

QUOTE MAGAZINE

Share It: Leaving a Legacy
That Outlives You

I was raised in a home with deep spiritual values, so I was trained from my youth that material things are transitory, at best. Still, an experience I had when I was 19 years old made an indelible impression on my young mind.

I was working one summer as the driver of a sightseeing tour bus in a city called Banff in the Canadian Rockies. I was assigned to drive a small group of foreign tourists for a 10-day tour through the most beautiful part of the mountains from Banff to Lake Louise and on to Jasper. The weather was superb and the scenery was magnificent. The leader of the tour was an elderly gentleman from the Philippines, accompanied by his wife and an entourage of about a dozen family members, friends, and business associates. It was a very interesting group. As the tour progressed I learned that this man was an extremely wealthy businessperson—a Mr. Lopez—with interests that included television stations, radio stations, a newspaper, and a large utility company in the Philippines. He was also well connected: His brother was vice president of the Philippines. I have no idea of the total value of his assets, but it had to be in the hundreds of millions—by today's standards well over $1 billion.

At the end of my tour, the old gentleman graciously asked me if I would like to leave my job as a bus driver and join his entourage as they continued their journey. I was flabbergasted. "But, I have no clothes for the trip," I stammered. "No problem," he replied, "We can arrange for anything you need." I called my father and informed him of my good fortune.

The very next day I was part of a billionaire's entourage, with a new set of clothing on my back and extra spending money in my pocket. It was like a fairy tale.

We stopped at the Lopez mansion in San Francisco long enough for me to obtain a passport and a visa, and then we were off to the Philippines. Upon landing in Manila, we were whisked through customs and immigration and driven immediately to the government palace, where we were granted an audience with First Lady Imelda Marcos. She accepted some expensive dresses as gifts and then posed for a photo with me. The next day the photo appeared in the Lopez-controlled newspaper—a gangling 19-year-old Canadian boy presenting gifts to the First Lady of the Philippines!

I moved right into the family mansion and began to enjoy all of the benefits of a life of luxury—maids, cooks, chauffeurs. After a few days, I was sent on a tour of the Lopez mansions in various parts of the country from Davao in the south to Baguio in the north. I saw the mansions, the cars, the accumulated assets firsthand. Impressive!

$$$
WIT & WISDOM
Life is just one big seminar (unless you order the tape set).
BILL MARTIN

After several weeks, the entourage wanted to continue its world travels, and I went along to Tokyo for another week of sightseeing, carte blanche. Having been raised in a small southern Alberta town of only 2,000 people, the experience was almost overwhelming.

The group was preparing to head for Europe when I informed my generous host that I had a previous commitment—I wanted to serve a two-year mission for my church—and I needed to return home to prepare. He handed me three crisp hundred-dollar bills—in 1967 a tidy sum—and sent me home. But not without arranging for me to stop in Honolulu for three glorious days at the Royal Hawaiian on Waikiki.

I received my mission call a few weeks later, to Tahiti (tough assignment!), and spent the next two years in French Polynesia.

A few years after my return, I was in San Francisco on business and dropped by the Lopez mansion to inquire about the family. The elderly Mr. Lopez, I was informed, had passed away. And his family had suffered a reversal of fortune. What they told me, I shall never forget.

Supposedly, when Marcos declared martial law in the Philippines in 1972, he seized more than mere power. He seized all of the media outlets—newspaper, TV, radio—and nationalized them, which is another word for legalized grand larceny. In doing so, he kidnapped the president of one of the television stations, who happened to be the son of Mr. Lopez.

$$$
WIT & WISDOM
In excellentia lucrum . . . in excellence is profit

Mr. Lopez received a phone call shortly thereafter in America and was given a choice: Relinquish his rights to all of his Philippine holdings or his son would be killed. I doubt the old man took more than a moment to make his decision. The son was released, the assets were transferred.

What would you do? Choose, now! Everything you own to spare the life of one of your children. Puts things in perspective, doesn't it?

You will probably never have to make such a drastic choice. Just make sure that you don't spend so much time accumulating assets and income streams that you neglect the most important relationships in your life. Be wise.

In the beginning of this book I challenged you to look at each dollar you spend through a microscope—to nurture each penny carefully. Now, as I close this book, I challenge you to look at money through the telescope of time—to realize how money can multiply with compound interest into enormous sums with the power to do much good for the world.

I challenge you to do what all great philanthropists have done: to be such a powerful steward over your forest of money trees that they can produce fruit to feed generations of people long after you have gone.

To this end, I wish you good luck and Godspeed.